W9-BWL-947

THE *Middle East* COLLECTION

THE *Middle East* COLLECTION

A SURVEY
OF THE
TURKISH EMPIRE

W.[illiam] Eton

ARNO PRESS
A New York Times Company
New York—1973

Reprint Edition 1973 by Arno Press Inc.

Reprinted from a copy in
  The Princeton University Library

The Middle East Collection
ISBN for complete set: 0-405-05310-X
See last pages of this volume for titles.

Manufactured in the United States of America

————◆————

Library of Congress Cataloging in Publication Data

Eton, William.
    A survey of the Turkish empire.

    (The Middle East collection)
    Reprint of the 1798 ed. printed for T. Cadell, Jun.
and W. Daviés, London.
    1. Turkey. 2. Eastern question (Balkan)
3. Great Britain--Commerce--Turkey. 4. Turkey--
Commerce--Great Britain. I. Title. II. Series.
DR425.E85 1973   914.96'03'1   73-6278
ISBN 0-405-05334-7

A

SURVEY

OF THE

TURKISH EMPIRE.

IN WHICH ARE CONSIDERED,

I.

ITS GOVERNMENT,

FINANCES, MILITARY AND NAVAL FORCE,

Religion, Hiftory, Arts, Sciences, Manners, Commerce, *and* Population,

II.

THE STATE OF THE PROVINCES,

Including the ancient Government of the CRIM TATARS,
The Subjection of the GREEKS,

THEIR EFFORTS TOWARD EMANCIPATION,

And the Intereft of other Nations,
Particularly of GREAT BRITAIN, in their Succefs.

III.

THE CAUSES OF THE DECLINE OF TURKEY,

And thofe which tend to the PROLONGATION of its EXISTENCE,
With a Developement of the Political Syftem of the late
EMPRESS OF RUSSIA.

IV.

THE BRITISH COMMERCE WITH TURKEY,

The Neceffity of abolifhing the LEVANT COMPANY,
And the Danger of our QUARANTINE REGULATIONS.

WITH MANY OTHER IMPORTANT PARTICULARS.

BY W. ETON, Efq;

MANY YEARS RESIDENT IN TURKEY AND IN RUSSIA.

LONDON:
Printed for T. CADELL, jun. and W. DAVIES, in the Strand.

1798.

PREFACE.

I Do not offer to the Public a complete Treatise; I have indeed materials, out of which I could have formed a much larger work; but thefe outlines will, I hope, reprefent in its true character the object to which I more immediately wifh to fix the attention of my readers.

As I reafon only from facts, I truft the impartial Reader will draw the fame conclufions; and as I fpeak of countries in which I have been long refident, and of events, to many of which I was witnefs, I hope my teftimony may have fome weight. To fhow that I have had opportunities of being acquainted with the matters of which I treat, I will only obferve, that in Turkey I have been a conful; that I have had indirect concerns in trade; and that, as a traveller, I have vifited moft parts of that empire; that in Ruffia I was, for feveral years, in the confidence of the

late

late Prince Potemkin, and in a fituation to know more of the fecrets of the cabinet than moft foreigners; and that for five years I did the bufinefs of fecretary to his Majefty's miffion at St. Peterfburgh: at the fame time I am convinced that I expofe myfelf to the cenfure of not being better inform-ed, and, on the other hand, of incur-ring, though I am confcious of not me-riting, the blame of betraying a con-fidence put in me; fo far, however, from this being the cafe, I rather appre-hend that the delicacy of my fituation, with refpeft to the two countries, and particularly to my own, may have ope-rated too reftrictively on my pen.

Many writers and travellers have feen things in a different light; and I am fenfible that I may be accufed of treat-ing the Turks too feverely, and parti-cularly by thofe who admire Lady Wort-ley Montagu's elegant defcriptions, and fimilar productions of a warm imagina-tion *. I draw conclufions from facts recorded

---

* The beft authors who have written on this fubject are, *Bufbec*, *Leunclav*, *Montecuculli*, *Marfigli*, and *Ricaut*; they fhow what the Turks were in their days. As to *Can-temir*, though he had found an afylum in the very heart of
the

recorded in their own hiftory. Indeed there cannot be a more horrible picture than that which they have, themfelves, delineated. The fentiments expreffed by the fultans and muftis, which will be found in the abridgement of their hiftory, in their own words, are fo repugnant to juftice, to humanity, to every principle of virtue, and to thofe laws which all civilized nations have refpected, that nothing can be faid worfe of them. The effects produced by this monftrous government in the provinces are fhocking to behold. We feek in vain for a population, fufficient to compofe thofe numerous kingdoms and ftates, which flourifhed when the Turks ufurped their dominion; we find the country literally a defert; we find vaft cities reduced to beggarly villages, and of many hundreds no traces remain.

The government of the Turks has undergone confiderable revolutions, which

the Ruffian empire, he wrote as if he ftill had been at Conftantinople. Other more modern authors are, *Bofcovifch, Bufinello, Guys, Le Bret, Sir James Porter, Riedefel* with *Dohm's* notes, *Ludeke, Stœvers, Ferrieres,* and *Volney,* and their picture of the Turks is not more favourable than mine. There are others, who have compofed in their clofets excellent hiftories, &c. of this people.

it

it will be neceſſary to inveſtigate. The
empire, in its flouriſhing ſtate, was one
vaſt camp. The firſt ſultans dated, and
their feeble ſucceſſors ſtill date, their
decrees from the imperial ſtirrup. The
iron ſceptre, imbrued in blood, could
only be wielded by warlike ſovereigns,
the idol and the terror of the ſoldiery,
whoſe diſcipline alone was their politics, and whoſe rapine alone their reſources.

Achmet III. father of the late Abd-
ul-hamid, firſt ſet the example of an
effeminate reign; and by not going out
himſelf at the head of his janizaries,
he became ſo much the object of their
contempt that they dethroned him.

Machmud, his nephew, terrified at
the fate of his predeceſſor, and finding himſelf unable to govern, determined to deſtroy the whole body of janizaries. The army, dreaded by the
ſultan, found in him an enemy more
powerful than all the hoſts of Chriſtendom; and he, without their co-operation, unable to wield his ſceptre, found
an enemy in the other ſlaves he called
in to aſſiſt him, ſtill more deſtructive of
his own power. The preſent reigning
ſultan, Selim, has fallen on a more gentle

tle method of abolifhing the *janizaries,*
but he ftill has the *ulema* to contend
with.

The abftract of their hiftory is moftly
from Ricault, whofe antiquated, though
faithful relation, I have often quoted in
his own language. I have only cited a
few facts to prove the truth of my general affertions ; to enumerate only all
the inftances of unprovoked aggreffion,
breach of oaths, treaties, and capitulations, maffacres, and acts of cruelty and
oppreffion, to be found in the bloody
pages of their hiftory, would alone make
a large volume.

The firft part of thefe papers has
been written fome time ; that which is
political, about two years ago, on my
return to my native country ; but it
was not then defigned for the prefs. It
may be objected, that there are matters
in it which ought not to be made public, as it contains information which
may benefit our enemies ; I anfwer,
that they being in poffeffion of the information which the late government
of France had procured, there is nothing effential in this book which will
be new to them ; nor had even that government, at any time, fo many fpies,

or fuch exact intelligence as the Directory now have.

With refpect to the Greeks, there
will be found much matter wholly new
to the Public, but not to the Directory;
for no one was better informed of the
ftate of Greece than citizen (heretofore
chevalier de) Truguet, lately minifter
of the marine department. He was for
a long time employed in the Archipelago, under the direction of Mr. de
Choiffeul Gouffier, and was fent to
Egypt to negotiate with the Beys for
leave to trade to India through that
country, and to counteract the Ruffian
intrigues with them.

I have endeavoured to prove, that the
interefts of Great Britain and Ruffia are
infeparable and reciprocal. This, indeed, has been generally granted; but
when the aggrandizement of that empire at the expence of the Turks has
been the fubject of difcuffion, that cafe
has generally been confidered as an
exception; on what grounds I fhall examine, and, I hope, plainly prove that
the expulfion of the Turks from Europe, and the re-eftablifhment of the
Greek empire, is more the advantage
of

of Britain than even of Ruffia itfelf;
that fo far from being an ufurpation,
it is an act of juftice; and that, according to the laws of nations, the Turks
have not, by length of poffeffion, acquired a right to the dominion of the
countries they conquered. The importance of the alliance of Ruffia appears every day more ftrongly, and I
rifk now, much lefs than I did a few
years ago, when I maintained, that the
falvation of Europe depended on engaging that power as a principal in the
war. The views of the French with
regard to Greece now too plainly appear, and the Emperor of Ruffia is in
danger of being attacked in the Black
Sea by a French fleet.

If it be faid that we ought, as much
as may depend on us, to prevent the
increafe of naval power in every other
nation, without denying the propofition, I affirm, that it is not applicable
to the prefent cafe: Ruffia never can
be formidable in the Baltic; nature has
forbid it. In the Black Sea fhe may,
and fhe will, in fpite of all we can do
to prevent it. The queftion then is,
fince we cannot prevent it, which is
the mode of its exiftence which will
be

be leaft hurtful to us? That the Greeks will emancipate themfelves from the yoke of Turkey is equally certain. If this event take place by the affiftance of the French, we fhall *certainly* have an *enemy* in Greece; if through Ruffia, and with our concurrence, a friend. There is, indeed, a poffibility, but not the leaft probability, that we may fometime or other quarrel with them, but not for a length of time, as there will exift a mutual intereft in friend-fhip. Why make a vain attempt, which will certainly create us enemies, when at leaft we ftand a fair chance of procuring friends?

What I have faid of Auftria at that time, I leave as I wrote; I fee no reafon to think I was then wrong.

The confiftency of the conduct of his Majefty's minifters, in firft oppofing the expulfion of the Turks from Europe, and afterwards making a war with Ruffia a *cafus foederis*, in the treaty of alliance with the Emprefs, in 1795, is fully proved by the different circumftances of the times. They have evinced, that they uniformly purfued the interefts of their country, and did not obftinately adhere to a fyftem, when

5   it

it no longer accorded with them. Let their antagonifts prove, that they themfelves did not facrifice the honour, as well as the interefts of this country, in oppofing, in an unprecedented manner, the meafures adopted by its government; that they themfelves are not the caufe of thofe calamities which they attribute to mifconduct in minifters.

I have added a few mifcellaneous papers without order or digeftion. They will fhow, in part, how far the Emprefs's vaft views of aggrandizement extended—they went to the entire conqueft of all European Turkey, a part of which was to be given to the Houfe of Auftria; the re-eftablifhment of the Greek empire, and placing her grandfon Conftantine on the throne of Conftantinople; of making Egypt an independent ftate; of giving to Poland a Ruffian for a fovereign, and ultimately incorporating it into her own empire; of making a conqueft of Japan and a part of China, and eftablifhing a naval power in thofe feas.

I have thought it neceffary to fay fomething of the character of the late Emprefs. Anecdotes of that Princefs appear daily in all languages. There are

doubtlefs

doubtlefs many truths in fome of them,
but they are generally fo defectively
related, and with circumftances which
fo totally mifcharacterife the action,
that few of them will ferve as materials for the accurate Biographer. Thofe
who wifh to know her real character,
and the character of the moft confiderable perfons of her court, would do
well to wait a little longer. As to the
hiftory of her reign, there are many
circumftances which cannot yet be dif-
clofed. Thefe anecdotes have the appearance of having been learnt in
Ruffia, but not committed to writing,
and the memory of the authors, fur-
charged with abundance of materials,
has confounded them; they appear
like mutilated ftatues reftored by un-
fkilful artifts; we find the trunk of
a Hercules or a Jupiter with the head
of an Apollo and the feet of a Satyr.

It is a difficult thing, at all times,
to difcover truth, amidft the mifre-
prefentations of courts, of minifters, of
commanders. Should any one write,
for inftance, the hiftory of the laft war
between Ruffia and Turkey, he would
take for his guide, in relating the firft
event, the fiege of Ochakof, the ac-

counts

counts publifhed by the court of Peterfburgh, and the reports of the commanders. There he would find a brilliant victory gained by Prince Naffau
over the Turkifh fleet in the Liman;
but if he could get the report made by
Paul Jones to the Admiralty of Cherfon, figned by all the commanders of
the fleet, he would find that no engagement took place (except a diftant
cannonade); that the Turkifh fhips ran
aground by their ignorance and bad manœuvres; and that Naffau with his *flotilla,* inftead of taking poffeffion of
them, fet them on fire. This journal,
which I have read, and taken an extract
from, was forbidden by Prince Potemkin
to be fent to Peterfburgh, and the whole
campaign, as it ftands on record, is nearly
a romance. The fortrefs might have
been taken the 1ft of July with more
eafe than the 6th of December, and the
commander in chief knew it. I was
at the opening of the trenches, and at
the ftorming of the place, and therefore can fpeak of facts to which I was
an eye-witnefs.

If, after all, I am miftaken, and have
loft my way in the wildernefs of politics, I have not erred intentionally; I
have

have been guided by no motive but the intereft of my country : and here I muft make a digreffion, which, I hope, will be pardoned.

A man who has been twenty years abfent from his native country may, I hope, be permitted to exprefs his afto- nifhment at the changes he finds on his return. Changes which feem not to ftrike fo forcibly thofe who faw the face of things every day.

When I left England, no man would have dared to ftand up to arraign his country, and publicly plead the caufe of France, and its enmity then was friendfhip compared with its enmity now; he would have been deemed a traitor, and the people would have treated him as fuch.

I hear minifters accufed of plunging the nation into a ruinous war, and per- fevering in it; I look to facts, and facts prove the contrary.

They are accufed of not humiliating their country before the enemy, and procuring fuch a peace as muft foon make England a province of France. I hope they are guilty.

I hear it publicly afferted, that the conftitution is changed; that liberty is
annihilated;

annihilated; that we are under a military government. I look to facts, and find a Hardy, a Thelwall, &c. &c. &c. cannot be punished. I see acquitted, at Haverford, men who were accused by five witnesses of high treason, because on their trial the witnesses cannot be *perfuaded* to speak out; and because their first positive, clear, and unequivocal deposition before a magistrate cannot be admitted. Where is the military government? The circumstance of an invasion would have justified it. How did they proceed in France, where liberty, equality, and fraternity are established? they punished *en maffe*. At Toulon, all those *fufpected* of having favoured the English were collected and fired on; at Lyons and other places, the same. Where were the juries? the counsel for the prisoners? where was the book of laws? where was the judge, who durst not interpret them one syllable beyond the letter? How would they have proceeded here? Not only the two men in question, but the whole town of Fifguard, would have been driven to the place where the French landed by invitation, and tried and executed by a regiment of soldiers, all *en maffe*, or in a lump.

XXVI   P R E F A C E.

lump. They would have proceeded in
the fame manner with a Thelwall and
his applauding audience. How did they
proceed with their oppofition? not an
oppofition to overturn the government
it had fworn to maintain, but an oppofition to ftop the progrefs of defpotic
power. The members of it were all
feized, and fent without trial to fome
place, nobody knows where, into exile,
perhaps to the bottom of the ocean.

In what page of hiftory, ancient or
modern, is fuch moderation to be found
as in this infulted government? I fee
here, *proved by facts*, men fubject only
to the law, and that law more powerful
than men. I find no fuch liberty any-
where elfe, neither in practice at this
day, nor in the records of hiftory.

Nor are my ears lefs fhocked to hear
a foreign dialect fpoken by a part of the
people of Britain. Our demagogues
have tranflated the French words *liberté,
egalité, fraternité, philantropie, philofophie,* by the Englifh words, liberty,
equality, fraternity, philanthropy, philofophy, and becaufe there is much refemblance in the founds, they would
perfuade the people that there is alfo
a refemblance in the ideas.

Facts

Facts teach us, that *liberté* fignifies the moft horrible tyranny, filencing all law, and violating all property; that *egalité* fignifies, murdering fovereigns and the higher claffes, and putting over the people men the moft low, ignorant, and wicked, invefted with power to infult, enflave, and drive them in flocks to be flaughtered, and placing them at a greater diftance than there exifted before between them and their fuperiors by birth and education. *Fraternité*, in France, fignifies being a Frenchman; applied to other nations, it fignifies, forcing on them a government, plundering their property, and taking their wives and daughters. *Philantropie*, is profeffing a general love to all mankind, and practifing cruelty to every individual. *Philofophie*, (which was the mother of all the French virtues,) fignifies the commiffion of every crime without remorfe; the extinction of every fentiment religious and moral, of every generous and focial feeling; the diffolution of every tie of kindred and affection; the annihilation of every quality which ornaments and diftinguifhes the gentleman, the fcholar, and the man of tafte; the banifhment of chaftity, mo-

b defty,

defty, fenfibility, and decorum from the female fex.

Every nation has thought it neceffary, in times of public danger, to punifh crimes, when the common law was infufficient, by a tribunal erected for that purpofe ; in Athens, this tribunal was compafed of the people affembled; in Rome, by judges appointed in confequence of a decree of the people. Have not the good people of Britain a right to look to their reprefentatives for protection againft thofe who *openly* and *fecretly* attack their government, and who *eftablifh fchools to diffeminate fedition* in the minds of their children, and yet defend the revolutionary tribunals in France, and the military defpotifm of the Directory, on the ground of public danger ? In all offences againft the nation, might not, (I afk, for I am not learned in the law) confiftently with our facred conftitution, the reprefentatives of the nation try and decide, rather than a jury of private perfons ? Such offences are not of a private nature between man and man: or might not that body which reprefents the party injured, the nation, be the accufer, and the Houfe of Lords the tribunal ? If this

*

manner

manner of proceeding be unprecedented, the neceffity of occurring to it
is alfo unprecedented.

I feel it incumbent on me to apolo-
gize to the Public for the repetitions,
foreign idioms, and other inaccuracies
and defects, which may be found in this
work, in confequence of its having been
too haftily prepared for the prefs.

ERRATA.

Page 66. line 4, *for* volontiers, *read* volunteers.
— 128. laſt line note, *for* melice, *read* militia.
— 156. line 22, *for* of, *read* off.
— 343, — 1, } *for* Fenal, *read* Fenar.
— 344, — 15, }

CONTENTS.

CHAPTER

CONTENTS.

CHAPTER V.—page 129.

Hiſtorical View of the Turkiſh Power.

Origin of its power. Cauſes of their former greatneſs. Character of their ſultans, and their ſyſtem of uſurpation ſanctioned by their religion. Othman I. Orkhan. Amurat I. eſtabliſhed the janizaries. His uſurpations. Bayazet I. ſtrangles his brother. Taken priſoner by Tamerlane, and kills himſelf. Mahomed I. kills his brothers. Amurat II. ſtrangled his brother. Horrid cruelties in his wars. Died of grief at his ill ſucceſſes againſt Scanderbeg. Mahomed II. murdered his two brothers. The greateſt monſter who ſat on the Turkiſh throne. Took Conſtantinople. Unheard of cruelties. He put to death above 800,000 Chriſtians. Bayazet II. His brothers eſcaped. Formed a project of cutting off the whole body of janizaries. Depoſed and poiſoned by his ſon. Selim I. murdered his father, brother, and his own children. Took Cairo. Died of a cancer a miſerable death. Soliman I. took Rhodes. His ſpeech to the grand maſter. Confeſſion of his ſentiments. Maſſacres in Hungary. Beſieged Vienna. Maſſacres. Took Bagdad, &c. Attacked Malta. Breach of capitulation. Killed his ſons and their children. Died of a flux. Selim II. ſet the example of not going himſelf to the wars. Took Cyprus. Ravaged Moldavia and took Walachia. Amurat III. murdered five brothers. Ravages committed in Poland and Ruſſia. Janizaries loſt their ſubmiſſion. Committed great ravages in the dominions of the emperor of Germany. Mahomed III. put to death nineteen brothers, and ten of his father's wives with child. Murdered the garriſon of Alba-regalis contrary to the capitulation. Several paſhas rebelled. He put to death his own ſon and his mother. Achmet I. unable to deceive, made peace with the Germans. His ſultana put his favourite to death. Muſtafa I. committed
mitted

CHAPTER

CHAPTER VIII.—page 284.

On the State of the Turkish Provinces.

CHAPTER IX.—page 334.

The Political State of Greece.

CHAPTER X.—page 391.

*The Turkifh Empire confidered with regard to its Foreign
Relations.*

POST-

A
S U R V E Y

O F   T H E

T U R K I S H   E M P I R E.

I N T R O D U C T I O N.

IT is the aim of the following fheets to
delineate the moral and political ftate of a
great empire, lefs accurately known to us than
its contiguity and relative importance demand.
The ftudy of human nature, under the various
influences of peculiar fituation, laws, and cuftoms, can in no cafe be uninterefting either to
the politician, the moralift, or the philofo-
pher.   If we confider mankind merely as
acted upon by fcience, as elevated to unufual
fplendor by the energies of intellect, or de-
preft to a brutal degradation by grofs ignorance, it muft render our fpeculations more
accurate, our judgment more diftinct, to try
the ftandard of theory by the teft of experience, and to view the effect produced on a

B   large

large community by the degree of knowledge
which they poffefs. If from fcience we turn
to morals, and would contemplate the efficacy of religious doctrines, of legal inftitutions, or of popular opinions, thefe cannot
be fairly tried but by referring to their effect
on the nation at large in which they exift.
Should it again be our defire to eftimate juftly
the political advantages of external and internal adminiftration, thefe are beft tried by
an appeal to facts: defpotifm or licentioufnefs appearing in their true colours give the
fureft, becaufe the moft rational means, of
appreciating the advantages of good government.

No one can doubt that thefe ends will be
greatly promoted by a review of the ftate of
Turkey, which muft prefent a picture no lefs
interefting, from the magnitude of its objects,
than from the peculiarity of their features.
It may indeed be objected, that this fubject
has been treated by many writers, apparently
well qualified to deliver faithful and complete
information; but it is not improbable that
the teftimony of an eye-witnefs, furnifhed
with a multitude of particular facts, would
even in that cafe be a defirable addition to the
mafs of evidence which is before the public.
The truth, however, is, that the multitude
of

of teftimonies, or the accuracy of information, is by no means fuch as to render further
accounts unneceffary : in many very_intereft-
ing points the principal authors do not agree;
fome are fwayed by perfonal or national intereft, and fome mifled by fuperficial obfervation or unfounded caprice. We have proofs
that even a long refidence in that country, and in a capacity which would appear
the beft calculated to afford information, that
of a public minifter, is not fufficient. The
numerous errors Sir James Porter has fallen
into demonftrate this. As to merchants,
their occupations feldom leave them leifure
or curiofity to be informed of matters foreign
to commerce, and diftant from their places
of abode. From travellers who run through
a country lefs is to be expected. " *Till a man*
" *is capable of converfing with eafe among the*
" *natives of a country, he can never be able to*
" *form an adequate idea of their policy and*
" *manners.*"

It is obvious, that a confiderable portion
of time and ftudy is requifite to obtain
a full acquaintance with the moral and
political ftate of a nation : he who would
obferve it with accuracy fhould have refided a long time in the country; he fhould
have poffeffed opportunities of penetrating

B 2   into

into the councils of the government, as well
as of noticing the manners and genius of the
people ; he fhould have feen them in war and
in peace, have noted their military fkill and
their commercial fyftem ; finally and above
all it is neceffary that he fhould have an accurate knowledge of their language, fo as to
cut off one great and almoft univerfal fource
of error in accounts of foreign countries,
arifing from the mifapprehenfion of the re-
lator himfelf.

In order to form a juft ftandard for
trying the comparative accuracy of different accounts, it will be neceffary to know
thofe prejudices which are moft likely, in
fpite of integrity, to infinuate themfelves into an author's work from motives of private or of public intereft.   With this view it
will not be unacceptable to notice a few particulars relative to two or three preceding
works of the beft reputation, which have
treated of the Turkifh empire in general :
(of earlier authors it is needlefs to fpeak.)
I know of no book from which more may be
learnt of the true character of that people,
and ftate of knowledge among them, than
from *M. De Tott*.   He fpoke their language
perfectly, he enjoyed their confidence, and
lived more intimately with them than any
                                    Chriftian

Chriſtian has lately done. It does not appear that he has wilfully miſrepreſented any one circumſtance. I never ſaw him, but what I have heard of him is much in his favour. His book diſobliged the French court, which did not wiſh to ſee them expoſed. He has ſpoken, perhaps, too much of himſelf, and made the moſt of what he did for the Turks, though the facts are indiſputable. Had he ſaid leſs of himſelf, we ſhould have loſt thoſe little ſtories he tells, which give more inſight into the true character of the people he was concerned with than volumes of diſſertations.

The egotiſm of modern travellers in relating incidents and adventures which might happen in any country, and which convey no information peculiar to that they are travelling in, is truly diſguſting; they are at beſt ſubjects for novels. The work of Baron De Tott is indiſputably the beſt and moſt accurate account hitherto given of the general ſyſtem, as well as the peculiar features of Turkiſh manners, and though it has been cenſured as a calumny, it is in fact a very moderate picture of real events.

To this teſtimony of De Tott is oppoſed that of M. Peyſſonel, a man undoubtedly learned and ſcientific, whoſe reſi-

B 3　　　　　　dence

dence in the empire and knowledge of its
language render him deferving of great attention, though his opportunities of acquiring information were by no means equal
to thofe of De Tott. Of M. Peyffonel
two things are to be remarked, the fuffrage which he gives in favour of Tott, and
the prejudices which were likely to affect
his own teftimony. In fpeaking of the Baron, he readily admits " *his profound know-*
" *ledge of the government, laws, manners, cuf-*
" *toms and character of the Turks, derived*
" *from a long refidence in the country, a clofe*
" *attention to the language, and from being em-*
" *ployed in affairs of the greatest importance.*"
What he profeffes is only to point out, " *pul-*
" *chro in opere nævos,*" fome imperfections
in a valuable work. After this fuffrage in favour of Tott, we need only refer to him for
a picture of Turkey, faithful enough to be
relied on, and yet fufficiently forcible to excite our difguft at fuch monfters in human
fhape. The fame M. Peyffonel quotes, as
writers of greater accuracy, Du Pan and
Montefquieu, who, he acknowledges, wrote
in their clofets accounts of a people whom
they had never feen.

In page 88 of M. Peyffonel's letter we
fee the true reafon of his defence of the
Turks:

Turks : " *It is* (fays he) *to endeavour to juf-*
" *tify a nation which has always been the ally*
" *of our own* ; *with whom we carry on a com-*
" *merce that is ſtill the objeȼt of envy and the*
" *vexation of our rivals.*"

Mouragia (now Chevalier d'Oraſſon) is perfectly equal to the extenſive work he has undertaken, which will contain more knowledge of Turkey than any book which was
ever written; but he will not touch the ſubjeȼt
of their decline and approaching fall : his object is to repreſent them in the moſt advantageous light, and he will not prove what they
are, but what they poſſibly might have been :
he is an Armenian, and Turkiſh is his mother tongue : he was once literally a ſans cu-
lotte : his promiſing genius, when a boy, procured him the patronage of a rich Armenian
merchant; intrigue, talents, and the protection of the French directory, raiſed him to the
poſt of Swediſh miniſter at Conſtantinople.

Other authors have only lightly touched on
thoſe matters which are the ſubjeȼt of this
book, and which it is my intention to inveſtigate more fully.

CHAPTER I.

On the Turkiſh Government.

TO point out thoſe relations which a country bears to its neighbours, or to the general intereſts of ſociety, is perhaps no very difficult taſk: the features are ſtriking, the moral and phyſical differences are eaſily diſcernible, and the ſtandard of general politics is, perhaps, accurate enough to determine, with ſufficient nicety, the reſult of ſuch an analyſis; but if we carry our inveſtigation into thoſe more minute cauſes which affect the proſperity or decline of a nation from internal circumſtances, we ſhall find the queſtion more deep and intricate, the deciſion more vague and doubtful. Without ſuch data, however, it is impoſſible to build up a moral or political ſpeculation of any magnitude or importance ; it is impoſſible to reaſon with accuracy on the great intereſts of nations, or to form grand and comprehenſive plans embracing the general advantage of ſociety. Nor is it leſs true, that internal cauſes are always

the

the moſt immediate motors in national elevation or decay: as, on the one hand, no feeble ſtate was ever elevated to extraordinary
eminence by the mere aid of alliances, however powerful; ſo, on the other, ſcarcely any
great nation ever periſhed by means of external violence, unleſs it had ſomething within
itſelf vicious and unſound. I ſhall, therefore,
in a future chapter, take a view of the Turkiſh Empire from without, as it ſtands related
both to the general ſyſtem of Europe, and to
the ſeveral European powers; and in the
mean while I will proceed to diſcuſs its internal ſituation.

From the nature of man, from the extent
of his faculties and the variety of his powers,
it is evident that he is at the ſame time operated upon by cauſes the moſt heterogeneous
and diſſimilar. With the progreſs of ſociety
new powers and new faculties are daily called forth; they continually modify each other,
and produce that action and re-action which
conſtitutes the complexity of the vaſt ſocial
machine. To abſtract and generalize theſe
various motions, to reduce them to their pri-
mary and elemental principles, is the buſineſs
of ſcience; but it unfortunately happens but
too often, that the philoſopher, who may with
much care and obſervation have made this
analyſis, will build upon it ſpeculations the
moſt

moft unfound and irrational. The error into which thefe dealers in fyftem frequently fall (an error which has very unjuftly thrown a general odium upon all the fyftematic labours of fcience) is to conceive that the divifions which they have themfelves eftablifhed in theory are ftrongly marked in fact, or, in other words, that the different habits and cuftoms of mankind are lefs intimately interwoven than experience daily proves them to be. When, therefore, we trace the diftinct fources from which the peculiar character and circumftances of the Turkifh nation have originated, we muft be careful at the fame time to remember, that the events which have flowed from thofe fources have been fo mixed and compounded together, and act at the prefent day with fuch an aggregate force, as to produce a far greater effect by combination than by their feparate power. So much is neceffary to be obferved before we begin to delineate the peculiar features of Turkifh policy: we now proceed to the tafk of difcrimination.

The modern European, accuftomed for the moft part to confider all the fubjects of one empire as alike entitled to the protecting care of government, alike invefted with the political rights of citizens, can with difficulty accommodate his feelings to a ftate of manners

ners refulting from the divifion of the poli-
litical body into conquerors and conquered,
oppreffors and oppreffed. This is, however,
the diftinction moft broadly marked in the
Turkifh Empire; a diftinction fupported by
every kind of prejudice which can influence
focial manners, and confirmed by the inveterate habits of ages. To the celebrated governments of antiquity this exaltation of one
part of the community upon the degradation
of the other was by no means unknown;
we fee it inftanced in the *Helots* of Sparta,
and in the inftitutions of many of thofe nations who moft loudly vaunted of their fancied liberty: happily for modern ages it has
generally, in Europe, given place to political
equality; but Turkey is the refuge of fana-
tical ignorance, the chofen feat where fhe
has unfurled her bloody banner, and where,
though torpid with age, fhe ftill grafps her
iron fceptre. That happy union, and equality of right to the protection of laws, which
tempers the variety of individual interefts by
the general utility, is the only bafis of focial
happinefs. How far the dereliction of thefe
principles in the Turkifh government weakens the power of the community, whilft it
perpetuates the mifery of the individual, will
appear from a comparative view of the different fects in that country, and from a furvey

vey of the ftate of its provinces. The *Turks*, properly fo called, are the followers of Mahomet, defcended from the Tatarian conquerors of thefe beautiful countries, who being now the actual mafters of the empire, and the only perfons who feem to have a real intereft in its exiftence, their fituation, moral and phyfical, firft demands our notice. The great outline of their character, as diftinguifhed from the other inhabitants of this extenfive empire, is the fuperiority which they claim on the grounds of conqueft and religion. To apply to a nation, barbarous as the Turks, any rule of rational policy drawn from the law of nations, would, perhaps, be deemed abfurd ; but the enlightened obferver muft ever remark, that the fancied right of conqueft is nothing but the right of the fword, which is never legitimate but when fanctioned by juftice. In the hiftory of the world there have been frequent inftances of mighty nations, who, after conquering their opponents by force of arms, have received from their captives the fofter yoke of fcience. It was thus that, in the words of Horace :

> " Græcia capta ferum victorem cepit, et artes
> " Intulit agrefti Latio."

Nor have there been wanting examples of the introduction of arts by the conqueror himfelf,

himfelf, who has thus made amends, by the
bleffings of civilization, for the havock which
he had caufed by the fword. The Turks,
however, like barbarians, invaded Greece,
and fwept before them the mighty monuments of ancient fcience ; and, like barbarians, they hold their captives, to the prefent
day, under the benumbing yoke of ignorance
and flavery. Inftead of promoting the mutual advantage of both nations, by an intercourfe of knowledge and benevolence, they
ufe the privilege of conqueft only to the extinction of the common powers of intellect.
A politic conqueror, in augmenting the happinefs of his new fubject, increafes his own
power ; a barbarian invader weakens his own
refources by the continued oppreffion of his
captives. Abderahman (or Almanzor) who,
in the middle of the eighth century, founded
a kingdom in Spain of the provinces which
had been fubject to the kalifs, promoted intermarriages between Chriftians and Mahomedans. The Arabs, who had been as
great enemies to the fciences as the Turks,
now cultivated them with great fuccefs, and
had acquired a confiderable portion of knowledge and politenefs, while the reft of Europe was degraded by ignorance and barbarifm. But the haughty Turk is not merely
exalted above his fubject Greek as a conqueror ;

queror; he confiders himfelf ftill more highly
elevated as the favorite of heaven, and the
greater part of his ferocity as a tyrant is
owing to the arrogant and barbarous dictates
of his religion.   It is in vain that the pane-
gyrifts of Turkey would affure us of the fpirit
of toleration, which, according to them, the
difciple of the fanguinary Mahomet cherifhes
in his bofom.   Every feature of the Turkifh
character, every circumftance of their public
and private cuftoms, contradicts the affertion.
Mankind are not at the prefent day to learn,
that the human character is formed by its
education, and that a great and important
branch of that education confifts of political
inftitutions. Were there any doubt of the
truth of this principle, the ftrong exemplifi-
cation of it afforded by Turkey would obviate
every objection.   There it is, more than in
any other country, that the dogmas of the
legiflator and the prieft are continually prefented to the mind of youth as well as of age;
that they occur in every rank and condition
of life, and act with a force the more powerful, as they are united in one and the fame
code.   Such are the obfervations which arife
on the firft view of the Turkifh character :
in proceeding to particularize its individual
features, we have to contemplate the various
caufes, moral and phyfical, which have an
influence,

influence, either immediate or remote, upon it ; always remembering, that they are to be viewed, not merely as fimple powers, but as acting with that mutual and reciprocal force which fo greatly augments their aggregate effect. The local and material objects which contribute to the rife and fall, the importance or weaknefs of nations, are, *climate, fituation, productions,* and *population* ; but thefe are in part or altogether fubject to the energies of mind, and mind takes its peculiar bent from *religious* and *political inflitutions,* from *hiftorical events,* from *arts* and *fciences,* and from thofe general *manners* which are the refult of all the other caufes combined.

In the following fketch I fhall endeavour to develope, firft, the *moral* caufes, and from their action it will not be difficult to account, in the fecond place, for the *natural* phænomena obfervable in the prefent ftate of Turkey.

The religion of the Turks is, perhaps, the predominating principle, which, above all others, ftamps the character of their minds ; but as its power in this refpect is chiefly owing to its political authority, and as it is not my intention to enter into a metaphyfical inveftigation of a fyftem whofe abfurdity is obvious to all enlightened, Europeans, I fhall confider this part of the fubject as dependant

on

on the political inftitutions, which will therefore firft demand attention.

Political inftitution is a fpring always in action, a motor univerfally prefent, forming the character of the individual, and guiding the operations of the community. Would we then caft our eyes over the moral map of Turkey; would we juftly eftimate the internal powers of that nation, either as an enemy or ally, our notions muft be regulated by the degree of purity or error obfervable in its political œconomy.

Much has been faid in affertion and denial of the *defpotifm* of the Turkifh government; and arguments the moft abftrufe and far-fetched have been employed, rather to confound the meaning of terms, than to eftablifh the authenticity of facts. But if by defpotifm be meant a power originating in force, and upheld by the fame means to which it owed its eftablifhment; a power fcorning the jurifdiction of reafon, and forbidding the temerity of inveftigation; a power calculated to crufh the growing energies of mind, and annihilating the faculties of man, in order to infure his dependence, the government of Turkey may be moft faithfully characterized by that name. All permanent power, extended over a large community, muft have fomething more than the mere force of arms

C

to

to rely on; or rather that very force muſt depend, in the ultimate reſort, on popular opinion. It is a vain objection, therefore, that the deſpotiſm of the ſultan cannot extend beyond the ſuperſtition of the people: that very ſuperſtition ſerves it as a baſis, and the more firmly rooted are their religious prejudices, the more terrible is the deſpotiſm which ſprings from them.

Equally vain and fruitleſs are the conteſts concerning the particular character of this deſpotiſm. It has been called a *military* government, from the nature of its origin, and the means moſt frequently employed in its adminiſtration; and it has obtained the denomination of a *theocracy*, becauſe its fundamental code is the Koran. Each of theſe ſtatements contains ſomething that is erroneous. A military government ſuppoſes the dictates of an arbitrary chief, requiring implicit obedience in every inferior, and preſcribing a certain and inevitable puniſhment for neglect or tranſgreſſion; it excludes all formality and delay, and it is enforced by military power. In theocracies, the will of the leader has not (or at leaſt pretends not to have) the direction of the ſtate: himſelf an inſtrument in the hands of a ſuperior being, he communicates to the people, at various times and as occaſion requires, the commands
mands

mands of the Divinity. The Turkiſh government bears evident traces of both theſe
ſyſtems, derived from the character of its
founder; but there are ſome points of difference which prove it to be, *ſui generis*, an he-
teroclite monſter among the various ſpecies
of deſpotiſm. In the Mahometan ſyſtem of
policy we may trace three æras. The *firſt*,
which was of that kind uſually denominated
a theocracy, continued during the life-time of
the prophet himſelf, who, like Moſes and
Joſhua among the Jews, appeared in the double character of a military chief and an in-
ſpired legiſlator. The *ſecond* was the government of the Saracen kalifs, his immediate
ſucceſſors: they bore indeed the double ſceptre of temporal and ſpiritual power; but as
they pretended to no perſonal communica-
tions with the Almighty, all the ſanctity of
their character conſiſted in being the deſcendants of the prophet, and the guardians and
expoſitors of his law. The preſent Turkiſh
conſtitution forms the *third* gradation : like
the preceding, it has an inviolable code in
the ſacred volume of its religion ; like them
alſo its reliance is on the power of the ſword,
and the modes of its adminiſtration are military ; but it has a great eſſential difference in
the ſeparation of the temporal and ſpiritual
authorities. This *diviſion of power* origi-

nated

nated in the political error of the Ottoman
princes, who, eager only for military glory,
and perhaps wifhing to caft a fpecious veil
over their ufurpation, when they finally fup-
preffed the kalifat, did not affume to themfelves all its functions, but refigned into the
hands of the theological lawyers the fpiritual
fupremacy. No defpotifm was ever more
profoundly politic than that, which, wield-
ing at once the temporal and fpiritual fword,
converted fanaticifm itfelf into an inftrument
of fovereignty, and united in one perfon the
voice and the arm of the Divinity. But it
muft be remembered, that when the power
of the kalifs began to decline, other princes,
befides thofe of the race of Othman, affumed
an independent fovereignty; and it is probable that moft of them, with a fhow of moderation, which they thought politic, invefted
the priefts with the adminiftration of all
their fpiritual affairs. Such was the origin
of the authority given to the *ulema,* or body
of lawyers, and their chief, the *mufti,* or high
prieft, to whom is entrufted the expofition of
the Mohammedan law in all its branches.
Thefe men poffeffing, like the priefts under
the Jewifh theocracy, the oracles both of law
and religion, not only unite in themfelves the
power of two great corporations, thofe of the
                                        law

law and of the church, but alfo fhare with the fovereign the direct exercife of the legiflative, executive, and judicial powers. Previous to the Ottoman æra, there were indeed muftis; but their power was only of a judicial, not of a political nature, exactly refembling that of the muftis, who are now appointed in the feveral provinces, and whofe office is fomewhat fimilar to that of kadi or judge; for it muft not be forgotten, that the judicial and facerdotal characters are in Turkey the fame. The chief engine of this hierarchy is the *fetva* of the mufti, a fort of manifefto, which, like the bulls of the Roman pontiff, originating in ecclefiaftical power, has been applied to the moft important political purpofes.

The kalifs, with a view of enfuring the prompt obedience of their fubjects, were accuftomed to give to the principal acts of their government the fanction of religion, by affixing to their decrees (fuch as thofe of war and peace) the facred feal, which affured to the true believers, acting under it, the honour of fupporting their faith, if triumphant, or the palm of martyrdom in cafe of death. The Othman princes, in order to obtain a fimilar end, were obliged to require the aid of the priefthood, which they had eftablifhed. They applied, therefore, to the mufti, who,

by

by the advice of the heads of the ulema,
publifhed the facred ordinance called *fetva*,
which declares the act of government, to
which it is affixed, confonant to the Koran,
and obligatory on all true believers. The
power which the priefthood thus acquired
was at firft inconfiderable; it refembled the
enregiftering of edicts by the French parlia-
ments, which was a meafure rather judicial
than legiflative; but they doubtlefs perceived in it the feeds of future greatnefs and authority. So long as the fceptre was fwayed
by warlike princes, the mufti was eafily made
to fpeak as the fultan directed, and the power
of the ulema, under their warlike monarchs,
was fcarcely perceived. It does not appear
that they attempted any refiftance to the will
of the fovereign before the reign of Amurath IV. That prince, one of the moft ferocious that ever fate on the Ottoman throne,
irritated at the oppofition of a mufti, caufed
him to be thrown into a huge mortar, and
pounded to death. He conceived this kind
of punifhment in order to obviate, by a cruel
irony, the privilege which the ulema enjoyed, that no member of their body could
have his blood fhed as a punifhment. This
example fufficiently proves how little the
men of the law were, at that time, able to

                               oppofe

oppofe a fovereign whofe defpotifm was fupported by the fcimitar.

But upon the decline of the military fpirit
of the fultans, that, which was only a political fpring in the hands of the fovereign, has
become a fundamental law of the empire,
creating and confirming a power, which, if
not in actual oppofition, is always in balance
againft him. The utility of fuch a balance
of power in the more enlightened governments has been ftrenuoufly fupported on the
grounds of a liberal policy; but, whatever we
may think of fuch arguments, they cannot
apply to the ftate of Turkey, where the balance is only a balance of intrigue and artifice, whilft there is, in both parties, a perfect
accordance of defpotifm, a mutual defect
both of the means and inclination to benefit
the community. On the part of the fultan,
it may be obferved, that he would, long fince,
have become the mere creature and tool of
the mufti, but for the power which he has
referved to himfelf, of nominating and depofing the holder of that dignity. This it is
which gives him a counterpoife againft the
mufti, by creating for him, among the
ulema, as many partifans as there are candidates afpiring to the pontificate. The ulema,
on the other hand, are, in their collective capacity, jealous of preferving the influence

which

which they have thus obtained in the government; and that religion, which served the firſt ſultans as a mean of adminiſtration, has become a ſource of terror and ſubjection to their feeble ſucceſſors. The fetva is now ſo indiſpenſable a preliminary to any political act, that the ſultan, who ſhould dare to omit it, would be declared an infidel by a fetva iſſued by the mufti *motu proprio*; and ſuch a proceeding would be ſufficient to excite againſt him both the populace and ſoldiery, and to precipitate him at once from his throne. So far is this jealouſy carried by the ulema, that they oppoſe, with all their power, the ſultan's departure from the capital, leſt, at a diſtance from their manœuvres, he ſhould be able to conciliate the army to his intereſts, and aſſert his independence. The late ſultan Muſtafa, anxious to be at the head of his army, was prevented from taking the field only by the fear of a revolt, which the men of the law could eaſily have excited in his abſence.

Another apparent check on the authority of the ſultan, is formed by the *great council*, conſiſting of the great military officers, the heads of the ulema, and the principal miniſters of the empire. No important act of government can be undertaken without a previous diſcuſſion in this aſſembly, at which the

the grand feignior, or his chief vizir, prefides; but every queftion is decided by a plurality of votes. It is unneceffary to expatiate on this body, as forming a diftinct political power, becaufe, from the nature of its members, it muft be fwayed either by the party of the fultan, or by that of the priefthood, and it, therefore, ferves rather to determine the relative power of thofe two diftinct bodies.

That much political knowledge cannot be expected from the minifters of ftate, is evident from the manner in which they attain their fituations. Rifing from the meaneft ftations, they advance progreffively to the higheft pofts ; not by means of fuperior genius or knowledge, but by petty intrigue, and by flattering thofe on whom they depend. The vizir *Yufef*, who commanded in 1790 againft the emperor, was raifed by Gazi Haffan from a ftate of the mereft indigence. He fold foap, in a bafket on his head, in the ftreets, before he became the fervant of Haffan, who, after employing him in that menial office, made him fucceffively clerk in the treafury of the arfenal, his own agent at the porte, (kapi kahia) pafha of the Morea, and, laftly, grand vizir.

There is, indeed, a regular eftablifhment for educating youth for the fervice of the fultan in a fchool at Pera, called *Galata Serai:*

Serai: when they come thither, they are placed in different claffes, according to their abilities and the line to which they are def-tined. But this inftitution has fo far dege-nerated, that few but the fons of perfons belonging to the feraglio are fent thither, where their education is of fmall importance, as any one, whether he has paffed through this college or not, may attain any office in the feraglio by means of intrigue and bribery. It may be worth while here to notice a fin-gular error, which is generally entertained in Europe relative to the term *feraglio*, which is fuppofed to mean the apartments of the wo-men : it literally means *palace*, and is, there-fore, applied by way of eminence to the vaft range of buildings inhabited by the grand feignior and all the officers and dependents of his court. Here is tranfacted all the bufinefs of government ; the council itfelf is called the *divan*, and the place of public audience the *porte*, or the gate. Of the officers of the feraglio the *vizir* is chief (as being the prime minifter of the fovereign) ; this is alfo a term given to him by way of eminence, as it fig-nifies a counfellor in general ; every pafha of three tails (that is of the firft clafs) is a vizir : the pafha or vizir who refides at the porte, or with the fultan, is called the grand vizir, or vizir azem. Befide the vizir, all the

the other great public officers of the empire,
refident at Conftantinople, inhabit the feraglio, or, at leaft, have their offices there; all
the minifters, pafhas, &c. without exception,
belong to it, and their poffeffions revert at
their death to the fultan, their mafter and
their heir, of whom they are ftiled the *flaves*
(kul, or kool) fo that their defcendants have
no advantage over thofe of the meaneft mechanics, except what they may cafually derive from the notice of the fovereign, or
from having been introduced by their parents into the fchool of the feraglio.

From the preceding obfervations it appears, that the legiflative and executive powers are, in the higher acts of policy, divided
among different bodies: the executive acts
of an inferior order are fuch as regard *financial* and *military* operations, or matters of
general *police*. The two former of thefe
branches, though of fmall import in the
individual acts, are, each in its aggregate,
of fufficient importance to claim a feparate
confideration; to each of them, therefore, I
fhall devote a future chapter, and for the
prefent pafs on to a curfory view of the internal police. However diftinct the *principle*
of the Turkifh government, as it at prefent
exifts, may appear, its forms of adminiftration, and all its internal police, are purely
military.

military. This is fo thoroughly the cafe, that the grand feignior is ftill fuppofed to reign, as formerly, in the midft of his camp; he even dates his public acts from his *imperial ftirrup*, and fimilar inftances are difcoverable in all his other formalities. The government of diftant provinces is committed to *pafhas*; their dignity is military, and the whole defpotic power of the fultan is delegated to them. A flight view of the hiftory of the janizaries will fhow of what kind is the dependence placed on them, as well in the maintenance of the police as in the exercife of war. The force of arms firft fubjugated the countries which form their empire; the force of arms alone could retain them in fubmiffion; and it is owing to the decline of the military fpirit of the Turks, that the members of fo vaft a body are, at the prefent day, fo feeble and difunited.—To wield the iron fceptre with effect required a warlike fovereign ftained with blood, the fcourge of his people, and alone the idol and the terror of an obedient foldiery.

Such were a long while the characters of the fultans, and of the janizaries, the faithful minifters of their defpotifm. From the moment that the latter beheld their chief no longer animated with a brave and warlike fpirit, the machine of government was thrown into

into diſorder; the moving power was no
longer the ſpring which ſhould have directed,
and the re-action of the exterior parts toward the centre was totally deſtroyed. The
janizaries, then, ſeized themſelves that power which a weak and cowardly ſultan could
not wield; they depoſed their monarch, and
placed upon the throne one in whoſe valour
and abilities they had greater confidence;
but a more refined policy on the part of the
deſpot annihilated the power of theſe pre-
torian bands, by a ſyſtem of corruption and
enervation. The moſt eminent of their lea-
ders were taken off, either by ſecret fraud or
open accuſation, and their places ſupplied
by the meaneſt and moſt devoted creatures
of the court. In the meanwhile the corps
itſelf was baſtardized and rendered contemptible by the introduction of a herd of the
vileſt of the people; men occupied in the
loweſt employments, and even ſtained with
the moſt infamous crimes, who would have
been formerly expelled from the ſervice
with the greateſt indignation. The ſultans
have, indeed, ſucceeded in extinguiſhing every
ſpark of that fire which they dreaded; they
have annihilated all traces of a military ſpirit; but they have, at the ſame time, para-
lyzed their own hands, and left themſelves
                                    without

without the powers neceſſary for the ſupport
of a deſpotic government. Many of the
paſhas, having little to fear from the vengeance of the grand ſeignior, proceed to the
moſt·violent abuſes of their authority, and not
unfrequently appear in open rebellion. The
defection ſpreads from province to province,
and little remains, in this vaſt empire, but
the ſhadow of an union without real ſtabi-
lity, and of an obedience which mocks the
graſp of ſuperiority. In the regular adminiſtration of government, however, the ſultan is poſſeſſed of the moſt arbitrary power
over the lives of his ſubjects, and executes
criminal juſtice, either by himſelf or his vizirs, without proceſs or formality.

In regard to property his power is more
limited : over that of all his officers he has
the fulleſt right; he is their lawful heir ; but
in regard to that of his other ſubjects he is
reſtricted by the laws to greater moderation.
It is, nevertheleſs, eaſy to avoid ſuch reſtric-
tions ; and we ſhall, in fact, ſee that the in-
ſecurity of property in Turkey is one very
powerful cauſe of the ignorance and vices
of its inhabitants. The ſultan delegates his
power in this reſpect to the vizirs and paſhas
in the provinces, and, in a leſs degree, to governors and officers of different ranks and denominations.

nominations. Pretexts and fuppofed crimes are always to be found to deftroy or to ruin a fubject. This part of the government is therefore truly defpotic; and when the prince or his reprefentatives are tyrants, it is defpotifm in a form the moft cruel and infulting to the rights of mankind.

Having examined the legiflative and executive branches of government, it remains to fpeak of the *judicial*. This branch is founded, like the others, on religion; but a divifion fuited to the barbarous nature of its origin feems to obtain in it. The offences againft the ftate, or fuch as affect the public peace, are wholly under the jurifdiction of the fovereign, and feem to be excluded from the judicial forms; whilft the difpenfation of juftice by formal procefs feems to be intended only for offences and difputes of a more private nature.

The excellence or defect of a judicial fyftem depends upon the *code* of law; upon the *commentaries* or precedents which are received as poffeffing authority; upon the *perfons* appointed to adminifter juftice, and upon their *mode* of decifion. The fundamental law, civil and political, is the *koran*, whofe refpect is owing to its divine origin: from this is extracted a civil code, called the *multka*, to which are added certain commentaries called
the

the *durer* and *halebi* ; and befides thefe there are various collections of *fetvas*, or fentences, of the moft celebrated muftis, all of which together form, it muft be confeffed, a collection of legal knowledge more than fufficient for the inftruction of the judges. But as thefe judges are not bound by any preceding decrees, and have the application of the law in their own breafts, the more intricate it is rendered by the different compilations and commentaries, the more arbitrary is the power intrufted to them. Were the tribunals pure, and the mode of trial equitable, this laxity of interpretation would doubtlefs be an advantage to the caufe of juftice ; but the contrary is fo notorious in Turkey, that the iniquitous decifions of the judges are proverbial, and often furnifh the fubjects of their burlefque comedies. Peyffonel complains of the unfairnefs of Baron de Tott in citing different inftances of Turkifh injuftice, and obferves, that fimilar examples may be found in the hiftory of every country ; but it is not neceffary in Turkey to recur to paft ages, or to fingle out particular examples ; it is the prominent feature in the character of their tribunals, and every day's experience confirms the cenfure of Tott, by repeated inftances of corruption.

The dexterity of the Turkifh kadis, or judges,

judges, to decide in favour of thofe who have paid them, is often very ingenious; many pleafant ftories are told of them, and it is generally a fubject for a kind of comedians, who act in coffee houfes or in private houfes, but without drefs or fcenery, one of them performing the part of a kadi, and two others the plaintiff and defendant.

An Arab who had hired out his camel to a man to travel to Damafcus, complained to a kadi, on the road, that he had overloaded his camel; the other bribed the kadi. " What has he loaded it with?" afks the kadi—the Arab anfwers, " *with cahué (coffee) and mahué,*" *i. e. coffee et cetera* (changing the firft letter into *m* makes a kind of gibberifh word, which fignifies *et cetera)* " *fugar and mugar, pots and mots, facks and macks,*" &c. going through every article the camel was loaded with; " *he has loaded it twice as much as he ought*;" " then," fays the kadi, " let him load the cahué and leave the mahué, the fugar and leave the mugar, the pots and leave the mots, the facks and leave the macks," and fo on to the end of all the articles enumerated, and as the poor Arab had told every article, and only added et cetera, according to the Arab cuftom, without there being any &c. he took up the fame loading he had before.

D   A chrif-

A chriſtian ſubject of the Turks was carried before a judge at Aleppo, accuſed by a Sherif of having one evening in the bazar, or market place, knocked off his green turban, for which he would have been put to death—the judge was himſelf a Sherif (they have in moſt places the privilege of a judge of their own race.) The Chriſtian ſent ſecretly, bribed him, and informed him of the truth, which was, that the Sherif's turban was of ſo dark a green that he took it for a dark blue, a colour which a chriſtian friend of his wore, and for whom he had taken him in the dark of the evening, and had knocked off his turban in a joke. The accuſed was brought before the judge, and the plaintiff came into the judge's hall with a great number of other Sherifs. The judge addreſſed them ; " *Do you come here in ſuch numbers to aſk juſtice, or to take it yourſelves ; go out all but thoſe who are witneſſes, and you chriſtian,*" ſaid he, addreſſing himſelf to the accuſer (who had been privately pointed out to him) " *go you out, I ſuppoſe you are a witneſs for the accuſed; you ſhall be called when you are wanted.*" The man exclaimed, that he was not only a Mahomedan, but a Sherif, and the accuſer himſelf ! " What," ſays the judge, " you a Sherif and wear a turban of a colour that I myſelf in the day time took

for

for that of an infidel; how could the poor
infidel in the dark diftinguifh it. You ought
to wear the holy *grafs* green of the prophet,
and not be afhamed of it.   He acquitted the
Chriftian, and ordered the plaintiff to be baftinadoed for not wearing a proper green turban.   It would, without this turn, have been
difficult to have appeafed the violence of the
Sherifs affembled; but he was well paid for
it, and for money they will run any rifks.

If the Turkifh judges difplay great ingenuity in diftorting the rules of equity, it
muft be owned that they fometimes fhow
equal fkill in the advancement of juftice.
When the famous Kuperly was grand-vizir,
an old woman brought to an Armenian
money-changer a cafket, containing jewels
of great apparent value, faid they belonged
to a fultana, and borrowed money on them,
depofiting the cafket after fhe had fealed it.
The money was to be paid again in a certain time. The woman not appearing a long
while after the time was expired, he opened
the cafket, in the prefence of feveral refpect-
able perfons, when the jewels were difcovered to be falfe. The Armenian went to
the vizir and related the ftory. The fultana
had not fent any jewels to be pawned. He
ordered him to remove from his fhop, in a
private manner, every thing valuable, and

D 2

on

on such a night to set it on fire; that he would be near with proper people to prevent it spreading; that then he should constantly sit before his shop, and lament to all who passed his having lost a casket of jewels of immense value in the fire. In a few days the old woman appeared, and demanded to release her jewels. She was carried to the vizir, who showed her her casket, and told her she should be immediately put to death by the most terrible torments, if she did not confess the whole. She discovered her accomplices; they were put to death, and the Armenian got back his money, deducting the vizir's share. This fact is known at Constantinople.

The panegyrists of Turkish jurisprudence adduce in its favour the custom which is called *burning the mat*, by which any individual, whether Mahometan, Jew, or Christian, may appeal to the justice of the grand seignior from the oppression or injustice of his officers. The petitioner, on these occasions, appears in the street, near the mosque to which the sultan is going, and has on his head a bit of burning mat, at the same time bearing aloft his petition, which is lifted up to the officer, whose business it is to receive and put it into a bag. The extreme of violence often produces a remedy no less violent

in

in its nature ; it is thus with the burning of the mat, which is never practifed but on great occafions, when a complaint is lodged, in a defperate manner, againft a vizir, or other great perfon, and the fultan is thereby cautioned to take the fuppliant under his protection. Such petitioners have, generally, a party of malcontents to fupport them ; and they adopt this mode to warn the fultan of the danger of not receiving their complaints, which, indeed, without fome fuch precaution, feldom meet with any attention.

It appears from the preceding confiderations, that the evils arifing from the mode of government afford little hope of reform. Such an attempt would in vain be undertaken, even by a fovereign of the greateft abilities and moft patriotic inclinations. Were a fultan, equal in military talents to Amurat the fourth, to fit on the Ottoman throne, it might be poffible to rekindle that martial genius in his forces, which has been fo long extinguifhed, and to reduce to fubmiffion thofe rebellious pafhas, who have been fo long independent. This indeed would be an herculean labour ; but even this would be rendered ineffectual by the prevalence of the ulema. A powerful priefthood, in oppofition to the fovereign, muft, in fuch a country as Turkey, thwart all his views, and render in-

D 3　　　　　effectual

effectual his moft ftrenuous exertions. To introduce an unity into the government, this ambitious body fhould be wholly extirpated; but fuch a ftep as this fcarcely any fultan who has fat on the throne, would have dared to have taken; how much lefs is it to be expected from the daftardly and enervated fovereigns who now fpring from the feraglio.

Much ftrefs has been laid by fome authors on the limitation of the fultan's power by law, with refpect to property of individuals, to prove that his government is not wholly defpotic. The fact, however, is fimply, that with regard to fome kind of property, as houfes which are poffeffed by inheritance, the fovereigns have fometimes thought it dangerous to violate the common law openly, by depriving the owner of their property by force; in fuch cafes, when the object has been defirable, we have feen them take a fhorter way, by putting the owner to death; and againft this exercife of power no one objects; and fometimes they have fubmitted to the law to make their reign popular. This oppofition to the will of the fultan, as has been obferved, is not to be underftood of the officers of the porte, for with thefe no ceremony is obferved. The pafhas in the provinces are, however, lefs delicate than the fultan in the capital.

CHAPTER II.

On the Turkish Finances.

THERE is no matter of internal policy which affords a wider scope for
the display of abilities than finance; it is to
a skilful application of its powers in this respect, that the rise and the continuance of a
great empire is chiefly to be attributed; and
from a failure here may be deduced most of
the evils which bring on its decay and downfal. It would be a narrow view of this subject, which should regard only the debtor and
creditor side of the account, the positive or the
relative magnitude of the imposts; it is not
so much the *sum* raised or expended, as the
mode of its levy and application, which is to
be regarded as the test of political ability.
The following sketch will, therefore, embrace a view of the different public treasures,
together with observations on the mode of
raising them, on their application, and on
their present situation.

The Turkish system of finance may be divided into two great branches, the public
treasury or *miri*, and the sultan's treasury

or

or *hafni,* each of which has its peculiar
fources of revenue, and its particular appro-
priation of expenditure.

There are, indeed, other treafures of confiderable magnitude, which deferve the attention of the politician, though not properly
included in the fyftem of finance : thefe are
the treafures of the *ulema* and thofe of the
mofques, fums taken from the active and efficient capital of the nation, and either wholly
unemployed, or appropriated to ufes which
cannot be fuppofed to have a very direct relation to the neceffities of the ftate.

The public treafure or exchequer of the
ftate firft demands our attention, as that in
which are to be expected the moft methodi-
cal regularity, the greateft fairnefs in the impofition, and judgment in the application of
the taxes. The revenues of this treafure are
of two kinds, the fixed and the cafual, the
former of which may be divided into the
karach or tribute paid by Chriftians, and the
farms of the empire in general; the latter
confift of certain articles, which will be
mentioned in the fubjoined detail.

The expenditure embraces a variety of
objects, *viz.* the expences of the army and
navy, in war as well as peace; the pay of all
officers, civil and military; the erecting and
repairing of fortifications, of public edifices,
high-

high-roads, bridges, &c. together with a great part of the expences of the fultan's houfehold, and feveral other extraordinary difburfements.

The following detail will comprife the ordinary revenue and expenditure of the public treafury of the Ottoman empire, from the moft authentic documents, together with a view of its debts and credits in the year 1776, at the conclufion of a ruinous war with *Ruffia*.

ANNUAL REVENUE of the MIRI.

This comprehends the different tributes, taxes, and cuftoms, called the karach, mukatá, bedeli-nōuzōul, avaragíhané, gebeluyan, gebeluyan-embak, gebi-humayun, havafihumayun, eukaf-humayun, pifkés-zaifé, meokuf, tarap-hanei, anciré, haremein hafinefi, fherifein hafinéfí, &c.

1. FIXED REVENUE.

The firft branch is the *karach*, a capitation tax, or annual redemption of the lives of all thofe males above 15 years of age, who do not profefs the Mahometan religion.— It is farmed in the different diftricts as follows:

EUROPEAN CITIES and PASHALIKS.	Purfes Rumi of 500 dollars or piaftres.	Piaftres.
Conftantinople and its environs This karach was augmented to this fum in the year 1776, by the addition of 360 purfes (or 180,000 piaftres) of which augmentation only 100 went to the public treafury.	2,916	
Adrianople and its environs -	1,750	
Sophia - - - - -	320	
Tattar-bazargik - - -	250	

	Purfes Rumi.	Piaftres.
Philippopolis - - - -	280	
Salonico - - - -	530	
Ufkiup - - - -	260	
Kiofdentil - - -	226	
Terhale - - - -	450	
Yenitfher Kinar - - -	270	
Avlonia - - - -	350	
Ohry - - - - -	250	
Delviné - - - -	170	
Elbiffan - - - -	160	
Bania - - - - -	450	
Kifria - - - - -	250	
Ozi (now in the poffeffion of Ruf-fia; called Oczakow by the Poles)	90	
Siliftria - - - -	170	
Varna - - - -	170	
Babadahg - - - -	100	
Paravadi - - - -	160	
Karinabad - - - -	180	
Egribozak - - - -	190	
Rufchuk - - - -	220	
Shumna - - - -	170	
Hezargarad - - - -	90	
Niceboli - - - -	390	
Harmen - - - -	260	
Viddin - - - -	300	
Iflemie - - - -	150	
Ufunge abad Hafkioy - -	176	
Gallipoli - - - -	240	
Orfe - - - -	70	
Yenebanti - - - -	210	
Negroponte - - -	500	
Ifdiu - - - - -	96	
Belgrade - - - -	180	
Nifia - - - -	196	
Alaffonia - - - -	170	
Tif - - - - -	45	
Kiordos - - - -	70	
Athens (Seitin, or land of olives)	90	
Yeniké - - - -	220	
Napoli di Romania - -	225	

	Purſes Rumi.	Piaſtres.
Hatevmis - - - -	120	
Calamata - - - -	130	
Enghily Kaſry - - - -	170	
Livadia - - - -	70	
Tancara - - - -	90	
Donigé - - - -	80	
Aleſſandria - - - -	290	
Boſnia with its dependencies -	1,495	
(Bender and Hotin are not included)		
Morea and its five juriſdictions -	3,560	
	20,015	
PROVINCES and CITIES of ANA-TOLIA.		
Hadé vendighiar Sangiaki - -	280	
The province of Kiatahie - -	480	
Gimis dizné of Eſkiſhehir - -	120	
Sultan Ony - -	130	
Kara Hiſſar - -	160	
The province of Angora - -	190	
The juriſdiction of Tuſſia -	180	
of Boli - -	90	
of Kiſlin -	75	
of Viran Shehir -	75	
of Hiſſar ony -	120	
of Akſhe-ſhehir	110	
of Cara-ſu -	55	
of Ghiul Bazar -	80	
The government of Caſtemony -	190	
The juriſdiction of Sinop - -	150	
of Tyr - -	50	
of Sultatnony -	70	
of Ghiuſel Hiſſar	90	
of Allaſhehir -	80	
of Metmen -	90	
The government of Menteſhe -	150	
of Smyrna -	320	
The juriſdiction of Akſne Shehir	120	
of Sahri-hiſſar -	125	
The iſland Kuſeh-adaſi - -	150	
The juriſdiction of Ghiul-hiſſar -	160	

	Purses Rumi.	Piastres.
The jurisdiction of Hamid -	300	
of Yalli-keffri -	80	
of Sandughi -	50	
The government of Breigha -	160	
of Caraffi -	40	
of Teké -	27	
of Glayé -	210	
of Ifenghemid -	450	
of Ala - -	110	
of Sivas -	490	
of Tokat -	260	
of Nikdé -	120	
of Yenifherry -	210	
of Yenni-il -	90	
of Amafia -	180	
of Bozauk -	70	
of Zurem -	150	
of Diyunik -	120	
of Dzanik -	800	
of Arabkir -	320	
The province of Caramania -	200	
of Ahfhery - -	210	
of Kaisarie - -	120	
of Akferai - -	120	
of Adana -	200	
of Silis - -	110	
of Iz·il - -	300	
of Ekin - -	90	
Tripoly in Syria - - -	120	
Damafcus (or Sham Sherif) -	400	
Aleppo (Haleb) - - -	600	
Kelis - - - - -	120	
Agras - - - - -	70	
Meras - - - -	200	
Anitab - J - - -	240	
The government of Malatia -	120	
of Rica - -	200	
of Ahmed -	110	
The government of Hifni Manfur -	80	
of Diarbekir -	300	
of Muffil -	300	
of Etzerun -	450	

	Purfes Rumi.	Piaftres.
The government of Trebifond -	300	
of Gelder -	200	
of Van - -	110	
of Karis - -	150	
Bagdat, Baffora, Merdin, and environs - - - - -	500	
The ifland of Tenedos - -	45	
of Meteline - -	180	
Shio (or Scio) -	380	
Stanchio - -	150	
Candia - -	560	
Kubrus (or Cyprus)	850	
Tino - -	45	
The iflands dependent on the capitan pafha - - - -	180	
Cairo (or Meffir) - - -	1,350	
Several other revenues, of which is a feparate account - -	1,455	
Total for the Karach for Romelia } and Anatolia - - - }	39,077 or	19,538,500

The SECOND BRANCH of the FIXED REVENUE comprizes the following general TAXES or FARMS of the Empire.

Mukata, (farms regiftered in the Bafh muhaffebé, &c.) - -	4,791	
The Ogialik of Bulgaria pays -	520	
The Agalik of the Turkomani -	450	
The body of Chingani (Gypfies or Bohemians) - - -	2,690	
Gebeluyan lokaf humayun render -	280	
Emlaki humayun - - D° -	350	
Gebeluyan of the Timar and Ziamet, poffeffed by aged or infirm perfons - - -	470	
Bedeli Nuzul of the Timar and Ziamet of Romalia and Anatolia	3,580	
Avarigi Hané *(per centage of immoveables)* - - -	2,959	

	Purſes Rumi.	Piaſtres.
Of tobacco, the mines of ſilver, &c. contributions of the admini-ſtrators -	2,300	
Mukata, mizan on ſilk, maſtic, oil, &c. of the country of Bruſa -	790	
Duty paid by the dealers in ſheep	780	
Salt pits or mines of Haſlar -	1,200	
Fiſh, woods, &c. of Metelino and its ports; tax on weight at Con-ſtantinople - - -	2,800	
Paid for the ſultan's kitchen, by certain cities, towns, and vil-lages - - -	1,300	
By the company of butchers -	600	
The cuſtom houſe of Conſtanti-nople - -	1,872	
*The duty on tobacco - -	1,287	

* N. B. This duty is aſſigned in the following
manner;
   855 purſes to the proprietors of the
         Malikané.
   232 to the muſti.
   200 to the imperial mint.

   1,287

	Purſes Rumi.	Piaſtres.
Rent of the houſes belonging to the arſenal - - -	1,280	
Duty on tobacco of Arabia and of Id - - - -	700	

Of which is aſſigned 400 to the proprietors
above mentioned 300 to the imperial
mint.

	Purſes Rumi.	Piaſtres.
Revenues of the farms belonging to Mecca and Medina - -	2,800	
Divers ſmall farms deſtined for cha-rity - - - -	2,995	
Annual Fixed Revenue - -	75,871	
or		37,935,500
Carried forward - -	75,871	
or		37,935,500

	Purses Rumi.	Piaftres.
Brought forward - -	75,871	37,935,500
II. Unfixed Revenue.		
From the Muagili and Mukata -	5,772	
Duty on tobacco - - -	3,065	
Cafual confifcations and inheritances - - -	1,327	
Farms of Cairo - - -	1,650	
On tobacco by a new regulation -	400	
The Zaëfé paid by the vizir and other minifters for their offices -	1,800	
Befides what is paid on the creating of a vizir on making any other minifter. - - -		
	89,885	
	or	44,942,500

Total of the Revenue of the Empire or public treafury, called the *Miri*, 44,942,500 piaftres, or about £. 4,494,250. fterling. Since this calculation was made, the exchange is ftill more againft Turkey, or, more properly fpeaking, this money has been much debafed.

The Revenues of Walachia and Moldavia are not included. They were to pay nothing during the three firft years after the peace with Ruffia was concluded.

ANNUAL EXPENDITURE of the MIRI.

	Purses Divani.	Piastres.
Pay of the city guards or militia of Constantinople - -	22,700	
Pay of the bostangis and of the people belonging to the sultan's kitchen - - -	700	
Pay of the agas and officers of the sultan's palace - -	1,700	
To the harem of the old palace -	1,800	
To the sultan's eunuchs - -	800	
To the aga of the seraglio of Galata - - - -	501	
Expences of the kitchen (purses rumi) - - - -	1,800	
To the chief of the butchers -	600	
Expences of the imperial stables	600	
Arbitrary assignments - -	1,250	
A donation to Mecca and Medina	9,000	
Pay of the sailors of the fleet -	2,700	
Provision for the fleet - -	800	
Expences of the admiralty -	1,800	
Pensions of the sultanas and of the deposed khans of the Crim -	1,372	
Pay of the garrison of Viddin -	1,250	
Pay of all the other fortresses of the Ottoman empire - -	18,000	
Pay of those of Bosnia - -	1,970	
For maintaining recruits -	472	
Expences of the lesser department called Kuchúk Kalem -	1,200	
Pay of those who guard the Danube - - - -	3,521	
Expences in maintaining the posts	1,700	
Total of the Expenditures of the Empire, paid by the public treasury or miri - -	76,236 or	36,968,133

Equal to about £. 3,696,813 sterling.

{ Revenue - £. 4,494,250 sterling.
Expenditure - 3,696,813
Surplus - - £. 797,437 sterling.

An

An ACCOUNT of the DEBTS and CREDITS of the MIRI, in 1776, *after the conclusion of the* RUSSIAN WAR.

	Purses Divani.	Piastres.
The Miri owed,		
To the treasury of Mecca and Medina - - -	- -	1,350,000
To the Hasnè - - -	- -	45,550,000
To the arsenal - - -	- -	6,500,000
To the Miri was owing,		53,400,000
From the tobacco customs -	3,786,000	
From several branches of the Revenue - - -	6,000,000	
A balance on the Yearly Payments to the treasury - - -	7,280,480	
		17,066,480
Balance, being the debt of the Miri, or about £. 3,628,350 sterling - - -	- -	36,333,510

The *hasnè*, or private treasure of the sultan, next claims our notice : in amount, indeed, it is vastly superior to the miri, but it contributes little to the exigencies of the state, except in times of war, or other great emergency, and even then it is generally made a creditor of the public treasury to the amount of its contribution.

The ordinary expenditure of this treasury is chiefly confined to the seraglio; it is, however,

E

ever, very confiderable, though greatly diminifhed fince the reform introduced by fultan Muftafa the third.

Its extraordinary expences have fometimes
been very confiderable, large fums being oc-
cafionally paid to fecure the fidelity of the
janizaries in times of popular commotion, or
on the acceffion of a new fultan to the throne
amidft the ftruggle of contending factions ;
it has alfo, in fome inftances, contributed
larger fums toward the profecution of a war,
than thofe for which it has been made creditor by the miri.

The receipts may be divided (as thofe of
the miri) into fixed and cafual; the former,
however, are very inconfiderable in comparifon with the latter.

The fixed revenues of the hafné confifted
of the following tributes :

From Cairo   600,000 piaftres.
   Wallachia   230,000
   Moldavia   260,000
   Ragufa   20,000
              _____
              1,110,000 piaftres, or £. 111,000 fterling.
              _____

Thefe, however, have either ceafed entirely, or are little to be relied on. The Ra-
gufan tribute, which is the only one paid regularly, confifts of 12,000 fequins, or £. 6,000
fterling

sterling every three years. Those of Moldavia and Wallachia are annihilated when there
is a war with Russia; and Cairo is so little
subject to the porte, that instead of receiving
a regular contribution from thence, large sums
are frequently sent thither to corrupt the begs,
and to ensure their obedience to the porte, by
fomenting quarrels amongst them.

The casual revenues of the hasné, are

1st. The revenues of the mines, which have lately much
  diminished.

2d. The sale (for they are really sold) of all places and
  posts, which are also diminished, as they do not
  bring in so much as they did, owing to the wretch-
  edness of the provinces. The pashalik of Cairo
  used to cost £. 75,000 sterling; that of a cadi
  in a great city 2 to £. 5000, and more.

3d. A duty of 10 per cent on all inheritances.

4th. The inheritances of the officers of the seraglio, and
  the porte (or empire,) the sultan being their heir,
  to the total exclusion of their children or relations.
  The ulema solely are exempted from this law.

5th. The confiscations of all officers disgraced or put to
  death

6th. The property of those who die without heirs, inherited
  by the law of escheat.

7th. Penalties.

8th. Presents from great officers and foreign courts.

Nothing can be more uncertain than a guess
(for a calculation is impossible) of the amount

of

of each of thefe branches of the private treafury; many of them are in themfelves highly
fluctuating, and others are fubject to immenfe
embezzlements. That they greatly furpafs
the revenues of the miri cannot be doubted,
fince it is the principal occupation of every
pafha to fuck out the very vitals of his province; and thefe men have no fooner amaffed
a great property, than they are cut off by the
fultan to enrich his treafury.

Every fultan leaves what is called his treafure in the vaults of the feraglio, and every
fultan thinks it a duty to leave as confiderable
a fum as he can—they attach even a vanity
to it.

The perfonal hereditary wealth of the individuals of the ulema forms, in the aggregate, a
very confiderable fund, which, in the ordinary
operations of government, cannot be applied
to any ufes of the ftate. The ulema, as we have
feen, is the only body of men who hold offices in the Turkifh empire, whofe property
is hereditary in their families; it may therefore be naturally fuppofed that they will become objects of the fultan's avaricious jealoufy: fuch, however, is their power, that
any invafion of their treafure would be
attended with the greateft danger. The
mere exiftence of fuch a treafure is, however, a fubject of great importance, both as
affecting

affecting the ordinary and extraordinary circumstances of the state.

In the former, it serves to support a body
of men invested with formidable power, in
oppofition to the fultan; but as these fame
men have little connection of intereft with
the people at large, their wealth feems to be
taken from the general ftock only to nourifh
an additional body of tyrants. In the event
of any great convulfion, it cannot be doubted
that even this treafure would be facrificed to
the prefervation of the ftate; but it feems
probable that this meafure would not be
adopted without fome ftruggle on the part
of the ulema, who will fcarcely be willing to
make fuch a facrifice until it is, perhaps, too
late.

The treafures in the mofques are very
confiderable : they arife from the revenues
appropriated to them at their foundation, and
by fubfequent bequefts; and as the fuperftition of the rich muffulmans frequently leads
them to fuch acts of oftentatious charity, the
aggregate of thefe fums throughout the whole
empire muft be immenfe. The whole of this
property, being under the feal of religion, cannot be broken in upon with impunity. The
ordinary revenues are, or ought to be, expended in the fupport of the mofque, and in
works of piety and charity; but there are be-

E 3   fides,

fides, in fome of their vaults, treafures which would be very confiderable, were it not for conftant malverfation on the part of the guardians. The whole of thefe treafures, though ftrictly forbidden by law to be applied to any other ufes than thofe of religion, may be reforted to when the feat of empire itfelf is in imminent danger, an event in which the interefts of the Mahometan religion are fuppofed to be involved.

Such are the fources, and, as nearly as it can be calculated, the amount of the Turkifh revenue and expenditure. The mode of its collection, and the probable confequences of its prefent fituation, afford room for obfervations of the higheft importance, which, indeed, are fufficiently obvious to the enlightened European, but which the ignorant Turk would with difficulty comprehend or arrogantly deride.

The want of clear and accurate views on the fubject of finance gives the court that rapacity, which fpreads to all the fubordinate officers, and tends to the impoverifhment of the people without augmenting (but on the contrary diminifhing) the refources of the government. It has become a fixed fource of revenue to fet to public fale offices of every denomination; nor is it only to the treafury that thefe fees, fometimes to a very high

amount,

amount, are paid : in the intrigues of the feraglio, by which the difpofal of all places is regulated, every thing is done by means of bribes ; and if this is attended, as we have feen, with the worft confequences in the diftribution of juftice, it is no lefs pernicious in the department of finance.

Hence it is, that the pafhas fent into the diftant provinces exert to the utmoft their power of extortion ; but are always outdone by the officers immediately below them, who, in turn, leave room for the ingenuity of their fubordinate agents ; and the circle is only completed by the power of the defpot, who, from time to time, fqueezes into his own coffers the fpunge, with which this herd of plunderers had abforbed the property of the people.

As the Mahomedans themfelves pay no perfonal tax or capitation, and in general contribute very little to the revenues of the ftate, the pafhas are obliged to find other methods of exacting money from them ; but the Chriftians always fuffer moft.

The mildnefs of the Turkifh government is argued from their permitting foreigners to pay lower duties than their own fubjects ; this circumftance is, however, only a proof of their ignorance in matters of commerce ; for furely a wife and politic fovereign would, by

all means, cherifh the commercial fpirit in
his own fubjects rather than in ftrangers.
The duty paid by foreigners is 3 per cent.
whilft that paid by the natives varies in different places from 5 to 7 and 10 per cent.
The loweft is a duty of 5 per cent. paid at
Conftantinople and Smyrna, on fome articles
of foreign produce; but in moft parts of the
empire the legal duty on merchandize in general is 10 per cent. Peyffonel, who cor-
rects Tott on this fubject, is himfelf fo far
from being accurate, that (contrary to his
affertion) the common duty is called *afheria*,
or the tenth (from the Arabic *afhir.)* But
the legal impofts are but a fmall part of what
the merchant pays: foreigners indeed are,
in all countries, more liable to impofition
than the natives; but that even the latter
are fubjected to heavy impofitions is certain,
from the inftances cited by Tott, which are
by no means uncommon.

From the total feparation of the public
treafury and that of the fultan, it refults,
that whilft the former is in the moft im-
poverifhed ftate, and unable to pay for the
moft neceffary expences of the empire, the
latter abounds with money, which is lavifhed
on the moft frivolous objects. However the
fplendor of the fovereign may be fuppofed to
be connected with the glory of the ftate, the
neceffities

neceffities of the latter have furely a para-
mount claim ; but in Turkey it is confidered
of more importance to provide diamonds for
the fultan's harem, than to conduct the moft
ufeful operations, military or commercial. If
the prefent ftate of the Turkifh finances
feems incompatible with the permanence or
profperity of the ftate, the future profpect is
ftill lefs promifing.

The debt of the miri, in 1776, cannot be
confidered as very enormous, if we take into
the account how great had been the exertion,
and how ruinous the expence, of the preceding war. The fleet, which had fuffered fo
greatly from the difafter at Tchefmé, was
alfo re-eftablifhed on a more formidable footing than it had been previoufly to that event,
and the treafury feemed to have effected all
its moft burdenfome operations. Neverthelefs the expenditure has fince increafed, and
it is not probable that the miri can difcharge
its debts without a donation from the treafury of the fultan, a meafure which does not
enter into the policy of the feraglio. Here
then we are to confider the probable confequences of a deficiency in its treafury, to a
government which knows nothing of the
financial provifions of modern politics, and,
confequently, will be totally unprepared for
fuch a conjuncture.

The

The revenues of the empire are diminish-
ing, and as the extortions of the pashas increase, and the means of satisfying them de-
crease in a degree alarming to the porte, op-
pressive even to the Mahomedans, and shock-
ingly distressful to the poor Christian subjects,
some great crisis cannot be very far off, when
the sultan must (notwithstanding every reason he may have to the contrary) open the
treasures of the seraglio, and, last of all, have
recourse to the sacred deposits of the mosques,
and the riches of the ulema. What disorder,
confusion, and alarm, this will occasion, what
revolutionary events it may produce in the
provinces, from the distress and consequent
weakness of the porte, may be easily foreseen; universal anarchy must prevail, and
every pasha will aspire at being an independent sovereign.

That there would be resources in the empire no one can doubt; but to employ them
would require another system of government
—a system incompatible with the policy, the
habits, and perhaps the fundamental laws of
the Turkish government.

The revenues have lately been considerably
augmented by improvements in the administration of the different branches, and particularly the farms.

The debasement of the current coin has
sometimes

fometimes been reforted to by fovereigns as a meafure of finance. In this point of view the following obfervations on the Turkifh money may not be unacceptable:

The alloy in the GOLD COIN is filver (not copper.)

The zurmachbub of Conftantinople, a gold coin of Machmut, Ofman, and Muftafa, weighs 13 karats, and is $\left\{ \begin{array}{l} 22\frac{1}{2} \text{ carats fine} \\ 1\frac{1}{2} \text{ alloy filver.} \end{array} \right\}$ The mitcal, or 24 carats of pure gold, is worth $6\frac{1}{2}$ dollars. Thefe pieces go for $3\frac{1}{2}$ dollars.

The zurmahbubs of Abdulhamid and Selim are 19 carats fine, and go for $3\frac{1}{2}$ dollars.

Thofe of Cairo weigh 13 karats, and go in Turkey for $3\frac{1}{4}$ dollars; they are from 17, 18, to 19 carats fine.

The fundukli of Machmut and Muftafa weigh $17\frac{1}{2}$ carats, are 23 carats fine, and go for 5 dollars,

SILVER COIN.

1 pound of filver equals 100 drachms.

In the piaftres there are but 40 drachms pure in the pound.

Thofe of Abdulhamit 34 drachms—they cheat 2 carats at the mint, which the money is lefs than the ftandard.

That of fultan Selim, the prefent reigning fovereign, is ftill worfe.

CHAPTER III.

Of the Turkish Military Force.

THE state of the Turkish military forms a very interesting branch of enquiry, since it is that by which their empire has risen, and upon which it seems to depend. In developing the weakness of this disorganized mass, I shall first recur to the causes which formerly gave it power, and which, having ceased to operate, leave it, at the present day, only the semblance of its ancient greatness. From this survey we shall turn to a delineation of its present state, and after giving a detail of the land forces, shall consider their present military character, their tactics, and laws of warfare; from the united consideration of which will be seen, what estimation the Turkish armies justly deserve. The naval force will merit a separate attention; and here we shall notice those attempts at its amelioration, from which, if effectual improvement could be at all hoped in Turkey, it might have been, with some probability, expected. Lastly, I shall notice the state of the Turkish fortifications, particularly of those which are, or are supposed to be, of the last importance to the defence of the empire.

It

It is undeniable that the power of the Turks was once formidable to their neighbour not by their numbers only, but by their military and civil inftitutions, far furpaffing thofe of their opponents, who were never united in a rational fyftem; governed often by courtiers, priefts, or women; poffeffing no rational fyftem of finance, no great refources in cafes of exigency, no fyftem of war even comparable to the Turks, a feudal government, internal diffentions, no wife or folid alliances amongft each other; and yet they all trembled at the name of the Turks, who, with a confidence procured by their conftant fucceffes, held the Chriftians no lefs in contempt as warriors than they did on account of their religion. Proud and vain-glorious, conqueft was to them a paffion, a gratification, and even a mean of falvation, a fure way of immediately attaining a delicious paradife. Hence their zeal for the extenfion of their empire, or rather a wild enthufiafm, even beyond the pure patriotifm of the heroes of antiquity; hence their profound refpect for the military profeffion, and their glory even in being obedient and fubmiffive to difcipline.

The Ottoman empire was governed by great men from Othman I. to Mahomed IV.
The

The exceptions, if any, were always fo fhort, that the military genius of the people did not decline, but was like a fire fmothered, and always broke out in the next reign with redoubled fury. To fultan Amurath I. is owing the rife of a permanent military among the Turks ; he it was, who, after extending the fphere of his conquefts from the Helle-fpont to the Danube, formed the more po-litic project of preferving his empire by a body of militia, accuftomed to difcipline and attached by peculiar privileges to the fer-vice.

For this purpofe he took every *fifth child of the Chriftians* in his power, above fifteen years old, and committed them to the care of hufbandmen for two or three years, to be inured to hard labour, and inftructed in the Mahometan religion. They were then taught the ufe of arms, and to accuftom them to flaughter they were made to practife the ufe of their fabres on their prifoners or crimi-nals. When every movement of compaffion was worn out, they were inrolled in the body of *yenifheri* (new troops) or janizaries, and formed the flower of the Turkifh army. The inftitution of the janizaries gave at that time a decifive fuperiority to the Turkifh arms, as they prefented a fyftem of difci-pline, and a permanency of organization, till then

then unknown in Europe. Thefe haughty
and celebrated legions were long the terror
of furrounding nations, and continued to be
looked upon as formidable until the middle
of the feventeenth century. At that time
the Turkifh power ceafed to aggrandize itfelf; it made a paufe in its conquefts, a paufe
prophetic of that downfal toward which it
has fince fo rapidly verged, and which feems
now to threaten a fpeedy approach. The
fteps which led to this degradation are eafily
difcernible. The difcipline of this ferocious
foldiery could only be upheld by fovereigns
equally ferocious : no fooner did the fultans
quit the fatigues of the camp for the debaucheries of the harem, than the janizaries,
difdaining their command, broke out into
fedition, and dethroned the monarch who
appeared unworthy of empire. It was the
policy of fultan Mahmud, who dreaded
their military and turbulent fpirit, to debafe
this corps; he therefore permitted the loweft and moft infamous of the people to en-
rol themfelves as janizaries; hence their
number has been greatly fwelled, but their
character has been more than proportionally
degraded, and many of them are notoriously
ftigmatifed for cowardice, theft, and the vileft
crimes, whilft others, enervated by a city life,
and the practice of the loweft trades, have

nothing

nothing military but the name of janizary. In the abftracts of their hiftory will be feen the attempts that were made to cut them off entirely.

Peyffonel makes a pompous enumeration of the diftinctions which take place in the army, and of the military canons of fultan Soliman, which determine its regulation and difcipline.

That there are fuch diftinctions follows from the very nature of an army, as the *fag kol* and *fol kol* (right wing and left wing) the *ortas*, *buluks*, and *feymens* (different names for corps) as alfo the titles of the officers, as *janizar aga*, *feymen bafhi*, *koul kiaiaffi*, &c.; but thefe forms prove nothing with regard to the minutiæ of tactics. It is the general characteriftic of the Turkifh government to be loaded with forms and regulations, which are of no effectual fervice; thus the canons of fultan Soliman indeed exift, but no one ftudies them, and to attempt enforcing them would be abfurd.

I fhall therefore proceed to ftate the following

CALCULATION of the TURKISH ARMY,

As far as its utmoft extenfion at prefent admits, from the concording teftimony of feveral

veral perfons who had the moft intimate acquaintance with it, from an application of many years, and with means of acquiring the beft information.

INFANTRY.

	Men.
1. Janizaries - - - -	113,400
2. Topgees, artillery men; according to the ancient inftitutions there fhould be 18,000, but there never exifted more than	15,000
3. Gumbaragees, bombardiers - -	2,000
4. Boftangees, guards of the gardens; they now guard the palace - - -	12,000
5. Mehtergees, who erect the tents and place the camp - - - -	6,000
6. Meffirlis, fent from Egypt—infantry and cavalry	3,000
7. Soldiers, from Walachia and Moldavia - -	6,000
8. Leventis, marines; few in peace, in war at moft - - - -	50,000

Infantry - 207,400

CAVALRY.

	Men.
1. Spahis—paid regulated - - -	10,000
2. Serragis, for the fervice of the infantry and their baggage, enrolled by the pafhas in the provinces. They are a corps de referve in great neceffities - - -	6,000
3. Zaims and timariots, feudal troops - -	132,000
4. Gebegis, armourers, who guard the powder, arms, and magazines, occafionally ferve as a corps de referve of cavalry; they fhould be, according to the canons of the empire, 30,000, they now are fcarcely - -	13,000

Carried over - 161,000

F

5. Miklagis,

C A V A L R Y.

Men.

	Men.
Brought forward -	161,000
5. Miklagis, who attend on the spahis - -	6,000
6. Segbans, who guard the baggage of the ca-} valry - - - -}	4,000
7. Volontiers, with their horses, never more than	10,000

Cavalry - -	181,000
Infantry - -	207,400

Total -	388,400

From these should be deducted,

1. The leventis, who belong to the fleet, and can only be employed } 50,000
near the coast where the fleet is - }

2. For the garrison of Constantinople, though so many in time of war, } 20,000
are not always kept there   -   - }

3. Garrisons of the fortresses and fron- } 100,000
tiers in Europe and Asia   -   - }

4. The bostangees, when the grand } 12,000
seignior does not go into the field }

                                182,000

Troops to take the field   -   206,400

The miklagis, and such as serve the vizir, the beglerbegs, and pashas, never go into } 20,000
the battle, and only increase the number; these may be computed nearly at   - }

Total   -   186,400

The remainder of effective men will therefore amount only to 186,400 men.

As

As it will foon appear how little the Turkifh arms are ftrengthened by difcipline, the
confideration of numbers becomes doubly important, and indeed it is upon them that the
porte at prefent entirely relies. Yet even
here its power evidently fails to an alarming
degree : it has often found it difficult to af-
femble 100,000 men ; and in 1774, with its
utmoft efforts, it could only bring into the
field 142,000.

Thefe numbers too are greatly leffened by
defertion. In 1773, the porte fent 60,000
janizaries toward Trebifond, to be embarked
for the Crimea, where not 10,000 arrived,
the reft having difperfed themfelves on their
route. Befides thefe regular troops, the
Turks were formerly affifted by numerous
hordes of Tatars, whofe mode of warfare
exceeded even their own in barbarity : this
fupply is now cut off by their ceffion of the
Tatar provinces to the emprefs, fo that they
will not in future·be able to cope with Ruffia even in the number of their troops.

The laft reliance of the porte is upon the
volunteers ; but a few obfervations will fuffice to fhew how little confidence can be
placed in fuch forces.

Formerly, when the whole nation was in
fome manner inflamed with the warlike genius of the janizaries, when the people were

F 2 inflated

inflated by fuccefs, and every one knew more
or lefs the ufe of arms, thefe were often
found ufeful and valiant troops ; but at prefent they confift chiefly of an undifciplined
rabble, inftigated either by a momentary
rafhnefs or a defire of plunder. Some go,
becaufe they are afhamed to ftay at home, on
account of the ridicule of their neighbours ;
others, to fecure the privileges and pecuniary
advantage which they derive from being attached to a chamber (or company) of janizaries ; another part of thefe volunteers
are robbers, and the outcaft of the Turks,
who go to plunder on their march, as well
going as coming, under the fanction of their
military profeffion.

The mollahs and mouhazim cry from the
minarets of the mofques, in time of war, that
all good mufelmans muft go to fight againft
the infidels, with a long enumeration of the
obligations on all true believers to take the
field.

Hence, a young man is often feized with
a fit of enthufiafm, (I have perfonally known
many fuch in Afia) he takes a pair of richly
furnifhed piftols (if he can afford it, for in
the richnefs of their armour is their pride) a
fabre covered with filver, and a carabine, and
mounts his horfe to conquer the infidels, and
make them become mufulmans, and to bring
back

back with him young girls for his harem. If he does not repent and turn back before he fees the camp, nor when arrived at the army, he foon learns from others the danger there is, and the difficulty of vanquifhing the infidels ; and when he has been a witnefs of it, and feen that there are only hard blows to be gotten, he generally fets fpurs to his horfe, and rides off. Thus by whole troops, in every war, thefe volunteers return, plundering the poor peafants, and often murdering them, particularly if they are Chriftians, to be able to fwear, when they return home, how many infidels they have killed. The Afiatic foot foldiers defert in the fame manner, and by thoufands, though they are moft of them janizaries.

There is, it is true, a confiderable difference in the foldiery : the Turks of Europe are the beft foldiers; but far above all, thofe of Bofnia, Albania, Croatia, and towards the emperor's frontier ; they are a very robuft and warlike people, accuftomed from their infancy to arms, and are almoft continually fighting with one another, or againft the porte, or plundering on the roads. The emperor had to do with a much worfe enemy than the Ruffians; and befides, they had to defend their families and homes, and confe-

F 3   quently

quently had an intereſt in the war, which the Aſiatic troops have not.

Many authors have contended, that it is poſſible to inſpire the Turks anew with their ancient military ſpirit, and to elevate their forces to their former ſuperiority, by inſtructing them in European tactics. The attempts which have ſo frequently been made by French officers to this purpoſe, without the leaſt ſucceſs, are convincing proofs againſt ſuch a ſuppoſition. The celebrated Bonneval, whoſe adventures were matter of much notoriety in the beginning of this century, laboured at this undertaking, as did the Baron de Tott ſince his time; yet, notwithſtanding the ability and perſeverance of the latter, all his pains were rendered fruitleſs by the unconquerable bigotry of the Turks themſelves. An attempt is now making on a better principle; not by endeavouring to diſcipline the old ſoldiery, but by raiſing a new corps, of which notice ſhall hereafter be taken. If theſe inſtances were not ſufficient to ſhow the impracticability of ſuch an attempt, a very ſlight view of the real ſtate of their force would ſuffice to ſet it in the cleareſt point of view.

Their force lies in their attack, but for that they muſt be prepared; taken unawares

6   the

the fmalleft number puts them to flight.
The Ruffians always conquer when they
attack them, and therefore avoid being attacked, which is generally very eafy. At
prefent the attack of the Turks (terrible indeed as it appears to thofe who fee it the firft
time) is no longer new to the Ruffians ; they
know how to receive it, and therefore do not
dread it. Had the emperor followed the
Ruffian fyftem, he would have been equally
fuccefsful, in the beginning of the laft war,
as he was when he changed his plan of operation.

Befides that the Turks refufe all me-
lioration, they are feditious and mutinous ;
their armies are incumbered with immenfe
baggage, and their camp has all the conve-
niencies of a town, fhops, &c. for fuch was
their ancient cuftom when they wandered
with their hordes. When their fudden fury
is abated, which is at the leaft obftinate refiftance, they are feized with a panic, and
have no rallying as formerly. In proportion
as the march of the army, advancing in the
field, was flow, fo is it rapid in its retreat.
They leave their baggage, abandon every
thing to the enemy, and do not even nail up
their cannon. The cavalry (which is the
only part of their army that deferves the
name of troops) is as much afraid of their
own foot as of the enemy; for in a defeat

they

they fire at them to get their horfes to efcape quicker. In fhort, it is a mob affembled
rather than an army levied. None of thofe
numerous details of a well-organized body,
neceffary to give quicknefs, ftrength, and regularity to its actions, to avoid confufion,
to repair damages, to apply every part to
fome ufe; nothing, as with us, the refult of
reafoning and combination; no fyftematic
attack, defence, or retreat; no accident forefeen, or provided for.

To thefe reafons might be added the opinion of Gazi Haffan, the celebrated captain-
pafha (of whom I fhall have occafion to fay
much hereafter) who, after repeated endeavours to improve the army, found all his attempts ineffectual. He faw it was impoffible to difcipline the Turkifh army, and gave
up all hopes of it, but propofed a new order
of battle.

He would have divided an army of 100,000
men into ten different corps, which were to
attack feparately, and fo arranged that the
retreat of the repulfed corps fhould not over-
whelm and put in diforder thofe which had
not attacked. He affirmed, that though the
artillery of an European army would make
great flaughter, yet no army could withftand
ten Turkifh attacks, which are furious, but
fhort if they do not fucceed, and the attack
of

of 10,000 is as dangerous as of 100,000 in one body, for the firft repulfed, the reft, on whom they fall back, immediately take to flight. But any one who knows the Turks would fee the impoffibility of leading on the other corps after a defeat of the firft, as the fpirit of their army now is. The old janizaries are no more ; befides, the Chriftian army, encouraged by fuccefs, would have time to recover from any diforder. Haffan himfelf was as brave as a lion, but he could not infpire into the troops his own fpirit; he tried nineteen years, and had all the time unlimited power. If he therefore performed nothing in a reign, where he virtually was fovereign, what is to be expected now or hereafter? Centuries may pafs away before another fuch man arifes with fuch means.

The Turkifh weapons require fome notice. The artillery which they have, and which is chiefly brafs, comprehends many fine pieces of cannon; but notwithftanding the reiterated inftruction of fo many French engineers, they are profoundly ignorant of its management *.

Their

* In fpeaking of their artillery I ought not to omit mentioning an Englifhman in the fervice of the porte ; his name is Campbell, and he is related to a great Scotch family. When very young, he came to Conftantinople (the caufe of his quitting Scotland is faid to be a duel) and, without making himfelf known to any European, he went

to

Their mufket-barrels are much efteemed; but they are too heavy; nor do they poffefs any quality fuperior to common iron barrels, which have been much hammered, and are of very foft Swedifh iron. They are thus made: round a rod of iron they twift foft old iron wire, and forge it; then they bore out the rod, part of which often remains, according as the wire was thick or thin, and the bore large or fmall.

The art of tempering their fabres is now loft, and all the blades of great value are ancient; however, their fabre is fuperior to any of ours in its form and lightnefs. It is a great error in all the cavalry in Europe to have heavy fabres; I have often heard old

---

to the porte and turned Turk. He advanced by flow degrees till he became general of the bombardiers (the place which Bonneval had) and then only he became acquainted with his countrymen, and other Europeans. He was many years at the head of the foundery of ordnance; and though at home he knew nothing of the art of cafting cannon, he foon far furpaffed Mr. de Tott, over whom he had great advantages, as he is a Mahomedan. He is a good claffical fcholar, and fpeaks the modern languages with correctnefs. He is perfectly a gentleman, and is univerfally refpected by Europeans for the honour, integrity, prudence, and humanity of his character. The Turks know little how to efteem a man of fo much worth; for after rendering the moft important fervices to the porte, he was treated with ingratitude, and now, being advanced in years, is wholly neglected.

German

German foldiers complain of it, and an old foldier is a good judge. It feems prepof-terous indeed to make all the fabres in a regiment of equal weight, without regard to the ftrength of the arm to ufe it; befides, a *fharp light* fabre will make a deeper cut than our heavy fabres now in ufe. Among the Turks, every foldier choofes his own fabre, and takes fuch a one as he can ma-nage with eafe; thus, if he miffes his ftroke he can recover his guard, whilft a man with a heavy fabre is loft. The part grafped by the fingers in European fabres is much too thick, and weakens the hold. Much is talked in Europe of the balance of a fabre by making it heavy in the hand*; this cannot be the cafe in any degree, except the knob or pom-mel project out of the hand towards the elbow, which will enable him to raife up the point quick by the force of the wrift, after he has given a blow; but the weight of the fall of the blow is diminifhed in both cafes. Let any man ftrike a blow with a

---

* The fulcrum is the fore-finger, and the back part of the hand preffes down the pommel; but a man in battle does not keep his hand at one height; he lifts up his arm, and confequently has the weight of the handle of his fabre to lift up, and the power is in the elbow and fhoulder, not in the wrift alone. It cannot be expected that men in action, particularly new troops, will ufe their fabres in the fame manner they do on field days.

fabre heavy in the hand, and then take out
the blade, and put on it a light fmall handle,
and ftrike another blow with it, and he will
find the difference. Let him ftrike with each
fifty blows as quick as he can, and obferve
the difference of time, and the fatigue, and
he will be convinced. The fharpnefs of the
edge of the Turkifh fabre, and the velocity
which the arm gives to a light weapon, com-
penfates for the weight of the fabre. All
their attention has been paid to the fabre
for ages (with it they conquered their empire) and it certainly deferves fome attention
for cavalry. The edge of our fabres is never
fharp enough, and the angle of the edge
is too acute. In regard to its crookednefs
it has an advantage, as a blow ftraight down
gives a drawing cut; and it is a good defence, for the arm being held out horizon-
tally with the fabre upright in the hand,
a fmall motion of the wrift turning the edge
to the right or left, covers the body by the
crook of the fabre; the fhoulder of the edge,
not the edge itfelf, forms the parry. Fencing
with the crooked fabre was formerly taught
to the janizaries. The pufh with the fabre
is alfo a good attack. If, however, the pufh
only is preferred for cavalry, the lighter and
longer the fabre is the better, and the nearer
it is to a fpear or lance. The blow upwards
is

is efteemed the moft dangerous by the Turks, as it is the moft difficult to parry.

Many of their cavalry make ufe of the fpear, which, for a clofe regular front, is perhaps the beft weapon ; but as the Turkifh horfe wheel round in full fpeed, and are never in a regular ftraight line, perhaps no weapon is fo advantageous as their light fharp crooked fabre. No body of cavalry that keeps together, and makes its evolutions without being broken (that is keeping a clofe front in a line) can give a fhock to the Turkifh cavalry; they wheel about and retreat much fafter than regular cavalry can advance, and this not in a body, but each man turns his horfe round in his place. Much might be faid for and againft their cavalry ; it is foreign to my prefent purpofe, and would require a long differtation to put them and our cavalry in a comparative view. Only let it be remembered, that though their infantry can neither be oppofed to European cavalry or infantry, nor their cavalry to European infantry, yet their cavalry is generally fuperior to all the cavalry they have been oppofed to hitherto ; I mean the better kind of their cavalry, which is now not very numerous, and can make no effectual oppofition to an European army of good infantry with cannon.

Their

Their beſt Turkiſh ſabres have one great
defeĉt, brittleneſs; they are apt to fly like
glaſs by a blow given injudiciouſly, though
a perſon uſed to cut with them will, without
any danger of breaking a ſabre or turning
its edge, cut through an iron nail as thick
as a man's finger. Few accidents happen in
conſequence of ſabres breaking among the
Turkiſh cavalry, but very frequently amongſt
the infantry, from ignorance of their uſe.
In regard to this I will cite a faĉt which
fell under my particular knowledge. At the
ſtorming of Oczakow, a lieutenant of the
fleet of the Black Sea, a Mr. Fox, an Engliſhman, ſerved as a volunteer, and marching at the head of a column of 200 Ruſſian
grenadiers, was oppoſed by a body of Turks:
he was a man of prodigious bodily ſtrength
and great courage; he fought at the head
of the column in the line, with a Turkiſh
ſabre; it was ſoon broken, and the ſoldiers
ſupplied him with others they picked up
from the ground, belonging to the Turks
that were killed, moſt of which, from his
want of ſkill, he broke, till the Turks retreated. He killed a number of Turks, and
eſcaped without a wound, defending himſelf
with the remainder of one ſabre till he was
ſupplied with another. None of theſe Turks
had the leaſt notion of parrying the blows.
This

This Mr. Fox was a volunteer afterwards at the ſtorming of Iſmail, where he was killed. He is remembered in the Ruſſian army to this day as a great hero. As ſoldiers, even the beſt taught to uſe the crooked ſabre, are not always ſo calm in action as to make the beſt uſe of it, a blade tempered in the manner of the beſt blades in Europe is preferable, provided the edge be *perfectly ſharp*, and the angle of it *not too acute*; and as to the crooked form, it alſo requires coolneſs and knowledge to uſe it, for if the part which bends moſt forward and the point do not deſcend in a ſtraight line, the point will turn the ſabre ſideways by its weight, as ſoon as the crooked part ſtrikes, and prevent its cutting; for this reaſon a ſtraighter blade, in an ignorant or timid hand, is preferable; but a light blade and thin hilt is abſolutely neceſſary for the ſafety of the ſoldier. It may be remembered that the Romans, with their ſhort ſwords, had a great advantage over the Gauls, whoſe long heavy ſwords ſoon tired them. A Turk, with his light ſhort ſabre proportioned to his ſtrength (for they are not long taking the chord of the ſegment) will not tire ſo ſoon as an European with his long heavy ſabre. I ſpeak of cavalry, for the ſabre, after the invention of the bayonet, is a bad weapon for infantry.

Their

Their laws of war are thofe of the moft ferocious barbarians: believing, from the prejudices of their religion, that they have a right to carry fire and fword at pleafure among the infidels, they are checked in their bloody career by no ideas of mercy. They have a right, as they imagine, to put to death all their prifoners, of whatever age or fex, whether they throw down their arms, capitulate, or by whatever method they are taken, and this right extends, not only to the moment of capture, but for ever afterward, unlefs the captive embrace the Mahometan religion. The heads of the enemy's fubjects are valued by the government at a certain price, and for every one that is brought in five fequins are paid out of the treafury. This is frequently a fource of the greateft crimes, as it is impoffible to diftinguifh the head of an enemy from that of a wretched peafant or unfortunate traveller, who has been affaffinated for the fake of the reward. It is the common cuftom after an action, when the grand vizir returns to his tent, for the foldiers to line the path with heads which have been thus chopped off.

The barbarous law of Turkifh warfare, which condemns all their prifoners to death, is not indeed always practifed; but it is not humanity which prevents it; avarice or brutal
desire

defire are the caufes of prolonging to the flave a miferable exiftence. At other times the ferocious conqueror butchers in cold blood his captive, or drags him along loaded with injury and infult. Such is the faithful picture drawn by Count Ferrieres and others of the treatment of the Auftrian prifoners (many of them officers of diftinction) in their way to Conftantinople. Thofe who fell fick on the road, or appeared incapable of being converted to the purpofes of labour, were cruelly mangled by the *common waggoners*, who chopped off the heads of fome, and maimed others from the impulfe of mere barbarity; and the proceeding of the common waggoners was *lawful*, and conformable to cuftom.

The naval force of the Turks is by no means confiderable. Their *grand fleet* confifted of not more than 17 or 18 fail of the line in the laft war, and thofe not in very good condition; at prefent their number is leffened. Their *gallies* are now of no ufe as fhips of war; but there are about twenty large veffels called *caravellas*, which belong to merchants, and in time of war are frequently taken into the fervice of the porte, and carry forty guns. Thefe were the veffels, of which feveral were loft, during the laft war, in the Liman, and between Kilburon and Ochakof. Their fhips in general are roomy, and larger, for the num-

G   ber

ber of guns, than ours. In regard to their
conftruction, they are built of good oak wood,
but the timbers being too far afunder, they are
very weak. From the flightnefs of their make
they are liable foon to become hogged; to
prevent which, they build them with their
decks curved up, fo that when the two ends
fettle, the veffels become ftraight. Such fhips
do not laft long, and are fubject to be leaky.
In 1778, the fineft fhip in the fleet foundered
in the Black Sea; being too weak, fhe worked
her caulking out, and leaked between all her
planks. The famous captain pafha, Haffan,
attributed it to the bad caulking, and when
the fleet came back into the port of Conftantinople, he ordered all the captains of the
fhips of war to attend in perfon the caulking
of their own fhips all the time, on pain of
death. One of them, being one day tired of
fitting by his fhip, went home to his houfe,
not above a quarter of a mile off. The captain pafha happened to go himfelf to the arfenal to fee the work, examined the caulking,
found fault, and afked for the captain; the
truth was obliged to be told him; he fat down
on a fmall carpet, fent one man for his blunderbufs, and another to call the captain; as
foon as the unfortunate man came near him,
he took up his blunderbufs and fhot him dead
without fpeaking a word to him. " Take and
9   " bury

" bury him," he faid, "and let the other
" captains attend him to the grave, and the
" caulking be fufpended till they return."

The fhape of their fhips bottoms is confidered by all thofe who are judges (fuch as
French fhip-builders and Englifh feamen,
whofe opinions I have heard) as the moft perfect. It is certain they are very faft failors,
but their upper works are very inferior to the
fhips of other nations. It is for the fake of
ftrength, and the improvement of their upper
works, that they have fometimes employed
French fhip-builders. I was acquainted with
Mr. Le Roy, who built them fome fhips at
Conftantinople ; he affured me, that he took
as models for the bottoms, Turkifh veffels.

They build their fhips at Meteline, Stanchio,
Sinope, or at Conftantinople. Thofe at Sinope coft (a fhip of the line) only £. 9,000,
without their guns and rigging. Their guns
are always of brafs. It appears therefore that
the Turks might eafily have fhips of the beft
conftruction ; but they have no nurfery for
feamen. The Greeks navigate their veffels,
together with a few Maltefe and other flaves,
and thefe are very timorous, for on the fmalleft
accident the captain hangs them. The
Turks fight the guns, and fome of the loweft
clafs affift in getting up the anchors, pulling
at the end of a rope, &c. They, however, row

and

and manage their narrow fharp boats in the channel of Conftantinople better than any other people. They get their beft failors from the coaft of Barbary, but not in great numbers; thofe employed in the trade of the Black Sea, and who belong to the coaft of Anatolia, are wretchedly bad; they navigate veffels of the worft conftruction poffible, which can never fail but before the wind; when the wind changes they run into port; this is the reafon fo many mercantile veffels are loft in the Black Sea, and not from the dangerous navigation of that fea.

The famous captain pafha (before mentioned) collected all the good failors he could engage from Barbary, the Adriatic gulph, Idrea (famous for a faft failing kind of cutters) and other parts, but ftill his fleet was badly manned, and without the Greeks never could have put to fea in 1778.

As the eftablifhment of the navy has been moftly taken from the Chriftians, and has not the authority of their ancient inftitutions to plead for its abufes, there would be a great poffibility of its improvement, were it not for that habitual indolence which leads the Turk quickly to abandon any arduous undertaking.

Never was there fo great a profpect of improvement in the Turkifh marine, as that afforded

forded by the exertions of the celebrated
Haſſan, captain paſha or high admiral, who
was promoted to that important office for his
military talents, and the bravery which he
diſplayed at Tcheſmé. He employed all the
influence which his official and perſonal character both gave him, and which, under ſultan
Abdul Hamid, was almoſt unlimited, to introduce various reforms into the Turkiſh navy,
and, had he been properly ſeconded, would
have certainly raiſed it to conſiderable importance, though not to an equality with the
Ruſſian fleet now in the Black Sea.

I cannot avoid making a ſhort digreſſion
relative to him. The name of Haſſan
being very common among the Turks,
there have been ſeveral Haſſan Paſhas, who
have borne the ſupreme command in their
marine; it will therefore be proper to dif-
tinguiſh this illuſtrious man by his ſurname
Gazi, or Conqueror, given him by the ſultan—this appellation exactly anſwers to Imperator during the Roman republic. Two
reaſons particularly induce me to delineate
his character; the aſperſions which have been
caſt upon it, and the ſtriking inſtances which
it diſplays of the inefficacy even of the
greateſt talents under ſuch a government as
that of Turkey. It is uncertain what country gave him birth. He was brought up at Algiers, where he raiſed himſelf to a conſidera-

ble

ble office in the fervice of the dey. M. de
Peyffonel, who is interefted in prefenting the
beft pictures of Turkifh manners, eagerly
feizes the opportunity of mentioning this
great man, and though in fome inftances rather too partially, he upon the whole gives a
much more juft impreffion of his character
than what we gather from Baron de Tott,
who had a perfonal enmity to him. The natural abilities of Gazi Haffan Pafha were
great ; his defects were thofe of education.
In perfon ftrong and vigorous, he improved
his conftitution by temperance, and hardened
it by the fatigues of a military life. The
acts of bravery, which defervedly elevated the
name of Gazi Haffan above that of any modern Turk, are too numerous and ftriking to
need repetition ; they bordered indeed fometimes upon rafhnefs ; and it is upon this account that Tott cenfures his daring attempt at
Lemnos. His conduct, however, on that occafion, well deferves the applaufe given to it
by Peyffonel; it was one of thofe daring enter-
prizes, which by their audacity feem to en-
fure fuccefs. The Ruffians were furprifed,
unarmed and unprepared, and were forced to
embark with the moft difgraceful precipitation ; it feems however a myftery, why their
fleet, formidable as it was, fhould fet fail,
and it can only be accounted for from the
panic

panic with which the bold exploit of Haffan had filled them. It has been infinuated that he was addicted to the unnatural vices too frequent among his countrymen; but this afperfion is altogether unfounded: he had one wife only, and no other amour *of any kind.*

The ridicule which Tott has thrown upon him for a want of fcientific knowledge is no more than applies to his countrymen univerfally; but though poffeffing little fcience himfelf, he by no means defpifed it in others, and the improvements which he fuggefted in the Turkifh marine difplay, if not an extenfive acquaintance with firft principles, at leaft a bold and vigorous grafp of native genius. Cruelty alfo has been laid to his charge, but without fufficient allowance for the ftate of things in which he was placed. The command of an undifciplined and tumultuous force is not always to be preferved by lenient meafures; his difcipline therefore was fevere, his punifhments ftriking, and often fanguinary, but never wantonly cruel; he put fuddenly to death, but never tortured.

Where a fimilar feverity was not called for, he difplayed a clemency unufual in a Turk. Though ftrictly religious, he was mild and equitable to Chriftians in general; the inhabitants of the Greek iflands under his dominion, ever found in him a protector, and

G 4   the

the Greeks of the Morea, through his influence, were preferved from total extirpation.
His refpect for Europeans, proceeding from
his acutenefs and liberality, was known to all
thofe refident at Conftantinople, and to none
more than to the Britifh ambaffador *, who
poffeffed his particular friendfhip, and had
great influence over him. The reforms and
improvements which this great man introduced, and which he would have carried
much farther, were very comprehenfive, including both the conftruction of the veffels,
the education of officers, and the fupply of
feamen.

As to the veffels themfelves, he entirely
altered their rigging, and lowered the high
poops, which held a great deal of wind, and
were very unwieldy and inconvenient in battle; thefe improvements were conducted by
an Englifhman, who rigged the veffels in the
Englifh manner.

He alfo gave them regular tiers of guns:
formerly there were guns of all fizes on the
fame deck; they now only keep on the
lower tier, two, four, or fix of their large brafs
guns, fome of which carry a fhot of one hundred pounds, and are placed in the middle of

---

* I cannot help obferving, that Sir Robert Ainflie poffeffed, in general, a greater influence at the porte than any
Britifh ambaffador before him.

the tier. What was of infinitely more important to the Turkiſh marine, was the reform which he endeavoured to introduce in the mode of collecting ſailors, and keeping them at all times ready for ſervice. It is uſual, as ſoon as the fleet enters the port of Conſtantinople in autumn, to lay up the ſhips in the harbour, and diſmiſs the ſailors, who all go to their homes till St. George's day, O. S. (4th May, N. S.); for in moſt maritime matters they follow the Greek calendar, their own year being compoſed of lunar months, and its periods ſubject to much variation. Before this day the fleet never ſails, ſo that during the winter it lies quite defenceleſs, and the Ruſſians might come down the Black Sea, and deſtroy it in the port of Conſtantinople without oppoſition.

Haſſan, foreſeeing this, propoſed building a large edifice at Conſtantinople for the ſailors to live in, as in barracks, that they might be always at hand. The porte not furniſhing the ſums neceſſary, he built one on a ſmaller ſcale at his own expence; but it is little uſed ſince his death, as the ſailors go to their own homes in different parts of the empire as before.

It is ſaid that the vizir, and other great officers of the porte, were fearful of ſeeing the grand admiral with ſo great a force conſtantly at his diſpoſal in the city. He, indeed,

deed, very probably had in view, to have a body of men at his command capable of keeping the janizaries in awe; though without this he was dreaded by them, and no riots happened, in his time, of confequence; the few that did, he quelled in an inftant, and flew without mercy all the ringleaders. In 1776 (or thereabouts) he eftablifhed a feminary and an academy at Conftantinople, for giving a regular education to young men for officers for the navy; but it came to nothing, as all innovations in Turkey ever muft, from prejudice, from envy, jealoufy, and fear of fome unforefeen and imaginary baneful confequence to the porte. Since that another fruitlefs attempt has been made.

The beft mode of eftimating the importance of the Turkifh navy will be by a comparifon of its conduct with that of its opponents. For this purpofe I fhall fubjoin a few obfervations on fome of the moft memorable naval tranfactions of the laft and preceding wars.

Gazi Haffan Pafha, who fo much diftinguifhed himfelf in the memorable affair of Tchefmé, was at that time the Turkifh admiral's captain, or *capitana*, called alfo vice admiral by the Europeans, but improperly. That the conduct of Gazi Haffan on this occafion difplayed equal judgment and refolution

tion cannot be doubted; he would probably have fucceeded in boarding and taking admiral Spiritoff's fhip, but for the taking fire and blowing up of both veffels. This event has been attributed to the defperation of the Ruffians; but as I was informed by admiral Krufe (who was then captain of Spiritoff's fhip) it arofe accidentally from the wadding of the Ruffian guns, which fet fire to the Turkifh veffel. (See Peyffonel, 101.) The event of the conteft at Tchefmé is well known: the Turkifh fleet was totally deftroyed, owing to the ill conduct of the captains, the cowardice of the men, and to the ignorance of Jaffer Bey, who was afterwards degraded from the poft of captain pafha, and his place fupplied by Gazi Haffan.

In the fubfequent war, Gazi Haffan himfelf commanded in the Black Sea; yet notwithftanding his exertions, his talents, and the great powers with which he was invefted (more than any of his predeceffors ever poffeffed) the Turkifh fleet remained in a ftate of impotence. During the whole of the fummer of 1788, the captain pafha lay with feventeen fail of the line off the ifland of Berizan. The Ruffian fleet, confifting of three fail of the line (with only their lower tier of guns in) and a number of fmall veffels, lay at a little diftance from him, be-

tween

tween Kilburon and Ochakof, to protect the fiege, and block up the port of the latter place. The captain pafha knew very well that the guns from Kilburon Point could not hurt him, as they were mafked by the Ruffian fleet; he was alfo well acquainted with the channel, and poffeffed undoubted bravery himfelf; yet he never dared to fail in and attack the enemy, becaufe he could not rely on his own fhips doing their duty, and manœuvring properly. The Ruffians expected an attack, and thought the event dubious. The remainder of their fleet lay in the port of Sebaftopolis, under the command of admiral Wainowitz, and though not one fourth as ftrong as the Turks, it failed to attack the captain pafha, who went out to meet it, and a running fight enfued, which ended to the advantage of the Ruffians, though they put back to Sebaftopolis; and even for this meafure the admiral was cenfured.

In the laft campaign of the war, the whole Turkifh and Ruffian fleets met, and fought at fea; and notwithftanding the very great inferiority of the latter, they were victorious, and purfued the Turks, who were flying ignominioufly before them into the Bofphorus of Conftantinople. The Ruffians were already in fight of the entrance, when a frigate reached their admiral with news of the conclufion

clufion of peace, which put an end to the purfuit.

I might have mentioned the action in the Liman the fame year, in which the Turks loft the greateft part of their veffels; but that was owing more to accident than any other caufe. If fuch was the event of a conteft, when the fuperiority was greatly in favour of Turkey, what is not now to be expected, when the Ruffian fleet at Sebaftopolis is fo confiderably augmented? It is now ftrong enough to rifk the lofs of one half of its numbers in an attack on Conftantinople, and the remainder alone will be more than a match for the fultan's navy.

As the laft hope of the Turks lies in their fortreffes, particularly in thofe of the Dardanelles, which they believe impregnable, I fhall add the following obfervations on this fubject.

They are ignorant of the art either of fortifying or defending, and, above all, of attacking places. They have not one fortrefs in the empire well fortified by art; a few are ftrong by nature, but none fo much fo that the Ruffians could not now take them either by a regular fiege or by affault. Prince Potemkin, had he chofen, could as eafily have taken Ochákof on the 1ft of July, when he appeared before it, as on the $\frac{6}{17}$th of December,

ber,

ber, when he ſtormed it under augmented difficulties. It was a political ſiege.

The Dardanelles, ſaid to be ſo formidable, may be eaſily paſſed by a fleet, or the caſtles may be beaten down by batteries erected on ſhore, or by ſea, from ſituations on which the great artillery cannot bear on ſhips. There are, on each ſide the water, fourteen great guns, which fire granite balls ; theſe guns are of braſs, with chambers like mortars, twenty-two Engliſh feet long, and twenty-eight inches diameter of the bore * ; they are very near the level of the ſurface of the water, in arch-ed port-holes or embraſures with iron doors, which are opened only when they are to be fired ; the balls croſs the water from ſide to ſide, as they are a little elevated. Theſe mon-ſtrous cannon are not mounted on carriages, but lie on the paved floor, with their breech againſt a wall ; they cannot be pointed, but the gunner muſt wait till the veſſel he intends to fire at is oppoſite the mouth, and they are at leaſt half an hour in loading one of theſe guns. All veſſels coming from Conſtanti-nople are obliged to ſtop at theſe caſtles, and ſhow their firman, or order from the porte, to let them paſs ; but there are examples of

* A gentleman, who has meaſured them ſince me, ſays, they are only twenty-three inches ; one of us muſt have made a miſtake.

veſſels

veffels in bad weather failing through the
channel without receiving any harm, though
the Turks have fired at them. It is true,
that in going with the ftream, which with a
northerly wind runs ftrong, it is eafier for a
veffel to pafs them, yet with a foutherly
wind the current runs up, though not fo
ftrong, and I believe an Englifh fleet with a
brifk gale would pay little attention to thefe
terrible batteries, the guardians of the Turkifh capital; they are, like the Turks themfelves, formidable only in appearance*. There
are other batteries of good cannon, but by no
means dangerous; fome of them at fuch a diftance, and on fuch high hills, that they are
quite ufelefs. The following circumftance
proves that the batteries in the channel of
Conftantinople, and at the entrance from the
Black Sea, cannot hurt a fleet failing in with
a fair wind. In the firft campaign, one of
the Ruffian veffels (a 64 gun fhip) was feparated from the fleet cruifing in the Black
Sea, and being difmafted in a gale of wind,
was forced into the channel of Conftantino-

---

* There is in the arfenal of Conftantinople the breech
of a cannon which was melted in a fire a century ago, of a
moft enormous fize (I am forry I have not the meafure of
it) but thofe of the Dardanelles are diminutive in comparifon to it. It was one of thofe ufed at the fiege of Conftantinople.

ple;

ple; though only under jury-mafts, and mov⸗
ing flowly, the Turks, by an inceffant fire
from all their batteries, were not able to fink,
nor even to hurt her; fhe caft anchor in the
bay of Buyukderé, after having paffed all the
moft dangerous batteries, and then furrendered herfelf.   The captain was an Englifhman; he was blamed for not continuing his
courfe, and faiking quite through to the Archipelago.

Another fortrefs, whofe importance has
been the fubject of much difcuffion, is Ochákof (fpelt by the Poles Oczakow, and called
by the Turks Ozi) I fhall therefore take
occafion to rectify a common miftake refpecting it.

It is afferted by fome, and denied by others,
that this fortrefs defends the entrance into
the Liman.   The report of mafters of merchant veffels has been infifted on, on one fide,
and that of thofe who have obferved the
courfe fhips of war take on the other fide.
They were both in the right.

Merchant fhips, if they are fmall, as thofe
in the Black Sea generally are, may fail out
of the channel, and go within reach of the
guns of Ochakof, but the channel for fhips
of war is at leaft four miles from Ochakof,
and within fifty fathoms of the point of Kill-
buron (not the caftle) on which the Ruffians
have

have erected strong batteries, the platforms
of which are only two feet above the level
of the sea. These batteries were erected
after the Turkish fleet entered the Liman, in
June 1788, and before all the remainder of
it got out again after their defeat. The consequence was, that not one large ship did,
after that, get out. Six of them attempted
to force the passage, and were sunk (though
they were not large vessels) opposite the batteries of the point. This obliged the remainder in the Liman, which were smaller
vessels, to take shelter under the guns of Ochakof, in a small port on the opposite side, within the Liman, where they were burnt by the
Russian fleet the 1st of July. That small
vessels may sail out of the channel, and out
of the reach of the guns at Killburn Point,
and even of the fleet in the channel, the
captain pasha proved. On the 22d of August,
he sent twenty-two small vessels (having
2,500 men on board, and provisions for the
garrison) from his fleet (with a wind which
prevented the Russian fleet going out to sea
to meet them) between the channel and the
shore of Ochakof; they arrived safe without
the Russian fleet having fired one gun at them;
two of them run ashore near the town, the
rest sailed out again as they came, the same
night.

H   Had

Had the Ruffian batteries been conftructed on the point of Killburn before the Turkifh fleet entered the Liman, it could not have paffed them till the Turks had made themfelves mafters of them : it follows that the point of Killburn, and not of Ochakof, is the key of the Borifthenes *.

The prefent reigning fultan, Selim, has made an attempt to introduce the European difcipline into the Turkifh army, and to abolifh the body of janizaries ; an attempt, which, whatever fuccefs it may ultimately be attended with, will form a memorable epocha in the hiftory of the empire.

A trifling circumftance gave rife to it. The grand vizir, Yufef Pafha, in the late Ruffian war, had a prifoner who was by birth a Turk, but being carried early in his youth to Mofcow, he had become a Chriftian, and found in a Ruffian nobleman a patron who gave him a good education, and placed him in the army. He was a lieutenant when he was taken prifoner, and had the reputation of being a good officer. The vizir took pleafure in converfing with him, for he had not wholly forgotten his mother tongue. He

---

* This place is often called Kinburn ; its proper name in Turkifh is Kill or Küll-buron ; that is, Hair-point, from its fhape. The Ruffians write it Kilburn.

reprefented

reprefented the advantages of the European difcipline, not only in battle, but in every other point of view, and particularly in fecuring the army from mutiny. By his perfuafion the vizir formed a fmall corps, compofed of renegadoes and a few indigent Turks, to whom the prifoner taught the European exercife, which they ufed to perform before the vizir's tent to divert him.

Peace being concluded, the vizir returned to Conftantinople, and conducted this corps with him. They were left at a village a few leagues from the capital. The fultan hearing of them, went to fee *how the infidels fought battles,* as he would have gone to a puppet-fhow; but he was fo ftruck with the fuperiority of their fire, that from that inftant he refolved to introduce the European difcipline into his army, and to abolifh the janizaries; he therefore caufed the corps to be recruited, fet apart a branch of the revenue for their maintenance, and finally declared his intention of abolifhing the inftitution of janizaries. This ftep, as might be expected, produced a mutiny, which was only appeafed by the fultan's confenting to continue them their pay during their life-times; but he at the fame time ordered that no recruits fhould be received into their corps.

The new foldiery are taught their exercife

H 2 with

with the muſket and bayonet, and a few manœuvres. When they are held to be ſufficiently diſciplined, they are ſent to garriſon the fortreſſes on the frontiers. Their officers are all Turks, and are choſen out of thoſe who perform their exerciſe the beſt.

What they may become in time it is difficult to foretel; at preſent there is no other knowledge in the army than is poſſeſſed by a drill ſerjeant; nor indeed can more be expected from them, till they have gained experience in actual war; and it muſt be remembered that they are ſtill Turks, a very different people from thoſe whom Peter the Great taught to conquer the Swedes. Their ignorance of thoſe manœuvres, which, more than numbers or perſonal bravery, decide the fate of battles, will make their defeat eaſy to the Ruſſians, ſhould ever they become numerous enough to form an army, the firſt time they meet in the field: it will then be ſeen whether they can make a retreat, or are to be rallied, and whether the new diſcipline will not all at once be abandoned. They have hitherto no confidence in it; and they are devoid of the enthuſiaſm and *eſprit de corps* of the janizaries. In the firſt campaign, however, they probably will be driven out of Europe.

Merely the inſtitution of this melice is an important

important event; and Selim may, perhaps, effect by policy, what several of his ancestors have attempted by force. Could he put himself at the head of a disciplined army, he would conquer the ulema as easily as the janizaries, and the Turkish power, though it would never again be formidable to Europe, might be respectable in Asia. The ulema see their danger, and oppose these changes with all their might. The whole is too new, has too many difficulties to encounter, and has made too small a progress for us to form an opinion how far the sultan will ultimately succeed.

The man who was the cause of this revolution in the military system, the Russian prisoner, and who had again become a Mahomedan, was rewarded for his services in the Turkish manner; for some misdemeanour, real or imputed, his head was struck off.

CHAPTER IV.

Of the Turkish Religion—Its Effect upon the Law, upon the Transactions of the Government, and upon the People at large. The Character, Learning, and Distinctions of the Ulema.

THE philosophic observer of mankind regards, as a chief object of his speculation, the manners of a nation ; it is from them, in general, that political institutions emanate, and it is to them that they always owe their efficacy. But manners themselves will be found to be marked with the character of previous institutions, and of the historical events of the people among whom they predominate. Thus there is a continual action and re-action of causes ; and the human character is alike formed by general manners and by particular incidents. The connection between these is so intimate, that we may almost with certainty determine the state of the one from a knowledge of the other. The beauteous fabric of political liberty cannot be upheld by a corrupt, an effeminate, or a dastardly

tardly people; nor can defpotifm give birth to a noble and ingenuous frame of mind.

The moft ftriking, as well as the moft difgufting feature of Turkifh manners, is that haughty conceit of fuperiority, arifing from the moft narrow and intolerant bigotry. There have been but too many inftances in hiftory, of nations who, having proudly arrogated to themfelves the title of favourites of the Almighty, have on that account exercifed an infolent difdain toward all who were without the pale of their religion. In no inftance, however, has this folly appeared more difguftingly confpicuous than in the Turkifh nation; it marks the public and the private character; it appears in the folemnity of their legal acts, in the ceremonies of the court, and in the coarfe rufticity of vulgar manners. As it is not my intention to enter into a metaphyfical difcuffion of the Mahomedan dogmas, I fhall, under the head of religion, only enquire into the various operations of the extenfive principle throughout the different orders of fociety.

If we liften to the dictates of their law, dictates which ought to have been conceived with caution and uttered with calmnefs, we hear nothing but the accents of intolerance breathed forth with all the infolence of defpotifm.

H 4

Every

Every *raya* (that is, every fubject who is not of the Mahomedan religion) is allowed only the cruel alternative of death or tribute; and even this is arbitrary in the breaft of the conqueror. The very words of the formulary, given to their Chriftian fubjects on paying the capitation tax, import, that the fum of money received, is taken as a compenfation for being permitted to *wear their heads that year*.

The infulting diftinction of Chriftian and Mohamedan is carried to fo great a length, that even the minutiæ of drefs are rendered fubjects of reftriction. A Chriftian muft wear only clothes and head-dreffes of dark colours, and fuch as Turks never wear, with flippers of black leather, and muft paint his houfe black, or dark brown. The leaft violation of thefe frivolous and difgufting regulations is punifhed with death. Nor is it at all uncommon for a Chriftian to have his head ftruck off in the ftreet for indulging in a little more foppery of drefs than the fultan or vizir, whom he may meet incognito, approves.

If a Chriftian ftrikes a Mahomedan, he is moft commonly put to death on the fpot, or, at leaft, ruined by fines, and feverely baftinadoed; if he ftrikes, though by accident, a *fherif* (or *emir* as they are called in Turkifh,

i. e.

i. e. a defcendant of Mahomed, who wear green turbands) of which there are thoufands in fome cities, it is death without remiffion.

The teftimony of Chriftians is little regarded in courts of juftice; at beft, two teftimonies are but confidered as one, and are even overborne by that of a fingle Mahomedan, if reputed at all an honeft man.

The Chriftians can build no new church, and not without great fums obtain a licence even to repair old ones. If a Mahomedan kills a Chriftian, he is generally only fined. At Conftantinople indeed they are (on account of the police neceffary in the capital) fometimes punifhed with death, according to the circumftances of the cafe, but always if attended with robbery, or by fecret affaffination in his houfe or on the highway, or in any manner fo as to difturb the police, which is properly the crime that is punifhed.

Sultan Muftafa, father of Selim, the prefent grand feignior, when he mounted the throne, propofed to put to death all the Chriftians in the whole empire; and was with difficulty diffuaded from doing it, on the ground of the lofs of capitation. This prince, however, in the courfe of his reign, appeared to be actuated by a love of the ftricteft juftice. What muft that religion and thofe principles

be,

be, which could induce a juft, at leaft a well-intentioned man, to maffacre whole provinces of defenceleſs ſubjects!

It is ſcarcely credible how far the littleneſs of pride is carried by the porte in all their tranſactions with the Chriſtian princes. Whenever they conclude any treaty, the inſtrument which remains in the hands of the Turks repreſents the other contracting powers as proſtrated at the foot of the ſultan's throne, and ſupplicating his favour and protection. The preſents which are made to the ſultan, on the arrival of an ambaſſador, or on any other occaſion, are regiſtered in the archives of the empire, as tributes paid by ſuch and ſuch *infidel karols* (the Poliſh or Slavonian name for king or prince, never given by the Turks but to infidels) to the ſublime porte for its protection. Theſe treaties, ſuch as they are, amount only to a temporary remiſſion of that implacable enmity with which their religion inſpires them againſt every thing which is not Mahomedan. To ſupport their faith, and to extend their empire, are the only law of nations which they acknowledge; and in ſupport of theſe principles they muſt be ever ready to direct the whole of their force againſt the arms of the infidels. It is indeed permitted them, whenever their own ſecurity is threatened,

*

to

to conclude a *truce*, for the fake of renovating
their ftrength, and enabling themfelves more
effectually to ferve the caufe of Mahomed ;
and this is the explanation which they give
to their own moft folemn treaties of peace.
In this they are much affifted by the nature
of the Arabic language, which they mix with
the Turkifh in their public acts, and which,
by the various application of its terms, literal
and metaphorical, enables them to give whatever interpretation they pleafe to any contract.   Thus, *fulch ebedy* properly fignifies a
perpetual peace, while *daim*, the term fyno-
nymous to *ebedy*, fignifies the fame thing, but
lefs forcibly : neverthelefs it coft the court
of Vienna, within this century, a long and
difficult negotiation to fubftitute the firft for
the other in a treaty which was, not long
after, broken by open hoftilities.

It has been contended by fome writers
with apparent probability, that the Turks,
reftlefs and diftracted as they are at home,
would be unwilling to augment their confufion by engaging in foreign contefts ; but
there are two obfervations which may be
made in anfwer to this argument ; firft, that
the government itfelf is too ignorant and in-
cautious to be fwayed by fuch confiderations.
We muft not look on the porte as a cabinet
under the guidance of enlightened politicians,
but

but of a fet of wretches continually fluctuating between the hope of amaffing plunder by means of war, and enjoying it in the tranquillity of peace; or of hot-headed fanatics, who confider the deftruction of infidels as the moft meritorious duty of a mufulman. Secondly, it may be doubted whether policy would not lead the minifters of the porte frequently to encourage wars, which would divert the turbulent fpirits from domeftic fedition to the hope of obtaining glory and plunder in a foreign conteft.

I fhall adduce but one inftance from hiftory in fupport of my opinion; it is the conduct of Turkey in the conqueft of Cyprus, as defcribed by the faithful and eloquent pen of the bifhop of Amelia.

Sultan Selim II. who at that period fate on the throne, neither endeavoured to extend by conqueft the empire his grandfather left him, nor to make it flourifh by policy. He left all the management of affairs to his vizir, and gave himfelf up to excefs in every kind of the moft beaftly debauchery. The people, difcontented at his unambitious reign, murmured fo loudly, that it was deemed neceffary by the vizir to fatisfy them: *they affirmed, that fultans were not fet up to enjoy peaceably what their predeceffors had left them; but to enlarge their empire by new conquefts, and*

*and finally reduce the univerfe to the Maho-
medan law* ; for this fpirit of conqueft and
pillage is the fpirit of the whole Turkifh nation, from the vizir to the peafant. It was
refolved to make war on the Venetians, and
to take Cyprus, though without any juft pretence whatever.

The powers of Chriftendom were at va-
riance among themfelves, and differences of
religion had caufed domeftic wars. France
was allied with the porte; Venice was in
great confufion by the blowing up of its arfenal, fuppofed to be done by Turkifh emiffaries ; there was a great fcarcity of corn alfo
in Europe; fo that the fultan, awoken from
his lethargy, thought now of nothing lefs than
conquering all Europe, and began with Cyprus. *They folemnly affured the Venetians*, that
the preparations they were making at Conftantinople were deftined to affift the Moors
in Spain; for oaths, and folemn affurances
and proteftations of public faith had always
been, and is to this day, with them ftate policy. The vizir, who for perfonal reafons
did not defire this war (he being bribed alfo
by the Venetians) objected to the violation
of a treaty which the fultan had fo folemnly
fworn to obferve. The ulema were hereupon
confulted, and unanimoufly anfwered " *that a
treaty made with the enemies of God and his
prophet*

prophet might be broken, there being nothing fo worthy a Mahomedan as to undertake the entire deftruction of Chriftians." This fentence ftands on record, with thoufands more of the fame kind.

The manners of the court itfelf, tinctured as thofe of all courts are with deceit, are not fufficiently polifhed to avoid a conduct, not merely haughty, but indecent, to the reprefentatives of chriftian fovereigns. The ftupid and incorrigible ignorance of the Turk makes him treat his moft favoured allies only as dependents ; hence their ambaffadors are received merely as deputies from tributary ftates. Every folemnity at which the foreign minifters affift in Turkey, occafions them a new fpecies of humiliation, in which they are led from indignity to indignity, a fpectacle to the ftupid populace, who infult them with the coarfeft language as they pafs, and meafure by this fcale the greatnefs of their fovereign. The minifter, who is to obtain an audience of the fultan, muft prefent himfelf at the porte by four o' clock in the morning, where, after three or four tedious hours occupied in unmeaning ceremonies, he is informed that he may be permitted to fee the refplendent face of the emperor of the world *(Gehan Padifha)* who among his other pompous titles bears that of *Alemum pennati, refuge of the*

the world; after which he is refeated in a folitary corner of the divan, on the left, near the door, and the vizir fends to the fultan a fhort note called *talkifh*, which is in fubftance, " that the infidel *(ghiaur)* of fuch a court, " after having been fufficiently fed, and de- " cently clothed, by the fpecial grace of his " fublime majefty, humbly fupplicates leave " to come and lick the duft beneath his il- " luftrious throne." The talkifhgee (or billet bearer) having returned with the anfwer of the emperor, the vizir and all his affiftants rife with refpect at the fight of the *facred* writing *(khat-ifherif)*, and the ambaffador is conducted to the audience, the ceremonies of which are too well known to need repe- tition. It may not, however, be amifs to no- tice, that the minifters and their fuite, who go into the audience chamber, are invefted with a *kaftan* or Turkifh garment, which covers entirely their own drefs, and reaches to the ground ; and that fome writers have abfurdly reprefented this robe as a mark of honour fhown to them ; the truth is, that the Turks wifhing them to appear in every thing as vaffals of their empire, obliged them formerly to be habited entirely in the Turkifh drefs, except the head, which was covered with a hat, and to let their beards grow previoufly to admiffion into the fultan's prefence, as their

tributaries

tributaries, the Ragufeans, do at the prefent day. This humiliating mafquerade was abo-lifhed by means of the ambaffadors of England and Holland, who acted as mediators in the treaty of Paffarowitz (in 1718) and who took advantage of the dejected ftate of Turkey to eftablifh the cuftom, that the European mi-nifters fhould appear in their national dreffes. The inveftiture of the kaftan is only a remains of the ancient ufage, and is no more to be confidered as an honour than the cuftom of wearing a hat at the audience, which is fo far from being a matter of favour, that no European minifter would be permitted to ap-pear otherwife before the fultan or vizir. The Turks confider a European's pulling off his hat exactly as we do a man's pulling off his wig.

Particular inftances of Turkifh infolence, even to the reprefentatives of their moft powerful allies, are frequent and ftriking.

It is not fifty years fince the grand vizir, Gin-Ali-Pafha, advifed the divan to confine all the ambaffadors to a fmall ifland near Conftantinople, as lepers, or other infectious and unclean perfons.

In 1756, the Sieur Du Val, drogoman to the French ambaffador, Mr. de Vergennes, having announced the double bond of alli-ance and marriage, which had united his court

court with the houſe of Auſtria, received
from the reis-effendi no other anſwer, than
:" that *the ſublime porte did not trouble itſelf*
" *about the union of one hog with another.*"
This marriage was not very agreeable news
to the porte. A ſimilar anſwer was given
by the vizir Kiuperli to the French ambaſſador, Monſieur de la Haye, even in the brilliant æra of Louis XIV. : when that miniſter
announced the ſplendid ſucceſſes of his ſovereign over the Spaniards, the vizir replied,
with the barbarous inſolence of an Ottoman
ſatrap, " *What care I whether the dog eat the*
" *hog, or the hog eat the dog, ſo that the intereſts*
" *of my ſovereign proſper.*" The ſame vizir
offered a more atrocious inſult to the ancient ally of the porte, in the perſon of the
ſon of Monſieur de la Haye, whom he cauſed
to be thrown into a dungeon, after receiving
publicly a blow, which broke one of his
teeth. The ſole cauſe of this outrage was
the refuſal of young De la Haye to explain
a letter, which he had written in cypher to
a friend at Venice.

It is not to be denied, that theſe degrada-
tions are frequently increaſed by the ſervility
of the miniſters themſelves, who, by a manly
reſiſtance, might generally avoid ſuch indignities ; for the barbarous inſolence of the
Turks, which is augmented by timidity,

I   ſhrinks

shrinks into nothing before a resolute and dignified firmness. Such was the conduct of
Monsieur de Ferioles, ambassador from France
in the last century, who having taken his
sword, either inadvertently or by design, to the
audience of the grand seignior, not only refused to lay it aside, but gave a kick in the
belly to an officer of the seraglio who attempted to take it from him by force; and
finding that he was denied admission, thus
armed, to the imperial audience, he returned
with his suite to his house at Pera, after
casting off the kaftan with which he had
been invested. Yet this ambassador remained
a dozen years longer at Constantinople, and
transacted the business of his office with credit to himself and advantage to his country.

In 1766, the porte, wishing to show some
mark of contempt to Poland, required the
Polish envoy to appear at the audience of the
vizir without a sabre; with this demand he
refused to comply, declaring that the sabre
was part of the Polish dress, and that as other
ministers wore their swords, he would not
appear at any audience in a manner contrary
to the ancient etiquette. The consequence
of his firmness was a compliance on the
part of the vizir, who received him with all
the usual ceremonies.

In

In the laſt war, it was offered to ſome Turkiſh priſoners to ſerve as volunteers in the Ruſſian flotilla againſt Sweden. On account of the pay, they accepted the offer with gladneſs, and behaved very well in ſeveral actions. On their return they were aſked, in my preſence, why they fought againſt their friends? their anſwer was, "*They* "*are all hogs alike to us, whether they wear* "*green or blue coats.*" The conformity of this anſwer with thoſe of the great officers of the porte is truly ſtriking.

It is not only in the formalities of the law, or in the etiquette of the court, that a barbarous inſolence is diſplayed. The peaſant, no leſs than the ſultan, thinks it unworthy of him to diſſemble the contempt which he bears towards all unbelievers. The very porter employed by a chriſtian merchant will return his addreſs with inſult; and ſo degrading is any connection with infidels eſteemed, that the janizaries employed as guards to a European have the general appellation of hog-drivers. No Turk of the loweſt condition will riſe from his ſeat to receive even an ambaſſador: to avoid this incivility in viſits from foreign miniſters, the vizir, or other perſon, comes into the audience chamber after the miniſter, and they both ſit down at the ſame time.

I 2

As

As a proof of the contempt in which the Turks hold all foreigners, and their perfuafion of their own fuperiority, which they even imagine is granted by other nations, I fhall mention one or two anecdotes, of which I myfelf was a witnefs.

A Turkifh prifoner of Ochakof, meeting at Cherfon, where he had liberty to walk about the town without reftraint, a Ruffian officer on a narrow pavement where only one perfon could pafs, and the ftreets being exceedingly dirty (over the fhoes) when he was within a few yards of him, the Turk, as if he had been in the ftreets of Conftantinople, made a fign with his hand to the officer to defcend from the pavement into the dirt. This appeared to the officer fo exceedingly ridiculous, that he burft out into a fit of laughter, upon which the Turk abufed him in the groffeft language, fuch as is ufed to infidels in Turkey, and ftill infifted on the officer's going out of his way; he, not being a violent man, only beckoned to a foldier, who pufhed him headlong off the pavement; to this the Turk fubmitted with filent refignation; but, unluckily for him, it was near the houfe of the governor, who had feen and heard the whole; he reprimanded the fellow for his infolence, and was threatened with the fame treatment as the

Ruffian

Ruffian prifoners endure at Conftantinople. The Turk's anfwer was, " *They are infidels, but "I am a Mahomedan.*" This procured him a good drubbing, but he all the while hollowed out, that it was not lawful to ftrike a mufelman; and as foon as he was fet at liberty, he went away fwearing vengeance againft the firft infidel he fhould meet when he got back to Turkey.

Some of the Turkifh prifoners, who were faved from the fury of the Ruffian foldiers at the ftorming of Ochakof, were put the next day, out of compaffion, promifcuoufly, into a warm fubterraneous room among the Ruffian wounded. When afterwards an officer came to remove them, and diftribute them to other different parts, fome Turks ftood up, and with an authoritative voice objected to the company being feparated, except in fuch parties as they dictated. Had their language been that of entreaty they would have been liftened to, for they wanted to put relations and acquaintances together. Nothing certainly is more cruel than in fuch circumftances to feparate friends and relations when it can be avoided. Prince Potemkin, who was a very humane man, had ordered exprefsly to alleviate in this refpect the hard deftiny of the captives. They were reminded of their own favage conduct on fimi-

I 3   lar

lar occafions, where wives and daughters were feparated from hufbands and fathers, and how otherwife they were treated. The anfwer was, " *They were not Mahomedans.*" Several of the women faid to the Turks, " LET " THEM *do as they will, they are our mafters* " *now.*" In the two firft words they expreffed the fame notion of their fuperiority as the men had done, but the remainder of the fentence is not uncharacteriftic of Turkifh women in general.

I have often been furprifed, at different extremities of the empire, and from different claffes of people, to receive anfwers in exactly the fame words; for example, every Turk will tell you, vizir or porter, at Belgrade or Bagdad, that they gained the empire by the fabre, and by the fabre they will defend it; and centuries ago they faid the fame.

The enervation of mind, fo common among the Turks, makes them at once fuperftitious and difinclined to bear up againft the evil which advances with giant ftrides againft their ftate. In the moment of popular apprehenfion, prodigies and predictions are eafily forged; to thefe the credulous Turks eagerly liften; the lower orders are at the prefent day perfuaded that the Ruffian ftandard will enter Conftantinople through a certain

tain gate, faid to be pointed out by an ancient prophecy, and the great men are fo
far from oppofing this weaknefs by fuperior
energy, that they look to the Afiatic fhore as
a fecure retreat from the fury of the conquerors.

It feems a kind of moral paradox, that
the fame people, who are thus averfe to taking the neceffary precautions againft evils of
fuch magnitude, fhould neverthelefs bear
them, when they arrive, with a fortitude and
refignation bordering upon apathy. The
caufe of this extraordinary conduct is to be
found in the predeftinarian dogmas of their
religion operating upon their minds, difpofed
by habitual inactivity and inceffant examples
of the inftability of fortune under their defpotic government, to acquiefcence in what
appears to be the will of providence. An
inftance which occurred to me is too remarkable not to deferve notice.

The Turkifh women and children (in
number about 400) who were brought out
of Ochakof, when the city was taken, to the
head-quarters of the Ruffian army, were put
all together the firft night under a tent. No
better accommodations could, under the preffure of the circumftances, be made for them,
though it froze exceedingly hard, and they
fuffered dreadfully from cold and nakednefs,

I 4 and

and many from wounds. As I fpoke Turkifh, I had the guard of that poft, and the fu-
perintendance of them that night. I obferved that there reigned a perfect filence
among them, not one woman weeping or
lamenting, at leaft loudly, though every one,
perhaps, had loft a parent, a child, or a hufband. They fpoke with a calm and firm
voice, and anfwered the queftions I put to
them apparently without agitation. I was
aftonifhed, and knew not whether to impute
it to infenfibility, to the habit of feeing and
hearing of great viciffitudes of fortune, or to
a patience and refignation inculcated by their
religion ; and at this day I am equally unable to account for it. One woman fate in
a filent but remarkably melancholy pofture,
infomuch that I was induced to offer her
fome confolation. I afked her why fhe did
not take courage, and bear misfortunes like a
mufelman, as her companions did ? She anfwered in thefe ftriking words, " *I have feen*
" *killed my father, my hufband, and my children* ;
" *I have only one child left.*" " Where is
" it?" I afked her with precipitation. "*Here!*"
fhe calmly faid, and pointed to a child by
her fide, which had juft expired. I and thofe
with me burft into tears, but fhe did not
weep at all. I took that night into my
warm fubterranean room as many of thefe
miferable

miserable women, perishing with cold, as it
would contain; they staid with me twelve
days, during all which time none of them
either complained aloud, or showed any signs
of exceffive internal grief, but each told
me her story (both old and young women)
as of an indifferent person, without exclama-
tion, without sighs, without tears.

Patriotism and public spirit are not to be
fought for in the Turkish character. It is a
spirit of oftentation and superstition which
has led to the foundation of so many mosques,
colleges, and caravansaries, and in those who
have lesser means, to the erection of numerous praying places for the use of travellers,
called *namas-ghiah*, which point out the direction of Mecca, as well as of fountains, in
the public roads and streets.

Having viewed the effects of the religion
itself on the manners of the different ranks,
it remains only to make some observations on
the teachers of that religion, especially as,
combining in Turkey the offices of priest
and lawyer, they form a body of so much
importance in the state.

The institutions of the clergy cannot but
have great influence on the manners of a
nation, and this influence is so much the
greater, by how much the superstition on
which

which it is founded is ftupidly grofs and univerfally prevalent. In Turkey, their political
power, it has been feen, is firmly rooted; nor
have they omitted any means of perpetuating
it, which could be founded on the ignorance
of the people. To found mofques, and endow
them with treafures, is held to be one of the
moft meritorious works of a mufelman; and
further provifion is made for the education
of youth deftined to the fervice of religion
and law, by the eftablifhment of *medreffés* or
colleges.

Thefe medreffés are ufually endowed, at
the time of founding a mofque, for the inftruction of youth in the elements of fcience.
They have *profeffors*, and they confer degrees,
from the *fohta* or ftudent to the *muderris* or
principal of a college; but in fact this is a mere
parade of terms. Children are admitted from
the *mektebs* or common fchools, where they
learn their alphabet, to feminaries which,
far from refembling the colleges of Eaton
or Weftminfter, much lefs of Oxford or
Cambridge, are fcarcely equal to the loweft
of our village fchools. A profeffor, for the
moft part ignorant of the firft principles of
fcience, fuperintends the inftruction; and it
is fuppofed to be neceffary for the members
of the *ulema* to go through all the *rutbés*

or

or degrees of office, both in the colleges and in the higher departments, which gradually lead to the ftation of *mufti* or high-prieft. Thefe degrees are *fohta* or ftudent, *muderris* or principal of the college, *naib* or judge's fe-cretary, *kadi* or judge, *molah* or fupreme judge, *kiabé-molahfi* or judge of Mecca, *iftambol-effen-difi* or chief magiftrate of Conftantinople, and *kadilafkir* or military judge, of which there are two (one for Europe and one for Afia).

Intrigue and party connections, however, render it eafy for the moft ignorant and in-experienced to attain the rank of *mufti*. Peyf-fonel afferts, that the pontificate has become a fort of heritage in fome great families; but there are no families which may properly be called great; it is true there are a few families who have, by means of cabal, had fome of the great offices of the ulema in their families for two or three generations. Though this corps has acquired a degree of ftability, the members of it are far from re-fembling families in Europe, whofe eftates are hereditary. The fultan is continually de-taching members of the *ulema*, by tempting them to accept offices of the porte, when they become his *kouls* or flaves, and he their heir at law. Nor is it only the fons of the ulema who enter into that corps by a regular progreffion through the offices : vizirs and

pafhas

paſhas often get their relations into the ulema, to ſecure an inheritance for their families
after their death, of what they have given
them in their life-times.

In the colleges, indeed, there is a pompous
detail of ſciences, which are profeſſed to be
taught, but which ſcarcely any one under-
ſtands. The pupils are few; thoſe of the
law have the greateſt pretenſion to learning,
but even they are groſsly ignorant. In their
libraries, indeed, exiſt ſome valuable books,
but they are unnoticed, except perhaps now
and then by a man of a ſingularly ſtudious
turn.

As to the particular ſciences, their juriſ-
prudence and theology conſiſts only of commentaries on the Koran; their aſtronomy is
aſtrology, and their chemiſtry alchemy; of
the hiſtory and geography of other countries
they are perfectly ignorant. Metaphyſics,
rhetoric, and grammar, are indeed taught,
but not upon rational principles. It is ſcarcely poſſible for an European not to over-rate
their learning, by reading theſe details of in-
ſtitutions, and the names of ſciences taught.

Were I, in ſhort, to deſcribe the learning
of a mufti, a kadi, or other regularly educated man of the law, in terms correſpond-
ing to his knowledge, when compared with
Engliſh literature, the picture would be nearly
as

as follows: he has, perhaps, read the Bible, and learnt enough of Greek to conftrue the Greek Teftament, without, however, knowing the grammar of the language, or being able to read the other authors. He has not learnt Latin, or purfued any claffical ftudies; but has merely confulted fome old commentaries on felect parts of the fcriptures, and is either a thorough defpifer of religion altogether, or a bigotted enemy to freedom of enquiry refpecting any of its articles. Befides thefe, he has probably met with tales of ghofts, genii, and the like, all which he implicitly believes; he has met with fome old fabulous hiftorian, like Geoffrey of Monmouth, to whom alfo he gives credit; and as well in hiftory, as in every other fcience, believes all the abfurdities which the people at large receive, and which I fhall hereafter delineate.

Of monks, which exift in Turkey, the great line of divifion is into thofe who refide in monafteries and thofe who have no fixed habitation; the former, called *mewliahs*, the latter *bektachis*, and each divided into different orders, with their peculiar cuftoms and laws. The mewliahs are chiefly diftinguifhed by the different ceremonies which they perform, fome howling until they fpit blood with the great exertions of their lungs, and others

others turning round to the found of mufic until they become delirious with the motion. Some perform hocus-pocus tricks with knives, hot irons, &c.

Of the *bektafhis*, fome attach themfelves to the fervice of the pafhas, fome to the different *ortas* or companies of janifaries, and fome are mere ftrollers, denominated *fhehhs* (or fantons), who pretend to miracles, prophecies, &c. and, roaming about the country, commit the greateft enormities under the cloak of religion. Thefe *fhehhs* are more highly efteemed in Afia than in Europe, and moft of all in Egypt. They pretend to be infpired, or frantic, and in thofe circumftances they feize on any woman in the ftreets in Egypt, and oblige her to fubmit to their embraces; indeed they never make any oppofition. The people cover the couple with mats for the fake of decency, and this conduct is looked on with reverence; the woman, fo far from being difhonoured, is complimented on the occafion, and even by her hufband. In Conftantinople this would not be permitted; the fhehh would be privately put to death; but they never are feized with thefe frenzies in Europe; the utmoft liberties they take there is to feign madnefs, and madmen (if they are not fo bad as to be obliged to be confined) are confidered as holy and infpired;

in

in this ftate they often tell the truth with
great freedom to the vizir, and fometimes
even to the fultan; but as there is ftill fome
rifk in that, they generally confine their liberties to thofe who have lefs power over
their heads.

The toleration of the Mahomedans has
been much vaunted. Hiftorians have faid:
" *The prudent policy of the Mahomedans, the
only enthufiafts that ever united the fpirit of toleration with the zeal for making profelytes,
offered the inhabitants of the countries they
conquered, their religion and laws on condition that they paid the eftablifhed capitation;
and fuch as embraced the religion of the conquerors were entitled to all their privileges,
&c.*" A fimple ftatement of their conduct,
as it appears proved by hiftorical facts, will
fhow whether their religion is tolerant or
intolerant.

They pretend to the right of fovereignty
over the whole earth, and to convert mankind to their religion.

Regardlefs of treaties, oaths, and all other
obligations, without provocation they attack
every country, when they fee a profpect of
fuccefs.

When they have conquered, they put to
death all ages, ranks, and fex; or they fpare a
few, who are reduced to a ftate of flavery, and

2   annually

annually obliged to ranfom their lives; they are deprived of the rights of citizens of the country they were born in; their property is taken from them; they are marked with infamy, are debarred all friendly intercourfe with the conquerors, and are continually perfecuted and maltreated if they do not deny their God and become apoftates; they take their children *, and bring them up in the Mahomedan faith, and make them fight againft their fathers and their fathers religion; for many imaginary or real crimes, fome of which, in Mahomedans, are not punifhable at all, they have the option only of death or apoftacy.

It has frequently been debated at the porte, to cut off all the Chriftians in the empire, who will not embrace Mahomedanifm. Every honour and advantage is offered to thofe who change their religion, and every fpecies of mifery and humiliation attends them and their pofterity who do not. Is this toleration?

* At prefent, however, they do not take children born in the country from their parents, to recruit the corps of janizaries. This cuftom ceafed, when the fultans wifhed to weaken that melice.

CHAPTER V.

An Historical View of the Turkish Power.

IN the detail of caufes which modify the character of nations, it will frequently be found neceffary to trace back the pages of hiftory, and purfue the chain of events through fucceffive ages, prefenting thofe ftriking events, whofe operations continue when their records are fcarcely to be found.

If the Ottoman empire is ftill vaft and extenfive ; if it ftill attracts the fear or the admiration of its neighbours, and fwells with ftupid vanity its fubjects, thefe effects are not furely to be attributed to the wifdom of its counfels, or to the valour of its forces, as they now exift, but arife from the fplendor of its former exploits, and the merited celebrity of its ancient character. It is true that thefe exploits were difgraced by perfidy and treachery, and ftained by violence and rapine ; and while their crimes exhibited an energy in purfuit, and a brilliancy in fuccefs, the claim of the Turks to national pre-eminence ftood undifputed ; but in the enervating lap of floth, the ferocious conqueror

K   has

has degenerated into a torpid barbarian, whofe only marks of former prowefs are to be traced in the infolence of his prefent demeanour, and the fullen affectation of his fancied dignity.

The Ottoman power and name originated in *Othman* (according to the Arabic pronunciation, or *Ofman* according to the Perfian) who, about the year 1300, affumed the title of *fultan,* and eftablifhed his empire at Prufa in Bithynia : but in order to take a view of the progrefs of the Turks, we muft trace their hiftory ftill higher up, and confider not only their own origin, but that of the Saracen kalifs, whom they fupplanted.

The vaft extent of continent, which, fpreading from the eaftern parts of Europe and the north of Africa, comprehends the greater part of Afia, has been the fource of many populous nations, and the feat of many extenfive empires, which have arifen with a rapidity only to fall as quickly into ruins. In the early hiftory of thefe countries, new irruptions and new conquerors continually fucceeded each other, and the power of founding an empire feems feldom to have been attended with the fkill requifite for maintaining it. Some, however, among the numerous hordes which then fucceffively prevailed, arofe to a greater height, and eftablifhed a more lafting name than others. The

The different branches of Tartars (or Tatars) from the north, and the Arabians from
the fouth, carried their arms over extenfive
regions, and founded great and permanent
empires.

It will not here be requifite to follow the
victorious prophet Mahomed, who, by the
fafcination of his religion, as much as by the
terror of his fword, fubjected fo many nations; fuffice it to fay, that his empire, fo
founded, was, within 200 years after his
death, extended by his fucceffors, the kalifs
or commanders of the faithful, over the north
of Africa and great part of Afia; befides
which they had made great progrefs in the
fouth of Europe, having overrun almoft all
Spain, and entered Sicily, Italy, and France.
The feat of their government was eftablifhed at Bagdad, whence iffued the man-
dates of their fpiritual defpotifm over this
wide extent of territory; but as an empire
fo haftily raifed, and fo unconnected in its
parts, was not eafily held together, and as
the commander of the faithful with the increafe of power acquired alfo habits of
luxury ill adapted to the art of governing,
their power was foon deftined to fall under
the fword of more hardy competitors.

Such competitors were found in the Tartar
(more properly Tatar) nations, by whom

K 2　　　　　　they

they were furrounded. The moft ancient records of this part of the world defcribe the Scythian or Tatar tribes as the invaders of their lefs ferocious neighbours. Their name has been very generally applied to the inhabitants of thofe vaft deferts and mountains fpreading from China to the Danube, and who, whether of fimilar or different origin, have at various times poured out their fwarms on all the furrounding countries. The Turkmans, or Turks, were a tribe of thefe Tatars, whofe original feat was beyond the Cafpian fea, from whence, incited by the defire of plunder, they defcended about the year 800, and feized upon Armenia, from them called Turcomania.

At this time the Perfian empire was ruled by governors, who were nominally fubject to the Saracen kalifs, but Mahmud, the Gaznevide, one of thefe governors, having extended his empire * from Tranfoxiana to Ifpahan, and from the Cafpian fea to the Indus, was invefted by the kalif with the title of fultan. Upon the fucceffion of his fon Maffud † to this dignity, a body of Turks under Tongrul Beg (known in fome of our hiftories by the name of Tangrolipix) either invited by the Perfians as auxiliaries, or at-

* A. D. 997.   † A. 1038.

tacking

tacking them as invaders (for the hiftorical accounts differ) obtained poffeffion of that kingdom. It is fuppofed to be about this time that the Turks embraced the religion of Mahomed, and the *kalif* having called them to his affiftance againft the rebellious *emirs*, conftituted the victorious Tongrul *temporal lieutenant of the commander of the faithful* *. From this dignity the ftep was fhort to the attainment of the whole power of the ka-lifat, to which a defcendant of Gengis-khan finally put an end, in the perfon of the kalif Muftazem †.

Meanwhile new opponents were rifing againft the Turks, who, fcarce fettled in their new conquefts, were obliged to yield them to frefh hordes of invaders. The more northern Tatars preffing upon the Turks, as one fwarm of thofe barbarians inceffantly protruded another, haraffed them in their newly acquired Perfian empire, and finally obliged them to relinquifh it in purfuit of frefh conquefts to the fouth. It was about the year 1200 that the Turks yielded the kingdom of Perfia to the Tatars; but pre-vioufly to this they had themfelves extended their arms over the greater part of Afia Minor, whither they now retreated, and fixed the feat of their empire at Iconium, in Ci-

* A. D. 1055.   † A. D. 1239.

licia,

licia, fince Karamania. Here too they were
preffed by the Tatars, and it was at this
time that the European mania of the cru-
fades having a fecond time broken out, the
Turks found themfelves obliged to cede the
whole of Paleftine to the Chriftians *. It was
not long before they regained this country,
taking Jerufalem †, *and putting to the fword,
without diſtinction or mercy, man, woman, and
child.*

The government which the celebrated Sa-
lah-uddin, (or Saladin) had eftablifhed, was
alfo about this time overthrown by the
Mamluks (who retained the independent
poffeffion of that country till the beginning
of the 16th century) and various other contefts arifing in the Turkifh empire, it fell
for a time into fmall independent fovereignties, and remained without a head until the
rife of Othman, who firft affumed the name
of fultan, and from whom therefore our account of the Ottoman race properly begins.

Before we proceed to an hiftorical detail
of the acts of the feveral fultans, I fhall
briefly notice the caufes of the former greatnefs of the Turks; which may be reduced
to the following heads:

1ft. Their conftant thirft after univerfal

* A. D. 1229.   † A. D. 1234.

monarchy,

monarchy, looking on the whole world as their property; and the propagation of their religion, excited by spiritual as well as temporal motives, never neglecting to seize on an advantage, as they were unreftrained by any fcruples of injuftice, or of breach of faith, oaths, or treaties.

2dly. Their concord in matters of religion and ftate.

3dly. Their perfonal courage in war, ftill increafed by fuccefs, and by the enthufiafm of religion.

4thly. Their general devotion to their fovereign, and the obedience of the foldiery and people to their fuperiors and commanders, to a degree hitherto unknown in hiftory.

5thly. Their ftrict obfervance of their ancient military difcipline, their military education, and the early acquaintance with arms, not of the foldiery only, but of the whole people.

6thly. Their great temperance, and confequent health and vigour of body.

7thly. The plunder of their enemies, the great rewards attending extraordinary valour, the crown of martyrdom waiting for thofe who died in battle, and the road of honour and power being open to every common foldier, who might hope to become grand

K 4 vizir,

vizir, and even to be allied to his fovereign.

8thly. The fevere and never failing inftantaneous punifhment inflicted on difobedience, difloyalty, diforder, or cowardice.

9thly. The military genius of their fovereigns, who always were at the head of their armies, and their power unreftrained either by civil or religious laws.

10thly. Their great refources for recruiting their armies, every Mahomedan thinking himfelf obliged, when called upon, to take the field, at the fame time that they had a continual fupply of troops in the children of their Chriftian captives, whom they educated in the Mahomedan religion, and trained to the ufe of arms.

Hence it is very eafy to account for the wide extent of their victories; nor ought we to be aftonifhed, that they conquered the whole dominions of the kalifs, the Greek empire, Macedonia, Epirus, Peloponnefus, Servia, Bofnia, Bulgaria, Syria, Paleftine, Egypt, &c. particularly when we recollect that their opponents were moftly very inferior to them in all the requifites for military excellence.

In thofe barbarous ages, when the Chriftian ftates, governed by courtiers, priefts,

or

or women, difplayed no traces of intellectual energy; when their feudal government, their ignorance of political œconomy, and their want of fyftem in financial and military arrangements, rendered them individually weak and contemptible; and when extended views of general politics, of mutual alliances, and of a balance of power, being unknown, they could not be confolidated into one powerful confederacy; it was then that the Turks exhibited a fuperior brilliancy of character, and built up a mighty and extenfive empire. Their civil and military inftitutions were far fuperior to thofe of their cotemporaries; their temperament of mind and body, naturally ardent, was inflamed by the precepts of a fanguinary religion, which incited them to conqueft by the moft flattering promifes of fenfual gratification; and they were led againft enemies they defpifed by chiefs of fingular fkill, bravery, and ambition. The Ottoman empire, governed by a fucceffion of great men, from Othman I. to Mahmoud IV. (with fcarcely a fingle exception) thus obtained an eminent reputation, whilft it widely extended the limits of its territory.

It muft be owned that their fame, however great as conquerors, has never entitled them to any other homage, has never ranked them among the benefactors or inftructors of mankind;

mankind ; they fcarcely deferve even to be reckoned among the fpecies. Intent upon victory, *they have ftopt at no means to profecute their plan of univerfal monarchy ; violating every principle of juftice and national faith* ; *attacking their neighbours without provocation, without claim, without even alledging a reafon for their conduct* ; *maffacring the vanquifhed without pity, or fparing their lives only to force them to a flavery the moft degrading* ; *feizing on their wives and daughters, felling or difhonouring them, regardlefs of the domeftic mifery of the unhappy fufferers.*

We have feen, in other countries, particular reigns or epochas marked with actions as difgraceful ; but that period or that reign was ever beheld by the nation itfelf, at leaft by the virtuous part of it, with the indignation it deferved; *but here is a fyftem of wickednefs and abomination transferred from the origin of the nation to its pofterity to this very day, confirmed by their religion, and approved by thofe who call themfelves the priefts of God.* Whereever the Turks have eftablifhed their dominion, fcience and commerce, the comforts and the knowledge of mankind, have alike decayed. Not only have they exemplified barbarifm and intolerance in their own conduct, but they have exinguifhed the flame of genius and knowledge in others, breaking
and

and defacing even the monuments of ancient art with a kind of favage exultation, and proving themfelves the real fcourges of the human race.

We now proceed to an hiftorical furvey of the ufurpations of their fovereigns, beginning with

OTHMAN I.

It was by degrees that this prince (a defcendent of the celebrated Gengis-Khan) reduced under his fubjection the different toparchies, or petty fovereignties, into which the Turkman empire of Karamania had fallen. When he firft affumed the title of fultan, he poffeffed the fovereignty of a fmall diftrict, the capital of which was *Kara-chifar.* Here he eftablifhed his government, and, purfuing his conquefts, took *Prufa* in Bithynia, and made it the feat of the Ottoman empire or kingdom (for not till the taking of Conftantinople did the fultans affume the title of imperator) which now extended over the greateft part of Afia Minor. He died in 1328, and was fucceeded by

ORKHAN.

This prince having taken Niké by furprife, and made flaves of all its inhabitants, removed his court thither. When he had extended

tended his conquefts to the Hellefpont, his ambition and zeal to propagate Mahomedanifm would not fuffer him to ftop there; he croffed it, and took Gallipoli. He died in 1359, having been a moft unjuft and inveterate enemy to the Chriftians.

AMURAT I.

Succeeded to his predeceffor's projects of ufurpation of the country, and extirpation of the religion of the Chriftians.

He took Adrianople in 1362, and made it the feat of his empire, as moft conveniently feated to extend his conquefts on the Chriftians. Amurat, as has been before obferved, formed the celebrated body of foldiers called yenifkari (or janifaries) which afterwards became the ftrength of the Turkifh army. He took Servia, and its capital Niffa, and Appolonia near Mount Athos. Having a quarrel with the fultan of Karamania, he fubdued his country, but did not dethrone him, as he was his fon in law, but thus laid the foundation of the extenfive empire of the Ottomans in Afia.

Amurat was ftabbed, in 1390, by a wounded Chriftian foldier, after he had gained a great battle, in which he gave no pardon, and *maffacred afterwards an incredible number of Chriftians*. Ever fince this event, all Chriftian

tian ambaffadors and their fuite, admitted to the fultan's prefence, are held by both their arms by two chamberlains during the time they are in the audience room. He fubdued a great part of Thrace, (or Romania) leaving to the Greek emperor little more than the city of Conftantinople.

BAYAZET I.

On his acceffion to the throne he immediately *ftrangled his younger brother Jacub.* This was the firft inftance of the fanguinary cuftom, afterwards fo frequent, of putting to death princes of the royal blood.

In the firft year of his reign he took Cratova in Servia, which was yielded to him on condition that the Chriftian inhabitants fhould depart with life and liberty; but he fent foldiers after them, and *murdered them all without mercy.* He entered into Bofnia, and brought away all the inhabitants whom he judged ufeful, and made flaves of them. He croffed the Danube (the firft time the Turks paffed it) and committed horrid cruelties in Walachia, from which he afterwards exacted a yearly tribute. He befieged Conftantinople twice, and had nearly taken it; but the great Tamerlane came to its relief, and overcame Bayazet in the greateft battle that was ever fought. Being taken prifoner,

he

he was put into an iron cage (as he told Tamerlane he would have done by him had he
been his prifoner) againft the bars of which
he beat out his brains in 1399. Nature has
not produced many more cruel and mercilefs
tyrants, nor ever a more inveterate enemy
to Chriftians, or to all countries he thought
he could conquer. The Turks were now arrived at the height of cruelty, treachery,
and thirft of conqueft.

MAHOMET I.

Soon after his acceffion he killed his brothers;
fome of them not till after a long civil war.
He regained all his father had loft, but had
not time to augment it much, as he died in
1422.

AMURAT II.

Eldeft fon of Mahomet. He ftrangled his
brother Muftafa. In 1432, he took Theffa-
lonica (or Salonica) and put men, women,
and children to the fword, except thofe referved for luft or hard labour. The cruelties here committed cannot be defcribed, any
more than the horrid ravages which he committed in Hungary. He invaded and fubdued Servia (contrary to his league with the
prince of it, his father-in-law) deftroying all
before him. He entered into Tranfilvania,
*

and

and killed men, women, and children, as far as he penetrated; he did the fame in Walachia, and burnt the villages and towns; all kinds of tortures and cruelty, in its moft dreadful fhape, was practifed on the Chriftians. The famous Scanderbeg, a native of Epirus, greatly checked him.

In 1445, Amurat took Peloponnefus and all Greece; he facrificed 600 prifoners to the foul of his father, ravaged the country, and deftroyed every thing pleafant, beautiful, and grand, and repeated his accuftomed cruelties. He greatly enlarged the Turkifh dominions, augmented the body of janizaries, and made them more formidable than they had been before. This cruel tyrant and invader of Chriftian ftates died of age, and grief at his ill fuccefs againft Scanderbeg, in Auguft 1450; he was, however, more faithful in obferving treaties than any of his predeceffors, or even than his opponent the king of Hungary; but he never made treaties but in diftrefs, and when he defpaired of conquering.

MAHOMET II.

The greateft warrior of all the Turkifh fultans, and the greateft monfter that ever fate on the throne of the Ottomans, or any other throne. Mahomet II. eldeft fon of the late Amurat,

Amurat, began his infamous reign by the murder of his two brothers. His next act was to offer a league with the emperor of Conftantinople and the defpot of Servia, his grandfather by the mother's fide, and at the fame time to make preparation for the fiege of Conftantinople. He never kept his word, his promifes, his leagues, or even his moft folemn oaths on the Koran, longer than fuited his purpofe. He was a monfter of perfidy, of cruelty, and injuftice, and he is " *the glory of the annals of the Ottoman race.*"

He took Conftantinople the 29th of May, 1453. " The emperor was, happily for him, killed in defending it. The barbarians entered the city, howling more horribly than the beafts of the foreft with thirft of blood ; they flew defencelefs men, women, and children, by thoufands, without the leaft refpect to dignity or beauty, to age or youth, to fex or condition. All who could fled to the church of St. Sophia, hoping that the facrednefs of the place would infpire refpect for the duties of man, of whatever religion he be ; they were there all flain, except a very few, referved for purpofes worfe than death ; and the church was converted into a ftable. Every common foldier had permiffion, for three days, to maffacre, to violate, and to pillage without reftraint. Riches

were

were worfe than poverty, and beauty worfe than deformity. A hundred thoufand barbarians fatisfied their avarice, their favage cruelty, and their brutal luft, or all. No tongue can defcribe their mifery. Three long days and three long nights the air was fhaken with their cries. The fultan heard it in his camp, and it lulled him to fleep. The dogs ran into the fields howling with compaffion, or leaped into the fea.

" After three days, the few Chriftians, fpared for the cruel purpofes of the conquerors, were driven like hogs into the fields. The fultan entered the city; his horfe was ftopped fometimes by heaps of the flaughtered, and fometimes waded through pools of blood. He made in the holy temple of St. Sophia a fumptuous feaft for his pafhas and officers, and as he fate banquetting he caufed to be killed, for his diverfion and that of his guefts, great numbers of his prifoners of the firft diftinction for birth, eminence, and learning, among whom were many of the late emperor's relations; and thefe feafts he repeated daily till he had deftroyed all the Grecian nobility, priefts, and perfons of learning or note, who had fallen into his hands, of both fexes and all ages. Many Venetian fenators, and Genoefe nobles, and rich merchants, were

L   among

among the prifoners ; they were in like manner murdered for his diverfion while he was
feafting, and to entertain his court."

Thus ended the Greek empire !

Thus was founded the feat of the Turkifh
empire, which Chriftian princes have fince
thought it juftice to defend from the attacks
of other Chriftian princes, and from the
ftruggles of the wretched remainder of an
injured and unhappy people, ever fince living in miferable bondage !

Unprovoked, the Turks attacked them, and
never ceafed till they had ufurped the throne
of their empire, as they had done thofe of
fo many other ftates and kingdoms, murdering millions in cold blood, and by tortures
of the moft unheard of barbarity.

He took Servia, and the empire of Tra-
pizonde, putting all the family of the emperor to death.   After triumphing over the
Venetians, he took Otranto in Italy, and
murdered all the inhabitants, according to
the Turkifh cuftom, except a few he chofe
out to make flaves of.

He died (by poifon as fuppofed) in the
year 1481, after having put to death above
800,000 Chriftians of both fexes.

BAYAZET

BAYAZET II.

Eldeſt ſon of the late ſultan, had a long
civil war to ſuſtain againſt his brothers,
whom he had not an opportunity of ſeizing
and putting to death when he ſucceeded to
the throne. He formed a projeſt of putting
to death the whole corps of janizaries, but,
as it was diſcovered, it became impraſticable.
He attacked without provocation the Venetians, and committed horrid maſſacres : he
alſo attacked the Egyptians. After a trou-
bleſome reign, he was depoſed by his ſon,
and poiſoned, in 1512.

SELIM I.

The greateſt monſter of this monſtrous
race. After poiſoning his father, he ſtrangled
his elder brother, and murdered his five ſons;
he caught another brother, and ſtrangled
him alſo. He made great conqueſts over
the Perſians, and in Aſia, and took Cairo
after a hard ſtruggle with the Mamaluks.
After a bloody reign, he died a lamentable
death of a cancer in his reins, as he was
planning an attack on Italy and Rhodes, in
September 1520. He commanded his ſon
to turn his arms againſt the Chriſtians, and
left him many bloody precepts.

L 2   SOLIMAN

SOLIMAN II.

Having freed himfelf from apprehenfion on the fide of Perfia and Egypt, he directed his attempts againft the Chriftians, and foon took Rhodes from the knights of St. John, who had held it for two hundred years. The fentiments of the Turks may be gathered from his fpeeches to the grand mafter, after he had figned, and fworn to obferve, the capitulation.

"Although I might *juftly* and *worthily* " infringe the articles I have prefcribed " with fuch an enemy *(that is, a Chriftian)* " from whofe deferved punifhment *neither* " *faith nor oath ought to ftay* a moft juft con- " queror ; yet I have determined to be gra- " cious and liberal to thee if thou wilt, by " well-doings, amend thy life, and I will " give thee great preferment in my fervice," &c. The grand mafter in a noble fpeech anfwered, " that he preferred death ;" which fo aftonifhed Soliman, that he promifed to obferve the articles of the capitulation. On the grand mafter's departure from Rhodes, Soliman told him, " What I have done unto " thee was not for hatred, but defire of fo- " vereignty."—" I need not war for riches" (in that he fpoke not truth, as the Turkifh hiftory proves by facts) " but for honour, " fame,

" fame, and immortality, and the extenfion
" of my empire ; for it is the property of a
" fovereign, royally defcended, by ftrong hand
" to take from others, and to invade others,
" not from a covetous mind, but from the
" honourable defire of rule and fovereignty ;
" for whilft my neighbour ftandeth I count
" it juft by force of arms to remove him."

He then attacked Hungary, took Buda,
and *murdered the garrifon*, which had *capitu-
lated*. He entered into Auftria with fire and
fword : " *The old were flain, the young led
" into captivity, women ravifhed before their
" hufband's faces, and then flain with their
" children, infants ript out of their mother's
" wombs, others taken from their breafts, cut in
" pieces, or thruft upon pointed flakes, and other
" incredible cruelties.*" He laid fiege to Vienna, but finding a moft defperate refiftance
raifed the fiege, and before he withdrew
*maffacred all his prifoners, men, women, and
children.* This fiege coft him 80,000 men.
He made John king of Hungary tributary
to him, entered again into Auftria, and repeated his cruelties, killing at one time
4,000 prifoners. He took, in 1534, Bagdad,
all Affyria, and Mefopotamia, formerly feparate kingdoms, but then belonging to Perfia.
He fent 200,000 men into Macedonia, to be
tranfported into Italy, and actually landed a

part

part of this army in Apulia, and took Caf-
trum. Turning his forces, however, from
Italy againſt the Venetians, he beſieged
Corfu, but not ſucceeding, he carried away
16,000 young people of the iſland into perpetual ſlavery, yet made other conqueſts on
them during a long war. He again came
to Buda, and converted Hungary into a
Turkiſh province, making an alliance with
the French to attack the Emperor. He
made a fruitleſs attempt on Malta, but carried off from Goza 6,300 young people into
ſlavery. The Turks then attacked and took
Tripoly, belonging to the order of Malta,
but did not keep the capitulations, as they
ſaid *no faith was to be kept with dogs.* Ali
Paſha of Buda invaded Upper Hungary, and
took Temeſwar, and, *contrary to the capitulation, murdered the garriſon.*

Soliman, being ſuſpicious of his ſon Muſtafa,
cauſed him to be ſtrangled in his preſence, but
afterwards found he was innocent; he ſtrangled alſo Muſtafa's ſon. Chihangar, another
ſon of Soliman, killed himſelf in deſpair. He
cauſed a third ſon Bayazet, together with
five of his children, to be ſtrangled. He
ſent a fleet and army againſt Malta, attacked
it a ſecond time, and took the fort of St.
Elmo; but meeting with great loſs raiſed
the ſiege. In ſhort, after doing in various

I   parts

parts of the world much mifchief to the Chriftians, and committing every where great cruelties, he died of a bloody flux, the 4th of September, 1566.

SELIM II.

Set the ruinous example to his fucceffors of not going himfelf to the wars, but carried them on by his lieutenants. He foon fought a pretence to declare war againft the Vene-tians, who, in this bloody conteft, loft Cyprus and a part of Dalmatia. He fent an army into Moldavia againft the waywode. At laft a peace was made, to which the Turks fwore *feven times*; yet the waywode was murdered by the pafha, unmindful of his oaths. They then overran all Moldavia, putting all the nobility, and many thoufands of others, to the fword; and all Walachia fell into the hands of the Turks, in 1574. The 9th of De-cember this fame year Selim died.

AMURAT III.

Eldeft fon of the late fultan, whofe death was concealed, as was ufual, till the new ful-tan was arrived. The janizaries, who had a cuftom in interregnums to plunder and even maffacre their fellow-citizens, Chriftians and Jews, were difappointed and murmured; he was obliged to give them large fums to

appeafe

appeafe them. He, on his acceffion, caufed
five of his brethren to be ftrangled in his
prefence. Though he was of a peaceful
temper, he continued his father's wars, becaufe he feared to be thought to degenerate
from the Ottoman princes, but went not
himfelf into the field. In October 1575, he
penetrated into Ruffia and Poland, and made
great flaughter. It was debated in the divan,
whether the league with the Chriftians or
Perfians fhould be broken; for they hold it
lawful, when it is the intereft of the empire,
to break all oaths and treaties with thofe of
a different faith with themfelves. It was
determined to make war againft Perfia. The
event of this war was favourable to him. It
was attended with their ufual cruelties. The
janizaries having now loft their fubmiffion,
and in a great part their difcipline, began to
kill their commanders whenever they were
diffatisfied with them. Amurat had permitted
their children to be enrolled in their corps.
He made war on the emperor of Germany,
and, as ufual, caufed much defolation. He
died the 18th of January 1595.

MAHOMED III.

Eldeft fon of the late fultan. He put to death
all his brothers (in number nineteen) and
ten of his father's wives, whom he fuppofed
might

might be with child. The janizaries, notwithftanding the new fultan's prefence, plundered the city, and had nearly killed their
fultan and plundered the palace. He carried on his wars againft the German emperor by his pafhas, but not being fuccefsful,
he went himfelf to Buda with 200,000 men,
and having taken Agria, returned to Conftantinople. This war was carried on with
various fuccefs, but with great fury. When
the Turks took Alba-regalis, by capitulation,
the Chriftians were to march out in fafety
with their arms, but the Turks put them all
to death, as well inhabitants as 3,000 foldiers.
The infolence of the janizaries became very
great, and they were continually mutinying
and fighting with the other foldiers. The
pafhas in many provinces rebelled, and the
fultan through fear made peace with them,
pardoned them, and confirmed them in their
offices; but he put to death other pafhas
who were in his power, which caufed thofe
who had any thing to apprehend to rebel again.
He put to death his own fon and his fon's
mother, on fufpicion of a defign to dethrone
him. The janizaries attempted to depofe
him. Whilft treating with the emperor of
Germany for peace, the fultan died at Conftantinople, in January 1604.

ACHMET

ACHMET I.

The fecond fon (the eldeft having been ftrang‑
led by his father) fucceeded to the throne at the
age of fifteen. The Turks were not earneft
with the negotiation for peace, but wanted to
deceive and fall on the Germans ; the war
therefore continued, but at length peace was
concluded in 1607. There was nothing
very remarkable in his other wars with dif‑
ferent nations. He died 15th November
1617 *.

MUSTAFA I.

The brother of the late fultan, who had been
preferved, but with fuch fecrecy that it was
fcarcely known whether he was alive or dead.
During his brother's reign, the council had
determined he fhould be preferved, as Achmet
was but fifteen years old, and there were only
thefe two heirs to the throne, but that he
fhould be kept in clofe confinement. Muf‑

* In his 23d year, he beat his fultana, who was mother
of a daughter, and wounded and trod on her, becaufe fhe had
ftrangled one of his fifters flaves, of whom he had become
enamoured. The fultana, having heard of this amour,
fent for her, ftrangled her, and put her clothes on one of her
own flaves, whom fhe fent to the fultan, and on her return
ftrangled her alfo, as fhe had done many others, who appeared
to be with child of the fultan.—*This anecdote fhews the de‑
fpotifm of this government, even among the women of the fe‑
raglio.*

tafa, being twenty-five years of age, was drawn out of a cell, and proclaimed fultan. He became uncommonly cruel; he caufed young Ofman, eldeft fon of Achmet, to be confined under a ftrong guard, and put to death the other fons of Achmet. He offered many indignities to the Chriftian ambaffadors—indeed, in the laft reign, the Europeans in Conftantinople were all ordered to be flain, but the vizir and other great officers diffuaded the fultan from this ftep. When Achmet had children of his own, it was determined to put Muftafa, his brother, to death; and though it was concluded in the council of the divan, yet Achmet was diverted from it by omens.

When an emperor mounted the throne, it was ufual to put to death his brothers and nephews; but when he had children grown up, he entrufted them with governments and the command of armies; this cuftom had now ceafed. When the father died, the vizir kept his death, if poffible, fecret till the new fultan arrived, who generally contrived to feize his brothers and put them to death; fometimes they fled, but they were generally caught fooner òr later, and put to death. It is for this reafon, that the fultan always goes to fome mofque in the city to public prayers every Friday, or fhows himfelf in public, for otherwife the

people

people imagine he is dead, and make a rebellion.

When the late fultan, Achmet, found death
approach, his counfellors advifed him to fettle the fucceffion. His own children were
young. He fent for his brother, and told him
his refolution of making choice of him to
fucceed to the throne, which much amazed
him, as the empire belonged to his own fon.
He recommended to him the children he had
by the fultana, entreating him to ufe them as
he had done him, leaving the children he had
by concubines to his difcretion.

Muftafa, by his cruelties, became fo odious,
that the grand-vizir, who was gone againft
the Perfians, returned with his army, depofed him, not having reigned a year, and fent
him to his prifon again, and placed Ofman
on the throne.

O S M A N I.

He fent a fleet into the Mediterranean,
landed at Manfredonia, and carried of 1,600
flaves. He made war againft Poland, and
marched himfelf at the head of 300,000 men,
with 300 field pieces and 100 double cannon,
but he had no fuccefs, and was reduced to fue
for peace.

Contrary to the will and advice of his
minifters, the fultan married, without any
pomp,

pomp, the grandchild of a fultana who had
been married to a pafha, only for her beauty,
which was ill-interpreted, his anceftors of
late years not ufually taking wives, efpecially
of a Turkifh race, on account of their relations.

The fultan, who had been difcontented
with the janizaries ever fince his difgrace in
Poland, meditated revenge againft them, and
the abolition of a corps now grown too formidable, mutinous, and meddling with the government, and having loft their ancient difcipline and fubordination. The janizaries
had, contrary to their inftitution, married, and
entered into trades; their children were alfo
janizaries, a privilege conceded them in a former reign, and they were more pleafed to ftay
at home, than to face the dangers of a foreign
campaign. His vizir promifed to provide
him a new foldiery of the Curds (who inhabit
the mountains between Smyrna and Mount
Lebanon,) 40,000 of whom were to be enrolled as his body guards; that the pafhas
of the provinces fhould train up to arms a
certain number of the inhabitants, to be
ready to ferve in foreign wars, and to conftitute a greater army than any of his predeceffors, and enable him to make greater conquefts at far lefs expence. It was agreed between the fultan and vizir, that the former
fhould

fhould go into Afia on fome pretence, as that of going to vifit Mecca, or to reduce Sidon, which had rebelled; but the fultan was not cautious enough in his preparations, melting metals, conveying away all his treafures, and ufing imprudent expreffions and threats to the janizaries. In the mean time the vizir had provided 20,000 men in Afia to be depended upon, befides the emir of Sidon, whom he had gained, under pretence of a war againft Perfia. At Damafcus, the fultan was to cut off all his guards, and ftay there till he had regulated his new army, then to return to Conftantinople, and root out the janizaries, fpahies, tamariots, and all their officers, to fettle a new government, and change the name of the city. He then hoped to conquer all Chriftendom, in the mean time he was to live in friendfhip with all powers.

Certainly this was a well-grounded defign, and the reformation of the army had become neceffary; the empire languifhed under infolent and lazy flaves, and the fultan found himfelf dependent on the janizaries for life or death, peace or war. A civil conteft, however, would have been produced; for the foldiery in Europe would have fet up another fultan; but he had all the treafure, and if he fucceeded, he would have faved an immenfe expence;

expence; for the janizaries confumed all the revenues of the empire.

The foldiery, however, oppofed the departure of the fultan, and threatened to fet up another in his place. They ran to the feraglio, but without arms, and demanded that he fhould remain in the city of Conftantinople; that he fhould deliver up the vizir and other great officers accufed by them of confpiring againft the ftate. The fultan confented not to go to Afia, but refufed to deliver up thofe whom they demanded, and perfuaded them to ftay till Saturday, which was council day—this happened on Wednefday, 7th May, 1622. The next day the tumult began again, and the vizir advifed the fultan to go to Afia in his own boats, but he refufed. The vizir appeared to appeafe them, but they cut him in pieces. The emperor then endeavoured to get over to Afia, but not fucceeding, he hid himfelf in a private place. The rebels demanded their fultan and more facrifices, and faid they muft have a fultan, and if he would not appear, they would make another: having waited fome time, they refolved to enter the palace, but took a folemn oath not to plunder it; they there killed the kiflar-aga, and not finding fultan Ofman, they demanded Muftafa, who had been dethroned; they

found

found him in a vault, where Ofman had put
him, with two negro women. They carried Muftafa to the old feraglio, and there
left him; Ofman came out after their departure, and having confulted with fome of
his friends, it was refolved to fend to the
women of the old feraglio to put Muftafa to
death; but he had a party among thefe women,
and the noife alarmed the guard, who refcued
him. The next day the fultan went to the
college of the janizaries, and by intreaties
had nearly prevailed, but for the indifcretion
of the janizary aga, who, being too zealous
for him, began to threaten the janizaries, who
thereupon flew him and others who came
with Ofman. Him they carried to the new
fultan, who only nodded confent to what
they propofed, and he was fent as a prifoner
to the Seven Towers. The new vizir made
by Muftafa knew the ftorm might pafs over
if Ofman lived; a confultation therefore was
held by the chief officers, and it was determined to fearch how many of the blood royal
were left alive, that if two remained Ofman
fhould be put to death. Two of his brothers
were found; one about twelve the other about
feven years of age, and the vizir then went
with executioners to the prifon, and ftrangled
Ofman. The foldiers, who did not intend to
go fo far, foon repented. The pafha of Erzerun

zerun broke out in open rebellion, and declared himself the avenger of his prince's
blood.

MUSTAFA I. *(re-enthroned.)*

On Saturday, 1ft June 1622, the capi-aga
or major-domo having received a fecret order
to remove the brothers of the late fultan
Ofman from their lodgings, and in the night
to ftrangle them ; as he was performing his
command, aided with a few of his executioners to carry away the princes, they cried
out; the pages running to the noife, and encouraged by the kiflar-agá, who had fome
fufpicion, without further examination killed
the capi-agá, almoft every order of men
having now rifen againft their own chief.
That night they fent fecretly to the janizaries
and fpahies. The foldiers returned in fury
to the court in favour of the pages, and demanded juftice againft thofe who thus would
have made an end of the Ottoman race,
only this Muftafa being left alive, who was
fo holy a faint that he would not people the
world with finners, nor endure any woman
near him. The innocent fultan protefted he
knew nothing of the matter; and that if fuch
command was procured, it was obtained frau-
dulently. He was eafily believed himfelf,
but his mother (another Livia) and Daout

M   Pafha,

Pasha, who had married her daughter, were vehemently suspected. This tumult was however appeased. The state of the empire was deplorable : the sovereign an idiot, the next heir a child, and all the great men and soldiers either destroyed, or mutinous, or corrupted.

The Persians seized this opportunity to recover the province and city of Bagdad. Had the Christian princes opened their eyes, they might also have regained much that they had lost.

The vizir took occasion to blame the janizar-aga, and to have him exiled to be strangled, and some other pashas, to make room for deposing Mustafa, and placing on the throne Murat, a child and brother of Osman's, many being of his party. The janizaries rose and rescued their aga. A new faction now arose between the reigning sultan Mustafa and Murat. No security was left for any man ; the rebellious soldiers had the government in their hands. The vizir retired. The soldiers adhered to the sultan of their own creating ; but the lawyers and churchmen (the ulema) planned a revolution, and affirmed publicly, that the constitution was subverted, the foundation of the state dissolved, the sultan unlawful, and all those who adhered to him guilty of heresy, in having despised the institution of Mahomed. This

This fpread all over the empire by correfpondence with their own body, and the
whole nation was divided in fentiment.

The foldiers ftill continued in their mutinous difpofition even in Conftantinople, and
their infolence grew to fuch a height, that
going in troops to the court, they demanded
all offices of profit, infifted on being ftewards
to the revenues of the mofques, (which
are great) demanded the farms of the cuftoms, and committed infufferable outrages.
The vizir durft deny them nothing; they
drank wine in the ftreets, contrary to their
law, and ftood in companies in the open
day, exacting money of all Chriftians who
paffed, to pay for their wine, and ftabbed
without mercy thofe who refufed to fubmit
to their extortions. None durft meddle with
men who had killed their own fovereign.
At Smyrna the janizaries affaulted the Chriftian confuls, and took money from them;
nor did they without difficulty efcape with
their lives. Rebellion appeared in feveral
provinces. The treafures were exhaufted by
the immenfe fums given to the janizaries at
each new acceffion to the throne, and by the
burden of feveral expenfive wars.

The fpahies demanded juftice for the death
of the late fultan, and the punifhment of the
vizir who had murdered him, but who had

M 2   fince

since abdicated that office. The janizaries protected him, but at length consented to his punishment, and he was carried to the same chamber where the sultan was strangled, and there met his fate; he even pointed out the corner where the regicide was performed, and desired to die there, which was granted.

On 20th January, 1622, a peace with Poland was signed by the mediation of the English ambassador.

The soldiers now openly plundered people when they wanted money, so that it was thought prudent to remove the royal mint into the seraglio, and coin all the metal they could find to satisfy the soldiery.

The pasha of Erzerun, with some others, raised a great army, and marched towards Constantinople, declaring his intention to reduce the janizaries of the city to obedience and discipline; to punish those who had murdered the late sultan Osman, and to settle a new sultan lawfully, who should be able to govern; asserting at the same time that Mustafa was an idiot, governed by a woman and by his vizir. The army at Constantinople refused to march against the pasha of Erzerun, and the empire was from one end to the other in confusion.

The chief cause of this evil was, that their three last emperors had not gone into the

field

field themfelves, excepting once, when Mahomet III. for the maintenance of his credit with the foldiery, went to Hungary, and took Agria. The people and minifters were defirous of depofing Muftafa, and placing on the throne Murat, brother of Ofman; but they feared that the vizir, who was in effect emperor, affifted by the janizaries, would maintain the fovereign they had placed on the throne; they alfo feared the low ftate of the finances, which would not allow of giving the ufual fums to the janizaries at the acceffion of a new fultan; but the report that the pafha of Erzerun had declared himfelf the avenger of the late fultan, had put to death all the janizaries that fell in his hands, with their wives and children; that he was advancing with an army; and that the foldiers fent againft him had difbanded, ftruck them with fuch fear, that they joined the civil power to depofe Muftafa, and place Amurat on the throne, and confented to relinquifh their ufual donations on a fultan's mounting the throne. Muftafa was therefore re-conducted quietly to his prifon, and

SULTAN

SULTAN AMURAT IV. (or MURAT)

In 1623, afcended the throne, being only fourteen years of age. The vizir fent againft
the pafha of Erzerun could or would do nothing; for the beglarbeg of Anatolia had
joined the pafha and the fpahies were on his
fide.

The Coffaks at this period entered the
Bofphorus with 150 fmall fhips and boats,
and deftroyed Buyukderé and Yenikoi, within
about twelve or fifteen miles of Conftantinople, on the European, and Stania on the
Afiatic fide. They returned the next night
quietly, having alarmed the capital. The pafha of Erzerun and the king of Perfia ravaged
the countries in Afia. Algiers and Tunis
began to caft off their allegiance to the porte,
and to become independent ftates. The pafha of Erzerun, however, was pardoned, and
admitted to another pafhelik, that of Bofnia;
for the porte thought it dangerous to bring
matters to the utmoft extremity, fo low was
it fallen; befides, they did not wifh the janizaries to triumph, and the grand feignior, fecretly, was not difpleafed at the pafha's conduct.

A. D. 1630. The government of the empire was chiefly in the hands of four pafhas,
who

who had married fifters of the fultan. The
fultan was much given to wine, and often
fhowed himfelf abroad, unlike a prince,
with debauched young men, fo that con-
fpiracies were formed againft him. The
people were difcontented with burthenfome
taxes, and the foldiery diforderly, and without
difcipline, and infolent at receiving no pay.
The pafhas in the provinces were almoft independent fovereigns, and the empire fhook
on its weak foundation.

The head of the fpahilar-agafi (general
of the fpahies) being cut off, the fpahies rebelled, and the janizaries joined them; they
threw ftones at and wounded the vizier,
whom they with threats obliged the fultan
to depofe, and deliver up to them, when they
cut him in pieces. They next caufed the
mufti to be depofed, and demanded to fee the
brother of the grand feignior, which was
granted; they then charged the new vizir
and mufti to become fecurity for his life.
The fedition was not appeafed till the foldiery had flain more victims. The fultan, in
the mean time, was contriving how he could
get rid of them, and wifhed to have killed
his brother, but the guarantee of the vizir
and mufti prevented it. He made another
vizir, and confulted with him how to weaken
the foldiery; and he really cut off a great
number of fpahies and janizaries fecretly,

M 4   fending

sending them on various pretences to divers parts, and affassinating them by night.

A. D. 1631. Being become now more manly, he went out on horseback often, with a martial appearance, exercised his soldiers, and reduced them to more obedience. In Asia and in Hungary there were still seditions amongst the janizaries, who, for want of their pay, killed their commanders.

A. D. 1632. Amurat had now borne him a seventh daughter; and though he was much troubled that he had no son of his favourite slave, yet he was so much in love with her, that he resolved to create her sultana, had not his mother declared against it, as a thing not usual for any woman to be honoured with that title before she had secured the inheritance by the birth of a male child.

He put to death two chiefs of the spahies, and eight principal janizaries, thinking to extinguish the spirit of sedition; but fearing another insurrection, he retired to Scutari, to the old seraglio, and fortified himself there.

He was so little regardful of the laws of nations, that he caused to be impaled a French interpreter, and put the ambaffador into prison, and committed other violences. Soon after he made peace with the Persians, but broke it again immediately. He also made peace with the emperor of Germany.

A. D. 1633. A fingular fight was maintained between two Englifh merchant fhips
loading corn (which was then prohibited) in
the gulph of Vola, againft the whole fleet of
the captain pafha's gallies. They killed 1,200
flaves and a great number of Turks, with the
captain pafha himfelf, and when they could
maintain the fight no longer, they blew
themfelves up. They funk three gallies, and
forced the fleet into port to repair. This
action is remembered, and talked of to this
very day in Turkey. The matter was compromifed at the porte on paying 40,000 dollars; but the Englifh only paid one third of
it, the French and Venetians paid the other
two-thirds, and why is not known.

A. D. 1634. Murat, growing now in
years, took the government entirely on himfelf, and determined to make himfelf feared.
He was fevere with his officers, and ex-
tremely fo with the foldiers, declaring that
he expected implicit obedience. The people mutinied at fome taxes, but he cut
off the heads of fifty ringleaders. He
hanged a kadi, to the great difpleafure of
the ulema; he went then to Prufa; he difpatched a boat to Conftantinople to bring
to him the mufti and his fon, both of
whom he immediately ftrangled. This tyranny ftruck terror into the whole empire;
for

for former emperors but rarely ufed to put
to death the muftis. The particular death
allotted for muftis is, by braying them in
a mortar ufed only for that purpofe; but
it is feldom practifed. Murat reflecting on
the ill effect that wine had on him, and the
dangers that it might produce on the people,
ordered all the wine in the town to be ftaved
out in the ftreets, on pain of death.

He hanged a Venetian merchant for having on the top of his houfe a high gallery, becaufe he fuppofed he might look into the gardens of the feraglio, and imprifoned all the
European merchants, who were not releafed till they paid 40,000 dollars. He
fearched all the houfes of the foreign minifters for arms, and took away even the
fword of the Englifh ambaffador. He attacked the Poles without declaring war. An
ambaffador was fent from Poland; Murat,
contrary to cuftom, fpoke himfelf, and told
him, "*that all Chriftian kings ought either to*
"*receive the Ottoman laws, or pay him tribute,*
"*or try the fharpnefs of his fword.*" He then
ordered war to be declared againft Poland,
though his war with Perfia was not finifhed;
but the Poles beat the Turks, and made
them fue for peace, which the Poles refufed,
till the pafha who entered their country was
put to death, and fome others. Peace was
then

then concluded. The captain pafha meeting the new French ambaffador at fea, going to Conftantinople, infulted him, and caufed him to go on board his fhip. After his arrival at Conftantinople, the French drogoman, who had brought complaints againft the captain pafha, was hanged by order of the fultan, and the ambaffador forced fuddenly and unexpectedly on board a fhip, and obliged to depart.

Murat fet out himfelf for the war in Perfia, at the head of 100,000 men, in April 1634, and when he reached Erzerun, he muftered his army, 300,000 fighting men, well difciplined, and rendered obedient by his feverity: he fet them alfo examples of frugality and patience, and became more temperate. He took Rivan, but entering further into Perfia, loft a vaft number of horfes. He utterly deftroyed Tauris by fire and fword, and returned, leaving his army at Aleppo and Damafcus, in December 1635. After his departure, the Perfians recovered what they had loft, and the people murmured again at Conftantinople. The janizaries were difpleafed at feeing the Boftangees take their places as guards of the grand feignior; the ulema were enraged, becaufe feveral of their corps, kadis and others, had been beheaded on pretext of faction.

Having

Having now eftablifhed his authority over
the military and the ulema, he gave loofe to
the utmoft violence and feverity on the moft
trifling occafions. He punifhed the ufe of
tobacco with death, and inflicted the fame
punifhment on his cook, for not feafoning a
difh according to his palate. To deftroy his
fubjects formed his daily amufement, either
by fhooting them with arrows, as he fate in
his kiofk, on the fhore of the Bofphorus, or
by firing a carbine at any one who looked
out of a window at him when failing in his
boat. To thefe crimes were added the loweft
debaucheries, and his chief companions in
drunkennefs were the revolted Perfian general, who had delivered up Revan, and an
Italian of the feraglio. Murat's uncontroul-
able violence now prompted him to attack at
once Ruffia and Perfia. Raifing, therefore,
a vaft army, he fet out on an expedition
againft the latter country, but previoufly
caufed one of his brothers to be ftrangled,
leaving alive only Ibrahim, the fole furvivor
of the Ottoman race, but weak both in mind
and body.

It was now that the vigour of Murat's
difpofition appeared in its beft light. He
took the field in May 1638, reviewed his
forces with care, difmiffed the invalids on
half pay, heard and determined all difputes in
the army, and preferved fo ftrict difcipline,
that

that the countries through which he paſſed
ſuffered none of the hardſhips uſually attending the march of a large army. The reſult
of this campaign was the capture of Bagdat,
the ancient Babylon, which event was ſoon
ſucceeded by a peace, and Murat returned in
triumph to Conſtantinople, on the 10th June
1639.

The Venetians having greatly ſuffered by
the piracies of the Algerines and Tuniſines,
ventured to make ſome repriſals, which ſo
much offended Murat, that he iſſued an immediate order to put to death the Venetian
ambaſſador, and all his countrymen in Turkey; and though this order was by the
prudent management of the vizir recalled,
yet Venice was threatened with a war, which
they could only avert by paying 250,000 ſe-
quins. The language of the *kaimakan*, on
this occaſion, was, " we know that the
" other powers of Chriſtendom are too weak
" to aſſiſt you, take your choice therefore :
" we ſell you peace at this price ; if you
" think it not worth your money, refuſe it."
Whilſt Murat was intent on new hoſtilities,
and raiſing forces, though he had not determined whom to attack, he returned to his
former debaucheries, and was ſuddenly carried off by them, on the 8th of February
1640, in the 17th year of his reign, and 31ſt
of his age.

Thus

Thus perished one of the most ferocious despots that ever insulted and disgraced humanity. Breathing vengeance against whole nations, he threatened to subdue all Christendom, and impose on it the yoke of Mahomedanism, and this not from motives of superstition, since he despised the dictates of that religion, and seldom fasted in Ramadan, or kept any other of its ordinances. So entirely was he a stranger to family affection, that he not only murdered his uncle and two of his brothers, but often expressed a wish to be the last of his race, and actually destined the crown for the khan of the Crim Tatars. The activity and energy of his mind had enabled him to suppress all sedition, and to render himself completely absolute; but this power he used only to the gratification of his own avarice, dying possessed of fifteen millions of gold, though the country was in a state of poverty.

IBRAHIM. (A. D. 1640.)

Notwithstanding a donation of the crown to the Tatar khan, made by Murat, in one of his fits of drunkenness, Ibrahim was unanimously raised by the pashas to the throne. This prince, who was deformed and weak in body, had his natural imbecility augmented by the long confinement which he had un-

dergone

dergone in a fmall room, with only a fingle window at the top. Coming thus unexpectedly to liberty and empire, he was intoxicated by the new pleafures which they prefented, and giving up the adminiftration of government to the former minifters, he devoted himfelf entirely to the luxuries of the harem. The vizir, thirfting for military glory, projected an attack on the Ruffian fortrefs of Afac (or Azof) but this ended only in difgrace. The following year, however, (1642) re-animated the Turks by the birth of an heir to the Ottoman throne. A peace was concluded with the German emperor, and a league with Perfia. The German peace was foon broken by the Turks, who made an unfuccefsful attempt to furprife the fortrefs of Rab (now called Giavanne.) The fears for the extinction of the Ottoman race were ftill further removed in 1643, by the birth of two more fons to Ibrahim, who daily devoted himfelf, with renewed avidity, to fenfual exceffes, exceeding whatever is related of Sardanapalus and Heliogabalus. The reftlefs difpofition of the divan led them, in 1644, to plan an attack on the ifland of Candia, but being then at peace with the Venetians, they concealed their defign under the femblance of amity, until their fleet was fitted out, and had failed toward that ifland. The

The Turks then threw off the mafk, and, in
June 1645, landed 74,000 men in Candia,
where, in their firft campaign, they took the
ftrong city of Cauca with their ufual violence
and flaughter, and thus began in injuftice a
long and bloody conteft, which lafted until
the end of that century.

The fultan, in the mean time, regardlefs
of every thing but his pleafures, continued to
give a loofe to the moft unbounded fenfuality;
and carrying his defires beyond the bounds of
the harem, went at length fo far as to feize the
daughter of the mufti. This outrage was the
caufe of his downfal. The great officers of
ftate and the foldiery embraced the caufe of the
venerable divine, and his ecclefiaftical power
was made the inftrument of vengeance againft
the tyrant. A fetva was iffued by the mufti,
charging the fultan to appear, and adminifter
juftice to his people ; and this being treated
with contempt, was followed by another,
declaring, " that he who obeyed not the law
of God was no true mufelman ; and though
the perfon were the emperor himfelf, yet
being become by his filthy actions an infidel,
he was, *ipfo facto*, fallen from his throne."
Upon the authority of this fetva, the janizaries quickly depofed Ibrahim, and fent him
to his former prifon, where, after fome days,
he was ftrangled, and his fon Mahomet exalted

alted to the throne. The weight and efficacy which, in this tranſaction, appeared to
be given to the fetva, was in fact owing to
the previous concurrence of the great officers of ſtate, and to the general contempt
into which the ſultan, by his ſenſuality and
cowardice, had fallen.

MAHOMET IV. (A.D. 1650.)

This emperor being but ſeven years old at
the depoſition of his father, it was determined that his minority ſhould continue ten
years longer, during which time his mother,
aſſiſted by the principal paſhas, undertook
the government. The Venetian war was
reſolutely purſued abroad; but at home great
diſſenſions took place between the different
factions. Murat, the predeceſſor of Ibrahim, a warlike prince himſelf, had promoted only brave and fiery ſpirits to command in the diſtant paſhaliks; but theſe,
during the reign of his weak and timid ſuc-
ceſſor, had aſſumed ſo much power as to become almoſt independent. To this ſource
of diviſion was added the mutual jealouſy of
the ſpahies and janizaries, the former aſſerting
themſelves as avengers of the death of ſultan Ibrahim, and claiming a precedency over
the latter in affairs of government. The
ſeraglio itſelf was farther divided by different

N

parties,

parties, fupporting the oppofite claims of the mother and grandmother of the young fultan to his guardianfhip; and all thefe caufes together concurred to render in a great meafure ufelefs the mighty preparations of the Turks to purfue the war in Candia. The minority of the fultan was one continued fcene of difcord and revolt.

In 1651, the fpahies of Afia marched toward Conftantinople, demanding the heads of the vizir and janizar aga; and this affair was compromifed by the difcharge of thefe officers from their employments.

In 1652, a rebellion broke out in Egypt and at Damafcus, but was foon quelled; and the following year the pafha of Aleppo marched with a great body of infurgents againft Conftantinople. This pafha, after caufing great terror in the capital, fettled the bufinefs by treaty, and though a rebel, was fo highly efteemed for his abilities, that on the death of the vizir, in 1655, he was elevated to that important poft.

The ill fucceffes of the Turkifh arms in the Venetian war fo much irritated the inhabitants of Conftantinople, that they came in a body to the gates of the feraglio, tumultuoufly demanding peace; nor was this rebellion fubdued by the divan without great difficulty, and by the facrifice of the new vizir.

In

In the year 1656, whilſt new preparations were making for war, a ſedition, more terrible than any of the preceding, broke out at Conſtantinople. The ſpahies and janizaries uniting, with the pretence of reforming the abuſes of the ſtate, ran in arms to the divan, and depoſed the grand vizir and other officers. They entered the imperial palace, plundered the treaſury of two millions of gold, and even threatened to depoſe the ſultan. The city was for ſeveral days given up to all the horrors of pillage, until the rebellion beginning to abate, through a want of union and of ſettled views among the ringleaders, authority returned to its former channel; the celebrated Kiuperli, paſha of Damaſcus, was called, at the age of eighty, to the poſt of vizir, and the grand ſeignior himſelf, attended by his chief officers, rode through the city to put to death the rioters, and to reſtore public tranquillity.

1657. The grand ſeignior from this time took the government into his own hands, and employed himſelf in forwarding the military preparations; but finding the janizaries mutinous on account of the non-payment of their arrears, he attempted to quell them, by puniſhing the ringleaders with death. The diſcontents at Conſtantinople, however, were augmented by the ſucceſſes of the Ve-

N 2

netians,

netians, until the vizir, going himfelf at the head of a very great force, took the iflands of Tenedos and Lemnos, which fuccefs elevating the grand feignior, he went with great pomp to Adrianople, where he offered peace to the Venetian envoys on condition of their furrendering Candia and Cliffia, in Dalmatia, and paying 3,000,000 crowns of gold; but this offer was too unreafonable to be accepted.

1658. The grand feignior was for a while diverted from his intended invafion of Dalmatia by the defection of the pafha of Aleppo, who having revolted, and marched toward Conftantinople, which was at that time afflicted with the plague, proclaimed a youth that was with him fultan, as fon of fultan Murat, and refufed to liften to any terms of accommodation.

1659. The power of the pafha increafing rapidly, the vizir marched at the head of a large army to give him battle, but was defeated with great lofs, and the grand feignior himfelf being obliged to take the field, the pafha offered to treat with him, which the fultan accepting, fent one of his creatures, who, under pretence of negociating, affaffinated the pafha. Some others, who afterwards attempted to profecute the plans of the deceafed pafha, were artfully difunited
and

and reduced by the management of the vizir.

1660. The porte now turned their efforts againſt the Venetians; but they being aſſiſted by a ſupply of French forces, proſecuted the war with vigour.

1661. Meanwhile having, under pretence of the rebellion of Ragotſki in Tranſilvania, reduced the important fortreſs of Varadin, contrary to the general peace concluded between the emperor and the grand ſeignior, a cauſe of war aroſe between Turkey and the German empire. This did not immediately break out, though the paſha of Buda, entering Tranſilvania, raiſed a faction there in favour of Turkey, and overthrew the leader of the oppoſite party. The old vizir Kiuperli now adviſed the grand ſeignior to remove his court to Adrianople, where he himſelf ſoon died, but not till after he had procured the nomination of his ſon to ſucceed him, who was no ſooner elevated, than he began to remove his moſt potent enemies by death or baniſhment. During theſe commotions the Venetian war was but faintly carried on.

1662. The revolt of the paſha of Magnatia and of the Georgians occupied the porte for ſome time, and the vizir being alſo employed in eſtabliſhing his own influence more ſecurely, the views of hoſtility againſt the

N 3 German

German empire were not profecuted with much ardour, until at the latter part of the year, the commotions being moftly terminated, the vizir prepared for war, and the pafha of Buda laid wafte great part of Tranfilvania, though it was fubject to the porte.

In 1663, after deceiving the Germans for fome time with a fhow of pacific intentions, the fultan openly declared hoftilities, by marching at the head of his forces from Conftantinople; and though the Germans made fair offers of peace, they were haughtily rejected by Mahomet. The fultan proceeded with the army as far as Adrianople, and then the vizir taking the command, marched toward the confines of Hungary. An inftance of his cruelty on this expedition deferves notice.

A chofen body of 8,000 Germans having attacked the Turks by night, and committed great flaughter, were at length repulfed, with the lofs of 400 killed and 1,800 prifoners. Thefe latter the fanguinary vizir condemned to death, and remained himfelf a fpectator of their murder on the fcaffold, until the murmurs of his army obliged him to defift, after having ftruck off 1,400 heads.

The Turkifh forces, continuing to advance, ftruck fuch terror into the emperor, that he retreated from Vienna with the records and other

other articles of importance; and by this timidity, no lefs than by the diftracted ftate of his councils, contributed much to exalt the arrogance of the Turks; but at length the valour of the German generals, and of their confederates the French, having turned the tide of war, and the vizir being beaten with great lofs, a peace was concluded, by which the Turks reduced their former infolent propofals to the ceffion of the fortrefs of Nieu Haufel.

This affair being fully fettled, in 1665, the fultan began to turn his thoughts to the poffeffion of the Ifle of Candia, and returned to Conftantinople, to prepare for the profecution of his defign. Hoftilities proceeded in the following year with great vigour on both fides, and the vizir with a great force landed on the Ifle of Candia.

The year 1667 opened with an embaffy from Poland, to complain that the Tatars, fubject to the fultan, had invaded that country, and carried off *an hundred thoufand* perfons into flavery; but of thefe complaints no notice was taken.

On the 11th of May, in this year, began the famous fiege of Candia by an army of 70,000 Turks, provided with every neceffary for the attack of fuch a place, and furnifhed with cannon, fome of which carried balls of

N 4

120 pounds weight. So certain were the Turks of fpeedy fuccefs, that great preparations were made at Conftantinople for rejoicing and illuminations on the capture of Candia; but that place refifted the moft furious and repeated attacks with heroic firmnefs, and the vizir was obliged to continue the whole of the winter in the trenches. A fecond year paffed in a repetition of the fame furious attacks, and the fame obftinate refiftance. In two affaults, the Turks loft 30,000 men; but by continual fupplies of men and ammunition, they were ftill enabled to prefs forward, and at length carried the outworks of the Chriftians.

The fultan finding, in the year 1669, that the great expence and exertion fruitlefsly made in this fiege produced nothing but difgrace, began to apprehend the elevation of his brothers to his throne, and therefore fent orders to have them ftrangled; but the people of Conftantinople taking up arms in their favour, for the prefent prevented his defigns from being put in execution. From thefe fears he was at length releafed by the furrender of Candia by a capitulation, which formed the bafis of a treaty of peace with the Venetians. In this celebrated fiege it was computed that 40,000 Chriftians, and nearly 120,000 Turks, were deftroyed.

In

In 1670, the vizir returned home in triumph, and joined the grand feignior in taking
fteps for the removal of his brothers. To this
end it was judged neceffary to difpatch the
moft turbulent of the janizaries on an expedition againft the Polifh frontiers, and
during their abfence prince Orkhan was privately ftrangled.

The year 1672 was fignalized by the Polifh war. The fultan, levying a great force,
and being joined by numerous bands of Tatars, entered Poland, fpeedily conquered the
Ukraine, and obliged the Poles * to pay a
yearly tribute of 22,000 ducats. The divan
was, however, diffatisfied with this peace,
and obliged the fultan to recommence the
war, notwithftanding the menaces of the
czar of Ruffia, who endeavoured to intereft
all the fovereigns of Europe in the defence
of Poland. Owing to domeftic difturbances,
the Turkifh army was very formidable. The
Poles repelled this fecond irruption more
bravely than the former; but in the fucceeding campaign, the Turks again gaining
the advantage, fwept away all the inhabitants
of the countries they invaded, diftributing

---

* The Turks and Tatars had killed or carried into
flavery more than 300,000 Polifh fubjects.

the

the captives of both fexes as flaves among the foldiery *.

In 1676 died the vizir *Achmet Kiuperli*, to whom was chiefly to be attributed whatever fuccefs had attended the reign of Mahomet, and whofe merits were moft admirably exemplified by being contrafted with the vices of his fucceffor *Kara Muftapha*. This new vizir practifed every fpecies of rapine and fraud to enrich and ftrengthen himfelf, and thinking war moft favourable to his influence (that with Poland being ended) in 1680, he called together a moft folemn council, in which he ufed every argument to prove, that a war would highly conduce to " the honour and advantage of the ftate," this being the only ftandard of political morality in Turkey. Though he was unfuccefsful at this council, he prevailed better with the grand feignior the following year ; perfuading him that the fituation of circumftances enabled him to fall on the emperor of Germany with advantage, and that the French court would favour his views. This may be called the crifis of the Othman power, when having attained the acme of its fame and

* The fine country of the Ukraine was rendered a defert. The Turks took Human, and of above 100,000 men, who were in it, very few efcaped.

5   fplendor,

fplendor, its own inordinate ambition, and
the prevalence of evil councils, pufhed it on-
ward to its decline.

The porte and the emperor were united
by a league or truce of twenty years, three
years of which remained yet unexpired, and
the infraction of this treaty was the firft ftep
toward that ftate of degradation, in which
the prefent age beholds this once mighty
empire.

As the prefent hiftorical fketch is intended principally to exhibit the means of
violence and blood, by which the Turkifh
fceptre has been fuftained; and as we have
now reached the point of its wideft extenfion, the remaining part of its hiftory will
require but flight notice; it will be fufficient to point out thofe leading events in
the reign of the fucceeding fovereigns, which
moft immediately affected the political ftate
of the empire.

The imperial war was long and bloody;
the Turks, at firft fuccefsful, penetrated to
Vienna, and laid fiege to that capital, but
were forced to raife it by Sobiefki. The
tide of their fortune now turning, Mahomet
was depofed by the janizaries, and the war
was continued, though with no better fuccefs,
by the two following fultans, Achmet II.
and Muftapha II. The latter, indeed, attempted to reanimate the military fpirit of
his

his fubjects by taking the field in perfon, but being defeated by the famous Prince Eugene, concluded the peace of Carlowitz in 1699, by which Tranfilvania was ceded to the emperor.

Thefe circumftances confpiring with others to render Muftapha unpopular, he was de-pofed, and fucceeded by his brother Ach-met III. who forced the Ruffians to cede, at the peace of Pruth, many important for-treffes. The inordinate ambition of this prince next led him to attack the Venetians and other Chriftian powers ; but his fuccefs herein was widely different, being reduced, by repeated defeats, to conclude, at Paffaro-witz, in 1718, a peace highly difgraceful to the Turkifh empire.

His war with Kouli Khan, the Perfian ufurper, proved no lefs unfuccefsful ; and the event of all thefe difgraces was, at length, a revolt, in which he was depofed, and fuc-ceeded by Mahomet V.

The year 1730, which produced the re-bellion of the janizaries, the depofition of *Achmet,* and the elevation of his nephew *Mahomet,* in its confequences was alfo pro-ductive of a confiderable alteration in the mode of carrying on the government.

From the time of Mahomet II. it had been ufual to delegate the whole adminiftration

tion to the vizir, but as this and the preceding rebellion had originated in the over-
grown power and ambition of thefe officers,
Mahomet, by the advice of his *kiflar-aga,*
an experienced man, took the power into
his own hands and determined to change his
vizirs frequently.

Mahomet, however, afterwards confided
much in the fucceffor of this kiflar-aga, a
man of the utmoft rapacity and infolence,
who, extending his attacks both againft the
janizaries and the ulema, thofe bodies con-
fpired his overthrow, and began to fhow
their intentions, by fetting fire to Conftantinople. The frequent repetition of thefe
fires at length aroufing the fultan, he confulted with the mufti, and by his advice
facrificed the kiflar-aga and all his dependents, and feized on their ill gotten
treafures, including a vaft quantity of precious ftones, and above 30,500 purfes
($£.$ 1,900,000) which was paid to the hafné.

The death of the *kiflar aga* gave another
change to the interior government. His fucceffor entered into a clofe connection with
the vizir, which lafted till 1754, when, on
the death of *Mahomet,* his brother *Ofman*
came from confinement to the throne ; and
the *kiflar aga* and his fecretary, the *jazigi effendi,*

fendi, gained the confidence of the new fovereign, and affumed their former power.

On the death of Ofman, in 1757, Muftapha, the fon of Achmet (before-mentioned) fucceeded, and he having an intimate connection with the vizir *Ragib Mehemet,* followed his counfel, and deprived the *kiflar aga* of his place and influence, and attached to the vizirat great part of the emoluments formerly given to the kiflar aga; fuch as the management of the revenues of the harem, arifing from large diftricts in Afia and Europe, and the appointment of all the officers. Since that time vizirs have been removed lefs frequently *.

From this digreffion to the fubject of adminiftrative government we return to notice the military affairs of the empire. Mahomet V. fucceeding to the conteft againft Kouli Khan, carried it on with no better fuccefs than his predeceffor, and was forced to an inglorious peace. Being afterwards en-

---

* The depofition of a vizir or effendi does not much affect the progrefs of public bufinefs; for the different departments are very minutely fubdivided, and the fubordinate officers continue in moft of them unaffected by a change of the fuperior. Thefe fubordinate officers of the feraglio amount to fome hundreds, and as they always pretend to follow precedent, they can expedite or procraftinate bufinefs at will, by means of this fubdivifion.

gaged

gaged in a war with the Germans and Ruffians, the latter advanced fo rapidly againft
him as to threaten his capital itfelf, and thus
forced him to conclude a hafty peace.

Ofman III. dying in 1757, was fucceeded
by Muftapha III. who, in the beginning of
1769, determining to attack the Ruffians, ordered the Tatars, under Krim Guerai, to invade their territory. The ravages committed
by thefe barbarian hordes I have elfewhere
defcribed ; they were fuch as the late emprefs, who then fate on the throne, could not
but view with indignation, and avenge with
power.

A bloody war commenced with the exploits of Prince Gallitzin, who attacking the
Turks at Choczim, in their intrenchments,
gained a complete victory, on the 30th of
April 1769. The fame general gained another important victory, near the fame place,
on the 13th of July following ; but was prevented from carrying the fortrefs of Choczim
itfelf by the prudent and cautious meafures
of the vizir. The undifciplined and turbulent ftate of the Turkifh forces, however,
agreeing ill with fuch prudence, this great
officer was facrificed to the clamours of the
janizaries, and fucceeded by a man no ways
his equal in military fkill.

The new vizir attempting to crofs the
Niefter

Niefter in the face of the enemy, on the 9th of September, was defeated by Prince Gallitzin, with the lofs of 7,000 men killed on the fpot. A fimilar attempt, renewed on the 17th of the fame month, met with fimilar fortune; the Turks were defeated, and obliged to abandon Choczim; and it was fuppofed that thefe two defeats coft them 28,000 killed, wounded, and prifoners, befides nearly 50,000, who deferted the army in its tumultuous retreat.

Prince Gallitzin retiring with honour, refigned the command to General Romanzoff, who, having fpeedily over-run Moldavia and Walachia, and received the oaths of allegiance, readily offered by its inhabitants, gained two fplendid victories over the Turkifh forces, on the 18th of July and the 2d of Auguft, 1770.

The enterprifing fpirit of the emprefs led her to adopt the more ftriking and novel meafure of fending a fleet into the Mediterranean, and thus attacking the Turkifh empire on both fides; and this meafure was crowned with fuccefs. The inhabitants of the Morea flew to arms on the approach of the Ruffians. But the moft brilliant action of this naval campaign was the victory of Tchefmé, an harbour on the coaft of Natolia, into which the Turkifh fleet being driven, were all de-

3 ftroyed

ſtroyed by fireſhips. Theſe, and other ſucceſſes of the Ruſſians, forced the Turks to
conclude a diſhonourable peace on the 21ſt
of July, 1774, ſhortly after the death of Muſtapha, and the acceſſion of his brother Abdulhamid.

We have thus brought down our view of
the Turkiſh hiſtory to our own times : the
peace of 1774 was the firſt great ſtep toward the limitation of an empire, which, as
we have ſeen, was originally founded on rapine and injuſtice. This blow was effectually followed up by the ſucceeding war,
which was terminated ſo favourably to Ruſ
ſia, in 1790 ; and it is ſcarcely to be doubted,
that another war, conducted on ſimilar principles, muſt totally extinguiſh the Turkiſh
power in Europe ; an event deſirable to moſt
Chriſtian nations, and particularly to Great
Britain.

I have ceaſed enumerating all the maſ
ſacres and breaches of faith the Turks have
committed for this laſt century and a half.
Their conduct has been uniform. Cyprus
and Candia would furniſh a volume.

O

CHAPTER VI.

Of Arts and Sciences, Commerce, and General Manners.

HAVING traced the outline of thofe grand leading caufes of national importance or decline, which arife from religious and political inftitutions, and from the events of paft ages, it may not be amifs to turn our view to the more domeftic circumftances or prejudices of a people, their knowledge or prejudices relative to commerce and the arts, and their habits of mutual intercourfe and affociation.

From what has already been faid of the caufes affecting the Turkifh character, it muft be evident that it affords but a fterile foil for the culture of the arts. All their habits tend to an indolence little favourable to the emanations of genius; hence refults a want of curiofity for the objects of fcience in general; and to thefe muft be added the reftraints of their religion and government.

A religion abounding in the groffeft ignorance and fuperftition, and which, at the fame time, teaches its followers that they
alone

alone are the favoured of God; that as their
faith is the pureſt, ſo are they, themſelves,
the wiſeſt of mankind, precludes them from
copying their more enlightened neighbours,
and even leads them to conclude that the
purſuits of infidels muſt be at leaſt frivolous,
if not immoral.

The ſuperſtitions of this religion have not,
like the ſplendid mythology of ancient Greece,
or the religious pomp of modern Rome, any
medium of communication with the arts, ſuch
as would be ſupplied by the decoration of
temples, or the pageantry of public games
and proceſſions : Mahomed ſtrenuouſly and
ſucceſsfully combated the idolatry of his
countrymen, and through fear of their re-
lapſe, ſtrictly forbade any appeal to the ſenſes
by ſtatuary or painting. However, the
Perſians, and ſome of the Arab kalifs, only
conſidered this prohibition as relating to the
repreſentation of figures as the object of
worſhip.

It is true, that this religion has not univerſally acted with ſo much force to the extinction of intellect. Under the ſplendid reign
of Abdurrahman, the founder of the Arabian
monarchy in Spain, it aſſumed a more civilized form. That political ſovereign promoted intermarriages between his Mahomedan and Chriſtian ſubjects, and favoured the

natural

natural propenfity of the Arabs to literature and fcience, at a time when the reft of mankind were funk in ignorance and barbarifm; but in all thefe proceedings he departed widely from the fpirit of intolerance and bigotry, which the Turks have uniformly attached to their religion, and he is to be viewed more in the light of a liberal politician than of a religious enthufiaft. The lively manners and ardent minds of the Arabs tempered the influence of a religion fundamentally barbarous and gloomy; but the Turks have not only given to fuperftition its full fway, but have even augmented its influence by circumftances of additional barbarifm.

The fufpicions of defpotifm muft ever tend to degrade and brutalize its unhappy fubjects. Few are the inducements which the torpid Turk has to apply himfelf to fcience, and thofe few are annihilated by the fear of exciting diftruft in the government. Travelling, that great fource of expanfion and improvement to the mind, is entirely checked by the arrogant fpirit of his religion; and intercourfe with foreigners among them, further than thofe immediately in their fervice, by the jealoufy with which fuch intercourfe is viewed in a perfon not invefted with an official character.

General

General knowledge is, from thefe caufes, little if at all cultivated; every man is fuppofed to know his own bufinefs or profeffion, with which it is efteemed foolifh and improper for any other perfon to interfere. The man of general fcience, a character fo frequent and fo ufeful in Chriftian Europe, is unknown; and any one, but a mere artificer, who fhould concern himfelf with the founding of cannon, the building of fhips, or the like, would be efteemed little better than a madman. The natural confequence of thefe narrow views is, that the profeffors of any art or fcience are themfelves profoundly ignorant, and that the greateft abfurdities are mixed with all their fpeculations.

I fhall elucidate this by detailing the opinions received, not only by the populace, but even by the pretended *literati*, in various branches of knowledge.

ASTRONOMY.—From the mufti to the peafant it is generally believed that there are feven heavens, from which the earth is immoveably fufpended by a large chain; that the fun is an immenfe ball of fire, at leaft as big as a whole Ottoman province, formed for the fole purpofe of giving light and heat to the earth; that eclipfes of the moon are occafioned by a great dragon attempting to devour that luminary; that the fixed ftars

O 3   hang

hang by chains from the higheſt heaven,
&c. &c. Theſe abſurdities are in part ſup-
ported by the teſtimony of the Koran ; and
the aſtronomers, as they are called, themſelves all pretend to aſtrology, a profeſſion ſo
much eſteemed, that an aſtrologer is kept in
the pay of the court, as well as of moſt great
men.

GEOGRAPHY.—Of the relative ſituation
of countries they are ridiculouſly ignorant,
and all their accounts of foreign nations are
mixed with ſuperſtitious fables. They dif-
tinguiſh different Chriſtian ſtates by different appellations of contempt.

E P I T H E T S which the Turks apply to
    thoſe who are not Oſmanlis, and which
    they often uſe to denominate their na-
    tion.

Albanians -   - gut-ſellers   -   - (*giguirgee*)
Armenians - t-rd-eaters, dirt-eaters - - (*bokchee*)
Boſniaks and ⎫
    Bulgarians ⎰ -   vagabonds   -   - (*potur*)
Chriſtians -   -   idolaters -   - (*purpureſt*)
Dutch   -   -   cheeſe-mongers - - (*penirgee*)
Engliſh - atheiſts - (*dinſis*) i. e. having no religion.
Flemmings -   -   panders - (*felamink, pezevink*)
French   -   -   faithleſs   - (*franſis, imanſis*)
Georgians -   - louſe-eaters -   - (*bityeyedſi*)
Germans - - infidel blaſphemers - (*gurur kiafer*)
Greeks of the iſlands - hares -   - (*tawſhan*)
Italians or *Franks* - many-coloured - (*firenki, baſſarrenki*)
                                                    Jews

Jews	-	- mangy dogs	-	- *(chefut)*
Moldavians	-	- drones -	-	*(bogdan, nadan)*
Poles	-	- infolent infidels	-	*(fudul guiaur)*
Ruffians	-	- mad infidels	-	*(ruſs, menkius)*
Spaniards	-	- lazy -	-	- *(tembel)*
Tatars	-	- carrion-eaters	-	- *(laſhyeyedgee)*
Walachians	-	gypfies	-	- *(chingani)*

Before the Ruffian fleet came into the
Mediterranean, the minifters of the porte
would not believe it poffible for them to
approach Conftantinople but from the Black
Sea. The captain pafha (great admiral) affirmed, that their fleet might come by the
way of Venice. From this, and a thoufand
fimilar and authentic anecdotes, their ignorance of the fituation of countries is evident;
and as to the ftories which they univerfally
believe, they are fuch as the following : that
India is a country far diftant, where there
are diamonds, fine muflins, and other ftuffs,
and great riches ; but that the people are
little known ; that they are Mahomedans
moftly, but do not acknowledge the kalifat
of their fultan ; that the Perfians are a very
wicked people, and will be all damned, and
changed into affes in hell, and that the Jews
will ride on them ; that the European nations are all wicked infidels, knowing an art
of war, which is fometimes dangerous, but
will all be conquered in time, and reduced to

O 4   the

the obedience of the fultan, that their women and children ought to be carried into captivity, that no faith is to be kept with them, and that they ought all to be maffacred, which is highly meritorious, if they refufe to become Mahomedans; yet they have among them a prophecy, that the *fons of yellownefs*, which they interpret to be the Ruffians, are to take Conftantinople; that the Englifh are powerful by fea, and the French and Germans by land; that the Ruffians are the moft powerful, and they call them the *great infidels*; but they are acquainted with no details of thefe countries.

ANCIENT HISTORY.—They have heard of an Alexander, who was the greateft monarch and conqueror, and the greateft hero in the world. The fultans often compare themfelves to him in their writings. Sultan Mahomed IV. in his letter to the Ruffian czar, Alexis Michaelovitz, calls himfelf " *mafter of all the univerfe, and equal in power* " *to Alexander the Great.*" They talk of him always as the model of heroifm to be imitated, but they know not who he was. Solomon, they fay, was the wifeft man, and the greateft magician, that ever exifted. Palmyra and Balbek, they fay, were built by fpirits at the command of Solomon.

POETRY

POETRY and GENERAL LITERATURE.——
They have a few poets, as they are called,
whofe compofitions are moftly little fongs
and ballads ; but in thefe, as well as their
profe writings, they differ widely from the
fimplicity of the Arabs, as they abound with
falfe conceits; and the language is a barbarous mixture of the Turkifh with Perfian
and Arabic, not unlike that " *Babylonifh*
" *dialeƈt*" of our puritans, which Butler
compares to " *fuftian cut on fatin.*"

Of the general tafte of the Turks, Tott
has given a juft defcription, when he fays,
" *a double meaning, or a literal tranfpofition,*
" *forms the extent of their ftudies and literature,*
" *and every thing that can be invented by falfe*
" *tafte, to fatigue the mind, conftitutes their de-*
" *light, and excites their admiration.*"

This leads me to a confideration of the
Turkifh language, a point on which I fhall
make fome obfervations rather more at length,
as it has not been hitherto treated with any
degree of accuracy. The origin of the Turkifh language was the *Zagutai*, a dialeƈt of
that Tatarian tongue, which has been fpread
fo widely by the hoftile incurfions of different barbarians.

The conjeƈtures of Tott on this fubjeƈt
are juftly correƈted by Peyffonel, whofe obfervations on the different origin of thefe
languages are deferving attention. Among
the

the barbarous hordes that have at different periods overflowed Europe and Afia from the north and weft, he diftinguifhes three great and diftinct nations, differing in origin and in language, the Celts or Teutons, the Fens or Slavonians, and the Huns or Tatars. It may be doubted, whether in the firft clafs he does not confound two very different tribes, as the remains of the Celtic and Teutonic languages ftill exifting in Europe certainly bear a marked difference. Thefe, however, he thinks (with juftice) were the firft of the barbarian invaders, including the Vandals, Goths, Oftrogoths, Vifigoths, &c. who all iffued from the countries between the Northern Ocean and the Baltic Sea. The fecond in order of time were the Fens, Venni, or Slavonians, who inhabited the borders of the Danube and the Euxine, and from whofe language the Slavonian, Ruffian, and Polifh of the prefent day are derived. The lateft of all were the Huns or Tatars, who, proceeding from what has been called the Platform of Tatary, have fpread from the fea of Japan to the frontiers of Poland, and have at different periods feized upon the Chinefe, Indian, Perfian, and Turkifh empires.

The Zagatai language, as muft neceffarily be the cafe with a tongue fpoken by fuch
barbarians,

barbarians, was poor and confined, and its deficiencies have been fupplied by the adoption of terms from the Arabic and Perfian.

The Turkifh language is the eafieft of any one we are acquainted with, becaufe it is the moft regular. It has only one conjugation of the verbs (excepting a difference of *ek* and *ak* in the infinitive, which the ear foon learns to diftinguifh) and but one declenfion of the nouns. There is no exception, nor any irregular verb or noun, in the language. The cafes and perfons are determined by the termination, as in Latin, but the phrafeology is much more eafy, and the tranfpofition is not carried to fo difficult a length. They have compound words, as in Greek, though they are more limited in their ufe. It is true, the Turkifh language is not very copious, yet it is manly, energetic, and fonorous. To fupply the want of words, or more frequently, from a defire of appearing learned, their writers introduced Arabic and Perfian, and thefe languages are now confiderably mixed with the dialects fpoken at the feraglio (or court,) and at the bar (or makami). The Arabic is moftly intermixed in topics of ethics, religion, or law; and the Perfian, in fubjects of gallantry, poetry, and at the feraglio. Had they only naturalized foreign words, and adapted them to the grammar

mar

mar of their own language, as we do in
Englifh, they would have enriched it, without making it more difficult, and have preferved its character; but thefe words and
phrafes preferve the grammar of the language
they belong to, which creates a real difficulty,
and renders it neceffary, in order to read a
firman, or a piece of poetry, to know fomething of the Arabic and Perfian grammars.
This will beft be demonftrated by an example: Suppofing the Latin to be Arabic, and
the Perfian French, a Turk would write, if
Englifh were his language, in the following
manner:

Language of a Mufti or Doctor.

I do not love *deplorare vitam*, as many, and
ii docti, fæpe fecerunt; nor do I repent that I
have lived at all, becaufe I have *ainfi vecu*,
as not *fruftra me natum exiftimem:* I do not
affert that *tædium vitæ* proceeds more from
want of fteadinefs in our true religion, than
from *atra bilis*. If a man deftroys himfelf,
he is either *infanus*, and a holy fool, or one
poffeffed *demonis*, or he is *un athée*—an infidel, or a Frank. Pray *deum* that he may
preferve you againft thofe who blow on
nodos funum, and whifper in the ear.

Language

Language of a Turkiſh Poet.

The eyes of *l' abbreuveuſe* * ineb ia e me more than *le vin*, and *ſes fleches* penet a e *la moële de mes os* quicker than thoſe from the bow.

This is the firſt couplet of a ſong in pure Arabic, (compoſed by an Arabian,) which I have thus written, to ſhew how a Turk would expreſs the ſame ſentiment with reſpect to the language; the genuine Turkiſh compoſitions are ridiculouſly hyperbolical.

It muſt be obſerved, that very few of thoſe, who lard their writings or diſcourſes with Arabic or Perſian phraſes, are much acquainted with thoſe languages; but they have learnt the phraſes and terminations moſt in uſe, and know the meaning of a ſentence, without underſtanding each word ſeparately, or having much idea of the grammar.

It is aſtoniſhing that they have not perfected their alphabet. They write generally without points, and it is then impoſſible to read their writing without knowing the language well. When they read foreign words or names, two people ſeldom read them alike. If the perfection of a written character be to repreſent words in a clear

---

* She who pours out the wine.

and

and unambiguous manner to the eye, they
certainly are farther from it than any other
nation, and they have remained in this ftate
of imperfection, without making the leaft attempt to improvement, fo long, that no effort
is now to be expected from them. Many
of the letters have each three different forms,
when they begin, are in the middle, or end a
word. The Arabic printed in Chriftian
countries, and on Mount Libanus by the
Maronites, is more diftinct and eafier read
than the written, though this is more elegant
in its appearance, which is but a fecondary
quality. It requires great practice to be able
to read the Arabic character quick.

Upon thefe different circumftances relating to the Turkifh language are grounded
the different opinions of the Baron de Tott
and M. de Peyffonel, the former of whom
juftly ranks, among the obftructions to fcience
in Turkey, the difficulty of writing and reading the language. To this Peyffonel oppofes
the facility with which the Baron himfelf
acquired a knowledge of the Turkifh language, without obferving that this knowledge only extended to *fpeaking* it, a tafk
which was comparatively eafy. Mr. de
Tott never acquired fkill enough to read it
readily. Peyffonel alfo adduces, as an additional argument, the ability of feveral European

pean interpreters, whofe names he mentions ;
but this eulogium was only applicable to the
celebrated M. Muragia, and not even to him
in its full extent ; nor does this prove any
thing in favour of the Turks themfelves, fince
the advantage which they poffefs as natives
is more than counterbalanced by their habits
of apathy and indolence. Peyffonel is equally
incorrect in comparing the different characters of the Turks to the different hands, the
italic, running hand, engroffing, &c. ufed in
other parts of Europe.

In thofe countries, the different hands have
all fuch a degree of fimilarity, that few are at
a lofs to write, and none to read them at all,
and a perfon who had only feen one hand, in
a few hours might learn the others ; but in
Turkey, fcarcely any perfon is verfed in the
different characters, except the *profeffed
writers*, and even among them thefe characters are employed each for its diftinct and peculiar purpofe : the *nefhki* is ufed in works
of fcience ; the *tealik*, for poetry ; the *divani*,
for ftate papers, commiffions, and epiftolary
correfpondence ; and the *falus*, for infcrip-
tions, devifes, &c. If the difficulty prefented
by thefe various characters feems at firft view
light, it muft be remembered, that a flight
obftacle, thrown in the way of an indolent

9   Turk,

Turk, becomes infuperable from his general difregard of fcience.

The art of *printing*, though often attempted, has never been introduced among the Turks, and this not owing to the difficulty of forming Arabic types, as has been by fome alledged, for the Chriftians of Mount Lebanon, as well as we, print books with Arabic characters : if they require the beauty of the written character, they might engrave on copper ; but the true caufe of this neglect, is the Turkifh indolence and contempt for all innovations.

Is it not matter of aftonifhment, that fince the firft eftablifhment of their manufactory of carpets, they have not improved the defigns, and particularly as they are not forbidden to imitate flowers ? The fame may be faid of their embroidery, and of the ftuffs made at Prufa, Aleppo, and Damafcus. Their carpets owe their excellency only to the materials they are made of.

In all the Turkifh arts, the traces of fuperftition are obfervable. Their *architecture* does not imitate that of ancient Greece, nor have they corrected one fault, or conceived any idea of proportion, from the perfect models they have daily before their eyes. In fhort, they have never ftudied architecture; and as to the practice of Europeans, it would

2   be

be derogatory to the Muſelman dignity to copy infidels. They have taken their notions of general forms from the Arabs, and have added nothing of their own. The church of St. Sophia, after it became a moſque, however, is the model by which moſt of the other moſques in Conſtantinople have been built; and this perhaps was owing to the architects being Greeks or Armenians. Though many of them have ſome notion of the rules of their own art, they are not permitted to purſue them beyond what the Turks conceive to be the *mahomedan* form; they look indeed with a kind of reverence on the noble ruins of Greece, believing them to have been built by devils or genii; they are alſo jealous of Europeans, who wiſh to obtain poſſeſſion of any parts of thoſe remains; but the only uſe they themſelves make of them, is to pull in pieces the marble edifices to burn them into lime. The plaſter of their walls, made of this lime, is very fine and beautiful; but who does not lament, that to produce it, perhaps the divine works of Phideas and Praxiteles have been conſigned to the furnace. This marble lime, mixed with pounded marble unburnt, forms a plaſter ſuperior in whiteneſs to the Indian chinam, but unequal to it in poliſh and hardneſs. Among the moſques and public buildings at

P   Conſtan-

Conſtantinople are to be found many fine edifices ; but they are copied from the Arabian buildings in Aſia, where there are much grander ſtructures than at Conſtantinople, though of as late a date *.

* On the origin of the moreſque and gothic architecture many learned diſſertations have been written. It is not to my preſent purpoſe to make extracts from them, for I ſhould have nothing new to ſay on the ſubject. With reſpect to the general form of the moſques, baths, caravanſaries, bazars, and kioſks, in the different parts of the empire, the maſs is, notwithſtanding many ſtriking defects, grand and impoſing ; the particular parts are devoid of all proportion ; their columns have nothing of their true character, being often twenty ana thirty diameters high, and the intercolumniation frequently equal to the height of the column. The capitals and entablatures are the moſt whimſical and ridiculous.

St. Sophia, at Conſtantinople, there is little doubt, was the model which the European architects copied, when they introduced the cupola upon four arches, than which nothing can be more prepoſterous. Thoſe who chuſe to ſee the falſe principles of theſe buildings expoſed, and how far they differ from the grandeur and ſimplicity of the ancients, may read *Friſe's Saggio ſull' Architettura Gottica, Livorno,* and in an excellent little German treatiſe annexed to the tranſlation of it, the peculiar excellencies of the gothic pointed out, excluſively of its defects.

It is worthy, however, of obſervation, that the interior of St. Sophia appears much larger, and that St. Peter's, at Rome, appears infinitely ſmaller than it really is. The cupola of this latter church is of the ſame ſize as the Pantheon ; the members of the entablature, which runs round the lower part of the cupola or lanthorn, are marked on the pavement below by different coloured marbles ; but no one can, without actual meaſurement, be perſuaded of this truth.

The

The noble productions of *ſtatuary* and *painting* are ſtill more fully ſuppreſſed. Theſe arts are anathematized as irreligious; becauſe a blind and ſtupid fanaticiſm has declared that it is impious to emulate the works of God. Hence the incitements to virtue and animation, which we experience in viewing the ſtatues or portraits of the benefactors of mankind, are wholly loſt ; hence too, the Turk can never be arouſed by thoſe flaſhes of genius, thoſe glowing energies of mind, which the hiſtoric pencil, in deſcribing ſome important ſcene, arreſts and renders immortal. So far is this bigotry carried, that neither the effigy of the ſovereign, nor the repreſentation of any imaginary being (as in the ancient medals) is permitted to be imprinted on their money.

The only uſe of theſe arts which is allowed, is the imitation of inanimate nature, in carving or painting the interior of a room. Even here they frequently uſe as ornaments paſſages from the Koran; but they generally paint the walls with flowers or landſcapes. Their ingenuity is, however, merely mechanical; and of ſcientific rules they are perfectly ignorant: perſpective is totally unknown to the painters themſelves.

The ſcience of the Turks in making aqueducts, has been vaunted by ſome authors; but

left

left it fhould thence be concluded that they
have a knowledge of hydraulics, I will here
ftate in what this fcience confifts. When water is to be conducted, they begin by laying
pipes of burnt clay underground, to the diftance of about a quarter of a mile, more or
lefs; they then erect a fquare pillar, and continue the pipe up till they find how high the
water will rife; then they carry the pipe
down the other fide, (leaving the top open)
and continue it underground to the next pillar; and fo on till they have brought the water to the place intended to be fupplied with
it. It fometimes happens that all their labour has been in vain; and they find by experience that the place to be fupplied is higher
than the place whence they wanted to bring
the water.

The principles of levelling are unknown
to them. It would be in vain to tell them
that the furface of water is not perfectly flat;
that there is fuch a thing as refraction; and
that a levelling inftrument alone will not
tell them the height to which water will rife.
The moft learned man among the ulema does
not know, that as the whole fine is to the
angle of refraction, fo is the diftance of the
object to its apparent elevation by refraction.
They have no means of calculating the late-
ral preffure of arches or of cupolas; though
they

they generally err on the right fide, yet accidents fometimes have happened. I once fucceeded in making a Turkifh mathematician underftand the principle of a catenarian arch, by fufpending a chain ; but when he endeavoured to explain it to an architect, who was erecting a confiderable building for the late captain pafha, Gazi-Haffan, he received for anfwer, that the figure defcribed by a chain hung up by the two ends might be applicable to the conftruction of the bottom of a fhip, but not to that of an arch of mafonry.

It is a certain fact, that a few years ago a learned man of the law having loft an eye, and being informed that there was then at Conftantinople a European who made falfe eyes, not to be diftinguifhed from the natural, he immediately procured one; but when it was placed in the focket, he flew into a violent paffion with the eye-maker, abufing him as an impoftor, becaufe he could not fee with it. The man, fearing he fhould lofe his pay, affured him that in time he would fee as well with that eye as with the other. The effendi was appeafed, and the artift liberally rewarded, who having foon difpofed of the remainder of his eyes, left the Turks in expectation of feeing with them.

The ufe of wheel carriages is almoft un-

known

known in Turkey. There is a kind of cart, ufed at Conftantinople, and in fome few other parts, moftly for women to travel in. In moft parts of the Afiatic provinces they have no idea of a wheel. All their merchandize is carried by horfes, mules, or camels, in every part of the empire.

The fultan has a coach or carriage, exactly of the fhape of a hearfe in England, but without any fprings; it was, when I faw it, drawn by fix mules. The pole was of an enormous thicknefs, as well as every other part. I enquired the reafon; the anfwer was, that if the pole, the axletree, &c. broke, the man who made it would lofe his head. The fultan never ufes a carriage as any kind of ftate; it is only in excurfions into the country that it follows him.

The people in Moldavia and Walachia, on the contrary, conftruct waggons for carrying merchandize on very juft principles of mechanics. Cafks too are not in ufe, except among the Greeks.

It may be inferred from Peyffonel, that the fcience of medicine has made confiderable advances, and commands a high degree of refpect in Turkey, when we find that the dignity of firft phyfician to the grand feignior is marked by the title of *hakim bachi effendi*; that he wears the large round turban
called

called *eurf*, the fame as that borne by men of
the higheft rank in the law; and that the
Mahometan who attains this dignity muft
have paffed through the *médréffés*, and have
reached the order of the *muderris*; but the
fact is, that the ftate phyfician is a mere no-
minal dignity, enjoyed by men of no fkill in
this fcience, whilft the man to whom the
care of the fultan's health is intrufted is always a Greek, a Jew, or an European, and
it is merely for form fake that the confent
and prefence of the *hakim bachi* muft be obtained for the adminiftration of remedies, of
whofe medical properties he is in general
profoundly ignorant. When the Turks take
a purgative medicine, they never commend
it except it be moft violently cathartic. They
have no notion of the falutary effects of a
gentle laxative.

Navigation, and the ufe of the magnet,
none have the leaft idea of but the people of
the navy, and they know fo little, that their
compaffes are made to point to the true north
with the variation allowed, and by the fame
compaffes they fteer their fhips in all feas.
Very few in the navy can take a meridian
obfervation.

The only people who have the fmalleft
idea of navigation, are the Algerines in their
fervice; and even theirs is chiefly practical

knowledge.

knowledge. They rely on the Greeks to navigate their ſhips of war. Their merchant ſhips take care not to loſe ſight of land; and this is the principal reaſon why ſo many of them are loſt in the Black Sea.

The want of field-pieces among the Turks, which induced Baron de Tott to undertake a new foundry, is a complete proof of the inactivity of this people. It is true that they had foundries of large braſs cannon; but they had not even attempted to caſt thoſe of a ſmaller kind, or of a different metal, although their furnaces are of *uſine*, which is particularly adapted to the caſting of iron. To the preſent day they are ignorant of the art of caſting iron, even for bomb ſhells; and this is the reaſon why all the Turkiſh cannon, both for land and ſea ſervice, are of braſs.

Though they have many fine large cannons at preſent, they are defective in the make of the carriages, particularly for field-pieces; and whilſt other nations are making daily improvements in this reſpect (by the conſtruction of flying artillery, &c.) the Turks, from their ignorance of mechanics, employ artillery the moſt awkward and inefficacious.

The defective ſtate of general ſcience in Turkey is owing to that want of union amongſt its branches, and to that deficiency

of

of combination, both in theory and practice, whose causes I have already traced out; but in every country individual exertion will do much, and insulated facts will be everywhere discoverable, like the casual flowers of the desert, which show what the human mind is capable of attaining, even in despite of accumulated obstacles. The great advantage which a highly civilized country possesses, is in the quick and ready combination of these facts, and in forming out of them general principles, which abridge the labour and facilitate the progress of the artist and the philosopher. It frequently happens, however, that the most barbarous people possess, in particular branches of art, an accuracy of principle, or a dexterity of operation, even superior to their more polished neighbours; and hence it will be found of use to collect detached information of this kind from every part of the globe. In the intercourse of mind, something is to be gleaned from a soil the most unpromising; I shall, therefore, make no further apology for the introduction of some unconnected remarks on detached instances of skill among the Turks in various arts and sciences.

It might reasonably be expected that a nation of warriors should have expert surgeons at least, and that they should have paid attention to the improvements and discoveries
made

made by other nations. Nothing of this, however, is the case. They perform no operations, nor will they consent to an European's making an amputation, though the loss of life be a certain consequence of omitting it. Their art is simply confined to healing, and at most extracting a ball and a splinter of a bone. It must be confessed that, as their habit of body is generally healthy, nature performs often wonderful cures. They rely much on balsams, mummy, &c. There is in Constantinople a Persian extraordinarily expert in the art of healing. The Arabs bury a person, who has received a wound in his body, up to the neck in hot sand for twenty-four hours.

I saw in the eastern parts of the empire a method of setting bones practised, which appears to me worthy of the attention of surgeons in Europe. It is by inclosing the broken limb, after the bones are put in their places, in a case of plaster of Paris (or gypsum) which takes exactly the form of the limb, without any pressure, and in a few minutes the mass is solid and strong. If it be a compound fracture, the place where the wound is, and out of which an exfoliated bone is to come, may be left uncovered, without any injury to the strength of the plaster encasement. This substance may be easily cut with a knife, and removed, and replaced

5   with

with another. If, when the fwelling fubfides the cavity is too large for the limb, a hole or holes being left, liquid gypfum plafter may be poured in, which will perfectly fill up the void, and exactly fit the limb. A hole may be made at firft by placing an oiled cork or bit of wood againft any part where it is required, and when the plafter is fet, it is to be removed. There is nothing in gypfum injurious, if it be free from lime; it will foon become very dry and light, and the limb may be bathed with fpirits, which will penetrate through the covering. Spirits may be ufed inftead of water, or mixed with it (or vinegar) at the firft making of the plafter.

I faw a cafe of a moft terrible compound fracture of the leg and thigh, by the fall of a cannon, cured in this manner. The perfon was feated on the ground, and the plafter cafe extended from below his heel to the upper part of his thigh, whence a bandage, faftened into the plafter, went round his body. He reclined back when he flept, as he could not lie down. During the cure, where they faw matter or moifture appear through the plafter coating, they cut a hole with a knife to drefs the wound, or let out the matter more freely.

On this occafion I cannot help mentioning the treatment of parts frozen in Ruffia,

not

not by the furgeons, but by the common
people, the fuccefs of which I was an eye-
witnefs to in feveral cafes, as well as to the
failure of the common mode of treating
frozen parts by the moft able furgeons of the
army.   I fhall fimply ftate the facts I relate
to.

After Ochakof was taken, I received into
my fubterranean lodging as many prifoners
as it would receive, all of which were either
wounded or had a limb frozen.   Among
them were two children, one about fix and
the other about fourteen years of age ; the
latter had one of her feet frozen to the ancle,
the other all the toes, and the fole of one of
her feet.   The fecond day the parts appeared
black (the firft day they were not much obferved.)   The French furgeon whom Prince
Potemkin had fent for purpofely from Paris,
and who was a man of note, ordered them to
be conftantly bathed with warm camphorated
fpirits ; the elder was removed to the hof-
pital, when   a   mortification began ;   the
younger I kept with me, and as we removed
into winter quarters, I carried the child with
me.   The mortified parts feparated, the bones
of the toes came off, and, after a long time,
the fores healed.   I fhould have faid, the
furgeon was for immediately amputating both
the limbs.

Near

Near to me were several women, whose feet had been in like manner frozen ; but as no surgeon attended them, the Russian foldiers and waggoners undertook the cure. It was also the second day when they applied their remedy, and the parts were perfectly black. This remedy was goose-greafe, with which the parts were smeared, warm, and the operation often repeated : their directions were, never to let the parts be dry, but always covered with greafe. The confequence was, that by degrees the circulation extended lower down, and the blackness decreafed, till, laft of all, the toes were only difcoloured, and at length circulation was reftored to them.

I can account for this no otherwife, than that the fat kept the pores fhut, and prevented the air from promoting putrefaction ; in the meantime the veffels were continually abforbing part of the ftagnated blood, till by degrees the whole circulation was reftored. It is known that extravafated and ftagnated blood will remain a long time in the body without putrifying, if it be not expofed to the air. I conclude alfo, that in thefe cafes of froft, the mortification firft begins on the furface, which is in contact with the air.

I only relate facts however, and leave it to others to account for them.

This

This is a general practice of the peasants throughout all Ruffia. If a part is difcovered to be frozen, *before the perfon comes into a warm room*, the froft may be extracted by plunging the part into cold water, or rubbing it with fnow till the circulation returns.

The wherries or boats of Conftantinople are conftructed much on the principle of the Deal boats, but they are more fharp and curved, not fo light, but very apt to overfet if people fhift their places in them unwarily. Their fhape is very elegant. The boatmen have a large marble weight for ballaft, which they place after the paffengers are feated. Though they are large, they row exceedingly faft, and were always efteemed the quickeft going boats in Europe ; but I faw a gondola, brought to Conftantinople by a Venetian ambaffador, keep pace with them. The gondolas, every body knows, are built on a contrary conftruction, being quite flat at bottom. The boftangi-bafhee (mafter of the police) has a boat of twelve oars, which rows with furprifing velocity ; but no one is permitted to build on that conftruction : this boat goes nearly twice as faft as the common ones, and confequently as the gondolas. They are dangerous fea boats, though they fail faft. It is not many years fince they were brought to fuch perfection, as may be feen by a boat

now

now preferved (I think, of fultan Achmet III.)
the merit, however, is their own. The Turks
row in general better than the Chriftian or
Jew boatmen.

The Turks ufe copper veffels for their
kitchen utenfils, which are tinned with pure
tin, and not, as in moft parts of Europe, with
folder compofed of tin and lead, which is
much fooner corroded by acids and fat ; and
though it has not been obferved that any violent diforders have been produced by the
veffels in common ufe (except from the
copper itfelf) as the quantity of lead diffolved
is fmall (the admixture of tin rendering lead
more difficult of folution) yet many chronic
maladies may be owing to this baneful metal
getting into the habit in fmall quantities, and
particularly of the nervous kind. There is
no country in Europe where the quantity of
lead ufed in tinning is fo great as in this
ifland ; an abufe which certainly merits the
attention of this government, as it did fome
years ago that of France, who prohibited at
the fame time, under pain of death, the ufe
of all preparations of lead in wine, or other
liquors ; a regulation very neceffary in England, as is alfo the eftablifhment of fome
means to prevent fuch part of the tea being
fold which comes in immediate contact with
the

the lead, in chefts where it happens to be corroded, as is frequently the cafe.

Nothing can be more clumfy than the door-locks in Turkey, but their mechanifm to prevent picking is admirable. It is a curious thing to fee wooden locks upon iron doors, particularly in Afia, and on their caravanfaries, and other great buildings, as well as on houfe doors. The key goes into the back part of the bolt, and is compofed of a fquare ftick with five or fix iron or wooden pins about half an inch long, towards the end of it, placed at irregular diftances, and anfwering to holes in the upper part of the bolt, which is pierced with a fquare hole to receive the key. The key, being put in as far as it will go, is then lifted up, and the pins entering the correfponding holes raife other pins, which had dropt into thefe holes from the part of the lock immediately above, and which have heads to prevent them falling lower than is neceffary ; the bolt, being thus freed from the upper pins, is drawn back by means of the key ; the key is then lowered, and may be drawn out of the bolt : to lock it again, the bolt is only pufhed in, and the upper pins fall into the holes in the bolt by their own weight. This idea might be improved on, but the Turks never think of improving.

The

The Greeks have a very curious manner of painting in fresco, which has many advantages. I also saw the ancient method of painting with wax, and fixing the colours by heat, practised by a Greek, and at a place I least expected it, at the Dardanelles; for at Constantinople it is unknown. Whether this be exactly the encaustic painting of the ancients it is hazardous to affirm, though I myself have not the least doubt respecting it. Thus much is certain, that it has, with regard to facility, very considerable advantages over the oil painting now in use; it has all its freedom, and the vivacity of its colours, added to solidity, and the durability which the experience of twenty centuries has proved wax painting to be possessed of. It was my intention to have treated on it in this place; but as it does not regard Turkey, the immediate subject of this work, and would be a dissertation of considerable length, I intend shortly to print it separately, with the Greek manner of fresco painting, in which all colours may be used on a lime-wall.

The Armenian jewellers set precious stones, particularly diamonds, to much advantage, with a foil, which, under roses, or half-brilliants, is remarkably beautiful, and is not subject to tarnish. Their method is as follows: an agate is cut, and highly po-

lished,

lifhed, of the fhape defired; in a block of lead
is formed a cavity of about its own fize; over
this is placed a bit of tin of the thicknefs of
ftrong brown paper fcraped bright. The
agate is then placed on the tin, over the cavity, and ftruck with a mallet. The beautiful polifh the tin receives is fcarcely to be
imagined. This is in general kept a fecret,
and fuch foils fell for half and three quarters of a dollar each.

The jewellers, who are moftly Armenians,
have a curious method of ornamenting watch
cafes, and fimilar things, with diamonds and
other ftones, by fimply glueing them on.

The ftone is fet in filver or gold, and the
lower part of the metal made flat, or to correfpond with the part to which it is to be
fixed; it is then warmed gently, and the
glue applied, which is fo very ftrong that the
parts never feparate.

This glue, which may be applied to many
purpofes, as it will ftrongly join bits of glafs
or polifhed fteel, is thus made:

Diffolve five or fix bits of maftic, as large
as peas, in as much fpirit of wine as will fuffice to render it liquid; in another veffel
diffolve as much ifinglafs (which has been
previoufly foaken in water till it is fwollen
and foft) in French brandy or rum, as will
make two ounces, by meafure, of ftrong glue,
                                                    and

and add two fmall bits of gum galbanum
or ammoniacum, which muft be rubbed or
ground till they are diffolved; then mix
the whole with a fufficient heat ; keep it in
a phial ftopt, and when it is to be ufed fet it
in hot water.

Cotton at Smyrna is dyed with madder in
the following manner :—The cotton is boiled
in mild alkali, and then in common olive
oil ; being cleaned, it will then take the
madder dye : and this is the fine colour we
fee in Smyrna cotton-yarn. I have heard
five thoufand pounds was given, in England,
for this fecret *.

A remarkable inftance occurred to my
knowledge of an individual fact, which might
have been of the utmoft ufe to fociety, but
which, owing to the ftate of knowledge and
government in Turkey, was wholly loft to
the world. An Arabian, at Conftantinople,
had difcovered the fecret of cafting iron,
which, when it came out of the mould, was
as malleable as hammered iron ; fome of his
fabrication was accidentally fhown to Mr.
de Gaffron, the Pruffian chargé d'affaires,
and Mr. Franzaroli (men of mineralogical
fcience) who were ftruck with the fact, and

---

* I communicated thefe two proceffes to a friend, who
printed them in the *Bee* four or five years ago.

immediately inftituted an enquiry for its author.   This man, whofe art in Chriftendom
would have infured him a fplendid fortune,
had died poor and unknown, and his fecret
had perifhed with him ! His utenfils were
found, and feveral pieces of his cafting, all
perfectly malleable. Mr. Franzaroli analized
them, and found that there was no admixture of any other metal. Mr. de Gaffron
has fince been made fuperintendant of the
iron manufactory at Spandau, where he has
in vain attempted to difcover the procefs of
the Arabian.

Europeans are much ftruck to fee the
Turks work fitting at every art or handi-
craft where there is a poffibility of it; car-
penters, for inftance, perform the greateft
part of their labour fitting. It is deferving
of remark, that their toes acquire fuch a
degree of ftrength by ufing them, and by
their not being cramped up in tight fhoes,
that they hold a board upright and firmly
with their toes, while with their two hands
they guide a faw, fitting all the while. Thefe
people are able to ftand on the end of their
toes, which will fupport the whole weight
of their body.

We have, in Europe, certainly falfe ideas
with refpect to the utility of fhoes, in preventing the feet of children from becoming
                                        too

too broad.   The Arabs, who when children wear no fhoes, and when they are grown up, only fandals or flippers, have the moft beautiful feet.

In fome parts of Afia, I have feen cupolas of a confiderable fize, built without any kind of timber fupport.   They fix firmly in the middle a poft about the height of the perpendicular wall, more or lefs, as the cupola is to be a larger or fmaller portion of a fphere; to the top of this is faftened a ftrong pole, fo as to move in all directions, and the end of it defcribes the outer part of the cupola; lower down is fixed to the poft another pole, which reaches to the top of the inner part of the perpendicular wall, and defcribes the infide of the cupola, giving the difference of thicknefs of the mafonry at top and bottom, and every intermediate part, with the greateft poffible exactnefs.   As they build their cupolas with bricks, and inftead of lime ufe gypfum, finifhing one layer all round before they begin another, only fcaffolding for the workmen is required to clofe the cupola at top.

At Baffora, where they have no timber but the wood of the date tree, which is like a cabbage ftalk, they make arches without any frame.   The mafon with a nail and a bit of ftring defcribes a femicircle on the ground,

Q 3　　　　　　　　　　lays

lays his bricks, faftened together by a gypfum cement, on the lines thus traced, and having thus formed his arch, except the crown brick, it is carefully raifed, and in two parts placed on the wall. They proceed thus till the whole arch is finifhed. This part is only half a brick thick; but it ferves them to turn a ftronger arch over it.

The cities of Bagdad and Baffora are moftly built of bricks dried in the fun, which ftand ages if kept tolerably dry. The clay is ufed in almoft a dry ftate, and beaten into the moulds with mallets. This gives them a wonderful degree of hardnefs.

At the entrance of the defert, coming from Aleppo, I found a village built in a very fingular manner; each room was a cupola, and refembled a hay ftack, fome of them a fugar loaf. The whole was of earth, as they have no wood. The inhabitants faid their town had been built by Abraham; that is, they did not remember when the oldeft houfes were built. They faid they were never out of repair, but that they fometimes plaftered the upper part, or rather beat earth on it. The walls were compofed of clay and gravel, and were exceedingly hard. The method they ufe is, to beat each layer of earth till it is very hard.

Such a method is ufed in the province of Lyons

Lyons in France, where they build houfes of feveral ftories, and very fpacious. The walls are always plaftered with lime and fand, and ftand fome centuries. Thefe are very fuperior to the mud walls of cottages in fome parts of England, where the earth is ufed very moift, and mixed with ftraw. The ancient Romans built in the fame manner as in France. The excellence of the Venetian plafter floors, fo much admired for their hardnefs and beautiful polifh, depends entirely on their being ftrongly beaten. The compofition is only frefh lime and fand, with pieces of marble, ufed almoft dry, and beaten till they are quite hard, then ground even and polifhed. Common earth as well as lime mortar acquires an incredible degree of hardnefs by compreffion, if it contains no more moifture than is neceffary to make its parts unite. A kind of artificial ftone may be made of gravel with a little lime ftrongly preffed, or beaten into moulds.

I have feen practifed a method of *filtering water* by afcenfion, which is much fuperior to our filtering ftones, or other methods by defcent, in which, in time, particles of the ftone, or the finer fand, make a paffage along with the water.

They make two wells, from five to ten feet, or any depth, at a fmall diftance, which

have

have a communication at bottom. The feparation muft be of clay well beaten, or of
other fubftances impervious to water. The
two wells are then filled with fand and gravel. The opening of that into which the
water to be filtered is to run, muft be fomewhat higher than that into which the water
is to afcend, and this muft not have fand
quite up to its brim, that there may be room
for the filtered water, or it may, by a fpout,
run into a veffel placed for that purpofe.
The greater the difference is between the
height of the two wells, the fafter the
water will filter; but the lefs it is the better,
provided a fufficient quantity of water be
fupplied by it.

This may be practifed in a cafk, tub, jar,
or other veffel. The water may be con-
veyed to the bottom by a pipe, the lower
end having a fpunge in it, or the pipe may
be filled with coarfe fand.

It is evident that all fuch particles, which
by their gravity are carried down in filtration
by defcent, will not rife with the water in
filtration by afcenfion. This might be practifed on board fhips at little expence.

The Arabians and the Turks have a preparation of milk, which has fimilar qualities to the kumifs of the Kalmuks: by the
firft it is called *leban,* by the Turks *yaourt.*

To

To make it, they put to new milk made hot over the fire fome old leban (or yaourt.) In a few hours, more or lefs, according to the temperature of the air, it becomes curdled of an uniform confiftence, and a moft plea- fant acid ; the cream is in great part fepa- rated, leaving the curd light and femitranf- parent. The whey is much lefs fubject to fe- parate than in curds made with rennet with us, for the purpofe of making cheefe.

Yaourt has this fingular quality, that left to ftand it becomes daily fourer, and at laft dries, without having entered into the putrid fermentation. In this ftate it is preferved in bags, and in appearance refembles preffed curds after they have been broken by the hand. This dry yaourt, mixed with water, becomes a fine cooling food or drink, of excellent fer- vice in fevers of the inflammatory or putrid kind. It feems to have none of thofe qua- lities which make milk improper in fevers. Frefh yaourt is a great article of food among the natives, and Europeans foon become fond of it.

No other acid will make the fame kind of curd : all that have been tried, after the acid fermentation is over, become putrid. In Ruf- fia they put their milk in pots in an oven, and let it ftand till it becomes four, and this they ufe as an article of food in that ftate,

2   or

or make cheefe of it, but it has none of the qualities of yaourt, though, when it is new, it has much of the tafte. Perhaps new milk curdled with four milk, and that again ufed as a ferment, and the fame procefs continued, might, in time, acquire the qualities of ya-ourt, which never can be made in Turkey without fome old yaourt.

They give no rational account how it was firft made ; fome of them told me an angel taught Abraham how to make it, and others, that an angel brought a pot of it to Hagar, which was the firft yaourt (or leban.)

It merits attention as a delicious article of food, and as a medicine.

I will here relate the manner the Tatars and Kalmuks make their kumis, or fermented mare's milk.

" Take of mare's milk of one day any quantity, add to it a fixth part of water, an eighth part of the foureft cow's milk that can be got, but at a future period a fmaller portion of old kumis will better anfwer the purpofe of fouring ; cover the veffel with a thick cloth, and fet it in a place of moderate warmth ; leave it to reft for twenty-four hours, at the end of which the milk will have become four, and a thick fubftance gathered at top ; then with a ftick, made at the lower end in the manner of a churn ftaff, beat it till

till the thick fubftance above-mentioned be blended intimately with the fubjacent fluid; let it reft twenty-four hours in a high narrow veffel like a churn. The agitation muft be repeated as before, till the liquor appears to be perfectly homogenous, and in this ftate it is called kumis (or koumis) of which the tafte ought to be a pleafant mixture of fweet and four. Agitation muft be employed every time before it is ufed. When well prepared in clofe veffels, and kept in a cold place, it will keep three months or more without any injury to its quality.

" It ferves both as drink and food; is a reftorative to the ftomach and a cure for nervous diforders, phthifis, &c."

The Tatars diftil this fermented milk, and obtain from it a fpirituous liquor, which they drink inftead of brandy.

The butter, which is moftly ufed in Conftantinople, comes from the Crim and the Kuban. They do not falt it, but melt it in large copper pans over a very flow fire, and fcum off what rifes; it will then preferve fweet a long time if the butter was frefh when it was melted. We preferve butter moftly by falting. I have had butter, which when frefh was melted and fcum'd in the Tatar manner, and then falted in our manner, which kept two years good and fine tafted. Wafhing does

does not fo effectually free butter from the curd and butter-milk, which it is neceffary to do, in order to preferve it, as boiling or melting; when then falt is added to prevent the pure butyrous part from growing rancid, we certainly have the beft procefs for preferving butter. The melting or boiling, if done with care, does not difcolour or injure the tafte.

To the lovers of coffee, a few remarks on the Turkifh manner of making it, in the beft way, may not be unacceptable.

Coffee, to be good, muft either be ground to an almoft impalpable powder, or it muft be pounded as the Turks do, in an iron mortar, with a heavy peftle. The Turks firft put the coffee dry into the coffee pot, and fet it over a very flow fire, or embers, till it is warm, and fends forth a fragrant fmell, fhaking it often; then from another pot they pour on it boiling water (or rather water in which the grounds of the laft made coffee had been boiled, and fet to become clear); they then hold it a little longer over the fire, till there is on its top a white froth like cream, but it muft not boil, but only rife gently; it is then poured backwards and forwards two or three times, from one pot into another, and it foon becomes clear; they, however, often drink it quite thick. Some put in a fpoon full of cold water to make it clear fooner, or lay a cloth

cloth dipt in cold water on the top of the
pot.

The reafon why our Weft India coffee is
not fo good as the Yemen coffee is, that on
account of the climate it is never fuffered to
hang on the trees till it is perfectly ripe ; and
in the voyage it acquires a tafte from the bad
air in the hold of the fhip. This may be
remedied in Italy, by expofing it to the fun
two or three months : with us, boiling water
fhould be poured on it, and let to ftand till
it is cold, then it muft be wafhed with other
cold water, and, laftly, dried in an oven.
Thus prepared, it will be nearly as good as
the beft Turkey coffee. It fhould be roafted
in an open earthen or iron pan, and the
flower it is roafted the better. As often as it
crackles it muft be taken off the fire. The
Turks often roaft it in a baker's oven while it
is heating.

The prefervation of yeaft having been a
fubject of much refearch in this country, the
following particulars may perhaps deferve attention. On the coaft of Perfia my bread
was made, in the Englifh manner, of good
wheat flower, and with the yeaft generally
ufed there. It is thus prepared ; take a
fmall tea cup or wine glafs full of fplit or
bruifed peafe, pour on it a pint of boiling
water, and fet the whole in a veffel all
night

night on the hearth, or any other warm place; the water will have a froth on its top next morning, and will be good yeaſt. In this cold climate, eſpecially at a cold ſeaſon, it ſhould ſtand longer to ferment, perhaps twenty-four or forty-eight hours. The above quantity made me as much bread as two ſixpenny loaves, the quality of which was very good and light.

A ſpring, which operates both on the individual and national character of the modern European with a force ſecond only to that of political inſtitution, is commerce. Upon the views entertained on this ſubject by a people; upon the extent and modes of their practice, and upon the character which they maintain with reſpect to it, depends much of their importance as a nation.

With regard to the general ideas entertained by all ranks in Turkey relative to commerce, they are no leſs narrow and abſurd than all their other opinions. "We " ſhould not trade," ſay they, "with thoſe " beggarly nations, who come to buy of " us rich articles of merchandize, and rare " commodities, which we ought not to ſell " to them, but with thoſe who bring to us " ſuch articles, without the labour of manu- " facturing, or the trouble of importing them " on our part." Upon this principle it is

that

that Mocha coffee is prohibited to be fold to
infidels. It is therefore no wonder that the
foreign commerce of the Turks is comparatively trifling ; their trade is moftly from
province to province, and even this is in-
conceivably narrowed by the want of mutual confidence, and the ignorance and fhort-
fightednefs of their views. They have few
bills of exchange, or any of thofe modes of
tranfacting bufinefs which the ingenuity and
enterprife of commercial nations have invented for the facilitation of commercial intercourfe.

The effects which the infecurity of property, and the watchful avarice of the government produce upon commerce, are ftill more
ftriking. In an extenfive trade capital and
credit muft be alike great, but from both
of thefe the Turk is cut off; he dares not
make a difplay of wealth ; and if he has
been fo fortunate as to accumulate a large
fum of money, his firft care is to conceal
it from view, left it fhould attract the blood-
fuckers of power. The neceffary confequence of this is, that credit, that vital
fpring of commerce, cannot be created, and
inftead of thofe commercial connections
which in this part of Europe ramify fo
widely, and render commercial operations fo
eafy, all bufinefs is tranfacted either by prin-
cipals

cipals themselves, or their immediate factors, in a way little different from the barter of the rude ages.

Nor is it only the insecurity of property while living which renders the Turk so averse to engage in undertakings of great extent and contingent advantage ; the disposition of it by will affords them little means of self gratification in viewing their inheritance transmitted to posterity. The merchants, and others of inferior rank, know, that a splendid fortune, at the same time that it renders their children objects of suspicion, will not raise them to posts of honour and respect, without putting them in a situation not to be able to transmit it another generation to their posterity ; those who hold any office of the porte know that they have the sultan for their heir, and his pashas or other officers for their executors; hence it is that posterity is of so little consequence in the eyes of the Turk, that he is seldom induced to consult much their welfare, and the hospitals, caravansaries, fountains, bridges, &c. built for charitable purposes, only originate in the ostentation or superstitious fears of their founders, who build them for the repose of their souls, or to perpetuate the reputation of their piety.

The natural result of this combination of circumstances is, that commerce is every where

where checked; no emulation takes place, no communication of difcoveries, no firm and folid affociation of intereft; their mechanical arts are in many inftances worfe cultivated now than they were a century ago, particularly the tempering of fabres; and fome of their manufactures have gone entirely to decay.

It remains only to fpeak of the moral character which they maintain as traders; and this has been varioufly reprefented. All ranks of people have fome flight kind of commerce, or rather a fort of pedling trade among themfelves, and confequently the diftinctive character of the different ranks will appear in this as well as in other circumftances. Amongft all of them a certain degree of artifice is common, and is fcarcely thought difhonourable, fuch as the corrupting of brokers and all thofe who are concerned in making bargains; but the officers and dependents of the porte are univerfally remarked as the moft venal and cheating fet of men on the face of the earth.

Honefty, however, it is faid, in fome meafure diftinguifhes the Turkifh merchant: this may perhaps be true, if we compare him with the crafty Greek, or ftill more fubtle Armenian, who, from the unjuft oppreffions under which they labour, are induced to re-

R   taliate

taliate by artifice, on their imperious mafters, the fource of half that tricking and deception commonly laid to the charge of the lower orders of fociety.

Much of the civilization of modern Europe has been with juftice attributed to the influence of female fociety; to this are owing the high and noble paffions which excite mankind to deeds of active patriotifm and benevolence, and the fofter pleafures which ornament and endear the focial circle. It will be worth while to confider how far then woman, " *laft and beft of all God's* " *works*," made to foften the ferocity of man, was made in vain for thefe barbarians; whofe love is fenfuality without friendfhip or efteem.

Polygamy is generally found to be deftructive to the finer feelings; it is fo in Turkey. The rich man (who alone is enabled to fupport feveral females) regards them only as the inftruments of his pleafures, and feeks their fociety with no other view; hence the women themfelves have no cultivation of mind, but live a ftupid folitary life, furrounded by flaves, or by women as ignorant and fpiritlefs as themfelves. Moral virtue and intellectual eminence are alike uncultivated by them, and the defcriptions of elegance and tafte difcoverable in their amufe-

ments,

ments, their gardens, and apartments, exift
only in the imagination of travellers, who,
like Lady Montague, aim rather to aftonifh
than inftruct.

The women in general only want an opportunity to become unfaithful to their hufbands, and the propofition generally comes
from them; but it is attended with great
danger. If a common Mahomedan profti-
tute even be catched with a Chriftian, fhe is
put into a fack and drowned, and the man
put to death, except he become a Mahomedan, which will not always fave both their
lives. Chriftians of the country have often
preferred death.

Marriage is with the Mahomedans merely
a civil contract; the wife brings no portion
to the hufband, but the hufband ftipulates in
the marriage contract, which is executed before a judge, to allow a certain portion to the
wife. The contracts are of two kinds, the
nikiah and the *kapin*; the former is the proper legal marriage, and every Mahomedan is
reftrained by the koran to four wives of this
defcription. This contract fpecifies a certain
fum, which is to be given to the wife in cafe
of repudiation, or of her hufband's death.
The other contract is only an agreement to
live together for a certain period, at the expiration of which a fpecified fum is to be

given

given to the woman. It is a juſt obſervation
of Baron de Tott, that the kapin or temporary marriage is a neceſſary conſequence of
the general inſtitution of polygamy. A ſeparation may be demanded by either party;
if it be by the woman, ſhe goes before the
judge, and pronounces the following for-
mula: " *Nikia-hum khalal, baſhum uzad,*"
i. e. " My dowry given up, my head is free."
The huſband, who repudiates his wife, muſt
repeat it either three ſeveral times, or three
times together, after which he cannot take
her back until he has ſubmitted to a peculiar indecent and immoral ceremony.

In converſation the Turks ſometimes diſ-
play good natural ſenſe; but the wit for which
they have been celebrated is no where to be
found. This is ſufficiently evident from the
exiſtence of the *muſahibs,* or profeſſed ſpeak-
ers, who are indeed little better than buffoons, but who are hired by the opulent to
amuſe their company. Can there poſſibly
be a greater imputation on the ſocial powers
of a people, than their adoption of ſuch a
practice? They cannot or dare not ſpeak ſo
as to keep up amuſing or inſtructive converſation, and they therefore call in the aid of
hired talkers. Derviſhes, particularly thoſe
who have the reputation of being mad, but
who generally are more rogues than fools,
often

often attach themfelves to the great, and amufe the company. Thefe people fome-times take very great liberties in their fpeeches, which is excufed in them on account of their holy frenzy.

A free people are a focial people, fond of friendly intercourfe. Cheerful converfe and unreferved communication of fentiment foften the nature, refine the manners, expand the heart, and enlarge the underftanding. Freedom of fpeaking and acting is the fource of civilization.

A nation of flaves is a nation difunited; no focial ties, no unbofoming of friendfhip; fufpicion and fear is in every breaft; converfation is uninterefting, and confequently not fought after; hired buffoons and low jefters are the fpeakers to the gloomy audience, or they fit in fad and ftupid folitude, fmoking a narcotic herb, or taking lethargic opium; infulting haughtinefs and ridiculous pomp take the place of that elevation of fentiment, and dignity of character, which alone exalts the man of high birth or office above his fellow-citizen; difguft and gloom hang over their countenances, and innocent mirth is deemed indecent.

When a Turk drinks wine, it is with an intention of being intoxicated; he therefore

fwallows

fwallows a large portion at one draught, or
repeats it till he is beaftly drunk ; or if he
is fearful of the confequences of being in that
ftate in the place he happens to be, at leaft
the quantity he prefcribes to himfelf to make
him *contented* (as they exprefs themfelves) he
drinks off all at once. Such a method of
drinking wine, and with fuch a view, certainly entitles drinkers to the contempt they
are held in in Turkey.

From thefe circumftances, which may be
confidered as forming the more ornamental
part of the manners of a nation, we pafs to
thofe more important points which conftitute
the bafis of their moral charaƈter.

And here it muft be obferved, that fo wide
and various an empire as Turkey cannot but
have ftriking varieties in the morals of its
inhabitants ; they, however, moftly agree in
the great leading points, and the variations
are to be accounted for from peculiar circumftances of fituation, origin, and habits.
I fhall therefore firft notice generally thofe
vices and virtues which belong to the Turks
as a nation, and then point out a few of the
moft ftriking differences obfervable in the
various provinces of the empire.

The moral charaƈter of the Turks has
been reprefented in a favourable light by
fome authors upon two principles ; the one,
a con-

a connection of intereſt between the Turks and their own country (which is the caſe of moſt of the French writers except Volney) and the other, from a wiſh to expoſe the vices and follies of other European nations by the contraſt. Of the writers themſelves I ſhall hereafter have occaſion to ſpeak ; the chief points of their deſcription will be included in the following obſervations.

Much has been ſaid of the equity of the Turks. If we look to the example of their ſultans, viziers, paſhas, and judges, ſelling juſtice, can it be ſuppoſed that theſe examples have not corrupted the people, though they were naturally good. The truth is, that they have ſo little idea of juſtice themſelves, that when they go to law (that is, appeal to a kadi) they rely more on bribes and cabal than on impartial judgment. Where the judge is not influenced, he is naturally juſt ; no man ſcarcely was ever ſo corrupted but he would be ſo. The European merchants, who have a better opportunity of knowing them than foreign miniſters, confined almoſt wholly to their reſidence, and ignorant of the country, or than travellers paſſing haſtily through the country, unanimouſly aſſure us, that they find them very cunning in their dealings, and full of deceit.

R 4 The

The people are faid to be humane : the peaceable citizen may be fo, as in other parts, or as man naturally is ; but the dictates of their religion, and the examples they fee, muft blunt their feelings ; and this citizen, in regard to an enemy, is as favage as a tiger. There is, after all (from whatever caufe) a ferocity in them which may eafily be awoken, and when they ftrike, it is with a dagger to the heart.

The temperance of the Turks, which is owing in a great meafure to their religion, produces its ufual good effect in rendering their intellects clear ; their grofs ignorance is not to be attributed to their want of natural fenfe ; the foil muft not only be in itfelf rich, it muft be cultivated. The Turk has indeed a good capacity, and an habitual prudence, but his government and religion are eternal bars to his improvement. Opennefs of mind and benevolence cannot exift where defpotifm renders every man fufpicious, nor can the votary of an intolerant and fanguinary religion cultivate liberality and fcience.

As to the politenefs afcribed to the Turks by fome authors, I never could difcover it : the Turkifh ferocity, perhaps, excited fear in them, and produced refpect : if a man

found

found himself alone with a tiger, and escaped unhurt, he would say it was a good-natured animal. The assuming superiority of the meanest Turk, the deference which is paid to him by all infidels who approach him, and by your own interpreters, impose and create respect; if the beast then only growls, but does not bite, he is praised for his civility. If you know their language, you will observe the difference of their expressions and their manners from those they use to their brother Mahomedans ; you will observe, at best, an insulting condescendence, which plainly bespeaks their contempt of you : they are ignorant of, and above practising the true principles of politeness. Madame de Genlis says, politeness consists in making others appear every thing, yourself nothing ; a Turk makes himself every thing, you nothing. We have only to observe the ambassadors they send to foreign courts (who are all people very low in office;) they neither learn the language, or gain any more knowledge of the country than the post-horses which draw them through it : when they return, they represent the men as monkies, because they are active, and the women as prostitutes, because they are unveiled, and live in society with men. Not one word of this is exaggerated. The language and the address
of

of the politeft minifter of the porte to a foreign ambaffador very much refembles the
civility of a polite German baron to his
vaffal.

Even their moft ftrenuous admirer, Peyffonel, acknowledges that Turkey remains two
centuries behind the reft of Europe in refpect to fcience ; that it has neglected naval
and military tactics and difcipline ; and that
it allows vices in many parts of its adminiftration to go uncorrected.

That there is a confiderable difference of
character and morals in the different parts of
the empire has been before obferved : the worft
are the people of Anatolia, particularly thofe
bordering on the Black Sea ; they are cowardly, treacherous, robbers, affaffins, and indecent ; thofe of Conftantinople are foftened
by a city life ; thofe of Aleppo are the moft
refined and civil among themfelves, and remarkably decent, but, like all the Afiatics,
hold Europeans in great contempt, and even
hatred ; at Damafcus they are furious zea-
lots ; the people of Smyrna are favage and
dangerous ; in European Turkey they have
fewer prejudices againft Chriftians, becaufe
they know more of them, or rather becaufe
they are lefs bigoted enthufiafts than at Damafcus, or in Egypt ; at Bagdad they are
lefs prejudiced by their religion, and more
open

open to inftruction, than in other parts of Afia; the people of Baffora, a mixture of Arabs, Perfians, and a few Turks, are mild and docile. It is fingular, that thefe people, from their communication with India and with Europeans, know infinitely more of our manners, arts, and arms, and are more inclined to adopt them, than thofe in the frontier towns in Europe, who are prejudiced, infolent, and proud. The Arabians of the defert generally pay nearly as much refpect to a European as to one of their own country, and more than to a Turk, whom they mortally hate.

CHAPTER VII.

On the State of Population in the Turkish Empire.

THE aim of all rational politics is to augment the numbers, and increafe the happinefs of mankind; and hence the ftate of population is generally the moft accurate ftandard of political error or improvement. From the preceding pages we fhall have feen fufficient reafon to apprehend that the population of the Turkifh empire cannot be, in the prefent day, at all proportioned to the extent of its territory. The religious diftinctions which deprefs into fo abject a ftate of flavery one great part of the community, and the infecurity of property, which affects every rank and condition, are both caufes, whofe combined operation muft greatly fubtract from the numbers of a people, which form the vital ftrength of a ftate. Where the cultivator is not fure of reaping the corn which he fows, he will fow only what the immediate neceffity of fubfiftence requires; the political ftate of the country prevents

prevents his accumulation of capital, and even that fmall portion which he may chance to poffefs, he will not hazard in fpeculations of fo very uncertain profit. In this languifh-ing ftate of domeftic agriculture, Conftanti-nople looks for a fupply of corn to foreign channels, particularly Egypt, Moldavia, Wa-lachia, the Crimea, and Poland.

From a view of the ftate of Egypt, it will appear that little dependence can be placed on the permanence of this fupply; ftill lefs would a wife government look to markets, which, like the others which I have enume-rated, are either immediately under the direc-tion of a hoftile ftate, or perpetually liable to its incurfions. The Ruffians are, indeed, wife enough, in time of peace, to invigorate their own agriculture, by fupplying Conftantino-ple with corn from their provinces. The Crimea, on which the porte ufed greatly to depend, has been deferted by moft of its Ta-tar inhabitants fince it fell under the impe-rial dominion; but the Ruffian and other adventurers, who now occupy it, are making great endeavours to revive its commerce and agriculture; thefe, however, as well as the fupplies of Poland, are in the hands of Ruf-fia, and in the event of a war fhe can not only withhold them, but perhaps cut off the fup-plies of Moldavia and Walachia, thus ex-
posing

pofing the Turkifh capital to the utmoft diftrefs. Notwithftanding thefe evident confequences of their prefent fyftem of policy, the
divan purfue thofe methods of fupply which
give them the leaft immediate trouble, totally regardlefs both of the decay of their
own agriculture and of the future deftruction which this fyftem threatens to their very
exiftence as a nation. It is not only in theory
that thefe evils are to be apprehended; a
comparifon of the prefent and paft ftates of
the Turkifh population will evince the truth
of the foregoing propofitions.

We know not what was the population of
this vaft empire in very remote ages; from
the evidence of hiftory it appears to have been
very confiderable; at prefent it is far from
being fo. Without going farther back than
the memory of perfons now living, it is eafy
to prove that depopulation has been, at leaft
in latter times, aftonifhingly rapid.

The great caufes of this depopulation are,
doubtlefs, the following:

1ft. The plague, of which the empire is
never entirely free.

2dly. Thofe terrible diforders which almoft always follow it, at leaft in Afia.

3dly. Epidemic and endemic maladies in
Afia, which make as dreadful ravages as the

4

plague itfelf, and which frequently vifit that part of the empire.

4thly. Famine, owing to the want of precaution in the government, when a crop of corn fails, and to the avarice and villany of the pafhas, who generally endeavour to profit by this dreadful calamity.

5th and laftly, the ficknefſes which always follow a famine, and which occafion a much greater mortality.

The plague is more mortal in proportion as it vifits a country feldom. At Conftantinople it is often a great number of years together: it is fcarcely perceived in winter, and frequently fhips fail to Europe with *clean bills of health*, though it is lurking in infected clothes, and in diftant and little frequented parts of the city. In fpring it breaks out again. No calculation can be formed of the numbers that die of it in the capital; for their want is never long perceived, there being a conftant influx of people from the country to the capital. Some years the mortality does not appear to be confiderable, but at other times they have what is called a *great ficknefs*, which carries off an aftonifhing number. The confumption of provifions has been reduced, during fuch a plague, to three-fourths of what it was when it began to rage.

It

It vifits moft parts of Afia every ten or twelve years, and carries off an eighth or tenth of the inhabitants, and fometimes a fourth or more. The farther eaft a country is fituated, the lefs frequently it is vifited. It is faid, it never goes where the olive tree does not grow. It reaches Baffora about every ninetieth year; but then this fcourge is moft dreadful. The laft plague carried off ninetenths of the inhabitants, and that city had been ninety-fix years free of it. Farther eaft it has not been known to go.

The plague, like the fmall pox, is a diforder never generated by foul air, or the like, but always produced by contagion. It, doubtlefs, comes from Egypt, though in Egypt it is frequently received back from Conftantinople.

Dr. Ruffel fays, the plague which afflicted Egypt in 1736, and of which it was faid that 10,000 died in one day at Cairo, " *was the* " *only one that happened in this century, which* " *was believed by the people of Cairo to have* " *been brought from Upper Egypt; the others* " *were always thought to have been imported* " *from Conftantinople or Candia, but never* " *from Syria or Barbary.*"

How eafily would not a regular *quarantine* and *fhutting up* deliver Turkey from this terrible fcourge !—but what is to be expected

but

but devaſtation from the Turks? No city has
better local ſituations for lazarettoes than Conſtantinople—I allude to the Princes Iſlands.
When the capital has been really free of it, it
always is brought thither either directly or
indirectly from Egypt (generally by the way
of Smyrna.)   Many people, not attending to
this circumſtance, have concluded that it was
generated in Conſtantinople, and talk much
of the bad air produced by the naſtineſs of
the ſtreets, which is without foundation.
The air of Conſtantinople is exceedingly pure
and healthy; but no infected or impure air,
loaded with the miaſma of putrefaction, &c.
will produce the plague, though it may fevers, both contagious and mortal, in a high
degree.

It does not appear from Plutarch's account
of the plague at Athens, that it really was
this diſorder which afflicted that city in Pe-
ricles time.   The true plague is never in the
air, perhaps (for I ſay this with ſome doubt)
not in the breath of a peſtiferous perſon, at
leaſt the breath cannot convey it above a few
feet, as the Ruſſian ſurgeons have ſufficiently
proved, when the plague was at Moſqua
(Moſcow) and at Cherſon more particularly,
where thoſe ſurgeons, who touched nothing
in the hoſpitals, and pulled off their ſhoes on
going out, all eſcaped.

S   The

The phyſicians at Conſtantinople ſay, the
more they ſtudy the plague the leſs they
know of it; and as it is there almoſt every
year, they have more opportunities of ſeeing
this diſorder than any others of the profeſſion. We learn nothing from the Ruſſian
phyſicians, who expoſed themſelves very much
in the plague at Moſcow, in 1771, and in
that which broke out in 1783 at Cherſon
(ſee Mertens's Obſerv. and Orreus's Deſcrip-
tio Peſtis; alſo Samoillovits's Memoire ſur
la Peſte;) nor is there any thing very ſa-
tisfactory with reſpect to the cure to be learned from Dr. Ruſſel's elaborate treatiſe on
the plague, nor from the more ancient authors. It is ſaid that friction with oil has
lately been diſcovered, in Egypt, to be a pre-
ſervative; ſo much is certain, that the plague
is unknown to thoſe nations whoſe cuſtom it
is to rub their bodies with oil. It has been
obſerved at Conſtantinople, that thoſe who
uſed mercurial frictions never catched the
plague, how much ſoever they were expoſed
to the contagion. May this not have been owing to the greaſe rather than the mercury?

Mr. Matra (who is now agent at Morocco)
gave James's powders to an Armenian family, about twenty years ago, at Conſtantinople, and they recovered. I alſo thought I
had performed cures with this famous medicine;

cine ; but it has had a fair trial in Ruſſia, without producing any ſalutary effect ; farther than what was to be expected from an emetic. There is, however, ſome reaſon to believe that it may prevent the plague, if adminiſtered *immediately after the infection*, though perhaps any other ſudorific would be equally ſerviceable.

There is one circumſtance, of which it is of importance to determine the truth, as it is of conſequence with reſpect to quarantine ; this is, whether the plague communicated *per fomitem*, (that is, by ſubſtances which, having imbibed the peſtiferous effluvia or miaſma, retain them in an active ſtate for ſome time,) be of a more mortal kind than that by immediate contact with a diſeaſed body ; and particularly whether the *fomes* become of a more deadly quality by its being long retained in the ſubſtance, than when newly imbibed by it.

Dr. Cullen ſays, " *It appears to me probable* " *that contagions, as they ariſe from fomites,* " *are more powerful than as they ariſe immedi-* " *ately from the human body.*"

Dr. Lind ſays, " *From a fixt attention to this* " *ſubject for many years, I ſay theſe laſt (wear-* " *ing apparel, dirty linen, &c. long retained in* " *that impure ſtate) contain a more concentrated* " *and contagious poiſon than the newly emitted*

S 2 " *effluvia*

" *effluvia or excretions from the fick.*" Van
Swieten was of the fame opinion.

On the other hand, Doctor Ruffel (Treatife of the Plague) whofe opinion with refpect to the plague is a great authority, thinks
differently; he fays, (page 205) " *I fhould be*
" *inclined to doubt that the peftiferous effluvia*
" *of a perfon labouring under the plague, after*
" *the having been fhut up fome time in a fubftance*
" *fitted to imbibe and confine them, would act*
" *more powerfully on a perfon difpofed to infec-*
" *tion, than the fame effluvia would have done*
" *at the inftant of their emanation from the mor-*
" *bid body.*"

It certainly would be a ridiculous pre-
fumption in one, who is not a medical man,
to decide between fuch great profeffional authorities; but do not facts, mentioned by
Dr. Ruffel himfelf, decide the queftion?
Page 97. fpeaking of the firft of the fix
claffes, under which he arranged the cafes
which fell under his immediate obfervation,
he fays, " *None of the fick recovered, and moft*
" *of them died the fecond or third day; a very*
" *few lived to the fifth.*"—" *Thefe deftructive*
" *forms of the difeafe prevailed moft at the*
" RISE *of the plague in* 1760, *and its* RESUS-
" CITATION *in the fpring of the two fubfequent*
" *years,* DECREASING ALWAYS AS THE
" DISTEMPER SPREAD: *and though they were*
                                    " *found*

" *found difperfed in every ftage of the peftilen-*
" *tial feafon, yet the number of fubjects of this*
" *clafs was proportionably very fmall, com-*
" *pared with that of others.*" Again (page
209.) " *But a greater difficulty than that*
" *of perfons not being equally fufceptible of*
" *infection, arifes from the ceffation of the*
" *plague at a period when the fuppofed con-*
" *tagious effluvia, preferved in apparel, furni-*
" *ture, and other fomites, at the end of a pefti-*
" *lential feafon, muft be allowed not only to*
" *exift in a much greater quantity than can be*
" *fuppofed to be at once accidentally imported*
" *by commerce, but in a ftate alfo of univerfal*
" *difperfion over the city.*"

It is an incontrovertible fact, in which
every author agrees, relative to the plague,
which, having ceafed in fummer or in autumn, breaks out again in the fpring, or
at any other time of the year, whether communicated by infectious fomites remaining
in apparel, &c. in the fame city, or brought
in merchandize, &c. from other parts, that
in the beginning fcarcely any one recovers
of the plague, that the diforder gradually
becomes lefs mortal, and laftly, that it entirely ceafes.

Quere? May it not be thence concluded,
that the reafon of the mortality in the beginning of the plague is owing to the fo-

S 3

mites

mites having been confined a longer time, and become thereby more poiſonous; that when the plague has raged ſome time, and the infection taken from peſtiferous bodies, or effects lately impregnated with *freſh* fomites, this is the reaſon why it is leſs malignant; that the diſorder thus becomes milder, and at length ceaſes to be infectious, till the fomites have again acquired an increaſed degree of malignity by time; that the examples mentioned by Dr. Ruſſel, (page 97.) of caſes of the firſt and mortal claſs, which ſometimes were found at every ſeaſon, were caſes where the ſick had caught infection from old fomites. This cannot be affirmed, but it cannot, I believe, be contradicted, and it would appear, from the gradual decline in malignity of the plague, to be probable.

It would appear that the plague, when it firſt breaks out, and is very mortal, not one in ten, and ſometimes in forty, recovering, is not ſo catching as when it is ſpread over the whole city. Perhaps later in the year, when the pores are more open by the warmth of the ſeaſon, people are more liable to be infected. Mertens (Hiſtoire de la Peſte de Moſcow en 1771) ſays, " *The great cold* " *which reigned during the laſt two months of* " *the year ſo enervated the peſtilential miaſma,* " *that thoſe who aſſiſted the ſick, and buried the* " *dead,*

" *dead, were lefs eafily attacked by the con-*
" *tagion, &c.*" It appears alfo from him, that
froft will in a very fhort time entirely deftroy the fomites : he fays, " *Dr. Poparetfky,*
" *told me, that the carriers of the dead clothed*
" *themfelves with fheep fkins, which had been*
" *worn by thofe who had had the plague, after*
" *having been expofed to a fevere froft forty-*
" *eight hours, and not one of them caught the*
" *plague.*"

It is natural to conclude, that the plague
fhould be more mortal in hot weather than
in cold ; but it would feem as if the degrees
of its poifon depended not fo much on the
ftate of the air as on the old or recent ftate
of the fomites ; and that the power of the
poifon was diminifhed by propagation, till
it became at laft little if at all mortal ; at
leaft experience in all places where the
plague has raged feems to prove this.

It alfo appears, that the fomites may be
preferved a long time in infected things,
which are not expofed to the air. Dr. Ruffel
quotes a fingular inftance of this from Dr.
Mackenzie of Conftantinople ; it is too interefting not to be repeated : " *Count Caftil-*
" *lane had, for three years running, perfons at-*
" *tacked in the fame manner, in the months of*
" *July and Auguft, notwithftanding all poffible*
" *precaution ufed in cleaning the room, and*

S 4 " *even*

" even white-washing it. At last, by my own
" advice to his excellency, he built a slight coun-
" ter-wall, since which there has been no ac-
" cident in that room, now five years ago.
It has never been determined how long the
miasma or effluvia of the plague, when shut
up in merchandize or effects, may remain
active ; there is reason to believe that it may
many months ; there are, indeed, proofs of
it in every lazaretto in the Mediterranean,
(as well as the contagion brought so far as
Holland and England in former times) where
there are often accidents happen to those who
open cotton bales and other packages ; and
this fomes, probably, was only the perspiration
or effluvia from infected persons, who laboured at the packing, or perhaps have lain down
on such merchandize, or fomes attached to
their clothes, though they themselves were
not infected ; but if by some accident cotton
embued with the pus of pestiferous buboes
or carbuncles should be by some accident
(which is not impossible) packed into the
cotton sent to Europe, how long such dried
pus would retain its infectious quality is
not known, but it is to be feared that it
might be very long, though it is to be hoped
that, like the matter of the small pox, it may
lose its contagious quality of itself in a certain
time without airing.

It

It is, however, evident that expofure to the air will deftroy this infectious quality; that great cold (as has been feen in the inftances quoted from Mertens) will deftroy it very fuddenly ; and it would feem alfo, that the rays of the fun and a drying wind will alfo, though not fo rapidly, arreft its poifon, and deftroy it : on this is grounded quarantine, the utility of which no rational man can now doubt, though formerly fuch doubts have exifted. But all quarantines are of no effect where the merchandize are not *opened and aired*; and as that is not the cafe in England nor in Holland, thofe lazarettoes are of no kind of ufe ; they retard trade without fecuring the country from infection. The quarantines in the Mediterranean only are efficient.

In a feparate chapter, treating on the Levant trade, I fhall have occafion to fpeak more at large on quarantine, and the neceffity of making other regulations in this country, than thofe which at prefent exift. Dr. Ruffel, indeed, has collected every thing that has been faid by others, and has turned this matter fo ably and fo fully himfelf, it may feem fuperfluous to fay more on that head ; but it appears to me, that he has not reprefented the danger fo ftrongly as he faw it ;

there

there now exifts a neceffity of fpeaking out more plainly.

We may add another caufe of depopulation, the tyranny of the pafhas, who, in fome parts of Afia, fo much impoverifh the people, that they prevent marriages being fo frequent as they are where there is lefs danger of being unable to maintain a family; and this gives rife to an abominable vice, which brings fterility with it, and when men are fo degraded as to become habituated to it, they lofe the natural inftinct in man for the fair fex.

Polygamy itfelf is an inftitution experience proves to be fo little favourable to population, that the Chriftian families are generally obferved to be more prolific than the Mahomedans.

Depopulation is firft perceived in the country. Cities are filled up with new recruits of inhabitants from the country; but when the cities become defert, and that not merely by the decay of a particular branch of commerce or manufacture, or any other fimilar caufe, but for want of people to emigrate from the country, we may eafily believe that depopulation has reached nearly its laft ftage. This is the cafe even in thofe parts of the Turkifh empire where manufactures exift;

where

where there is bread for thofe who will feek employment; even in thefe places the country is alfo defert, villages uninhabited, and fields, and gardens, and orchards lying wafte.

Let us take a view of the prefent ftate of fome of the moft confiderable cities of Afia.

Aleppo (Haleb) is the beft built city in the Turkifh dominions, and the people are reputed the moft polite. The late Dr. Ruffel (in his Natural Hiftory of Aleppo) calculated the number of inhabitants, in his time, at about 230,000; at prefent there are not above 40 or 50,000. This depopulation has chiefly taken place fince 1770. As this city is built of a kind of marble, and the houfes are vaulted, they are not fubject to decay and fall in ruins, though they remain uninhabited; they ftand a monument of the deftruction of the human race: whole ftreets are uninhabited and bazars abandoned. Fifty or fixty years ago were counted forty large villages in the neighbourhood, all built of ftone; their ruins remain, but not a fingle peafant dwells in them. The plague vifits Aleppo every ten or twelve years. About four years ago there was at Aleppo one of the moft dreadful famines ever known any where.

The whole coaft of Syria, which a few years ago was tolerably populous, is now almoft a defert. Tripoli, Sidon, Laodecia, are

infignificant

infignificant places, and the country around them almoft abandoned. Maundrell, about a century ago, complained of the rapid depopulation of Syria; but from his account it was then in a flourifhing condition compared with its prefent ftate.

Moful has loft half its inhabitants, and is in a ruinous ftate.

Diarbekir was the moft populous city in the Turkifh empire but a few years ago; it might ftill have been counted among the firft cities in the world for magnitude, and, notwithftanding the exaggerated accounts of Cairo and Conftantinople, it contained more people in its walls than either of thefe cities. In 1756, there were 400,000 inhabitants, at prefent there are only 50,000. In 1757, fwarms of locufts devoured all the vegetation of the furrounding country, and occafioned a famine; an epidemic ficknefs followed, which carried off 300,000 fouls in the city of Diarbekir, befides thofe who perifhed in the adjacent villages. The plague vifits this country every thirty or forty years.

At *Merdin* there are about 1,000 fouls. The ficknefs of 1757 was fatal to this city and its environs: the greateft part of the town is uninhabited; it is fubjeft to endemical ficknefles.

Bagdat contained from 125 to 130,000 inhabitants; at prefent there are fcarcely 20,000.

20,000. The plague of 1773 carried off two-thirds of the people. Here likewife are feen whole ftreets and bazars defolate.

Baffora (or Balfora, i. e. Bi-al-fura, called by the Arabs often Al-fura) contained, twenty years ago, nearly 100,000 inhabitants; the laft accounts from there mention only 7 or 8,000.

Between *Angora* and Conftantinople there is a conftant communication by caravans: there are old people at Conftantinople who remember forty or fifty villages in the road, of which no veftiges now remain. (In thefe parts the buildings are not durable, being chiefly timber frames filled with brick or earth, and plaftered over.) An Englifh merchant of my acquaintance, whofe trade as well as his father's was between thefe two cities and Smyrna, has a lift in his books of all the towns or villages in the road, of which about fifty are not known, even by name, to the prefent conductors of caravans. No longer ago than 1768, it was afferted, that upwards of two hundred villages in this part of the country had been forfaken, on account of the oppreffions exercifed over the inhabitants.

Though we fhould admit that the people in Turkey multiply as much as it is poffible for the human fpecies to do (which is how-ever very far from being the cafe) yet ftill it

is

is impoffible that the fruitfulnefs of the women can keep pace with the mortality of the
plague, and the other ficknefſes which afflict
this empire, particularly in Afia. If ftill
there be a confiderable number of people
difperfed over this vaft tract of country, what
muft not the population have been a few
centuries ago? Collectively indeed the number is fomewhat confiderable, but each diftrict, confidered feparately, is a defert compared with the moft thinly inhabited region
in Europe.

If we proceed to a regular calculation,
and take for a datum the greateft number of
inhabitants thefe countries could maintain
four centuries ago, and allow the greateft
number of births experience of the moft
prolific nations will juftify; and, on the
other hand, deduct at every period they are
vifited by the plague and other ficknefſes the
number of deaths which then take place,
the refult will be a much fmaller number of
inhabitants than there now really exifts; if we
reafon *a pofteriori*, we fhall find that four centuries ago there were a much greater number than it is poffible there could have been
in fact.

It is therefore reafonable to conclude, that
depopulation could not formerly have made
fo rapid a progrefs as at prefent; and that in
a century

a century more, things remaining in their prefent fituation, the Turkifh empire will be nearly extinct.

Smyrna is the only city in Turkey where depopulation does not appear; but how often are not its inhabitants renewed? It is the only place of confiderable trade in Turkey, and from the refort of foreign fhips, as it is the centre of export and import trade, muft long continue to flourifh.

It is worthy of remark, that the Curds in the mountains, and other independent or rebellious tribes, who do not mix with the Turks, are exempt from the mortality occafioned by all the calamities which afflict the countries more immediately under the iron fceptre of the porte.

I fhould have mentioned a part of Bulgaria, and a great part of European Turkey, except the countries towards the Adriatic and Hungary, as almoft deftitute of inhabitants. This ftate of the country is particularly ftriking on the road from Belgrade through Sophia, Phillippopolis, and Adrianople, to Conftantinople. The north or north-eaftern part of Bulgaria is populous.

In taking a feparate view of European Turkey, of Greece, and of Egypt, we fhall find fimilar traces of that devaftation, occafioned by the complicated evils under which

this

this empire has fo long groaned ; at prefent I fhall pay a particular confideration to
the ftate of the capital itfelf.

Conftantinople is the more deferving of our
enquiry, becaufe, erroneous as calculations of
the number of inhabitants in great cities
ufually are, none have been more exaggerated than the population of this city.

The caufes of this error were probably various, as, firft, the fituation of the city on
the afcent of a hill, which, fhewing every
houfe in it, and hiding the voids between
them, makes it appear to the greateft advantage.

Secondly, the crowd of people appears to
be prodigious in the ftreets leading to the
cuftom-houfe, to the harbour (to crofs which
the boats are all ftationed at a very few
landing places or *fcales)* to the great bazars
or markets, to the porte, to the baths, and to
the principal mofques ; but it fhould be obferved, that thefe are all fituated in the fame
part of the city, and that every one who goes
out, either for bufinefs or pleafure, paffes
through thefe ftreets, and travellers very
rarely go farther into the city, where they
would find ftreets nearly deferted, and grafs
growing in many of them, notwithftanding
their narrownefs.

Thirdly, ftrangers (and I include moft foreign

reign minifters, who are grofsly impofed on
by the ignorance of their drogomans or interpreters) are mifled by the accounts they
receive of the number of janizaries, of boftangees, of boatmen, of artifans, of fhopkeepers, &c. without knowing that one and
the fame perfon is commonly in two or three
of thefe capacities; for inftance, almoft every
boatman is a boftangee or a janizary, and
the greateft part of the fhopkeepers and artifans are janizaries. We muft rely on real
calculation.

Firft calculation.—In Conftantinople and
its environs there are daily confumed from
nine to eleven thoufand kilos of corn. Experience has proved, that one perfon con-
fumes nine kilos a year, one with another.
One kilo of wheat is twenty-two okes,
which renders eighteen okes of flour, of
which they make twenty-feven okes of bread,
as their bread is very moift, made into flat
cakes feemingly half baked. An oke is about
two pounds and three quarters Englifh avoir-
dupois weight. (In France, one pound of
wheat produces exactly one pound of bread
This was the rule obferved by their government with refpect to the price of bread.) According to this calculation, the medium number of inhabitants would be 426,000 fouls;
and this mifled Sir James Porter, formerly

T   Englifh

Englifh ambaffador at the porte, as it has done many others, who rely on the information received from interpreters.

It is the policy of the porte, or rather of the vizirs, to keep the price of bread low at the capital; and it is generally cheaper there than at a day or two's journey diftant. The *miri* folely diftributes the corn, not to the city only, as people have concluded, but to all its fuburbs, as *Pera*, *Galata*, the neighbouring villages, to the city of *Scutari (Efcudar,)* and all along the channel of Conftantinople, which is bordered with large villages to *Kuchuk Chikmagi*, commonly called *Ponte-piccolo*, and thence in a line to *Borgos* and to *Domufderé*, on the coaft of the Black Sea, to the *Princes Iflands*, to nine large villages in Afia behind Scutari, and thence in a line north, to all the country as far as the Black Sea.

Some years, from 14 to 16,000 kilos of corn have been confumed. A confiderable quantity muft be allowed for the confumption of veffels of all denominations that frequent the port, and when corn is dearer in the country than the price at Conftantinople fixed by the *miri*, it may reafonably be fuppofed that fome little contraband is carried on.

From

From all this it muſt appear, that not above one half of the corn is conſumed in Conſtantinople, and conſequently, that the number of inhabitants does not exceed 213,000 ; and if we take for our rule thoſe years in which 16,000 kilos were conſumed (and which by the by have always been thoſe when corn was dear in the country) ſtill the number will be but 292,000 ; the medium between the higheſt and the loweſt year, when there was no remarkable plague, is 230,000, which I believe to be near the real number of inhabitants.

Second calculation.—The *kaſſab baſhi* (or chief of the butchers) through whoſe office all cattle for ſlaughter muſt paſs, diſtributes to Conſtantinople, Scutari, &c. from 2,500 to 3,000 ſheep a week, or 130,000 to 156,000 a year. It muſt be obſerved, that the Turks eat very little beef; ſome fiſh indeed, and fowls, but the quantity is trifling to the mutton. At Paris they conſumed 10,400 ſheep a week, beſides beef, and 630 hogs, ſalt-fiſh, &c. and one million pounds of bread daily. The annual conſumption of Paris was about 12,800 muids of corn (36,864,000 pounds); 77,000 oxen; 120,000 calves; 32,000 barrels of herrings, 540,000 ſheep, and 32,400 hogs, beſides other articles.

Suppoſe

Suppose the French to eat only the same quantity of bread as the Turks, (and I believe there is not much difference,) the calculation, applied to Paris, would make the number of inhabitants to be about one million.

There are, however, a few sheep killed by contraband, that have not passed through the hands of the *kaſſab baſhi*, and the butchers dependent on him, but their number is very small, as the practice is attended with dangerous consequences, and the profit arising from it inconsiderable.

This calculation of meat produces fewer inhabitants than that of corn, and we must take rice into the account to make it anywise adequate; but it at least proves the former not to have been too low.

Third calculation.—From about 1770 to 1777, there was no plague at Conſtantinople. The dead, which were carried out of the gates of the city, where a regular regiſter is kept (except when, in time of the plague, they ſurpaſs one thouſand a day, after which they are not counted) amounted only to 5,000 one year with another. This number, multiplied by 36, the largeſt number which poſſibly can be taken, though Conſtantinople is very healthy, and the Turks temperate, gives only 180,000 inhabitants. It muſt be observed,

obferved, that fome confiderable people are
buried in the city, in their gardens or private
burial grounds, and fome are carried to the
cemeteries of Pera and Scutari, an account of
all of which is not taken, as feveral on that
fide of the city do not pafs the gates : if we
allow 1,000 a year for thefe, which is certainly much beyond the truth, by this calculation there would appear to be 216,000
inhabitants. As to the fuburbs of Pera and
Galata, if they are to be included as making
a part of Conftantinople, they are not very
confiderable, confifting only of a few long
ftreets. The number of fouls they contain I
have forgotten, and my memorandum is mif-
laid : I counted the houfes.

Fourth calculation.—The ground on which
Conftantinople ftands is not fo extenfive as
Paris. Count Choiffeul Gouffier, the French
ambaffador, had an exact plan made of it by a
Mr. Kauffer, a very good geometrician,
which proves this fact; and whoever walks
acrofs the city in different directions may
convince himfelf of its accuracy. The
ftreets in Paris are very narrow, the houfes
four and fix ftories high, and inhabited from
top to bottom ; the ftreets in Conftantinople
are alfo narrow. The churches, hotels, &c. of
Paris, do not take up near fo much ground as
the mofques, baths, palaces, gardens, (of

T 3 which

which whole ſtreets on the upper and back parts have one to each houſe), the ſeraglio, houſes of the great, ſhops, and bazars, where people do not live, &c. The houſes in Conſtantinople are ſpacious, except the very crowded quarter by the water ſide ; they are compoſed of a ground-floor *(rez de chauſſée)* which compriſes the kitchen, a ſtable, waſh-houſe, ſtore rooms, &c. a room to receive ſtrangers, and a yard in the centre, except in the above mentioned crowded quarter ; over this there is but one ſtory, where the family lives. This is the general conſtruction of all the houſes ; they differ only in ſize and the number of apartments. It is a very unuſual thing for two families to live in one houſe ; it would be an indecency, and amount almoſt to a crime, except it be two brothers, or a father and a ſon, among the poorer people. Hence it follows demonſtratively, that there cannot be above one fourth of the number of inhabitants in Conſtantinople, which there are in Paris, and whatever objection may be made to my otner calculations, this cannot be confuted.

We may therefore conclude, that the population of Conſtantinople is leſs than 300,000 ſouls at preſent, and that it never could have been much more within the walls, with their mode of building houſes.

In

In the year 1777, there were 5,700 private and public boats of all fizes in the port of Conftantinople, and in all the villages to the Black Sea. This number is great, but the fituation of the city muft be confidered, and that every one muft go in a boat who goes into the country, at leaft to the part frequented, which is acrofs the water, or to the villages, all built by the water fide, and almoft inacceffible by land; that there are fcarcely any kind of carriages; that the inhabitants of Conftantinople take great pleafure in going on the water, and great numbers have boats of their own, almoft all who can afford it; and that they make no ufe of carriages. In Paris, there were 12,500 coaches or carriages, and infinitely fewer people go in carriages in Paris, than they do in boats in Conftantinople.

The Turks tell you indeed, and perhaps believe it, that there are 72,000 mofques in Conftantinople. The Chriftians out of vanity, to make their fect appear confiderable, magnify their own numbers, but no credit is to be given to them; thefe affertions cannot be oppofed to calculations founded on facts.

Cairo is another city, the magnitude of which has been much exaggerated. Volney fays, the number of inhabitants are 250,000 fouls. I had an account of the population of

Cairo

Cairo from a very fenfible Armenian, who
had lived twelve years there, which agreed
nearly with Volney's ; he made the number
to be 230,000. Volney further fays (on
what foundation he does not mention) that
all Egypt contains 2,300,000 fouls—however, the population is there better known
than in other parts of Turkey.

The people of the country tell us of
300,000 dying in a year of the plague, in
Cairo, but no reliance is to be placed on
their calculations.

Various are the opinions of writers and
travellers with refpect to the number of
inhabitants in the Turkifh empire, and difficult, certainly it is, to make a calculation with any degree of accuracy, in a country where there are no regifters kept of births
and burials, (except at Conftantinople,) or
other events which concern the general Mahomedan population of the cities, and where,
in the country, not only the fize, but the
number of villages is unknown ; there are,
befides, wandering tribes and independent
diftricts, fuch as the mountains inhabited by
the Curds, as wholly unknown in Turkey as
in Europe.

With refpect to Chriftians and Jews the
cafe is different ; they keep regular regifters
of their births and burials ; but as they remain

main in the feveral places they are made, and
no account of them is tranfmitted to the government, it is impoffible for any individual
to collect them; nor indeed can one always
rely on the affirmation of the bifhops or
other perfons, who have the regifters, without actual infpection of the books; for fometimes out of vanity they augment the ftatement of their population, and fometimes out
of policy with regard to the Turks, they
diminifh the account of their numbers, as
they are often taxed or fined *in a body*, to pay
certain fums to a pafha (fuch unjuft demands
are called *avanias,)* and the fmaller their
numbers appear, they hope the lefs will be
the fum impofed on them; it therefore requires addrefs even to get at thefe regifters, which, after all, have not the accuracy of fimilar documents in Chriftian
countries.

The only datum which we can in anywife form a calculation upon, is the karatch,
or capitation tax, on all male Chriftians and
Jews above the age of fourteen or fifteen. By
knowing the fum this tax is farmed at
(which is lefs than the fum the collectors receive, and therefore not very accurate) and,
more or lefs, the fum each male pays, we have
fome kind of data to reafon from. This calculation gives nine million of fouls; but it is

to

to be remembered, that there is a part of the empire in which the inhabitants are independent, and confequently pay no capitation, as will be feen in the next chapter. The Greeks calculate their numbers to be feven millions in all parts of the empire, and there are not many in the diftant provinces far from Greece.

The only method of calculating the Mahomedan inhabitants would be, the proportion they bear to the Chriftians in the different cities and provinces, and of which there are fome vague accounts. In many places there are ten Chriftians to one Mahomedan, and in others ten Mahomedans to one Chriftian; in fome, their numbers are nearly equal. Were I to make a guefs (for a calculation I could not call it) my opinion with refpect to the whole population of the Mahomedans in the empire would as widely differ from the generally received notions, as it does with refpect to the particular population of Conftantinople.

If their numbers have greatly decreafed, we need feek no other caufe to account for it than the plague, though there are many others co-operating with great deftruction.

If we take for granted, that there were fifty millions of people on the continent two centuries ago; that the births are to the
burials

burials as twelve to ten, or that one in thirty-
fix die every year, in the common courſe of
mortality, or that the number of births to
the living are as one to 26, 27, or 28, or
any calculation more favourable to the in-
creaſe of population, we ſhall ſtill find that
the mortality occaſioned by the plague, taken
on an average (as its ravages are ſtated in
theſe pages) would reduce theſe fifty millions
to little more than ten at this day.

CHAPTER VIII.

On the State of the Turkish Provinces.

IT is not enough to confine our view to the metropolis, in order to form an accurate judgment of a great empire; there, indeed, is the centre of government and of opulence, there are placed the fprings which guide the whole, and thither are brought the products of the general exertion; but it is not from the apparent tranquillity and greatnefs of the capital that we can form a juft idea of the ftate of the provinces. Lulled into a fatal fecurity within the receffes of his palace, the tyrant frequently knows not the fcenes of ruin and devaftation which, under fanction of his name, are acted at a diftance by his creatures; he perceives not the increafing uneafinefs and difaffection of his oppreffed fubjects, until the tempeft of rebellion, rolling rapidly forward, breaks over his aftonifhed head.

The relaxation of the bands of power has gone too far in the Turkifh empire not to be, be, in some degree, perceived by the porte; they cannot but feel the weakneſs of their authority over moſt of the diſtant *paſhaliks*; but as ignorance is always confident, they, perhaps, over-rate their remaining power, and truſt to the ſhadow of a name whoſe terror has long ſince paſſed away.

Still, it muſt be acknowledged, that there are circumſtances which counteract the tendency of their political ſyſtem to fall in ruins; there are prejudices, habits, and local peculiarities, which ſerve to hold together the barbarous inhabitants of thoſe extenſive regions. In order to judge of their importance, it will be neceſſary to conſider, in detail, the ſituation of the different provinces, moral and phyſical; to trace " *mores hominum multorum* " *et urbes*," not merely the ſtrength and extent of the countries, but the ſpirit, manners, and diſpoſitions of the people.

Of the dependent provinces of the Turkiſh empire, the firſt rank in the eye of an enlightened European will be held by the deſcendants of that people from whom emanated the ſcience and the refinement of our hemiſphere; of the Grecians, therefore, I ſhall treat at large in another part of this work; and I propoſe to conſider them ſeparately, becauſe the diſtinctions, religious and political, exiſting between them and their Mahomedan

homedan conquerors, together with the relations they bear to the Chriſtian ſtates in general, will furniſh ample matter for a ſeparate
diſcuſſion ; I ſhall here only remark, that the
captain paſha, or grand admiral, is paſha of
the Archipelago, and the fleet, or a diviſion,
goes annually to collect the tribute : it is
then that the poor Greeks moſt feel the
weight of the iron ſceptre that governs them,
and all the inſults and oppreſſion of the vile
ſatraps of the tyrant.   When a ſhip of the
fleet arrives in a port, all the people who can,
fly to the mountains or into the country,
others ſhut themſelves up in their houſes,
without daring to ſtir out.   Every one on
the roads are plundered by the ſoldiers and
ſailors of the ſhips, and if they are not cut,
or wounded with a piſtol ball, or killed out-
right, they eſteem themſelves happy ; even
in the ſtreets it is the ſame.   Thus the poor
Greeks pay another contribution to the fleet,
which is heavier to thoſe on whom it un-
happily falls than that to the ſultan.

If a woman or a girl, or even a boy, is met
by them in any place not immediately under
the eye of their officers, or where they might
be expoſed to reſiſtance, they are infallibly
victims to their brutality.   In weak towns
and villages this ſometimes happens in the
ſtreets.   The officers cannot always, and of-

4   ten

ten will not reftrain them, except where the crime is too public, and complaint might be made to the porte. The captains and officers raife contributions for themfelves on the principal inhabitants under various pretences. The Greeks are generally prevented from complaining, out of fear that the next fhip which comes will take revenge. When the fhips of war are met at fea, they are little better than pirates to the Greeks and Ragufans.

With regard to the other countries which are, or have recently been fubjeéted to the Turkifh yoke, I fhall here give them a brief confideration, from which it will appear that their fituation, relatively to fubordination and internal management, is fuch as might reafonably be expeéted from the wretched fyftem of policy which we have previoufly invefti-gated.

Cafting our view over the pafhaliks or governments moft immediately conneéted with the feat of empire, we fhall find them diftraéted, diforganifed, and fcarcely yielding more than a nominal obedience to the fultan: fuch are the pafhaliks of Afia Minor and Syria. With regard to the more diftant provinces, they may be confidered conneéted with the porte rather by treaty than as integral parts of the empire. In this light I
view

view Moldavia and Walachia on the north, and Egypt on the fouth. Thefe unfortunate countries (unfortunate in their political regulation, however bleft by the bounty of nature) fuffer, though in different degrees, from the harpy touch of Turkifh defpotifm. I fhall confider them fingly, and add to thefe obfervations a review of the ftate of the Crimea, with fome remarks on thofe Tatar hordes, whofe ferocity has either been foothed or fubdued by a fubjection to Ruffia.

A flight fketch of the ftate of rebellion or independence of the chief pafhaliks will eafily demonftrate the weaknefs and inefficacy of the prefent political fyftem of Turkey.

The great pafhalik of Bagdad has been in reality independent, except at very fhort intervals, ever fince Achmet Pafha, who defended it againft Nadir Shah (the famous ufurper of Perfia.) The fultan only confirms the pafha the people, and principally the foldiery of Bagdad, have appointed to govern them with defpotic power; the firman, however, fent on thefe occafions, always mentions the pafha as being nominated by the fublime porte to this high and trufty office, in confideration of his virtues, and fome fignal fervice he has rendered to the empire; and this farce is kept up by a new firman fent every year to continue him in office, as
if

if the porte really had the power to remove him. The porte draws no revenue from this extensive province. The pasha, who has always a large army in his pay, and entirely devoted to him, sends regularly an account of the revenue of his government, which he always proves is entirely abforbed by the expences of the army, which he states as neceffary to be kept on a formidable footing, to serve the empire against any attacks of the Persians or Arabs, and by the reparation of fortreffes, which formerly existed, and of which no vestige now remains, &c. Whenever there is a war with an European power, and the pasha of Bagdad is called on to furnish his quota of troops, he pretends the neceffity of keeping them all at home, to defend the province against the attacks of the Arabs, and finds means to provoke some Arab nation to war; or, in connivance with the prince of the Montefiks (an Arab nation on the banks of the Euphrates) carries on a sham war. In short, the sultan is the nominal sovereign of Bagdad, but the pasha has the real sovereign independent power in his hands.

In Armenia Major, and all the neighbouring countries, there are whole nations or tribes of independent people, who do not

U   even

even acknowledge the porte, or any of its pafhas.

The three Arabias do not acknowledge the fovereignty of the fultan, who only poffeffes, in thefe countries, a few unimportant towns.

The pafha of Ahifka cares very little for the porte; and the famous Haggi-Ali-Ye-nikli-Pafha, of Trabifonde, was the mafter of all that country; he could bring a large army into the field, and often fet the porte at defiance.

In the country about Smyrna, there are great *agas*, who are independent lords, and maintain armies, and often lay that city under contribution. The porte never gains but a temporary influence, by fometimes intermeddling in their quarrels.

All the inhabitants of the mountains, from Smyrna to Paleftine, are perfectly independent, and are confidered by the porte as enemies, whom they attack whenever there is an opportunity. They are compofed of different nations, who have their own fovereigns or lords, and are even of different religions. Thofe near Smyrna are Mahomedans; farther down come the Cordes, a very ferocious and faithlefs people. In the neighbourhood of Aleppo there are various fects of religion. The mountains of Antilibanus are inhabited by by Drufes and Chriftians, and have, at times, been formidable to the porte; they have more than once taken Damafcus, and plundered it.

The nation of Drufes would here deferve particular mention; but as there are accounts of them already publifhed, which appeared to me, when I was in that country, very exact, I fhall forbear faying more about them; I cannot, however, avoid taking notice of a great miftake the Ruffians made in the laft war but one, in attacking thofe people in conjunction with Shech Omar al Daher, of Acri, between whom there never exifted much harmony. Had they reconciled their difference, which they might have done, they would have had for allies all the countries from Egypt to the Curdes, who, probably, would have joined the league, and the army they could have brought into the field would have been more numerous than that of the fultan; they would have been mafters of Damafcus, Aleppo, and all that part of the empire.

The very confiderable country, which was for fo many years under the jurifdiction of the fhech of Acri, never paid any revenue to the porte, and was by it even confidered as an independent ftate. Shech Dahar was befieged in his capital, after the conclufion of

the

the war, by the famous great-admiral, Haſſan Paſha; he himſelf was killed, and the
country reduced to obedience. The porte
appointed a paſha to govern it, and he has
now become as independent, and more formidable, even than was Dahar himſelf.

Between the country of the Druſes and
that of Acri there is a nation inhabiting the
mountains on the back of Tyre, (which alſo
belongs to them, though there are no houſes
now ſtanding on that once famous ſpot,) called *Metuali*; they are of the ſect of Ali, and
are ſuch inveterate enemies to the Turks,
that they murder every one who comes into
their country, or that they can ſurprize.

On the coaſt of Syria, the ſultan only
virtually poſſeſſes the ports of Latachia (Lao-
dicea) a ſmall ſhallow harbour and a ruined
town; Alexandretta (or Scanderon) the port
of Aleppo, a miſerable village, the air of
which is ſo bad, that it, perhaps, has not its
equal in the world for inſalubrity; Tripoli
and Sidon, Jaffa, and a few very inſignificant
places. The caravans, which go from Scanderon to Aleppo, are obliged to go by the
way of Antioch, as all the country, through
which the direct road leads, belongs to the
Curds, who will not ſuffer the Turks to
paſs it.

All Egypt is independent. The paſha ſent
to

to Cairo is in effect a prisoner during his government, which is only ·nominal; the porte draws little or no revenue from it, and no troops, except a few fanatics in time of war with the Christians. The Turks have at different times got possession of Cairo, but never could maintain themselves in the government. The last instance of their subjecting the capital was by the late Haffan, captain pasha, but it was soon lost again; yet Constantinople depends very much on Egypt for provisions, and above all for rice. The Russians, when they had a fleet in the Mediterranean, very much distressed the porte, by cutting off the communication with Egypt, and might have done it much more, had they not permitted many neutral vessels to supply them.

In Europe, the Morea, Albania, Epirus, and Scutari, are more or less in a state of rebellion; Bosnia, Croatia, &c. obey the porte only as long as it suits them, and the sultan reaps little benefit from them. These latter countries afford the most robust and warlike soldiers in the empire; they are accustomed to arms from their infancy, as they are continually fighting among themselves, district against district, and often even village against village, besides individual quarrels of families. These troops would be

U 3   of

of great ufe to the fultan in his wars, but
they will not go far from their houfes, and
ferve only when it is to defend their own
country: the emperor of Germany has had
to contend with them, while only the enervated and daftardly foldiery of Afia has been
oppofed to Ruffia.

Lately we have feen almoft all European
Turkey in arms againft the porte, Adrianople
in imminent danger, and even Conftantinople itfelf trembling for its fafety.

I have faid that Egypt is independent: a
few words on the peculiar relation of that
country to Turkey will not be improper,
perhaps. The divifion of the fpiritual dig-
nities of the Mahomedans took place, A. D.
970, in an early period of their religion, and
the Fatimite kalifs eftablifhed themfelves in
Egypt, claiming to themfelves the title of
commander of the faithful, heretofore borne
by the kalifs of Bagdad.

Both thefe kalifs fuccefsively yielded to
the force or policy of the Turkifh princes.
The laft of the Egyptian kalifs called in
the Turks to his affiftance againft the Chriftian crufaders, which fervice being accom-
plifhed, the new allies *turned againft the kalif
himfelf, and ftrangled him,* A. D. 1171, when
a new dynafty commenced in the perfon of
Salah-ud-din.

The

The Egyptian princes long maintained an independent power by the affiftance of their Mamaluk troops, until, in 1518, they were reduced to fubjection by Selim the fon of Bayazet, and have ever fince remained attached, nominally at leaft, to the porte ; but as their beys were not deprived of their power, and to this day each is governor, or rather fovereign of a diftrict, thefe in fact exercife a tyranny of the worft kind over a country, which would be one of the moft productive in the univerfe, were property protected, while they render little either of tribute or fubmiffion to the port.

This corps of *Mamaluks* is kept up, to this day, by *flaves* bought from the fame countries, viz. Georgia, Circaffia, Abaffa, and Mingrelia, and moftly purchafed at Conftantinople, for their children, born in the country, are not admitted into the corps ; indeed it is affirmed, and it is very remarkable, that they have but few children, and their families never extend beyond two generation. This is accounted for by their being greatly addicted to an unnatural vice.

The actual power refides in the Mamaluks, and the bey who has moft of them in his fuite is confequently the moft powerful. As to the pafha fent by the porte, he has at

different

different times had more or lefs influence, but is in general a mere cypher, obliged to fubmit to the will of the beys, who difmifs him when they pleafe. They have fome-times entirely thrown off all appearance of fubmiffion to the porte; and at prefent, as well as generally, their obedience is only no-minal, and the pafha is in reality a prifoner in the caftle of Cairo, which is the place fixed for his refidence.

The tribute which Egypt ought to fend the porte is frequently withheld, or, if tranf-mitted, it is diminifhed by deductions for the reparation of canals, fortreffes, &c. at the will of the beys. Yet a long proceffion of mules and camels fets out annually from Egypt, with the pretended revenue for the fultan, which, inftead of filver, confifts moftly of bags of rice, and, not unfrequently, ftones.

The janizaries and Arab foldiers in the fervice of the porte are but little able to enforce its authority, as they are few in number, and moftly compofed of artizans and perfons unaccuftomed to arms. The Mamaluks, on the contrary, muft be allowed to be moft excellent cavalry.

In the beautiful country and climate of Egypt, it is diftreffing to confider how little the advantages of nature are cultivated, and how

how much its evils are augmented by the ignorance and unaccountably grofs fuperftition of its inhabitants.

From a furvey of Egypt I turn to the northern part of the empire, to contemplate the provinces of Walachia and Moldavia, which, like the laft mentioned country, are rather attached to the empire by treaty than by abfolute fubjection, and who retain at leaft independence as to matters of internal regulation; their inhabitants are, however, more oppreffed than perhaps any people in the empire; nor could they poffibly bear fuch exactions, were it not for the wonderful fertility of their foil.

Their waywodes (or princes as they are generally ftill called) are Greeks, who purchafe their offices for large fums of money, the porte generally receiving about 80,000 pounds fterling for every nomination, and who are obliged to maintain themfelves in their pofts, by continually feeing thofe who can ferve or hurt them at Conftantinople; for befides the complaints which frequently are made againft them, other Greeks are continually caballing at the porte to get them removed, and to obtain their places. The waywodes muft, befides raifing large fums to defray all thefe expences, enrich themfelves, in order to live in affluence with a large train of dependents,

pendents, who follow them from Conftantinople, and to fecure a fafe and fplendid
retreat to themfelves when recalled from
their waywodfhips to their former homes,
where, though the fear of punifhment is
ever hanging over them, and deftroying their
repofe, they maintain within their own
houfes a weak and oftentatious magnificence.
It is eafy to conceive how much the miferable fubjects of their defpotifm, while in
office, muft fuffer from the impofitions neceffary to anfwer fuch calls of rapacity.

The boyars are obliged to furnifh money
to the waywode, and they in return opprefs
the people by all kinds of exactions, exclufively of the public taxes, which go immediately into the waywode's purfe, and
which are multiplied ad infinitum, and exacted with the utmoft feverity : thefe taxes,
which are not in proportion to the property of the people, aggravate them beyond
defcription ; they murmur, but muft fubmit
and pay.

Among the hardfhips of the Moldavians
may be reckoned their being obliged to furnifh a fupply of corn to Conftantinople, at a
certain price fixed when they firft came
under the Turkifh yoke : this was originally
eftablifhed as a favour to thofe countries,
but has now become an intolerable burthen,

as

as the price now bears no proportion to the
prefent value.

Another great caufe of complaint is the
paffage through their country, or refidence
in it, of a Turkifh army in time of war.
The exceffes which thefe undifciplined hordes
commit are beyond defcription, plundering
and laying wafte the country, and often
deftroying whole villages, and maffacring
their defencelefs inhabitants; hence it is
not unufual for the inhabitants to flee with
their moft valuable effects to the woods and
mountains for concealment, as foon as they
hear of the approach of an army : I was
myfelf a witnefs of the terror of the Moldavians for a fimilar event. Being a prifoner,
in 1778, at Galaz (when hoftilities had taken
place in fome parts, between Ruffia and the
Turks, which had nearly ended in a war)
I was awakened one night by the cries of
women, and the noife of the preparations
made by the whole town to flee, on a ru-
mour (which proved groundlefs) of the approach of a Turkifh army. I then learnt
that every family was provided with a wag-
gon, and one or more horfes, to efcape in
cafe of danger.

The Turkifh foldiery, if they ftay but a
fhort time in a place, caufe fo much havock,
that the unfortunate Moldavians and Wa-
lachians,

lachians, returning to their homes after thefe
monfters have withdrawn, are for a confiderable time unable to rebuild their houfes,
and procure feed and other requifites for
the cultivation of their corn fields and vine-
yards, which the Turks have rooted up.

The following circumftances will prove
how much reafon the Moldavians in particular have to prefer the dominion of Ruffia
to that of Turkey.

At the peace of Kainargi it was ftipulated,
that the waywode fhould not be removed
without the confent of the court of Ruffia,
in order to deliver the people from the oppreffion neceffarily attendant on a frequent
change of their rulers. The porte, however, in 1777, fent to the waywode Gica
a particular friend of his, who, pretending
illnefs, requefted Gica to pay him a vifit,
under pretence of communicating to him
affairs of fecrefy; the attendants of the waywode were fent out of the room, when a
band of ruffians rufhed into the apartment
from a private door, and murdered this unhappy credulous man. A fucceffor was immediately appointed, without confulting the
court of Ruffia, or its minifter at Conftantinople. This is the nation whofe fcrupulous
obfervance of treaties is fo much vaunted by
fome writers.

While

While Moldavia was in the hands of the Ruffians, during the laft war, Prince Potemkin treated the inhabitants with the utmoft indulgence, and exempted them from all kind of taxes, fo that they returned with great reluctance under the Turkifh yoke. It is little confolation to them to be governed by princes or governors of their own religion, for their fituation, if not their inclination, makes them as rapacious as Turks. The contemptuous and humiliating treatment all ranks meet with from the Turks is impatiently borne by a race of people naturally haughty, and afpiring for liberty and independence, and particularly the Boyars, who are treated by the Ruffians as equals and as gentlemen, and, if they emigrate, are admitted into the civil or military fervice.

If there were any deficiency of proof to eftablifh the miferable debility of the Turkifh government, with regard to its diftant provinces, and the horrible devaftation to which thofe provinces are fubject, we fhould find it in the eulogift of Turkey, Mr. Peyffonel. He was French conful in the Crimea, in 1758, when a rebellion broke out, occafioned by the extortions of the officers of the porte, relative to the *ichetirah*, or tranfporting of corn. The rebellious Tatars, to the number of eighty thoufand, pillaged and overrun,

overrun, in feven days, the province of Moldavia, carried off forty thoufand flaves, fpread
terror and defolation on all fides, and the
porte had no other means of fettling this
difturbance than by depofing the reigning
khan, Alim Guerrai, and placing in his room
Krim Guerrai, the rebel chief. At this time,
fays Mr. Peyffonel, we faw the plains of
Kichela, covered, as far as the eye could reach,
with male and female flaves of all ages, cattle, camels, horfes, fheep, and all kinds of
plunder, heaped together. The whole of this
booty was taken from a Chriftian province
fubjeƈt to the porte. Krim Guerrai, in return
for his exaltation, endeavoured to caufe the
effeƈts to be reftored to their proprietors, and
the prifoners to be fet at liberty; but, notwithftanding the vigorous and determined
meafures of this prince, he could only wreft
from the rapacious banditti under his command a fmall part of their plunder. Of the
flaves, many were fecreted or fold, and many
dead from brutal treatment, fo that only half
the number of the prifoners returned to their
country. This is the account of Peyffonel,
the friend of Krim Guerrai; but it is well
known, that he himfelf had a part of the
plunder, and that only fuch were fent back,
whofe age rendered them unfit for their purpofes. I was informed, in Moldavia, from
the

the regifters, that there were above thirty
thoufand fouls, the flower of their youth,
who never returned. Surely this picture of
defolating barbarity fufficiently marks the
character of the Tatar hordes ; and if we
add, that they were conftantly making incurfions into Ruffia, Poland, Circaffia, &c.
to carry off the inhabitants, plunder and
burn the villages, it fufficiently juftifies the
court of Ruffia in taking poffeffion of this
neft of thieves and murderers, and reducing
them to fomething like focial order and fubordination. Inftead of being blamed, as the
emprefs has been, by thefe Chriftians, who
always fympathife with Turks, and by thofe
politicians who think the duration of their
ufurped empire a defirable object, fhe ought
to receive the thanks of all men, of whatever
nation, and particularly of Chriftians, who are
not degraded by prejudices, or corrupted by
the practice of fimilar enormities. The
whole reign of the Tatars has been an infult
to mankind, and a difgrace to human nature,
not inferior to that of the Ottoman fultans.
Was it to be expected that a power like
Ruffia fhould fuffer itfelf to be thus infulted
by a horde of favages, when fhe could redrefs
the grievance ? and had fhe not a *right* as
fovereign, as a Chriftian, and as a friend to
humanity, to protect her feeble neighbours,

who

who had no other fupport to look to, and whofe plunder and depopulation ftrengthen her enemy as well as theirs? She had a facred right, and the mouth is unholy which dares to arraign it.

The connection of the Tatar hordes with the Turks, both in origin and religion, induces me to review the ftate of their moft celebrated feat, the Crimea (or Krim) though it has now paffed under the dominion of Ruffia, and has been abandoned by a great part of its former inhabitants. To this I am the more prompted by the erroneous ideas which have been propagated in Europe relative to that meafure, to the country in general, and to the nature of their ancient government, hitherto fo little known. To explain all this, it may be neceffary to prefent a fketch of the Tatar modes of warfare, and their fmall degree of civilization, and to notice the improved ftate of manners and commerce which is arifing under the foftering care of Ruffia.

The name of Tattar or Tatar, not Tartar, is common to a vaft number of thofe roving and uncultivated tribes, who inhabit the wide extent of country from the northern frontier of China to the borders of Hungary, and from among whom have arifen, in darker ages, the conquerors and the founders of many

many mighty empires. The tribes on the
north of the Euxine had, like many other
countries bordering on the Turkifh empire,
been fubjected to a kind of dependence;
they yielded little in time of peace, and in
war fupplied only a predatory banditti, little
lefs terrible to their friendly neighbours than
to the hoftile power.

In very early ages the empire of the Crimea (the ancient Cherfonefus Taurica) arofe
out of the ruins of the ftill more ancient and
extenfive dominion of the khans of Kapt-
chak. It took its name from the town of
Krim, of which little veftiges now remain,
and is at prefent called Efki-Krim (or Old-
Krim) but which was a place of great trade
in the year 1237, when the Mongul Tatars
eftablifhed their dominion in this peninfula.
Thefe princes were wholly independent, until the Genoefe, having eftablifhed themfelves
there in the 15th century for the fake of
commerce, obtained fuch an afcendency as
to depofe or elect the native khans at pleafure. Over the principal gate of Kaffa there
ftill exifts a Genoefe infcription and the arms
of the republic. The Turks having expelled
the Genoefe, began in like manner by refpecting the independence of the khans, efpecially as they had embraced the Mahomedan religion; but they foon affumed the

X   right

right of confirming their election, and finally, of nominating them to office. Under the hands of Turkey, the Black Sea, which had formerly been the fcene of a very active commerce, was fhut up by the narrow policy of the divan, and the ports of the Krim gradually loft that fplendor and magnificence now attefted only by their ruins. No friend of humanity can do otherwife than rejoice that fuch mafters have, by the events of war, been difpoffeffed of this important country, and that it has fallen under the control of a power, whofe more liberal and enlightened views tend to revive a decayed commerce, to polifh barbarian ferocity, and to render a portion of the globe, which had been almoft a defert, again fertile and productive.

Immediately as the emprefs got poffeffion of the Krim, fhe projected the recal of trade and manufactures to a fpot fo well fituated for them; fhe immediately, and at a great expence, formed new eftablifhments for that purpofe, fent a number of troops to protect her new dominions, and allowed the reigning khan to retire on a liberal penfion.

The following account of the former government of that country, which I had, in 1781, from Seid-Effendi, vizir to Shaheen Guerrai, the reigning khan, and which I found

found by other information to be perfectly
accurate, I prefent as the more deferving notice, as no juft account of that government
has hitherto appeared. To compare it with
the ancient feudal governments, and to offer
a number of conjectures which would arife
from an inveftigation of that fubject, would
be foreign to my prefent purpofe, and a tafk
I am not qualified to undertake, but it may
furnifh matter for the fpeculations of others.

The khan was always the eldeft male of
the *Guerrai* family, defcended from *Gengis
Khan*, except there was fome natural inca-
pacity which excluded him from the fucceffion, or that the country, which fometimes
happened, interfered, and elected another,
but always one of the Guerrai family, and
the eldeft and neareft to the right line of
defcent. Afterwards this family became very
numerous, and it was difficult to determine
who had the beft claim, fo that the khans
were latterly wholly elective. Thofe moft
concerned in the election were the beys and
the murfas; but the general opinion of the
nation was alfo confidered, as the nomination
of an unwarlike or unpopular khan would occafion an oppofition on the part of the people.

After the Turks became formidable to the
Krim Tatars, the porte eftablifhed a right
of approving the election, and afterwards of

X 2 appoint-

appointing the khan folely. The beys and principal murfas (or myrfas) fometimes wrote to Conftantinople to folicit the fovereignty for the prince whom they preferred, and fometimes the candidates bribed the porte.

The khan retained his fovereignty only during the pleafure of the Ottoman fultan, and annually a capugee-bafhi was fent from Conftantinople with a firman confirming him for the year to come. By the peace of Kainargi, in 1774, the Krim was declared independent, and the Tatars reftored to their privilege of electing their own fovereign.

If the khan was depofed, it was by a firman (or hatti-fherif) of the fultan, brought from Conftantinople by a capugee-bafhi. His depofition was often the confequence of complaints againft him by the principal people of the Krim, or of diffatisfaction on the part of the porte of his conduct in time of war, or tardinefs in fupplying the capital with corn; but he was never put to death.

The laft unfortunate khan, who reigned when I received this information, was an exception. He quitted Ruffia, and retired to Conftantinople, where he was at firft received with great diftinction, then exiled, and afterwards put to death.

The depofed khans were fometimes exiled

to a diftant part of the empire, or one
of the Greek iflands, but generally the
porte gave them a *chiftlik*, or kind of farm,
confifting of a country-houfe and cultivated lands, between Conftantinople and
Adrianople, whither they carried with them
their domeftics, and fuch as were attached
to their fortunes. There are at ·prefent
nearly three hundred princes of the family
refiding in thofe parts, who fometimes render the roads unfafe, as they or their people
cannot entirely abandon their old cuftom of
plundering. They are the next heirs to the
Ottoman throne, and the reigning family has
often been nearly extinct. At prefent there
are, befides the fultan, only two fons, ftill very
young, of his late uncle Abd-ul-hamid.
Selim himfelf has no children : he is much
addicted to a vice which generally carries
with it this punifhment.

When the fultan appointed a khan, he
wrote to the four beys, informing them that
he had named fuch a prince for their fovereign.

The khan was as defpotic as the Ottoman
fultan in the execution of the law, which in
common cafes was that of the koran ; in
extraordinary cafes, or where he did not
choofe to appeal to the law, there was no
reftraint on his power, except with refpect to
the beys families, as fhall be hereafter mentioned,

X 3

tioned, and in affairs which concerned the nation at large.

The khans had no land of their own, except a very little about Bagſhiſerrai.

All the ſons of the Guerrai family are ſtiled *ſultans*.

There was a council, or rather a ſtate *(état)* compoſed of the four eldeſt perſons of four families who have the title of bey (the ſame as the Arabic beg) or prince. The names of theſe families are Sherin, Barin (or Baron,) Manſur, and Sigevut.

The firſt family is very numerous; of the ſecond, two perſons only were living in 1782; of the Manſurs there are alſo many, but of the Sigevuts few. The Sherins, who are eſteemed the moſt noble, and to whom the ſovereignty would devolve, were the Guerrai family extinct, frequently marry daughters of the Guerrais, and ſometimes, though not often, out of the moſt conſiderable Myrſas families.

The khan was, by the conſtitution of the government, obliged to conſult them in matters of peace and war, and all matters which concerned the nation in general, and to confirm all matters of importance written by the khan to Conſtantinople, or any other courts, by their ſignature.

The khan could not put to death any one of the families of the beys, without permiſ-
ſion

fion from Conftantinople; he could only imprifon them. Formerly they were judged by the other beys and the khan, and if the other beys were implicated in his crime, by the murfas, or body of landholders.

Neither the beys, nor any of their family, could ferve the khan in any office whatever.

A bey could not fell, or otherwife alienate the family lands and poffeffions, which were inherited, not by his children, but by his fucceffor in office or dignity. The money and moveable effects the beys could leave to whom they pleafed, and it was in this manner that they provided for their children. All the individuals of the beys families were called murfas, except the perfon invefted with the dignity of bey.

In criminal cafes, the beys as well as the murfas, on whofe lands the crime was committed, feized the offender, and fent him to the khan or other officer of juftice. This is to be underftood of capital offences; in cafes of lefs importance they might punifh by beating.

There was another ftate, compofed of the murfas or proprietors of land, and who confidered themfelves as a feparate clafs from the people; their ideas of diftinction on this head exactly correfpond with thofe re-

X 4   ceived

ceived in Europe, of *gentlemen* or *nobles*. The word murfa (in Perfian *mirfa)* fignifies lord, or feigneur, and we fhould tranflate it *efquire, lord of the manor,* or *leffer baron,* while the beys are the *great barons* or *peers*.

The eldeft fons of the murfas inherited their father's lands, and not the eldeft males of the family, as was the cafe with the beys. Of their money or other effects they difpofed as they pleafed to their younger children. They had the fame jurifdiction as the beys in cafes of offences committed on their lands, that is, beating or imprifoning, and fending the offenders to the khan or other tribunals.

The khan could put to death a murfa, but he always, when the nature of the cafe admitted delay, judged the offender before the beys, or an affembly of the murfas, or fuch of his friends who infifted on feeing juftice done to him according to the koran.

In matters of national concern, or which might occafion a general difcontent, the khan affembled the *murfas* as well as the *four beys* ; the latter acting always as a check on the great power of the khan, and reftraining the power an union of the murfas fometimes had rendered too dictating. In former times the beys and the murfas depofed their fovereign, when his conduct had occafioned a general difcontent ; but this was confidered as fo dangerous

dangerous a step, that it was never recurred to, except in very urgent neceffities.

The peafants or country people, who formed the body of the nation, were free.

The peafant, who farmed a piece of land for agriculture or pafture, paid to the bey or murfa, who was the owner, twenty per cent of the produce for rent.

If the land was his own, he paid only ten per cent. to the bey or murfa, in whofe diftrict it lay.

The peafant difpofed of his property as he pleafed; if he died inteftate, the law of the koran decided the fucceffion.

When the khan raifed an army for war, he fent a fummons to the beys and murfas to furnifh their quota, which was fixed in proportion to the number of people who dwelt on their poffeffions. Every bey or murfa commanded the body he brought into the field. The khan gives the foldiers neither pay nor provifions; their officers or themfelves provided what was neceffary till they paffed their frontier, when they fubfifted on plunder, whether the country belonged to a friendly or an inimical power. Almoft every Tatar had a horfe and arms of his own.

A part of the booty, which they always made whenever they paffed their frontier, belonged to the khan, a part to their bey or

murfa,

murfa, and the remainder to themfelves, which was generally the moft confiderable.

The beys nor the murfa were permitted to make war with one another ; and the people were forbid to take a fhare in their perfonal quarrels.

There was another clafs of the people, who dwelt in cities and towns, and who paid no rent to the beys or murfas for the ground their houfes ftood on, or their gardens or fields, which belonged to themfelves, or they hired of other proprietors, as thefe lands or grounds belonged to the city or town ; nor were they fubject to be called out to war ; they often, for the fake of plunder, voluntarily joined the corps of fome bey or murfa.

There were fome other perfons in the Krim, who had the title of bey, but they did not belong to the *ftate* or *état,* and were in effect only common murfas.

There was a clafs of people alfo called *courtiers, kapu-khalki,* people of the *porte* or gate, that is, the court, becaufe juftice was anciently adminiftered by the judge fitting at his gate ; they confifted of the vizir, khuznadar-bafhi, defterdar, akhtagibey, kapigi-bafhi, &c. The khan appointed any perfon he pleafed to thefe offices, as murfas or their fons, merchants, Turks, &c. and when they had an office, if they were of an infignifi-cant

cant family, they were called aga, and their
fons took the title of murfa. The beys and
great murfas fometimes gave their daughters
in marriage to the courtiers if they were become perfons of confequence, but, however,
this was rare, and generally by the folicita-
tion of the khan.

The great officers of the ftate were

1. GALGA-SULTAN. He was governor of
the city of Akmedfchit, and its diftrict, where
he always refided. He was always of the
Guerrai family, and had in his diftrict power
of life and death, as the khan himfelf. No
perfon older than the reigning khan could be
appointed to this office. He had a court, and
officers of the fame denomination as the
khan, viz, a vizir, khaznadar, &c. It has
been always underftood by thofe who have
treated of the Krim, that galga-fultan was
the khan's eldeft fon; this is never the
cafe.

2. NURUDDIN-SULTAN. He alfo could be
of no other family but of the Guerrai. He
had the fame privileges as galga-fultan, but
could not put to death; he refided always
with the khan, but had no part in the adminiftration of juftice, or any other department, farther than giving his advice, or
tranfacting for the khan in his name fuch
bufinefs as he entrufted him with. His office
feems

feems to have been a kind of occafional lieutenant to the khan, always at hand.

3. Or-Bey (or ore-bey as it is pronounced) lived at Perekop, called Or. His privileges were the fame as thofe of galga-fultan ; except that he could not put to death ; he was not always of the *Guerrai* family, but fometimes a *Sherin*, in which cafe he had no *vizir*, but he had all the other officers of his court the fame as a fultan.

4. Ak-kirman-Seraskir was always a fultan, and had power of life and death. He refided at *Akkirman*, before the Turks took poffeffion of *Befarabi* ; he was alfo governor of the *Nogai-Tatars* before they emigrated from the plains to the north of Perekop to the Kuban ; he had the fame officers as *galga-fultan*.

5. Kuban-Seraskir had the fame power and privileges as galga-fultan, being always a fultan of the Guerrai family. Befides, every tribe of the Kuban-Tatars had a ferafkir, who adminiftered juftice in the tribe, but was under *kuban-ferafkir*, and could not put to death.

Befides thefe there were,

1. The Mufti in the Krim, appointed by the khan, and who refided with him at Bagchiferrai, but there was no body of ulema to check

check the power of the government, as at
Conftantinople. When the Turks were in
poffeffion of Caffa, they had a mufti there,
but he never was confulted by the Tatars,
or fuffered to meddle in their affairs.

2. A kadilafkir (or kaziafkir) in like manner appointed by, and refiding with the
khan.

3. Twenty-four kadis (or kazis) one in
every confiderable diftrict, befides kadis in
the Kuban, where every kadi had a diftrict of
feveral villages or encampments of tents.

Thus this fingular government feems originally to have been feudal, but was afterwards, when the Tatars became Mahomedans, modified by the adoption of the laws of
the koran. The Tatars acknowledged the
fultan of Conftantinople as kalif and head
of their religion. They never could be perfuaded to leave off eating horfefleth, which is
forbidden by the Mahomedan law to Mufelmans. The Turkifh muftis wifely decided,
that horfefleth was forbidden to all other
Mahomedans to eat, but not to the Tatars,
as they had been accuftomed to it, and that
thereby it ceafed to be a fin.

The REVENUES of the reigning Khans were,

1ft. TEN PER CENT. of the corn the No-
gais grew.

2. The

2. The produce of the SALT LAKES—very little falt was the property of individuals— they rendered him about one hundred thoufand dollars a year, that is, about twelve thoufand five hundred pounds fterling.

3. The DUTY on imports and exports, which ufually amounted to the fame fum of one hundred thoufand dollars, or twelve thoufand five hundred pounds fterling.

4. SUBSIDIES, which the Ottoman *porte* paid to the *khan* in time of war, and frequently other fums, to affift in armaments, and to keep the Tatars in good humour.

5. The fums annually fent by the Ottoman fultan to defray the expences of Galgafultan's court, and to pay the officers of the khan's court, as vizir, khafnader, &c. with a view to render them more dependent.

6. The pay of the *feimans*, a body of troops of about 1,600, who ferved as guards to the khan, was always fent from Conftantinople.

The Turks, in return, could always rely on a body of auxiliary cavalry from the Krim and the Kuban.

The Chriftians and Jews paid a capitation tax, as in Turkey, to the beys or murfas; but they were infinitely lefs vexed than in Turkey, enjoyed more protection, and were treated with lefs infolence and indignity.

The

The revenue of Shahзen-Guerrai-Khan, in 1781, amounted to 900,000 dollars, without calculating the fums ufually fent from Conftantinople; this fum makes about £. 112,500 fterling.

The number of inhabitants was then reduced to about 100,000 fouls in the Krim, and 600,000 fouls in the Kuban; two thirds of the inhabitants had emigrated to Turkey fince the beginning of that khan's reign, which was the laft. In the autumn of 1777, the Tatars of the Krim alone met the Ruffian army, under Prince Proforofsky, in the plains of Salguir, with forty thoufand men, all well mounted and armed. In 1782, the large city of Kaffa confifted only of 450 houfes inhabited.

It may not be inappofite to fay a few words on the reign of the laft khan of the Tatars, and the final extinction of the Tatar dominion in the Krim.

In the treaty of peace of Kainargi, concluded in July 1774, the independence of the Krim was ftipulated in thefe words. Art. III. *" All the Tatar people, thofe of Crimea, of " Budgiac, of the Kuban, the Ediffans, Geam- " bouiluks and Edifchkuls, fhall, without any " exception, be acknowledged by the two empires " as free nations, and entirely independent of any " foreign power, and fhall be governed by their*

" own

" own *fovereign of the race of Gingis-Khan;*
" *elected and raifed to the throne by all the*
" *Tatar people; who fhall govern them accord-*
" *ing to their ancient laws and ufages, render-*
" *ing no account whatever to any foreign power;*
" *it is for this reafon that neither the court of*
" *Ruffia nor the Ottoman porte ought not to*
" *meddle, under any pretext whatever, in the*
" *election of the faid khan, nor in their affairs,*
" *domeftic, politic, civil, and interior, but, on*
" *the contrary, acknowledge and confider the*
" *faid Tatar nation in its political and civil*
" *ftate, on the fame footing as other powers,*
" *which govern by themfelves, and are depen-*
" *dent on God alone. With refpect to the cere-*
" *monies of religion, as the Tatars profefs the*
" *fame worfhip as the Mufelmans, they fhall*
" *regulate themfelves with regard to his high-*
" *nefs, as grand kalif of Mahometanifm, accord-*
" *ing to the precepts which their law prefcribes*
" *to them, without, however, any prejudice to*
" *the confirmation of their civil and religious*
" *liberty, &c.*"—" *Ruffia engages to withdraw*
" *its troops, &c. and the fublime porte to re-*
" *linquifh all right whatever, which he might*
" *have to the fortreffes, cities, habitations, &c.*
" *in Crimea, the Kuban, or in the ifland of Ta-*
" *man, nor to keep in any of thefe places, gar-*
" *rifons, nor other armed people, &c. &c.*"

In confequence of this ftipulation, *Shaheen*
Guerrai

Guerrai was elected khan by the beys and murfas, with the approbation of the people, as it feemed, for no difcontent appeared among them.

The new khan, however, did not long keep his popularity. He wifhed to civilize his people, and introduce the European difcipline among his troops. He would have fucceeded, had he paid more refpect to the deep rooted prejudices of the people. He began by entirely abolifhing the old form of government; he raifed new foldiers and paid them, and appointed murfas for their officers. They had no ftanding army before, but every man was a foldier. He diminifhed the rent paid by the people to the murfas for their land, and appropriated it to his own ufe, allowing fuch murfas as would ferve in the army handfome falaries. He affected too much the manner of the Chriftians or Ruffians, though he obferved with punctuality all the ceremonies of his religion. His expences were thus increafed beyond his income, and he could not, like his predeceffors, apply for pecuniary affiftance to the Ottoman Porte, which had ceafed to pay the falaries of the officers of his court. He ftruck a new coin at an enormous expence; the mint was conducted by a German. He farmed out the different branches of the revenue to people

Y   who

who exacted the payment with a rigour
hitherto unknown. He eftablifhed a corps
of artillery, and endeavoured to form a marine ; but want of revenue prevented him
fucceeding in any one undertaking.

The Turks faw with jealoufy the independence of the Tatars, and lamented being
deprived, in all probability, of their affiftance
in any future war, as the khan declared his
intention of remaining neutral, as the only
means of making his people formidable, and
maintaining his independence. The Turks
laboured inceffantly by their emiffaries, who
were moftly religious enthufiafts, to ftir up
the people to rebellion. They fucceeded in
raifing fuch a fpirit of difcontent, that the
khan, fearful of his perfonal fafety, called in
a body of Ruffians. and placed fmall corps
in different parts of the country. The Turks
had, previoufly to this, fent a body of troops
to Taman, and beheaded one of the khan's
commanders.

I arrived at the Ruffian fortrefs of Jani-
kali, in October 1777, and was fetting out
for Bagfhirai, when news arrived that the
Tatars had fuddenly fallen on the difperfed
Ruffians in every part of the Krim and the
Kuban at the fame time, and had cut them
all off; the khan himfelf luckily efcaped to
the Ruffian head-quarters. The Ottoman
Porte,

Porte, at the fame time, had appointed a new
khan, and fent him to the port now called
Sebaftopolis, with five fhips of the line. A
Ruffian army foon entered the Crimea ; the
Tatars were defeated, and during the winter
reduced again to obedience to their khan.
The Ruffians are accufed of committing fome
cruelties on this occafion. If they cannot be
juftified as Chriftians for following the law
of retaliation, they are, as men, fomewhat
excufable.

The Tatars, though reduced to obedience,
could not be kept in that ftate by the few
troops the khan could rely on ; he was
therefore obliged to have an auxiliary army
from Ruffia, and the porte made feveral attempts to excite a frefh rebellion. The emprefs, at laft tired out by the continual alarms
they occafioned, and determined no longer to
fuffer her fubjects to be expofed to the calamities the incurfions of thefe barbarians occafioned, feized on the Krim and Kuban in
1783. The khan retired to Kaluga, in Ruffia Minor, where he was allowed a very large
penfion by the emprefs, and treated in every
refpect as a fovereign ; but, unaccuftomed to
a quiet and inactive life, he quitted Ruffia, and
went to Conftantinople, where at firft he was
received with great diftinction, but was foon
fent into exile to a Greek ifland, and one day,

as

as he was in his bath, he was feized and
ftrangled, and his head fent to Conftantinople.

I beg the reader will excufe a fhort digreffion refpecting myfelf, as it may throw fome
light on the character or morals of the people
I was among. The $\frac{10}{21}$th December, 1777, I
failed from Janicali, in a fmall veffel, for
Kaffa, (the road by land being unfafe) which
had juft been taken by the Ruffians, under
General Balmaine, by ftorm, and many
Turks, who were at Kaffa, had been put to
the fword by a Greek corps from Janicali,
who alfo robbed my fervant of all my baggage, to a very confiderable amount, and
which I never recovered. Inftead of making the port of Kaffa, we were driven by a
ftorm along the coaft, and after lofing our
bowfprit and all our anchors, we were in
great diftrefs for water, being eighty perfons
on board, all military men. We made feveral
defcents on the coaft to procure water, but
were always beaten off by the Tatars; at laft
we paffed Belaklava, and lay to in the gulph
of Giosléve, oppofite the port of Sebaftopolis, where we faw the Turkifh fleet at anchor.
The mafter of a Turkifh mercantile veffel
came out to us, and we bargained with him,
for about fifty pounds fterling, for a cafk of
water, which he promifed to bring us off in
the

the night; but as foon as he got on fhore, we obferved one of the Turkifh frigates loofening her topfails to come out. It was nearly night, and we put to fea and bore away for the Danube, the only port we could reach with the wind we had, preferring to throw ourfelves on the mercy of the Turks to perifhing by thirft. I was the only perfon in the veffel who could navigate her out of fight of land. The captain, who was a Greek, had become mad. I found two Turkifh charts of the Black Sea, which differed in the latitude of the Danube a degree. I examined the coaft of Anatolia, which I had furveyed that fummer from Conftantinople to Kitros, and by that judged which was the beft.

We arrived fafe off Sulina-mouth, but the wind not permitting us to enter, a Turkifh boat came out to us; and here I cannot enough commend the humanity we experienced from the crews of feveral Turkifh merchant veffels. We had only a hawfer and a boat anchor to hold the fhip. The water was very fmooth. It was already night. They fent out five large boats manned to tow us in, if there fhould be any danger, and they remained with us all night. We got fafe into the river in the morning.

Y 3

The

The next day I set off for Galatz, intending to go by land to Ruffia. In the river I found two new Turkifh 50 gun fhips, without their guns or crews. I had known the captains at Conftantinople, and was received with kindnefs by them.

The 1ft January, 1778, I went to the Greek governor, to pay him a complimentary vifit: I found a very cold reception from him; he was feated on his fopha with a Turk, in appearance of fome diftinction, who immediately produced a warrant from the pafha of Ebrahil to cut off my head and thofe of 26 perfons who were come with me from the veffel. The executioner was ftanding in the room, with a bag to put our heads in, and a heap of fawduft was laid in the court before the houfe to abforb the blood. My Greek interpreter was fo terrified, that he could utter no other word than *quel facco*, pointing to the bag in which his head was to be put. Luckily I was not intimidated; but I was obliged to fpeak for myfelf as well as I could, and with great difficulty perfuaded the officer, who was filiktar (fword-bearer) to the pafha, that I was an Englifh-man, and came with no ill intentions; that were I an enemy, in the fituation we came into the Danube the cuftom of all nations

granted

granted us an asylum. He then told me, we were accused of coming into the Danube with a design to burn the two Turkish ships of war. In short my arguments, and a few thousand dollars in Russian bank notes, prevailed on him to go back to the pasha for fresh instructions, and to send to the captains of the Turkish ships of war, who engaged to answer with their heads that I was an Englishman, and a friend of the captain pasha's. It was a lucky circumstance that they had seen me with the captain pasha, and knew that I really was an Englishman.

I afterwards learnt that the Greek governor, who had at first received me with great civility, was our accuser.

We remained prisoners at large in the town three months, when an order from the captain pasha came to let us depart, and " *that we should be so little molested, that if a* " *bird perched on the mast top it should be driven* " *away.*"

While I was in the quarantine at the Russian frontier, in September 1778, there passed 75,000 Christians, obliged by the Russians to emigrate from the Crimea (35,769 males.) The Armenian women, who came from Kaffa, were more beautiful, and, I think, approached nearer that perfect form which the

Y 4 Grecians

Grecians have left us in their ftatues, than the women of Tino. Thefe people were fent to inhabit the country abandoned by the Nogai Tatars, near the weft coaft of the fea of Azof (Palus Mæotis) but the winter coming on before the houfes built for them were ready, a great part of them had no other fhelter from the cold than what was afforded them by holes dug in the ground, and covered with what they could procure : they were people who all came from comfortable homes, and the greateft part perifhed ; feven thoufand only were alive a few years ago. A colony from Italy to the banks of the Boryfthenes, in 1783, had no better fate, owing to the bad management of thofe who were commiffioned to provide for them, and not to the climate ; nor have colonies of Germans been more fortunate in Ruffia—but this is a digreffion.

I fhall here take the opportunity of correcting a few errors into which fome writers of celebrity have fallen.

With refpect to the title of fultan, borne by the Gengifkhan family, and to that of khan (written frequently by the French, who do not diftinguifh the found of an *m* from an *n* when not followed by a vowel, *kam* and *cham*, as they write Edimbourg, &c.) Baron de Tott has made fome obfer-

§   vations

vations which require correction. His errors, which are not entirely cleared up by Peyffonel, arife from not having obferved the different force which thefe words have in the different countries where they are ufed. They are both words of command, and (contrary to Tott's affertion) are ufed by the Turkifh emperors to exprefs fovereignty, as is evident from the Arabic infcription on the Ottoman money : *Sultan, ebn ul fultan, Abdulhamid khan, damé mulkhu. Sultan, fon of a fultan, Abdulhamid the khan, whofe reign be perpetual.* Thefe terms, however, are ufed very differently in Perfia ; *fhah,* which among the Tatars is equivalent to *khan* or king, is the only title taken by the Perfian monarch : in that country *khan* anfwers to the Turkifh *pafha,* and is therefore taken by the governors of provinces, whilft *fultan,* which there fignifies fimply commander, is a title given to a captain of horfe. In my time, a man was made *khan* or governor of Benderrik, and his fon, who commanded a body of cavalry, was called *fultan.* I fpeak of the prefent acceptation of thefe words, not of their more ancient fignification.

Tott is erroneous in ftating, that the bey of the Sherins conftantly reprefents the five other beys. In the *kinguefhés,* or extraordinary affemblies, as well as in all the public convocations,

convocations, the bey of the Sherins, though firſt in rank, repreſents only his own family; the beys of the other houſes are alſo preſent, and repreſent each their own family.

The *hiſtorical journal* of the affairs of the Crimea, which was kept at *Bagtſhiſerrai*, is probably a valuable document: Peyſſonel ſeems to doubt of its exiſtence, or at leaſt to ſuppoſe, that it is little more than a compilation from general traditions, made by ſome Tatar of learning; it is, however, certain that ſuch a journal was regularly kept there by a family, who have handed it down from father to ſon with the ſame regularity as a ſimilar journal is kept at the porte at Conſtantinople: the khans often referred to it.

The caverns found in different parts of the Crimea, particularly at Tepekirman, half a league from Bagtſhiſerrai, have given riſe to much curious ſpeculations: from their ſituation on the ſides of ſteep, and often perpendicular ſides of rocky mountains, as well as from the regularity of their ſtructure, it is evident that they have been excavated by human art, but whether as ſepulchral monuments, as fortreſſes, or as places of refuge for cattle in time of invaſion, or for whatever other uſe, is at the preſent day doubtful. The objection of Mr. Peſſyonel, who thinks it impoſſible for cattle to have climbed to

ſuch

such a height, is certainly erroneous as to its practicability, since the Tatars. at present actually do put herds of goats every night into some of them, by means of steps cut in the rock, which, had he passed a night, as I did, in that beautifully romantic vale, he might have been an eye witness of; others, indeed, have no such access, and might serve as a refuge to the masters of the flocks themselves.

What has been said sufficiently illustrates the political state of the Tatars. In their education, there was little to supply the mind with knowledge, and whatever marks of sagacity are discoverable among them, are to be attributed to natural genius, and the effect of an active mode of life, which, even among savages, bestows a sharpness and accuracy of intellect. Their acquired information is very limited: reading and writing constitute their highest branches of education, and in the sciences in general they are less informed even than the Turks themselves. Like most barbarians, their own country is to them at once the pattern of excellence and the boundary of knowledge; and the chief officers of state themselves were ignorant of the geography or relative situation of every other country.

The Tatar mode of fighting has no re-
semblance

femblance to European tactics; it is one continued fcene of confufion and tumult, though it gives occafion to the difplay of great agility, and no fmall portion of a barbarous kind of fkill. Alternately flying and advancing in detached parties, many kinds of conteft are carried on at once; the fabre, the pike, and fire arms, are all employed, and they fight alike on horfeback or on foot, though the former is their moft common mode. The regularity and difcipline of the modern European battles has greatly contributed to produce a correfpondent mildnefs towards the conquered; but in this defultory warfare the paffions of the individuals are let loofe, perfonal fury augments the favage horror of the fcene, and the enemy is never fpared, unlefs he be fufficiently unhurt to become valuable as a flave.

It is not furprizing, that on the emprefs's obtaining poffeffion of the Krim, a great number of its Tatar inhabitants fhould emigrate from their country. Befides the religious prejudices of thefe people, their unfettled and turbulent habits rendered them little adapted to that induftry and civilization, which it was her endeavour to introduce into her newly acquired dominions. Thofe who chofe to leave the country, had

leave

leave to fell their lands and other property, which was protected by the Ruffians. She did not act with them as the Turks and Tatars ever did to the inhabitants of the countries they conquered; thofe who chofe to remain, were left in the quiet poffeffion of their property and their religion, and enjoyed every protection and privilege as a Ruffian Chriftian fubject.

The Tatar hordes now no more fwell the Turkifh army, nor mark their road with fmoking villages laid in afhes, and murdered inhabitants; thofe hordes, who penetrated even into Pruffia and Silefia, ravaged Poland, Hungary, and Ruffia, deftroying by fire and fword every habitation, every living creature they could not carry off, tying their prifoners to their horfes tails, and thofe prifoners were the flower of their youth, led away, never more to return from flavery and violation to their friends or their country; thofe hordes are now either difperfed among their brother favages in Afia, or civilized by their conquerors.

CHAPTER IX.

The Political State of Greece.

THE political ftate of Greece has long
announced to the attentive obferver
that explofion which late events feem to
have rapidly promoted. Greece can no
longer fubmit to the Turkifh yoke; fhe pants
for emancipation, and already afpires to be
ranked among the independent ftates of Europe. The rife, or rather the renovation of
her power will form an important æra in
European politics: to appreciate its probable confequences we muft confider the paft
and prefent circumftances of that famous
country; we muft recur to the eclipfe of her
former fplendor by the Turkifh conqueft, to
the long night of barbarifm and oppreffion
in which fhe has been whelmed, and to thofe
ftruggles which of late years have fhown
that fhe is about to awake to the affertion of
her native rights.

It is not here my intention to trace the details of claffic ftory, to defcribe thofe heroic
ages, when the fplendor of genius and the
illumination

illumination of fcience feemed to be concentrated within the narrow boundaries of
Greece, and by their irradiation to communicate animation and improvement to
furrounding nations ; it will be fufficient for
me to call to the remembrance of the fcholar
fome of the brighteft pages in the hiftory of
mankind ; it will be fufficient to cite the
names of thofe poets and orators, thofe ftatef-
men and moralifts, whofe illuftrious deeds
and whofe admirable precepts ftill extort the
applaufes of the univerfe. To Greece belonged an Homer and a Demofthenes, a
Phocion and an Ariftides, a Socrates, a Plato,
an Ariftotle, a Phidias, and an Apelles ;
in fhort, in whatever path the ardent and
eccentric imagination of man has fought for
fame, in that the Grecian name ftands eminently confpicuous, if not arrogating to itfelf
an unrivalled fuperiority.

India and Egypt had for many preceding
ages cultivated the arts ; but thefe countries
were only the cradle of knowledge ; when
tranfmitted to the genial climate of Greece,
foftered by her political freedom, and animated by her vivacity and enterprize, it
quickly attained the fublimeft heights, and
invefted the human character with a dignity
before unknown. By what gradations their
ancient fimplicity, temperance, modefty, and

good

good faith funk away, and how the decay of
their virtues involved the ruin of their genius,
their hiftory will fhew : let the philanthro-
pift, perufing the inftructive leffon, weep
over the fall of human greatnefs, or rather
let him collect from the fatal example, new
incitements to energy and perfeverance in
the caufe of private and public virtue.

Ancient Rome, the victorious rival of
Greece in arms, caught from her captive the
infpiration of genius ; but fhe never reached
a fimilar degree of fublimity ; fhe imitated,
but never equalled, the poets, the orators,
the hiftorians, the artifts of Greece, according to the ingenuous acknowledgment of the
firft of Latin poets :

" Excudent alii fpirantia mollius æra,
" Credo equidem : vivos ducent de marmore vultus;
" Orabunt caufas melius, cœlique meatus
" Defcribent radio, &c.

Indeed no nation ever arrived fo nearly at
perfection in every branch of fcience. The
genius of the ancient Grecians feems to
have been endowed with as preternatural a
ftrength as the bodies of Homer's heroes.
Their poetical imagery was fplendid and
fublime, their oratorical tropes bold and energetic, their fpeculative philofophy manly and
comprehenfive. Of the effect of their paint-
ings we can judge only from hiftory, but
their

their ftatues have reached to the prefent times; they poffefs a dignity more than human; they feem the *ne plus ultra* of genius, tafte, and execution, and though often imitated defy the hand of the copyift.

Such a nation could not have fallen under the yoke of a Turkifh conqueror, had fhe not been prepared for that difgrace by a long period of debafement and fuperftition. When this laft and moft terrible cataftrophe arrived, fhe faw her cities and palaces laid in afhes, and the magnificent monuments of her ancient glory levelled with the duft by the rude ftrokes of thofe ferocious barbarians; fhe faw her fons, a race who had graced and dignified fociety, flaughtered without diftinction and without mercy, or fubjected to a captivity ftill worfe than flaughter; yet ftill her weeping genius feemed to linger among the melancholy ruins, and reluctantly to leave them, to carry with her the faint remnants of learning and tafte into more fortunate regions, where fhe fowed the feeds of that civilization and fcience which at the prefent day fo eminently flourifh in Europe.

Conquered Greece polifhed Rome, but the conquerors were Romans. Conquered Greece did not polifh Turkey, for the conquerors were Turks. The infenfibility of thefe barbarians is aftonifhing: living amid the effulgence

Z

gence of genius, they have not caught one
ſpark; they gaze with unfeeling ſtupidity on
the wonder and boaſt of art, on their glorious monuments, on their temples, and conclude they were built by genii, and then
deſtroy them, to burn the marble for lime
to make ſtucco for their own taſteleſs houſes,
whence the fine arts are baniſhed; where
ignorance, tyranny, ſuperſtition, and groſs
ſenſuality only dwell in ſad and ſtupidly-
ſolemn pomp, or iſſuing out with ſavage
fury, lay waſte the country round, and imbrue
their hands in the blood of the helpleſs, murdering without remorſe thoſe they have conquered.   Thus the fineſt countries in the
world are become deſerts; part inhabited by
ſavage beaſts, and part by more ſavage men;
the poor aborigines ſkulking in hiding places
like the timid hare (which epithet the Turks
give them in deriſion) while thoſe beaſts of
prey roam abroad.

Every objeƈt moral and phyſical, the fair
face of nature and the intelleƈtual energies
of the inhabitants, have alike been blaſted
and defiled by the harpy-touch of Turkiſh
tyranny. As an inſtance of thoſe changes
which the country has undergone, we need
only confider the iſland of Cyprus, now an
almoſt uninhabited deſert, which was, not
only in ancient times, but when it was taken
by

by the Turks from the Venetians, populous
and exceedingly rich. The gentry lived like
princes in fplendor, and even the peafants
had each of them at leaft a filver cup, fpoon,
knife, and fork. The number and excellency of its productions were wonderful. At
prefent only a little cotton, fome filk and
wine, and a few drugs, are its produce, all
to no great amount. Even the falines (or
falt-works) which were fo great a branch of
revenue and commerce to the Venetians, have
produced nothing fince the Turks poffeffed
it.

Of the defects of the Grecian character
fome are doubtlefs owing to their ancient
corruptions; but moft of them take their
rife in the humiliating ftate of depreffion in
which they are held by the Turks. This
degradation and fervility of their fituation
has operated for centuries, and has confequently produced an accumulated effect on
the mind; but were this weight taken off,
the elafticity and vigour of the foul would
have wide room for expanfion; and though
it cannot be expected that they would at
once rife to the proud animation of their
former heroes, they would doubtlefs difplay
energies of mind, which the iron hand of
defpotifm has long kept dormant and inert.
It is rather aftonifhing that they have re-

tained

tained fo. much energy of character, and are
not more abafed, for like noble courfers
they champ the bit, and fpurn indignantly
the yoke ; when once freed from thefe, they
will enter the courfe of glory. The truth of
thefe obfervations will appear, whether we
confider the Greeks in their common character as one people, or whether we confider
them according to their local and peculiar
diftinctions.

When we view the Greeks in their more
comprehenfive character as a nation, their
fuperiority over the Turks in knowledge is
furprifingly great; they poffefs a great degree
of genius and invention, and are of fo lively
an imagination, that they cannot tell the
fame ftory twice without varying the em-
bellifhments of circumftance and diction ;
added to this, both men and women fpeak
much, and with wonderful volubility and
boldnefs, and no people are fuch natural
orators ; numbers of them fpeak Italian, but
all have an activity and fprightlinefs which
ftrongly contrafts with the ftupid and pompous gravity of the Turks ; an European
feels himfelf as it were at home with them,
and amongft creatures of his own fpecies,
for with Mahomedans there is a diftance, a
non-affimilation, a total difference of ideas,
and the more he knows their language the
more

more he perceives it ; on the contrary, the more intimately he knows the Greeks, the more fimilar does he find them in habits and manners to other Europeans : their bad reputation is more owing to the flander of the French (their mortal enemies) than to fo great a degree of demerit. In general, they are an agreeable and a ferviceable people, but they are much given to levity, immoderately ambitious, and fond of honourable diftinctions ; but this very ambition, now a weaknefs, when they have nobler objects to purfue will lead them to greatnefs.

From the account given by Tott (vol. i. p. 118) of the difturbances excited by the patriarch *Kirilo*, it would appear that the Greeks have not yet entirely abandoned that fpirit of fuperftition and bigotry, which was, perhaps, the main caufe of their former downfall.

It muft be obferved, however, that thefe difputes are not fo much foftered among themfelves, as they are owing to the efforts of the Latin church, which was the cafe in the inftance alluded to, where the foundation of the conteft was a bull of the pope, directed againft the Greek church.

They bear the Turkifh yoke with greater impatience than other Chriftians (who have long ceafed to ftruggle againft it) and poffefs a

Z 3   fpirit

fpirit of enterprize which, however ridiculed
by fome authors, often prompts them to noble
atchievements. Their ancient empire is frefh
in their memory; it is the fubject of their
popular fongs, and they fpeak of it in common converfation as a recent event.

That they poffefs a firm and manly courage, notwithftanding the infinuations of
their calumniators, has been too often tefti-
fied to be in the leaft doubtful; the inftances
which they have difplayed in the Ruffian
fervice have been truly ftriking. They are
paffionate, and fometimes given to affaffination; but, except in Zante and Cephalonia,
the ftiletto is not fo frequent with them as
with the Italians, whom they in general refemble, the beft of them, if we add more
energy, being very fimilar in character to the
Venetians, and the worft to the Genoefe.

The moft obfervable difference in the
Grecian character is between thofe of Conftantinople and their countrymen of the
iflands. The merchants and lower orders of
the Conftantinopolitan Greeks have indeed
no very marked character; they are much the
fame as the trading Chriftians in all parts of
the empire, that is to fay, as crafty and frau-
dulent as the Jews, but lefs fo than the Armenians, who are the moft fubtle of all
ufurers.

But

But there is (in a *suburb called* the Fenal)
a race of Greeks who call themfelves nobles,
and affect to defpife thofe of the iflands ; they
are certain opulent families, from which are
generally appointed the drogomans of the
porte, and the waywodes of Walachia and
Moldavia. They have kept thefe places
amongft them, as they are moftly allied together, and keep up a conftant connection
with the officers of the porte. They are
continually intriguing to get thofe in office
removed, and obtain their places ; even children cabal againft their fathers, and brothers
againft brothers. They are all people of
very good education, and are polite, but
haughty, vain, and ambitious to a moft ridiculous degree, confidering the contempt they
are treated with by the Turks. As to their
noble extraction, it is a matter of great uncertainty; moft of them bear the names of
thofe families which were illuftrious when
the Turks took Conftantinople, but they
would find it difficult to prove their defcent.
They have in general all the vices of the
Turks of the feraglio ; treachery, ingratitude,
cruelty, and intrigue, which ftops at no
means. While they are drogomans of the
porte, they are obliged to behave with great
caution and prudence, but when they

become waywodes, they are in nothing
different from Turkiſh paſhas in tyranny;
nor is it to be wondered at, when men
are obliged to look up not only to tyrants,
but to the very ſervants of tyrants, for honour and conſequence; to flatter their ignorance and ſtupidity, their foibles and their
vices, and to tremble for their lives at their
frowns, that cunning takes the place of wiſ-
dom, vice of virtue, and treachery of fortitude. In ſuch a ſituation the mind muſt
loſe its vigour, the heart its generoſity: the
abaſement of man by ſuch cauſes was never
more ſtrongly exemplified than in the inſtance of the Greeks of the Fenal; they
do not weep over the ruins which they cannot reſtore, nor ſigh to rear others of equal
magnificence.

Strange as is the infatuation which induces
theſe Greeks to aim at the poſt of waywodes,
it is perhaps no leſs aſtoniſhing than many examples which daily occur in other nations of
the power of ambition. Though ſtyling
themſelves noble, and affecting a ſuperiority
over the other Greeks, they are the only part
of their nation who have totally relinquiſhed
the ancient Grecian ſpirit; they ſeem not
anxious, as the iſlanders are, for liberty, but
delight in their falſe magnificence, and in
the petty intrigues of the ſeraglio; and their
pride

pride is to appear in their drefs like Turks; and yet the fituation which they are thus eager to obtain is befet with perils, and fcarcely one who holds it efcapes depofition and punifhment. No fooner is a waywode appointed, than he fets out in great ftate for his government, attended by a crowd of relations and dependents, for all of whom, as well as for his own fplendor, he muft provide by oppreffing the unhappy fubjects of his tyranny. Meanwhile his countrymen at Conftantinople are engaged in continual plots for his removal, and it becomes neceffary for him to accumulate a large fum to bribe the minifters and others on his return, and to avert the perfecution, which continues for years afterward to hang over him.

Thofe of Macedonia, &c. are robuft, courageous, and fomewhat ferocious; thofe of Athens and Attica are ftill remarkably witty and fharp; all the iflanders are lively and gay, fond of finging and dancing to an excefs, affable, hofpitable, and good natured; in fhort, they are the beft; thofe of the Morea are much given to piracy; but it is not to be wondered at, confidering the cruel treatment they have met with, and the ftruggles they are continually making againft the Turks. Albania, Epirus, and in general the mountaineers, are a very warlike, brave people, but

3   very

very favage, and make little fcruple of killing and robbing travellers; a Turk cannot venture in their country alone; there is no man in the country but would make a merit of fhooting him—and is this to be wondered at?

The Greeks of Zante and Cephalonia, fubject to the Venetians, are famous for ftabbing with knives.

In fome iflands the people are not handfome. In Metaline, the women are remarkable for very large breafts. In Tino, the women are almoft all beauties, and there the true antique head is to be found.

In general, the people of the iflands have grand and noble features. From different faces you may put together, in walking through a market place, the heads of Apollo and of the fineft ancient ftatues.

It is fcarcely poffible for any perfon not to be miftaken in judging of the conduct of the porte towards its provinces, by any analogy from the political operations of other European nations. Amongft us, the unfuccefsful revolt of a whole province would indeed give birth to fome additional rigour, and to fome ftriking example of punifhment; but the ferocious Turk propofes nothing fhort of extermination, in order to free himfelf from the fear of future defection. It

was

was thus that, when the inhabitants of the Morea, who, inftigated by the defire of liberty, had taken up arms in favour of the Ruffians, returned again under their yoke, a deliberate propofal was made in the divan to flaughter them in cold blood; nor was this the firft time that the maffacre of all the Greeks had been fericufly debated; it was, however, in the prefent inftance, fuccefsfully oppofed by Gazi Haffan, both on motives of humanity and policy *.

It has been faid, that long poffeffion of a country gives an indifputable right of dominion, and that the right of the Turks to their poffeffions has been acknowledged by all nations in their treaties. As to treaties between the Turks and other nations, who had no right to difpofe of the countries ufurped by the Turks, they cannot be binding to the Greeks, who never figned fuch treaties, nor were confulted, or confented to their figning.

* The chief argument which he ufed, and which alone carried conviction to his hearers, was, *if we kill all the Greeks, we fhall lofe all the capitation they pay.*

Even without fuch a provocation, fultan Muftafa, predeceffor and brother of Abdulhamid, on his acceffion to the throne, propofed to cut off all the Chriftians in the empire, and was with difficulty perfuaded to defift. Is this a nation which merits that Britain fhould enter into a war for its defence?

When

When one nation conquers another, and they become incorporated, by having the fame rights, the fame religion, the fame language, and by being blended together by inter-marriages, a long feries of years renders them one people. Who can in England diftinguifh the aborigines from the Romans, Saxons, Danes, Normans, and other foreigners ? They are all Englifhmen.

The Greeks were conquered by the Turks, but they were attacked (like all other nations they conquered) by them without provocation. It was not a war for injury or infult, for jealoufy of power, or the fupport of an ally, contefts which ought to end when fatisfaction or fubmiffion is obtained ; it was a war, having for its aim conqueft, and for its principle a right to the dominion of the whole earth ; a war which afferted that all other fovereigns were ufurpers, and that the depofing and putting them to death was a facred duty. Do the laws of nations eftablifh that fuch a conqueft gives right of poffeffion ? They, on the contrary, declare fuch conqueft ufurpation.

The conquered were never admitted by the Turks to the rights of citizens or fellow fubjects, unlefs they abjured their religion and their country ; they becames flaves, and as, according to their cowardly law, the Turks

Turks have a right at all times to put to death their prisoners, the conquered and their posterity for ever are obliged annually to *redeem their heads*, by paying the price set on them : they are excluded from all offices in the state. It is death for a conquered Greek to marry a Turkish woman, or even to co-habit with a common prostitute of that nation ; they are in every respect treated as enemies ; they are still called and distin-guished by the name of their nation, and a Turk is never called a Greek, though his fa-mily should have been settled for generations in that country. The testimony of a Greek is not valid in a court of judicature, when contrasted with that of a Turk. They are distinguished by a different dress ; it is death to wear the same apparel as a Turk ; even their houses are painted of a different colour ; in fine, they are in the same situation they were the day they were conquered ; totally distinct as a nation ; and they have, there-fore, the same right now as they then had, to free themselves from the barbarous usur-pers of their country, whose conduct to all the nations they have conquered merits the eternal execration of mankind.

In the war between Russia and Turkey, which continued from 1769 to 1774, where-ever the Russians appeared the Greeks took

up

up arms and joined them. The hiſtory of this war, and the part which the Greeks took in it, is too well known for it to be neceſſary that I ſhould enter here into any particulars. The progreſs that was made againſt the Turks was very conſiderable, and their fleet being deſtroyed at Chiſhmé, the capital might have been attacked by the victorious Ruſ-ſians. Had the Ruſſian admiral been a man of any experience, or of an enterpriſing cha-racter, that war muſt have terminated in the expulſion of the Turks from Europe.

Nothing can place the Turks in a more deſpicable light, than the progreſs the Ruſ-ſians did make, notwithſtanding the ſlowneſs of all their motions, their never profiting of any advantage, the opportunities they loſt of ſtriking deciſive blows, the want of plan or combination in every enterprize, and the un-military conduct in the execution; the bra-very of their troops indeed, when there was a poſſibility of ſucceſs, always ſecured them victory. The Ruſſians and Greeks, to this day, make reproaches to each other of miſ-conduct; but as the accounts hitherto pub-liſhed are taken from the relation of Ruſ-ſians, we may ſafely conclude that juſtice has not been done to the Greeks. In this laſt war, when they acted alone, they fought like true

true defcendants of their heroic anceftors in the little diverfion they made.

It was folemnly ftipulated in the 17th article of the peace of Kainargi (figned $\frac{10}{21}$ July, 1774) that " *The empire of Ruffia reftores* " *to the fublime porte all the iflands of the* " *Archipelago, which are under its dependence*; " *and the fublime porte, on its part, promifes,* " 1*ft. To obferve* SACREDLY, *with refpect to* " *the inhabitants of thefe iflands, the conditions* " *ftipulated in the firft article, concerning a ge-* " *neral amnefty and eternal oblivion of all crimes* " *whatever, committed or fufpected, to the pre-* " *judice of the fublime porte.* 2*dly. That* " *neither the Chriftian religion, nor its churches,* " *fhall be expofed to the fmalleft oppreffion, and* " *that no hindrance fhall be put to their con-* " *ftruction or reparation; nor fhall thofe who* " *officiate in them be oppreffed or infulted.* 3*dly.* " *That no payment fhall be exacted from thefe* " *iflands of the annual taxes to which they* " *were fubjected, viz. fince the time which* " *they have been under the dependence of the* " *Ruffian empire, and alfo, in confideration of* " *the great loffes which they have fuffered dur-* " *ing the war, for the time of two years to* " *come, to count from the time of their reftora-* " *tion to the fublime porte.* 4*thly. To permit* " *thofe families which would quit their country,* " *and eftablifh themfelves elfewhere, to depart* " *freely with their goods; and to the end that*
" *thofe*

" *thofe families may put their affairs in order,*
" *the term of one year is granted to them for*
" *this free emigration, counting from the day of*
" *the exchanging of the prefent treaty.*"

Notwithftanding this folemn engagement, the Turks, almoft as foon as the Ruffians had evacuated their conquefts, and, relying on the faith of treaties, had delivered up the inhabitants to their domination, fell upon their victims, unprepared to refift them, and maffacred an incredible number, particularly in the Morea, where their vengeance fell with all its weight. Whole diftricts were left without a fingle inhabitant, and this fine country is now almoft a defert. The Greeks upbraid the Ruffians with abandoning them ; the Ruffians anfwer, they relied on the faith of treaties. They ought to have known, that the fetva of the mufti had often announced, that *no faith is to be kept with Chriftians* ; hiftory furnifhed them with numerous inftances of their putting in practice this precept ; indeed I know of no inftance when they have not, if it appeared to them that it was their intereft fo to do ; and yet we find writers who vaunt the fcrupuloufnefs of the Turks in obferving their treaties ; they fhould always have added, *when it was their intereft,* and their ftatement would have been juft.

So ardent was the wifh of the Greeks to regain

regain their liberty and independence, that neither difcouraged by the abandonment of the Ruffians, nor deterred by the apprehenfion of again incurring the dreadful vengeance of the Turks, as foon as a frefh war broke out between thofe powers they again took up arms.

A fleet was fitted out at Cronftad, and failed for the Archipelago under the command of a brave, prudent, and experienced officer, Admiral Greig, an Englifhman, who had ferved in the former war, and greatly diftinguifhed himfelf under Count Orlow; who, from an officer in the guards, where he faw no other *honourable* fervice than quelling a riot at a brandy fhop, was raifed to the fupreme command of a fleet and an army, and entrufted with an expedition which required the greateft experience and talents. The king of Sweden rendered to the emprefs the effential fervice of detaining her fleet in the Baltic, by attacking it in that fea, and thereby putting into her hand the naval fuperiority which, by its abfence, would have paffed into his. This ill-timed diverfion of the king of Sweden retarded the fate of Turkey, and the interference of other courts faved it for this time; at leaft they obliged the emprefs to make peace; but that peace would have been but of a few months duration, had

A a   not

not the death of Prince Potemkin and some other circumstances intervened, which shall be spoken of in this place.

In the mean time the empress sent manifestoes to all parts of Greece, as she had done in the former war, inviting the inhabitants *to take up arms, and co-operate with her in expelling the enemies of Christianity from the countries they had usurped, and regaining them their ancient liberty and national independence.*

A Greek of the name of Sottiri was sent to Epirus and Albania, to distribute manifestoes, and combine an insurrection with the chiefs. An army was soon raised; their head-quarters were at Sulli. They marched against the pasha of Yánina (Janina) and completely defeated his army in a pitched battle, in which his son was killed, and despoiled of his rich armour, which they sent to the empress.

They collected a sum of money by voluntary subscription of individuals, and fitted out at Trieste an armament of twelve small ships, under the command of Lambro Canziani, a Greek, with which they sailed to the Archipelago. They were everywhere victorious, and the impression was so great and alarming to the porte, that it had nearly drawn the whole Turkish navy out of the Black Sea, and left the capi-

5   tal

tal expofed to the attack of a formidable Ruffian fleet, then in the ports of the Crim.

The emprefs had fent a captain Pfaro to
Sicily, to eftablifh magazines for the fleet
coming out under Admiral Greig, and feveral other perfons, to furnifh the Greeks with
money and ammunition, and to remove the difficulties the Venetians, ftill unwilling to of-
fend the porte, had thrown in their way, and
the obftructions they had put to their communication by means of their port Prevafi,
the neareft to Sulli. In this ftate of things
the Greeks fent three deputies to St. Peterfburgh, with complaints againft the perfons
commiffioned to this fervice by the emprefs.
They prefented the rich armour of the pafha
of Yanina's fon to her imperial majefty; but
were prevented, by the intrigues of thofe who
feared an enquiry into their fcandalous pecu-
lations, for feveral months from prefenting
their petition, and explaining the bufinefs of
their miffion; at length they fucceeded in
obtaining a private audience of the emprefs,
to which they were conducted by Mr. Zou-
bov, the favourite. They prefented a memorial in Greek, with a tranflation in French,
of which the following are exact copies:

T₀

Τη ὑψολότατη, ἐνδοξοτάτη, κὴ Θεοσεβεσάτη
Αὐτοκρατορισση, κὴ Βασιλισση πασῶν τῶν
Ρωσιῶν, κὴ τα εξ. κὴ τα εξ. κὴ τα εξ.

ΚΑΙ τῦτο ἐ πρὸς ἕτερον τὶ εἰμὴ τὸ διὰ μάκρος χρόνε,
ματέως δενθέντες, τοῖς ὑπεργοῖς τῆς ὑμέτερας Αὐτοκρα-
τορικῆς Μεγαλειότητος πρὸς ἀπόκρισιν, ἀναφορὰς ἀν προ-
χρόνε αὐτοῖς προσεφέρομεν. ἐκ ἀπιτισάμενοι δὲ, καὶ
μάλα, ἐν ἐσχάτη ἀπελπισεία φερόμενοι διανοῦντες τας
φρικτὰς συμφοράς, ἀς ἡ ταύτης βραδυτης προξενεσιαν τοῖς
ἡμετεροις συμπατριοτες, οἱ γαρ ελκυσθεντες παρὰ τῶν
προδήλων κλίσεων τῆς αὐτῆς Αὐτ. Μεγ. ἐφερον τα ὅπλα
κατα τε κοινῦ ἐχθρῦ τῦ Χρισηανικῦ ὀνομάτος, ἀπεσηλαν
ἒν νῦν ἡμᾶς προσφέρειν, τοῖς ποδοῖς τῦ ὑψηλῦ αὐτῆς
Θρόνε ὡς σημεῖον κὴ δῶρον τῆς ἡμῶν ευλάθειας, τὴν ζωῆν κὴ
περιῦσιαν αὐτῶν.

Νκι Βασιλησσα κὴ Κυρία· τῦτο ἐ πρὸς τί ἕτερον ἡμὴ
ἀπολολόντες πᾶσαν ἐλπίδαν μιᾶς ταχεας αποκρισεως,
τολμῶμεν γόνυ κλίνοντες προσφέρειν τὴν ταπινὴν ἡμῶν,
αναφορὰν, πρὸς τὰς πόδας τῆς αὐτῆς Αὐτ. Μεγ. ὅπως
τῆς εκ τῶν αδελφῶν ἡμῶν αἱμάτων ρύακας ξηρένειν, οἳ ἤδη
ἀναμφιβύλως ρέεσιν.

Ἕτερον Εν ιερὸν ὤφλημα ἡμῶν τὸ κὴ κύριον εἶδος τῆς
ἡμῶν παραγγαιλίας, ὃν κὴ ἠρέθησε ἡμᾶς ἐν ταύτη τὴ
τολμειρᾶ επιχειρήσει, εςὶν ὅπως ἐξαπατήσομεν, τὴν αὐτῆς
Αὐτ Μεγ. ἐξ ὧν ἔτολμισαν απατεῖν (ὡς δε κὴ οἱ μεγιςάνες
αὐτῆς) εγνωμεν γαρ, ὅτι ὁ ὑππεὺς Ψάρος ανὴρ βδελερω-
τατος εκ τῦ ἡμῶν ἔθνες, ἕνεκεν τῆς κραιπάλης αὐτῦ, ἀς
ἐξήλθεν κὴ εις ἀν ευρισκέται. Ὁ γαρ δὲ ἐὰν μὴ πλανῶν,
ανεπεσχειντως τῆς ὑπεργῆς αὐτῆς πισὼν αὐτοῖς ἑαυτὸν, ως
ἄξιον μεγάλων κατορθυμάτων, ἀ ποτὲ ꞷκ ἔποιησε. ꞷτος
ἐν κὴ ἔτι ἐγείρεται ὡς ἄρχων κὴ ὁδηγὸς, τῦ ἡμῶν ἔθνες,
καυχομενος

καύχομενος ότι ἐμένομεν τὴν παρασίαν αὐτῶ ἐπὶ τῆς ἡμῶν γῆς, ινα κυρήξομεν ἡμῖν αὐτὸν ἀρχιςρατιγον. καυχήσεις ἁς μόνον γράφει κ̀ ὖκ ἐργαζέται. θεωρισείαν ἡ αὐτῆς Αυτ. Μεγ. ἐν τῆ ἡμῶν ἀναφορᾶ τί ἔτος ἔποιησε ἡμῖν, ἔγνωκαμεν γαρ ὅτι, αὐτὸς λαβὼν ἀπείρης ποσοτήτας χρημάτων, φημίζει ὅτι ἔδαπανησε αὐτὰ ὑπὲρ ἡμῶν. δυναμεθα πληροφορησαι τὴν αὐτῆς Αυτ. Μεγ. ὅτι ὖδε αὐτὸς ὖδέ τὶς ἄλλος σπῶ εἰς ἡμᾶς ἀπελσάλθη εκ τῶν σῶν ὑπεργῶν δ'δωκε ἡμῖν Ἑν μόνον ῥάμπλιον. ἡ μικρὰ φλοτίγλια, κ̀ ἔτερε ναῦς τῶ Λάμπρω, κατεσκεύασησαν κ̀ ὁπλισθησαν διὰ τῆς τῶν ἡμῶν χρημάτων δαπάνης. εἰς μόνος εξ ἡμῶν ἔασας τὴν κρηνικὴν αὐτῶ κοίτην, ἔδαπανησε δέκα κ̀ δύο χιλιάδας χρυσὰ νομήσματα ἐκ τῶν ἰδίων αὐτῶ χρημάτων, ὁπλίσας δύο ναῦς, ἑνεκεν τάτη οἱ Οθωμανοι ἀπεκτειναν τὸν ἀδελφὸν κ̀ τὴν μητέρα αὐτῶ, τῶ ἔλεηλατησαν τὰ ὑπαρχοντα κ̀ τῶ ἔφθειραν τῶς ἀγρῶς.

Οὐκ ἔτησαμεν ποτὲ κ̀ ὖκ ἐτῶμεν τῶς σᾶς θησαύρας, ὖκ ἔτησαμεν εἰμὴ πυριον κόνιν κ̀ σιδήριας σφέρας (α ὖδυναμεθα ὀνήζειν) κ̀ ἐν τῶ ὀδιγείν ἡμᾶς εις τὴν μάχην.

Εξ ἐναντίας ἀπεσηλαν ἡμᾶς προσφερειν σοὶ τὴν ζωὴν κ̀ τα κλήματα αὐτῶν, κ̀ ὖκ ετεῖν τῶς σᾶς θησαύρας.

Νεύσον, ὢ κρατεὰ Βασιλινησσα, δόξα τῆς τῶν Ἑλλήνων πίςεως, νεύσον δεόμεθα αναβεινόσκειν τὴν ταπινὴν ἡμῶν ἀναφορᾶν. Ὁ Οὐρανὸς ἐφυλαξεν τὴν ἡμελέραν ἀπολύτροσιν προς δόξαν τῆς σῆς Αυτ. Μεγ. ὑπὸ τὴν αὐτῆς προςασίαν, προσδοκῶμεν λυτρόσαι, τὴν αὐτοκράτοριαν ἡμῶν χρωμένην, τὴν πατριαρχίαν κ̀ ιεραν θρησκείαν, καταφρονιθίσαν κ̀ καταπατιθίσαν εκ τῶν βεβήλων, κ̀ βαρβάρων Οθωμανῶν· προσδόκωμεν σοι, λυτρόσαι τῶς τῶν Αθηναίων, κ̀ Λακαιδεμονίων ἀπογόνας, τῶ τυρραννικῶ ζυγῶ, τάτων τῶν ἀγρίων, ὑφ' ὧν σενάζει, Εν Εθνος, ὖ το πνευμα ὖκ απεσβεση, ὃ ὁ ἱρως ὑπερπολεῖ τῆς ελευθεριας, ὖκ ἐδυνηθησαν γαρ αἱ σιδεραὶ ἁλισαι τῶν βαρβάρων αποσβεννειν, ἔχει δε προ τῶν αὐτῶ ὁμμάτων

τὴ

τὴν εἰκόνα τῶν ἡρωικῶν πραξεων τῶν αυτε προπατορων
ἕως νῦν.

Αι λαμπραὶ ἡμῶν ἠκοδομαὶ ἀναγινόσκεν ἡμῖν τὴν πα-
λεὰν ἡμῶν μεγαλίοτητα· οἱ ἄπιροι λιμεναι, η ευφυνη τῶν
αγρῶν μὰς, ὁ Ουρανὸς ὁ ἀένναως γελῶν εφ᾽ ἡμὰς, ἡ ακρα
Θερμότητα τὴν ἡ φύσις εμπνέει ἒ μόνον τοῖς νέοις αλλὰ,
κὴ τοῖς πεβαρεμένοις γηραλέοις ἡμῶν, λεγει ἡμῖν ὅτι μας
ἔςι πρόχειρη ὡς κὴ προς τες προγονες ἡμῶν.

Νεύσον ἒν Κυρία διδόναι ἡμῖν σὸν ευγκονα Κονςαντίνον
διὰ ἄνακτα ἡμῶν, τ̄το μόνον τὸ γένος ὅλον ημῶν ετεῖ δεο-
μενον· (γενος γαρ τῶν ημῶν αυτοκρατορων αποσβεςη) κὴ
ἔσεται ὡς τες προγονες αυτ̄.

Ημεῖς ἐκ ἐσμέν εκ τῶν ἀπατιλῶν οἱ τίνες ετόλμησαν απα-
τίσαι τὴν μεγαλοψηχότερην τῶν ἀνάκτων· ἡμεῖς εσμὲν οἱ
ἀπελςαλμένοι τῶν λαῶν της Ελλαδος προμηθευμένοι απο-
λυτε δυνάμεως, ὡς δὲ τοιετοι προσπιπτόντες τοῖς ποσῖν
αυτῆς ἣν μετὰ Θεὸν σωτήρα ελπιζόμεν, ωμνυόμεν δε ἴσεσθαι
μέχρι τελευτέας ἡμῶν ἀναπνοῆς,

Οι τῆς ὑμετέρας Αυτοκρατωρικῆς Μεγαλιότητος
πιςότατοι δετλοι, κὴ τα εξ.

Πετρετπολη,
Απριλιτ, 1790.

Πανος Κιρη,
Χρίςος Λαζοτῖι,
Νικολαος Πάνκαλος.

Madame,
    " Ce n'eft, qu' après avoir folicité long-tems en
vain, les miniftres de VOTRE MAJESTE IMPE-
RIALE, pour une reponfe au memoire, que nous
avons eu l'honneur de leur prefenter, et poufsès
àu dernier déféfpoir par la reflexion des malheurs
affreux que ce retard, poura produire à nos compa-
triotes,

triotes, qui invités, par les manifeſtes de V. M. I.
ont pris les armes, contre l'ennemi du nom Chré-
tien, et nous ont deputé pour porter l'offre de
leurs vies et de leurs biens aux pieds de votre
trône imperial : ce n'eſt qu' aprés avoir perdu
tout éſperance d'avoir autrement une prompte
reponſe pour arrêter les ruiſſeaux du ſang de
nos fréres, qui ſans doute coulent dejà à cauſe
de ce retard, que nous oſons proſternés à SES
PIEDS preſenter à ELLE-MEME notre trés humble
memoire.

Un autre devoir, également ſacré pour nous,
et qui êtoit un objet principal de notre miſſion,
nous porte à cette demarche hardie : de déſabuſer
V. M. I. qui on oſe tromper, ainſi que ſes miniſtres : nous avons appris, avec indignation, que le
chevalier Pſaro, homme abhorré de notre nation,
de la crapule de la quelle il eſt ſorti *, et oû il
ſeroit reſté, ſi, en trompant les miniſtres de V. M. I.
avec une audace inouie, il ne s'êtoit pas fait
valoir par la repreſéntation des explois qu'il n'a
jamais faits, s'erige actuellement, en chef et con-
ducteur de notre nation. S'il n'y auroit de mau-
vaiſes ſuites que pour lui, nous attendrions avec
patience, qu'il ſe preſentât dans nos contrées.——
Fanfaronnade cependant, qu'il ne fera jamais que
dans ſes ecrits. Comme, il a agi envers nous
V. M. I. verra dans notre memoire. Nous en-
tendons qu'il a pris de ſommes immenſes, qu'il
pretend avoir depenſé pour nous : nous aſſurons
V. M. I. que, ni lui, ni perſonne de VOS officiers

---

* This man had been a livery ſervant in Peterſburgh.

envoyés

envoyés à nous, nous ont donné un feul rouble. I.a flotille et les autres armemens de Lambro ont été fait à nos fraix : un de nous a abandonné fon foyer paifible ; a armè à fes fraix deux vaiffeaux ; a depenfé 12,000 zechins pour des armemens, et les Turcs ont maffacré fa mère, fon frere, ont rafé fes poffeffions et defolé fes terres.

Nous n'avons jamais demandé Vos trefors : nous ne le les demandons pas actuellement : nous n'avons jamais demandé que de la poudre et des balles (que nous ne pouvons pas achêter) et d'être mênes en bataille. Nous fommes venus pour *offrir*, nos vies et nos biens ; pas pour *demander* des trefors.

Daignez O GRANDE IMPERATRICE! GLOIRE DE LA FOI GRECQUE! daignez lire notre memoire. Le ciel a refervé notre delivrance pour le regne glorieux de V. M. I. C'eft fous Vos aufpices que nous éfperons de delivrer notre empire ufurpé, et notre patriarchat, et notre fainte religion infulteés, des mains des barbares Mahometans ; de delivrer les defcendants d'Athenes et de Lacedemon du joug tyrannique de ces ignorans fauvages, fous lequel gemit une nation dont le genie n'eft pas êteint, que l'amour de la liberté inflame, que le joug de fer des barbares n'a pas avilie ; qui a devant fes yeux, toujours prefent, l'image de fes anciens heros dont l'example anime fes guerriers encore aujourdhui.

Nos fuperbes ruines parlent à nos yeux de notre ancienne grandeur : nos ports innombrables, nos beaux païs ; le ciel qui fur nous fourit toute l'année ; l'ardeur de notre jeunneffe, et de nos

decrepits

decrepits vieillards mêmes, nous difent que la nature nous eft auffi propice qu'elle l'êtoit à nos ancêtres. Donnez nous pous fouverain Votre petit-fils CONSTANTIN, c'eft le vœu de notre nation (la famille de nos empereurs eft êteinte) et nous ferons ce qu' êtoient nos premiers ayeux.

Nous ne fommes pas de ces gens qui ont ofé tromper LA PLUS MAGNANIMES DE SOUVE-RAINES; nous fommes les *Deputés,* munis de pleins pouvoirs et d'autres documens des peuples de la Grece; et comme tels, profternés au pied du Trône, de CELLE, qui, aprés DIEU, nous re-gardons comme notre SAUVEUR, nous proteftons d'être jufqu' à notre dernier foupir."

De V. M. I.

Le plus fideles et les plus
devoués ferviteurs,

St. Peterfbourg,
April, 1790.

(L. S.) PANO KIRI.
(L. S.) CHRISTO LAZZOTTI.
(L. S.) NICCOLÓ PANGALO."

TRANSLATION.

Madam,

It was not until we had long folicited in vain Your Imperial Majefty's minifters for an anfwer to the memorial, which we had the honour of prefent-ing to them; it was not until, driven to the utmoft defpair by the reflection of the dreadful evils which this delay might produce to our countrymen, who (invited by the manifeftoes of Your Imperial Majef-ty) have taken arms againft the enemy of the Chrif-

tian

tian name, and deputed us to lay the offer of their lives and their fortunes at the foot of Your imperial throne; it was not till we had loft all hopes of other-wife obtaining a fpeedy anfwer to ftop thofe ftreams of the blood of our brethren, which doubtlefs flow already through this delay, that we have at length dared to proftrate ourfelves at *Your* feet, and to prefent our humble memorial to Your Imperial Majefty in perfon.

Another duty equally facred, and which was a principal objeƈt of our miffion, induced us to take this daring ftep : it was to undeceive Y. I. M. whom (as well as Your minifters) there have been people audacious enough to miflead. We have learned with indignation, that the chevalier Pfaro now ereƈts himfelf into a chief and conduƈtor of our people; a man abhorred by our nation, out of the dregs of which he rofe, and where he would have remained, if he had not with an unheard-of audacioufnefs deceived Your Imperial Majefty's mi-nifters, and affumed a reputation by attributing to himfelf exploits he never performed. If no ill con-fequences would enfue but to himfelf, we fhould patiently await his appearance in our country, a boaft however which he never will perform but in his writings. How he has aƈted towards us Y. I. M. will fee in our memorial. We hear that he has received immenfe fums, which he pretends to have expended for us. We affure Y. I. M. that neither he, nor any of your officers fent to us, ever paid us a fingle rouble. The flotilla, and the other arma-ments of Lambro, were equipped at our own ex-pence. One of us (deputies) abandoning his peaceful

ful home, fitted out two veſſels at his own expence, and expended in armaments 12,000 zechins, whilſt the Turks maſſacred his mother and his brother, levelled with the ground his poſſeſſions, and deſolated his lands.

We never aſked for Your treaſures ; we do not aſk for them now ; we only aſk for powder and balls (which we cannot purchaſe) and to be led to battle. We are come to *offer* our lives and fortunes, not to *aſk* for Your treaſures.

Deign, O Great Empreſs ! Glory of the Greek faith ! deign to read our memorial. Heaven has reſerved our deliverance for the glorious reign of Y. I. M. It is under Your auſpices that we hope to deliver from the hands of barbarous Mahomedans our empire, which they have uſurped, and our patriarchat and our holy religion, which they have inſulted ; to free the deſcendants of Athens and Lacedemon from the tyrannic yoke of ignorant ſavages, under which groans a nation whoſe genius is not extinguiſhed ; a nation which glows with the love of liberty ; which the iron yoke of barbariſm has not vilified ; which has conſtantly before its eyes the images of its ancient heroes, and whoſe example animates its warriors even to this day.

Our ſuperb ruins ſpeak to our eyes, and tell us of our ancient grandeur ; our innumerable ports, our beautiful country, the heavens which ſmile on us all the year, the ardour of our youth, and even of our decrepid elders, tell us that nature is not leſs propitious to us than it was to our forefathers. Give us for a ſovereign Your grandſon CONSTANTINE : it is the wiſh of our nation (the

family

family of our emperors is extinct *) and we shall become what our anceftors were.

We are not perfons who have dared to impofe on the *moft magnanimous of fovereigns :* we are the deputies of the people of Greece, furnifhed with full powers and other documents, and as fuch proftrated before the throne of HER, whom, next to GOD, we look on as our faviour; we declare that we fhall be till our lateft breath,

YOUR IMPERIAL MAJESTY'S
　　　　Moft faithful and moft
　　　　　　devoted fervants,

St. Peterfburgh,　　(L.S.)　PANO KIRI.
　April, 1790.　　　(L.S.)　CHRISTO LAZZOTTI.
　　　　　　　　　(L.S.)　NICCOLO PANGOLO.

As thefe people are out of the reach of Turkifh vengeance, I have not fcrupled naming them.

　　　　　　　　　　　　　　　THE

---

* In Europe we are apt to think that thofe who bear the names of Comnenos, Paleologos, &c. are defcendants of the imperial family : the Greeks, however, themfelves have no fuch notions; they are either Chriftian names given them at their baptifm, or that they have taken afterwards, and they only defcend to the fecond generation. A man is called Nicolaos Papudopulo; the former is his name received in baptifm, and the latter a furname, becaufe he was the fon of a prieft; his fons take the furname of Nicolopulo (fon of Nicolaos) added to their Chriftian name, and their children the father's Chriftian name as a furname. Thofe of Fanar have, particularly lately, affected to keep
　　　　　　　　　　　　　　　　great

THE emprefs received them very gra-
cioufly, and promifed them the affiftance
they afked. They were then conducted to
the apartments of her grandfons, and offer-
ing to kifs the hand of the eldeft grand
duke, Alexander, he pointed to his brother
Conftantine, telling them, it was to him that
they were to addrefs themfelves; they reprefented to him in Greek the object of their
miffion, and concluded by doing homage to
him as their emperor (Βασιλευς των Ἡλλενων.)
He anfwered them in the fame language,
*Go, and let every thing be according to your
wifhes.*

With this memorial they prefented *a plan
of operation,* from which I fhall extract only
a few particulars :—They propofed, after the
emprefs had furnifhed them with cannon,
and enabled them to augment the fquadron
under Lambro Canziani, and fent them en-

---

great names in their families, which were only Chriftian
names, or names which they have taken of themfelves, or
were afterwards given them by their parents, relations, or
friends. The fame may be faid of fome names in the
Archipelago, particularly where the family has preferved
for fome generations more property than their neighbours ;
but their names do not add to their refpect among the other
Greeks, who all know the origin of them, and have not
the leaft notion that there is any lineal defcent to be traced
of their ancient imperial or noble families, notwithftanding
the pretenfions often of fome of them, who bear their names
when they come to Europe.

gineers

gineers to conduct the fiege of ftrong places,
to begin their firft operations by marching
from Sulli, where the congrefs was held, and
whence they had a correfpondence with all
Greece.—Their route was to be firft to Li-
vadia and to Athens, dividing into two corps.
In their march they were to be joined at appointed places by troops from the Morea and
Negroponte. To this ifland the fleet of
Lambro was to fail. They were then to proceed in one body to Theffalia and to the city
of Salonichi, where they would receive large
reinforcements from Macedonia. The whole
army being then affembled, they were to
march to the plains of Adrianople, with (as
they calculated) three hundred thoufand
men, to meet the Ruffians, and proceed to
Conftantinople, where they hoped the Ruffian fleet would be arrived from the Crim ;
if not, they efteemed their own force fufficient to take that city, and drive the Turks
out of Europe and their iflands.

In this plan the eftablifhment and the difpofition of magazines, and retreats in cafes
of difafter, were provided for. The force of
the Turks in different parts, and the different
movements to oppofe them, were calculated.
All their refources, and the amount of the
troops each place had engaged to furnifh,
were plainly ftated, as well as the means
they

they had adopted to carry on a fecret correfpondence with all parts of the country, both
with refpect to their own allies and the
movements of the Turks. To enter more
into particulars would not be juftifiable in
me.

The emprefs fent them to the army in
Moldavia, to Prince Potemkin, giving them
1,000 ducats for their journey thither. They
left Peterfburgh the $\frac{13}{14}$ May 1790. In Auguft they were fent to Greece by the way of
Vienna, and Major General Tamara with
them, to fuperintend the whole expedition,
and furnifh them with the affiftance they
required.

It merits attention, that the king of Pruffia had pofted an army of 150,000 men, in
June 1790, on the frontier of Bohemia ; that
the convention of Reichenbach was figned the
27th of July. The fentiments of the court
of London refpecting the war, and its probable interference in as ferious a way as Pruffia had done, were known at St. Peterfburgh.
It is to thefe circumftances we muft attribute
the flownefs with which the projects of the
Greeks were feconded. They were affured
that they fhould have every fuccour they required, and much more : money was fent,
but not much of it difburfed ; they were en-
joined to prepare every thing, but to undertake

take nothing, till the proper moment fhould arrive for their acting, which, they were told, depended on many circumftances, of which they were ignorant. Lambro in the meantime acted by himfelf, but could undertake nothing of any confequence. Things remained thus till after the campaign was ended, and Prince Potemkin came to St. Peterfburgh.

The fate of the armament commanded by the gallant Lambro deferves to be mentioned.

The Greeks proved on this occafion their love of liberty, their paffion for glory, and a perfeverance in toils, obedience to difcipline, and contempt of danger and death, worthy of the brighteft pages of their hiftory; they fought with, and conquered, very fuperior numbers; and when at laft they were attacked with an inequality of force, as great as Leonidas had to encounter, they fought till their whole fleet was funk, and a few only faved themfelves in boats.

Lambro had only refources left to fit out one fingle fhip: the news of a peace arrived; but boiling with indignation at the neglect he had experienced from the Ruffian agents, and thirfting for revenge, he failed notwithftanding, and attacked and deftroyed feveral Turkifh veffels: he was declared a pirate, and difavowed by Ruffia—but he was not intimidated

timidated—at length he was again over-powered ; he difdained to ftrike ; his veffel funk under him, and he again efcaped in his boat, and took refuge in the mountains of ·Albania.

The conduct of the Ruffian agents to him was the moft fcandalous. The peculation of all thofe entrufted at a diftance with the em-prefs's money was become fo glaring and common, that they looked on it as their own property. Lambro was fuffered to be im-prifoned for debts contracted for his arma-ments, and was only releafed by the contri-butions of his countrymen.

In the fpring of 1791, an armament was prepared in England to fail for the Baltic, to force the emprefs to make peace. The king of Pruffia was ready to co-operate by land. Inftead of the fleet, Mr. Fawkener arrived at Peterfburgh. It was ftill undetermined by the emprefs, whether fhe fhould brave Eng-land and Pruffia (though from the turn af-fairs had taken in England, and the arrival of another ambaffador, fhe was affured fhe had little to fear from our fleet, and, confe-quently, little from the Pruffian army) or make peace with the Turks on the condi-tions fhe had confented to when fhe was more ferioufly alarmed.

In this uncertainty a courier was kept ready to depart with inftructions to General Tamara. The king's envoy was informed of this circumftance, and would have learnt immediately the contents of the difpatch, which would have made him acquainted with the emprefs's refolution refpecting the profecution of the war, or confenting to peace. The courier, however, was not difpatched. The bufinefs was terminated with the king's joint envoys. Prince Potemkin departed for the army, and on his road learnt the victory gained by Repnin over the vizir's army, and the figning the preliminaries of peace. Secret orders had been fent to Repnin, as foon as the emprefs had refolved to conclude a peace, which he fortunately executed; and it is certain that he received a copy of the arrangement made with the king's minifters, before he figned the preliminaries. Impediments were thrown in the way of the departure of the meffenger difpatched to Conftantinople, fo that he did not arrive till any interference of our ambaffador could be of no effect.

It is plainly to be feen, that though the emprefs pretended fhe had of her own accord (and before the arrangement with His Majefty was known to her general) concluded a

peace,

peace, the interference of His Majefty in bringing about that event had a weighty effect.

When the news of the figning the preliminaries reached the Ruffian fleet, it had beaten the Turks in the Black Sea, and was purfuing them into the channel of Conftantinople, where they muft inevitably have been deftroyed. Had the Ruffian admiral been a man of more experience, they might all have been taken in the engagement.

Thus ended a war, which, had it not been for the interference of Great Britain and Pruffia, would have placed the emprefs's grandfon on the throne of Conftantinople; and, had not circumftances imperioufly prefcribed to them the part they acted, we fhould have had, in Ruffia and Greece, allies which would, long ago, have enabled his majefty and the emperor, in all human probability, to have humbled a foe, which now threatens all Europe with total fubverfion, and even to become the inftrument of emancipating Greece from the Turkifh tyranny, not to become an independent people, but to be oppreffed by a worfe tyranny, under the name of liberty.

The Suliotes ftill maintain their independence : they were often attacked by the Turks, but were as often fuccefsful ; they

fought

fought feventeen battles or fkirmifhes, the
laft of which had nearly been fatal to them,
as appears by the following paper, communicated to me by a drogoman, now in the Britifh fervice, which will throw much light on
the character of the inhabitants of Epirus;
and it contains, befides, very curious and interefting matter. The authenticity of what
he relates cannot be called in queftion, as it
very exactly agrees with every other account
I have received.

In 1792, being in the French fervice as
interpreter, I was fent from Salonico by the
French conful, Mr. Cofenery, on fome bufinefs regarding the confulfhip, to Ali Pafha,
at Yanina, the capital of Epirus. I arrived
there the 1ft of May, and found the pafha
making great preparations for war. I found
alfo there the French conful of Prevefa, Mr.
de la Sala (a defcendant of the Salas, who
betrayed the Morea to the Turks, when in
the poffeffion of the Venetians) and acting as
commiffary, not only to provide timber in
Epirus for the French navy, but alfo for re-
volutionizing that country.

He communicated to me his commiffion,
infinuating, that if I would affift him, I might
expect great rewards. One day, when we
were with Ali Pafha, our converfation turned
upon the French revolution, which was always
introduced

introduced with a view to excite him to throw off all obedience to the porte. The pasha said to us—" *You will see that Ali Pasha, the* " *successor of Piros (Pyrrhus) will surpass* " *him in every kind of enterprize.*"

The pasha continued to assemble troops without making known his intentions. In July, his army consisted of 20,000 good Turkish soldiers, who were the more formidable, as they were all Albanians. He then declared, that his design was to attack the Mahomedan town of Argirocastro, situated twelve leagues distant from Yanina, which would not be governed by a person he sent for that purpose, nor anywise submit to him. With this excuse he wrote to Captain * Bogia and Captain Giavella, two of the most considerable of the chiefs of the Greek inhabitants of the mountain of Sulli, praying them to meet him with all their soldiers or companions, to assist in his expedition. His letter was in modern Greek, of which the following is a copy, which I insert, that the learned reader may see how much, or how little, it differs from the ancient.

Φιλοιμε Καπιτὰν Μπόζια κỳ Καπιταν Τζαβελλα, ἐγὼ
ὁ 'Αλỳ Ππασίας σὰς χαιρετῶ, κỳ σὰς φιλῶ τὰ ματία,
επειδὴ κỳ ἐγὼ ξεύρω πολλὰ καλὰ τὴν ανδραγαθείαν σας

* The Greeks call their chiefs captains.

κ̀ πwhich ωαλλικαρίαν σας μ̃ε φαινέται ναχω μεγάλην χρειαν
ἀπὸ λογᾶσας, λοιπὸν μὴ καμετε ἀλλέως ωαρακαλῶ, ἀλλ
εὐθὺς ὁπᾶ λαϐέτε τὴν γραφὴν μ̃ε, νὰ μαζοξέτε ὅλασας τα
ωαλλικάρια κ̀ νὰ ελθέτε νὰ μὲ εὑρετε διανὰ ωαγω, να ωολεμήσω τᾶς ἐχθρᾶς μ̃ε. τᾶτη ἴναι ἡ ὅρα κ̀ ὁ καιρὸς ὁπᾶ
ἔχω χρειαν ἀπὸ λογᾶσας, κ̀ μένω νὰ εἰδῶ τὴν φιλιαν
σας κ̀ τὴν ἀγαπην ὁπᾶ ἐχετε διὰ λογᾶ μᾶ· ὁ λᾶφεσας
θελει ἴναι δυπλὸς ἀπ' ὅσον δίδω εἰς τᾶς Αρϐανιτας διᾶ τὶ
κ̀ ἡ ωαλλικαριάσας ξεύρω πῶς ἴναι ωολλὰ μεγαλότερη
ἀπὸ τὴν εδικὴν τᾶς. λοιπον ἐγὼ δὲν ωάγω νὰ ωολεμήσω
ωρὶν νὰ ἐλθετε ἐσεὶς, κ̀ σὰς καρτερῶ ὁλλιγορα νὰ ἐλθετε.
ταῦτα κ̀ σὰς χαιρετῶ.

VERBAL TRANSLATION.

" *My friends, Captain Bogia and Captain Giavella, I, Ali Pasha, salute you, and kiss your eyes,
because I well know your courage and heroic minds.
It appears to me that I have great need of you, therefore I entreat you immediately, when you receive my
letter, to assemble all your heroes, and come to meet
me, that I may go to fight my enemies. This is the
hour and the time that I have need of you. I expect to
see your friendship, and the love which you have for
me. Your pay shall be double that which I give to
the Albanians, because I know that your courage is
greater than theirs; therefore I will not go to fight
before you come, and I expect that you will come soon.
This only, and I salute you.*"

I was present when the pasha's Greek se-
cretary wrote this letter, and I took a copy of
it,

it, it not appearing to him or to me as a matter of fecrecy.

Ali Pafha is an Albanian of Tepé-dellen ; he is a fon of Veli Pafha, who governed a part of Albania ; though a Mahomedan, he underftands very little Turkifh, and fpeaks only Greek and the Albanian language, which is a mixture of Slavonian, Turkifh, Greek, and a few old French words, but per-feƈtly unintelligible to thofe who underftand all thofe languages.

On receiving this flattering letter, the chiefs held a council with their men. Cap-tain Bogia, and the majority of the foldiers, thought the pafha's propofal was only a ftra-tagem to get them into his power, and make himfelf mafter of their mountain. Captain Bogia, in confequence, wrote to the pafha, that he received his letter with great refpeƈt and fubmiffion, and was himfelf ready to obey his orders ; but as he could not perfuade his people to follow him, it was unneceffary foi him to go alone. Captain Giavella, eithei through avarice or ambition, was induced to comply with the pafha's requeft, and went to his army, though only with feventy men. He was received with great marks of friend-fhip. The pafha and his army marched four leagues on the road towards Argirocaftro, and encamped ; but he fent an advanced

B b 4 poft,

poſt, confiſting of 400 men, under a buluk-
baſhee, as far as the town, and the people
making a ſortie, a ſkirmiſh enſued. Giavelli and his men were now perfectly convinced of the paſha's deſign, and laid aſide all
ſuſpicion; but ſix days afterwards they were
all ſeized unawares, as they were diſperſed in
the Turkiſh camp, and put in heavy irons,
except three, who, getting their arms, defended themſelves till they were ſlain. The
men were ſent to Yanina, and impriſoned
in the ſmall iſland which is in the Acheruſian
Lake, on the banks of which Yanina ſtands;
but Giavelli was kept in the camp. The
paſha immediately turned his march towards
Sulli, and arrived before the mountain the
next day. The Suliotes, who are always on
their guard, had notice of the paſha's approach, and of the fate of their countrymen,
ſix hours before he arrived. They aſſembled,
and gave the command in chief to Captain
Bogia, whoſe abilities they knew.

The mountain of Sulli, or Caco-ſulli, ſo
called on account of the ill the Turks have
experienced from them, is ſituated eight
leagues from Santa-maura (or Leucas) in the
Ionian Sea, having Prevaſa (Nicopolis) to
the ſouth-weſt, diſtant ten leagues; Yanina
to the eaſt, twelve leagues; and ſouth-eaſt,
Arta, diſtant eight leagues.

To

To the fouth, this mountain joins the Chimæra mountains, which are inhabited alfo by independent Greek Chriftians, allies of the Suliotes. On the eaft, at the foot of the mountain, is a fine plain of about fix fquare leagues, which is very fertile; in it they have built four villages, for the purpofe of cultivating the land; but in time of danger the inhabitants fly to the mountain. There being no water in the plain, they have funk cifterns or refervoirs to collect the rain.

The mountain is a natural ftrong fortrefs. Three fides are perpendicular precipices to the bottom. The top of the mountain they call Tripa, which fignifies a cavity. There is only one narrow fteep paffage to afcend to it, and it is defended by three towers, nearly a mile diftant from each other, fituated on eminences, where the road is moft difficult. The afcent is about three miles long. In the firft mile there is a village called Kapha, which fignifies top or fummit.

On the fide towards Chimæra there is a fmall brook, formed by the melting of the fnow of thofe mountains, from which, in cafe of need, the inhabitants of Sulli get water, by letting down fponges, as the fides are not even enough to let down any kind of bucket or other veffel; and this water cannot be cut off

by

by the Turks, as it is defended by the heights
of the mountains.

Captain Bogia ordered corn to be carried
from the villages to the Tripa, for fix months
provifions, as it is always kept in readinefs to
be tranfported; then the four villages were
evacuated; half of the inhabitants went to
Kapha, and the others to Tripa, their laft
afylum, which will contain ten thoufand men;
then, having more time, he threw into the
cifterns hogs and lime, and other naftinefs, to
prevent the Turks ufing the water.

The pafhas encamped in the villages, and
furrounded the mountain at a diftance, to prevent their receiving affiftance of troops from
the Chimæriotes, or ammunition from St.
Mara or Prevafa, whence they are always
fupplied. The main body of the Turkifh
army in the villages was commanded in perfon by the pafha; the corps towards Chimæra by his fon Mokhtar, pafha of Arta
(of two tails) and Captain Prognio, who was
a chief of the Paramathian Albanefe; the fide
towards Prevafa, was commanded by Mamed
Bey and Ofman Bey his brother; that on the
fide of Arta, by Soliman Ciapar, another
chief of the fame Albanian town of Para-
mathia, a man of eighty-five years of age, tall,
and of a fine gigantic ftature, having no appearance of age but the fnowy whitenefs of
his

his beard; he had with him eleven fons from thirty to fixty years of age, all tall and ftrong like their father: their bodily ftrength and perfonal courage caufed them to be looked on as heroes, and gave them a remarkable fuperiority among their countrymen: they went together, that if one fell the others might revenge his death; for among thefe people it is the cuftom, that relations go to the war together to revenge each other's death. Thofe who have the greateft number of relations are the moft powerful families, and the fathers of the principal families are their chiefs.

I will fpeak a little on the fubject of thofe Paramathian Albanefe. Their town is fituated twelve leagues diftant from Yanina; they poffefs a territory of twelve leagues in circumference, and can bring into the field 20,000 men. Their country is fo mountainous and inacceffible, that they have never been conquered by the Turks. How they became Mahomedans they do not know themfelves exactly; fome of them fay, that when the Turks firft invaded thefe countries, they made peace, on condition of becoming Mahomedans, and procuring their independence. They fpeak Greek, and know no other language; they look on the Turks and other Albanians as effeminate, and hold them in

the

the utmoſt contempt. They have no regular
government ; each family or relationſhip
(clan) adminiſters juſtice among themſelves.
The largeſt clans have the moſt influence in
the country in all public or general matters.
They are careful not to kill people of another
kindred, as the relations revenge his death,
and when once bloodſhed is thus begun, it
goes on till one of the clans is extinct. They
always carry their guns with them, whenever they go out of their houſes, and never
quit them ; even at home they are not
without their piſtols in their girdles; at night
they put them under their pillows, and lay
their gun by them beſide. The ſame precautions are obſerved in all theſe parts, except the town of Yanina. There are amongſt
the Paramathians, however, a conſiderable
number of Greek Chriſtians, who live all in
the ſame manner. Thoſe who are Mahomedans know little of their religion, or pay
little regard to it; their women are not veiled;
they drink wine, and intermarry with the
Chriſtians. It is true, indeed, that they will
not eat pork ; but if the huſband and wife are
of different religions, they make no ſcruple of
boiling in the ſame pot a piece of pork and
a piece of mutton.

All ſtrangers, Turks, Europeans, Greeks,
or others, who happen to paſs on their terri-
5   tory,

tory, or are caught by them, are carried to their public market, and there fold.

Being one day at Yanina, at the Greek archbifhop's houfe, I faw a Piedmontefe prieft, who, travelling in thefe parts, had been feized by the Paramatheans, and fold; his ftory, as related to me by the prelate, is as follows: Soliman Ciapar being at his houfe one day on a vifit, told him, that he had bought a Frank for four piaftres, but that he was good for nothing, and though he beat him daily, he could not make him do fo much work as his bread was worth; he would therefore, he faid, when he got home, kill him as a ufelefs beaft. The archbifhop offered to buy him for the four piaftres he had coft, and to pay the money immediately, if Ciapar would give fecurity (for here no one trufts another). The bargain being fettled, the Frank was fent: he proved to be a man of learning, and the archbifhop eftablifhed a fchool under his direction at Yanina, for Greek children. When I was there, he gained fifty and fixty piaftres a month, and was fo pleafed with his fituation and the kindnefs of the archbifhop, that he had refolved to remain in that country, and marry.

A ftranger might travel into thefe mountains, and would be treated hofpitably by the inhabitants, if, while he was in a neighbouring

bouring country, he put himfelf under the protection of a Paramathian, who would give fecurity for his being brought back fafe.

But to return to the pafha's expedition. The fecond day after the army had encamped in the plains of Sulli, the pafha caufed Captain Giavella to be brought before him, and told him, that if he would inform him how he could get poffeffion of the mountain, he would not only fpare his life, but make him beluk-bafhee of the province. Giavelli anfwered, that if he would fet him at liberty, he would go to the mountain, and engage his party, and at leaft half the inhabitants, to fubmit to him, and take up arms againft Bogia ; that by thefe means he could introduce the pafha's troops into the Tripa, when the other party would alfo be glad to make their peace without fighting. The pafha afked him what fecurity he would give for his performing his promifes. Giavella anfwered, he would give him as an hoftage his only fon, a boy of twelve years of age, who was dearer to him than his own life, that if he deceived him he might put his fon to death. Giavella accordingly called his fon down from the mountain; but as foon as he got to the mountain himfelf, he wrote to the pafha as follows :

" *Ali*

" *Ali Pasha, I am glad I have deceived a traitor ;
I am here to defend my country against a thief. My
son will be put to death, but I will desperately revenge
him before I fall myself.* • *Some men, like you Turks,
will say I am a cruel father to sacrifice my son
for my own safety. I answer, if you take the mountain, my son would have been killed, with all the rest of
my family and my countrymen ; then I could not have
revenged his death. If we are victorious, I may have
other children, my wife is young. If my son, young as
he is, is not willing to he sacrificed for his country, he
is not worthy to live, or to be owned by me as my son.
Advance, traitor, I am impatient to be revenged. I
am your sworn enemy, Captain Giavella.*"

The Greek original was :

Αλι Πασια, χαιρομαι οπȣ εγελασα έναν δολιον, ειμαι
δῶ να διαφευλευσω τὴν ωατριδα μȣ εναντιον εις ευαν κλεπῑην.
ὁ γος μᾶ θελει αποθανει εγὼ ὁμως απἑλπιϛως θελω τον
ἑκδικεισω ωριν να ἀποθανω. καπιοι Τȣρκοι καθως εσενα
θελȣν ειπᾶν ὅτι ειμαι ασπλαχνος ωατερας μετο να θυ-
σιασω, τὸν γον μȣ διὰ τὸν εδικον μȣ λιτρομον αποκρινομαι,
ὅτι αν εσυ ωαρεις το βȣνὸν θελης σκοτοσης τον γον μȣ
με το επιλιπον της φαμελειας μȣ κὴ τȣς συνπατριοτες μȣ,
τοτες δεν θα μπορεσω να εκδικησω τον θανατον τȣ αμή-
αν νικησωμεν θελει ἑχω ἀλλα ωεδια ἡ γενεκα μȣ ἦναι νεα.
εαν ὁ γος μȣ νεος καθὼς ἦναι δεν μενει ευχαριϛήμενος να
θυσιαϛὴ δια τὴν ωατριδα τȣ, αυτὸς δεν ἦναι ἄξιος να
ζηση κὴ να εγνωριζεται ὡς γος μȣ. ωροχορησε ἀπιϛε ειμαι
ανυπομονος να εκδικηθω.

Εγὼ ὁ ομοσμενος εχθρος σȣ,

Καπιταν Τζιαβελλας.

The

The pafha did not think proper in his rage to put the hoftage immediately to death, but fent him to Yanina, to his fon Velim-bey, who governed in his abfence. I was prefent when the boy was brought before him : he anfwered the queftion put to him with a courage and audacioufnefs that afto-nifhed every one. Velim-bey told him, he only waited the pafha's orders to roaft him alive. I don't fear you, the boy anfwered; my father will do the fame to your father or your brother if he takes them. He was put in a dark prifon, and fed on bread and water.

The pafha attacked the village of Kapha, and was repulfed three different times with great lofs, but Captain Bogia confidering the difparity of numbers, as the Suliotes had only 900 men in the Tripa, refolved to abandon this poft, which the Albanefe took poffeffion of the next time they attacked it, though with confiderable lofs, the Seliotes firing at them from among the rocks in fafety.

The pafha's troops, fuffering very much through want of water, which was brought to them fix leagues on horfes, as all thofe who attempted to fetch water from the brook under the Sulli mountain were killed by ftones the women rolled down on them, or fhot by the men, began to mutiny ; the pafha there-fore

fore determined to ftorm the Tripa the next day, and having affembled the principal officers, and chofen 800 Albanians, he expofed all his treafure in his tent, which confifted of Venetian ducats, and told them, it fhould all be diftributed among them if they took Tripa ; and that, befides, they fhould have all the immenfe riches which it was known were there. The next day the 800 Albanians, having at their head Mehmetember, and in the main body two fons of Soliman Chapar, and in the rear Captain Brogno, marched to the affault, and drawing their fabres, declared they would not fheathe them till they were victorious.

Captain Bogia left 400 men to garrifon Tripa, and fent four hundred to lie in ambufcade in the foreft on each fide of the road, with orders not to attack till the fignal agreed on was made from the fecond tower, in which he fhut himfelf up with fixty men, and from whence, by means of fignals, he commanded the movements. Giavella went with the troops into the foreft like a common foldier, the better to take his meditated revenge. The ambufcade was commanded by Demetrius, Bogia's fon.

The head of the Albanian column advanced without moleftation as far as the fecond tower, which they furrounded, and fum-

moned

moned Bogia to furrender. He replied, he could not truft himfelf to them, but would fubmit to Captain Brogno when he arrived; they therefore marched further up towards Tripa, leaving him, as they thought, a prifoner. The pafha's army, feeing the Albanefe had advanced without refiftance to the top of the mountain, and fearing to be deprived of a fhare of the plunder of Tripa, left their tents, and ran up the mountain with fhouts of victory. When Bogia faw that the enemy, in number about 4,000, had advanced to the third tower, which was near the Tripa, he rang a bell, the fignal for a general attack, which was a general flaughter: the ambufcade prevented any returning. They were in every part expofed to the fire of the Suliotes, who were covered by the rocks or the trees, and from the fecond tower Bogia made great havoc. The women from the heights rolled down great ftones, which for that purpofe are always piled up. The enemy defended themfelves, when the Suliotes came out to meet them, with great obftinacy; they were, however, all killed, except 140, who furrendered themfelves prifoners. Among them was a fon of Soliman Chappa, and many officers. The Suliotes had fifty-feven killed and twenty-feven wounded. Giavella was among the flain. After fhooting from the ambufcade a great

number

number of the enemy, he fallied out with fome of his friends, to avenge the fuppofed death of his fon, and to fight till all the enemy were killed, or he himfelf fell. After making a great havoc among the enemy, into the thickeft of whofe ranks he had ran forward with defperate valour, he fell, covered with wounds, and furrounded by heaps of flain.

The bodies being thrown down from the rocks into the Turkifh camp, ftruck the remainder of the army with fuch a panic that they fled with great precipitation towards Yanina, and abandoned the pafha. Bogia profited of their diforder to fend 200 men, who, falling on the rear, cut off great numbers. The pafha himfelf efcaped with difficulty, and killed two horfes before he got back to Yanina. All the baggage, ammunition, arms, provifions, and the pafha's treafure, fell into the hands of the Suliotes, befides four large cannon, which they drew up to the Tripa, and which were a great acquifition to them.

The other corps, towards Prevafa, Arta, and Chimæra, followed the example of the main body, and reached Yanina in great hafte. So great indeed was their panic, that none of them ftopt till they got within the

C c 2   walls

walls of the city, thinking they were still purfued by the Suliotes.

In the mean time, the communication
being opened with the Chimæriotes, the
Sulian army increafed in two days fo much,
that they found themfelves ftrong enough to
offer the pafha battle in the open plains.
They marched to an eftate of the pafha's
near Yanina, and took poffeffion of it,
whence they fent him a letter, threatening
to take him prifoner in his haram. They
purfued the Paramathians into their country,
where they cut down the trees, and drove
away vaft herds of cattle and flocks of fheep
to Sulli.

The pafha, apprehenfive for the fafety of
his capital, fent a bifhop to propofe peace
to the Suliotes. It was concluded on the
following conditions :

1ft. That the pafha cedes to the Suliotes
all the territory as far as Dervigiana (fix
leagues from Yanina) inclufively.

2. That all the Suliotes, who were prifoners, fhould be fet at liberty. (Then Giavella's fon returned fafe to Sulli.)

3. The pafha fhould pay 100,000 piaftres
as a ranfom for the prifoners the Suliotes
had made.

With the Paramathians they concluded a
                                    feparate

separate peace, as they are not dependent on the pasha.

The conditions were, that they should in future be allies, and that they should on all occasions succour the Suliotes, both with men, arms, and provisions, when they were at war.

Returned home to their mountain, the Suliotes divided the booty, and the 100,000 piastres, into five parts : one was destined to the repair of churches, which the Turks had damaged, and to build a new one on the Tripa, dedicated to the holy virgin ; the second part was put into the public box for the service of the community ; the third was equally divided among all the inhabitants, without distinction of rank or age ; the two other parts were distributed to the families of those who had lost men in battle.

This peace was soon broken by the pasha, who was twice afterwards defeated, and the Suliotes gained still greater honour.

The writer of this journal further says, that in this country there are ten Greeks to one Turk ; that the Sulian army always consists of about 20,000 men, including their nearest neighbours on the Chimæra mountains. He points out how easy it would have been for them to have put in effect

what

what their chiefs had concerted with the Ruffians. But I avoid entering into particulars, as I might give information to thofe who would make a bad ufe of it.

It was afterwards difcovered, that the French conful, Mr. de la Salas, had advifed the pafha to get poffeffion of Sulli and Chimæra, as then he would have nothing to fear from the porte, if he threw off all obedience ; and that the French could then fupply him with artillery and ammunition, &c. Mr. de la Sala was one day fhot dead in the ftreet at Prevafa by a captain of Lambro's fleet.

CHAPTER X.

*The Turkish Empire considered, with regard to
its Foreign Relations.*

THE preceding pages have shown the
internal situation of the Turkish empire; they have traced the progress of a power
founded in violence and rapine, growing up
in tyranny and injustice, and ultimately verg-
ing to corruption and decay. But it is not
enough to expose the defects of internal constitution and administration; to the politician
it must be matter of serious enquiry to learn
what are the foreign relations to which these
domestic arrangements give birth; what rank
in the scale of political importance such an
empire has obtained; and how its existence
has affected, and its approaching annihilation
will affect the interests of other states. This
view of the subject must, however, be taken
with great caution.

In the system of Europe, great and important changes have taken place, and the
balance of power, once a subject of so much

contention

contention and jealoufy, has received, and
is daily receiving, fuch fhocks as feem to
threaten its total fubverfion.

In the midft of this chaos we may ftill,
however, perceive the outlines of two grand
combinations of interefts dividing Europe
by their mutual oppofition.   At the head of
thefe confederacies may be placed the two
ancient rivals in opulence and glory, Great-
Britain and France; and however we may
be inclined, with philofophers, to lament that
there exift irreconcileable interefts, or political prejudices, which fow eternal difcord
between nations, on account of their vicinity
and power, it muft be reluctantly acknowledged, that fuch interefts and fuch prejudices
not only do exift, but are likely to become
ftill ftronger on the part of the French re-
publicans, who, while they preach univerfal
liberty, fraternity, and toleration to all mankind, act with a fpirit of inveterate hatred,
defpotifm, and infufferance, which the nar-
roweft prejudices, and the deepeft depravity
of human nature could only produce.

It may be obferved, that thefe two powers,
as well as moft of thofe that rank in the firft
clafs, have nearly the fame relationfhip of
interefts as heretofore; but the inferior ftates
are moftly thrown from their balance, many
of them either totally or partially annihilated,

lated, and feveral induced to form alliances
diametrically oppofite to their former principles of policy.

In order to explain the conneftion of
Turkifh politics with the general fyftem of
Europe, it will be neceffary to take into
confideration the particular interefts of the
different powers, and to fhow their relation
to the prefent or any future ftate of that
empire. Previoufly to this, however, a general fketch of the prefent fituation of things
may tend to elucidate our further difquifi-
tions.

The attachment of France to Turkey is
rationally founded on the great commercial
advantages which fhe enjoys from that nation ; on the ufe fhe makes of the porte to
form a diverfion in her favour, whenever the
fituation of her affairs on the continent requires
it ; and on her particular jealoufy of Ruffia,
which, by obtaining poffeffion of the paffage
from the Black Sea, might fend a naval force
into the Mediterranean, to the evident diminution of the French power and commerce.
The local fituation of the poffeffions of the
houfe of Auftria has ever made it an objeft
of jealoufy to France ; fhe has, therefore,
laboured to crufh, or at leaft to curb that
power, and finds an additional bond of friendfhip with the Turks in their hoftility to the
emperor.

emperor. Much light is thrown on this fubject by the papers printed at Paris fince the
revolution, entitled *Politique de tous les Ca-
binets de l'Europe pendant les Regnes de Louis
XV. et XVI.* It there plainly appears (did
we want proofs to convince us) that France
confiders Spain, Pruffia, and Turkey, as its
beft and moft natural allies; and that whenever it was connected in bonds of amity with
Auftria, it never confidered that alliance
otherwife than as a temporary convenience,
and fecretly entertained fentiments hoftile
to the profperity of that houfe; that it regarded the prefervation of the Turks as a
matter infinitely more important to her than
Poland or Sweden; that its jealoufy and
hatred to Ruffia, even when it courted her
friendfhip, and concluded a treaty of commerce with her, could only be equalled by
its hatred and its jealoufy of Great Britain.
We have no reafon to believe, that the republic thinks differently.

France then being by fyftem the avowed
or fecret enemy of the two imperial courts, it
is to her that the powers which have to dread
either of thofe courts will naturally look for
fupport.

Pruffia, whofe views of aggrandizement
depend in a great meafure on the ruin of the
houfe of Auftria; and Sweden and Denmark,

mark, who both look with envy or apprehenfion on the ftill growing power of the Ruffian empire, muft be induced by fuch motives to attach themfelves, when they dare, to France, and of confequence muft be inclined to fupport the Ottoman power.

It is by other views of policy that the nations in the fouth of Europe are directed in forming their alliances with France. Moft of the Italian ftates, by their comparative infignificance, are rendered neceffarily dependent, and by their fituation muft be led, either through fear or policy, to court the protection of that power, while Spain, ever jealous of the Britifh naval fuperiority, ever apprehenfive for the fate of her colonies, fees in France alone an ally fufficiently powerful to difpel her fears and to defend her interefts.

The reafons alledged for the connection of different nations with France will, in their converfe, point out the motives for alliance with Britain. Among the fecondary powers attached to us are Portugal and Naples; the one by long commercial habits, and a fear of its more potent and dangerous neighbour, Spain; the other, by a like apprehenfion of the French enmity, fecret or avowed.

On the fide of Auftria we fee an ancient
ally

ally again united to us by a recent treaty, and by a fimilarity of intereſt, which muſt continue as long as the ſecret or avowed connection ſubſiſts between France, Pruſſia, and Turkey.

Ruſſia, which has riſen to its preſent importance, even more by the policy of its monarchs than by the greatneſs of its population or territory, vaſt as they are, may in ſome meaſure be conſidered as removed, by its northern ſituation, ſo far from the ſphere of European politics, that it may occaſionally, and at its option, either enter into them, or preſerve a neutrality, as beſt ſuits its purpoſe; an advantage which no other ſtate poſſeſſes, and of which the empreſs is perfectly aware, having frequently avoided taking part in thoſe very conteſts which tended to promote her intereſts. Though Ruſſia has not long been raiſed to the ſituation ſhe now occupies, her army is the moſt formidable, and has many advantages over every other military eſtabliſhment in Europe: beſides a great naval force in the Baltic, ſhe has obtained a complete ſuperiority over the Turkiſh fleet in the Black Sea, both by the number and excellence of her ſhips, and the ſkill and courage of her ſailors, ſo that ſhe can open to herſelf a paſſage into the Mediterranean, and is now poſſeſſed of all the means, ſo long and

and fo perfeveringly purfued from the time
Peter the Firft took Afoph to this day, of
annihilating the monftrous and unwieldy defpotifm of the Ottoman fceptre in Europe.
The emprefs has alfo conceived the vaft and
generous defign of delivering Greece from its
bondage, and of eftablifhing it under a prince
of its own religion, as a free and independent nation. It was not long ago the policy of the Britifh cabinet to counteract thefe
fchemes of the emprefs (with what reafon
we will not now confider); but a conviction
of the fimilarity of her interefts with our own
now prevails; the Turkifh claufe (in all preceding treaties) was given up in the treaty
of 1795, and a war between Ruffia and Turkey now becomes a cafus fœderis with Great
Britain, and fhe is juftly confidered as our
moft valuable and moft natural ally.

If this general fketch of this fyftem of
Europe be juft, it will afford a clue to the
motives which have actuated, and are likely
to actuate the conduct of different powers in
their individual relations.

To return to FRANCE.—This nation,
ever verfed in intrigue and fertile in politicians, has appeared under all circumftances
to be beft inftructed with regard to the real
ftate of Turkey, and has fhown a conviction
of the weaknefs of its ally, at the very time
when

when it was moſt neceſſary to ſupport its
importance. Thus it was, that when the
Count de Vergennes (who by a long reſidence at the porte as ambaſſador, had obtained a thorough knowledge of the reſources
of the empire) was directed by the Duke de
Choiſeul to excite the Turks to war againſt
Ruſſia, he ſtated the moſt forcible reaſons
for an oppoſite line of conduct. Theſe reaſons, which were concluſive with the miniſter, were founded on the real weakneſs of
the Ottoman empire, and the falſe ideas of
its ſtrength entertained by ſeveral courts in
Europe, which it would have been ſo impolitic in France to have removed, by ſuffering
the Turks to engage in a war deſtructive of
their reputation. The ſame Count de Vergennes, when he became miniſter, inſtructed
Monſieur de St. Prieſt, to uſe every argument
which might induce the Turks rather to
yield to the demands of Ruſſia than to engage in a war.

The arrangement of the diſpute with Ruſſia in 1778 was attended with ſome ſingular
circumſtances. The Turks had, contrary to
the treaty of Kainargi, appoined a new khan
of the Crim, and ſent him with a fleet of
ſhips of war, in the latter end of 1777, to the
port now called Sebaſtopolis, to ſupport the
Tatars, whom they had before excited to

2   rebel

rebel againſt their lawful khan, Shaheen-Guerrai. On theſe grounds a war had nearly broken out, when the porte, after holding a ſecret divan, ſuddenly reſolved on peace, and notified their determination to Mr. Stachief, the Ruſſian envoy. He applied to the Engliſh ambaſſador, Sir Robert Ainſlie, to aſſiſt at the conference to be held, and act as mediator at the ſigning of the accommodation. Sir Robert, however (doubtleſs for good reaſons) refuſed, and Monſieur de St. Prieſt was ſent for, who readily accepted the office, and France appeared, on no other ground than the refuſal of our ambaſſador, as mediatrix. From this time Monſieur Stachief was ſo much governed by the French ambaſſador, that his court thought it neceſſary to recal him, as the empreſs by his conduct plainly perceived the tendency of the French councils to ſupport Turkey.

In 1783, when Ruſſia found it abſolutely neceſſary for her own ſafety, and the tranquillity of her ſubjects, who were continually expoſed to the incurſions of the Tatars, to take poſſeſſion of the Crim, and annex it to the empire, the French ſtill perſuaded the Turks to yield for the time to neceſſity, and rather to give up the Crim than run the riſk of loſing Conſtantinople itſelf.

The late emperor Joſeph had formed with the

the emprefs the plan of expelling the Turks
from Europe, and had obtained, as he
thought, the acquiefcence of France; but
that artful power unwilling to hazard, and
at that moment unable to fupport an open
conteft in favour of the Turks, employed all
its engines in fecret manœuvres for their
caufe.

The imperial courts difcovered thefe defigns, but not before France had prevailed on
Sweden to declare war againft Ruffia, after
the porte had imprudently, and contrary to
their advice, done it, and had by means of
M. de Choifeul-Gouffier negociated a fubfidy from Turkey to the Swedifh monarch.
The part too which they took, not only in
acquiefcing, but in urging Great Britain and
Pruffia to oppofe the progrefs of Ruffia, and
fupport the king of Sweden in that war, was
well known to the two imperial courts.

Since that time Auftria and Ruffia (other
circumftances having intervened) turned their
views to an alliance with his Britannic Majefty, and which has ftill been ftrengthened
by the declaration or triple alliance figned in
September 1795. Towards them, therefore, France muft retain an hoftile difpofition, while her connections with Spain, Pruffia, Sweden, and Turkey, refult from mutual
and natural interefts, as that with other ftates
does

does from motives of dependence and felf-prefervation.

SPAIN, notwithftanding the extent of her territories, and the immenfity of her refources if well managed, feems to have been degraded almoft to the rank of a fecondary power. Her colonial poffeffions, the fource of her apparent fplendor and of her political degeneracy, have become an object of fo much apprehenfion to her, that, unable to rely on her own force for their prefervation, fhe muft court the alliance of a more powerful neighbour. Of the two chief naval powers, Britain excites the greater jealoufy, as pretending to the command of the fea, and appearing ever intent on the extenfion of her commerce and foreign poffeffions. This antipathy is heightened, on the one hand, by the refentment with which Spain views on her own coaft the Britifh fortrefs of Gibraltar, as, on the other, her attachment to France has been cherifhed by intimacy, and by the mutual intereft which they have, to keep the northern powers out of the Mediterranean.

Of the influence of political opinions (whether monarchical or republican) in confolidating the union of the different parties, I forbear at prefent to fpeak, becaufe the principles which are here laid down as the

bafis

bafis of fuch union apply to the countries under whatever form of government they exift. So long as different nations retain the fame relations, commercial and political, which they now bear to each other, fo long will the general outlines of the fyftem of Europe, and its grand divifions of intereft, remain nearly as they are here reprefented. Opinion may, in fome inftances, be a motive more forcible than the permanent diftinctions of intereft, as in the cafe of the late war between Spain and France for the re-eftablifhment of monarchy; but thefe caufes are merely temporary, and however the difpute may terminate, recurrence will ever be had to thofe principles, which, being founded on local and effential diftinctions, have the greateft poffible degree of permanency. The French republic have proved, that they have the fame notions with refpect to the alliance with Spain as the monarchy had ; (the family compact was framed entirely by intereft ;) they look on it as " *the* " *moft effential as well as the moft natural* " *which France can form.*" Were monarchy to be re-eftablifhed in France, fhould we have made an ally of Louis XVIII. or a friend of one fingle emigrant?

PRUSSIA, which has been led forward to its prefent eminence by a train of fortunate
events.

events, muſt chooſe that ally which will beſt
enable it, not only to preſerve its ſituation,
but purſue its never-ceaſing projects of aggrandizement : it has, perhaps, ſometimes
to chooſe between France and Ruſſia ; but it
cannot rely on the latter ; tranſitory events
may unite their intereſts for a moment, perſonal predilection of ſovereigns may influence the option for a time, but no ſolid alliance can be formed : the partition of Poland
has ſown the ſeeds of diſcord, which, ſome
day or other, will ripen. With France no
ſuch circumſtances exiſt ; it is the country
which can procure to Pruſſia more advantages than any other, and in return receive
more from it. From Ruſſia and from England it has drawn occaſional means of aggrandizement, but it has always, even in
the moment of receiving their aſſiſtance,
looked on them with a ſuſpicious eye. Should
Pruſſia be ſeriouſly allied with Ruſſia, Auſtria muſt be leagued with France ; and ſhould
then a quarrel take place between the two
former, Pruſſia might not have it in its
power to break the Auſtrian alliance, and
join France in the moment of diſtreſs. It
is not probable this wily cabinet will throw
itſelf into the hands of a power, on which,
from many circumſtances, it can never for
any length of time rely. The aggrandize-

ment

ment of Pruffia muft be at the expence of the Houfe of Auftria, and the fyftem of the cabinet of St. Peterfburgh never will be to ruin that houfe.

Pruffia will temporize with the emprefs, but its prefent and future fyftem undoubtedly will be an alliance with France; for if Ruffia at any time be ill-difpofed to it, it has no other refource to rely on. The jealoufy of Auftria, at this moment, muft be excited to the higheft degree, by the concurrence of Pruffia with France in endeavouring to annihilate the Germanic confederacy. This conduct muft leave Pruffia without any other fupport but the directory, and, however matters terminate, will leave a deep rooted enmity in every part of Europe, which may ultimately have fatal confequences, and renew a combination againft a country which has loft its tutelar genius. To preferve his dominions from his powerful neighbours required all the talents of the great Frederic, and even he with difficulty was able to fave it from deftruction. Such talents are not again to be expected in a fovereign. That both France and Pruffia confider themfelves as *the moft* natural allies is obvious; that they confidered themfelves fo, even while other alliances exifted, is equally obvious. We need only to look to what has, in the latter part of this

this century, happened between France and
Auſtria—between Ruſſia, Auſtria, and Pruſſia—to be convinced that natural alliances will
ultimately prevail over temporary ſyſtems. It
would be ſuperfluous to enter into details ſo
well known. If the king of Pruſſia joined
Auſtria in the preſent war, it was to ſecure
the friendſhip of the monarchy, which he
then thought would be reſtored; when he
ceaſed to think that event practicable, he as
readily allied himſelf with the republic; his
object was the ſame, an alliance with *France*.
Pruſſia by this conduct prolonged the miſe-
ries of humanity; for ſhe cauſed a campaign
to fail, which would have ended them, and
turned a defenſive war in France to an offen-
ſive war out of it, which has nearly ruined
Europe. What is the fruit ſhe has reaped?
In this one campaign ſhe loſt the conſequence
which forty years of ſucceſs had given her.
The ſeeds of democracy and rebellion are
ſown in Pruſſia; moſt of the literati ſpread
them broadly, not to ſay a very great portion
of the officers of the army, and there is not a
country in Europe more ripe for revolution.
The treaſures which the great Frederic left
behind, and, what is ſtill a much greater loſs,
that ſpirit in the army, that emulation of
glory, that devotedneſs to their ſovereign's

D d 3 cauſe,

cause, which, more than its difcipline, made it fo formidable, have totally difappeared.

In 1791, the king of Pruffia had a ftanding army of above 200,000 men ready to act; the people fatisfied with their government, and attached to their king; the army had ftill the warlike fpirit which the great Frederic had breathed into it, and the treafures he left were not yet diffipated; he had fupplanted the emprefs in her influence in Poland, which was become formidable.

SWEDEN would fcarcely be efteemed of any confequence in Europe, did not its local fituation enable it to make a diverfion in favour of Turkey, by a war with Ruffia; to France it, therefore, has always appeared in the light of an ufeful ally, and has ever been affifted by her with fubfidies, and fupported with all her intereft; but, fince its decline, the fervices it is able to render are thought inadequate to its burthen, and the old connection is fupported, rather to prevent its forming new ones, than from the real affiftance it can afford.

If Sweden would purfue a line of ftrict neutrality, Ruffia has little temptation to difmember it any further; but another war would, moft probably, make the Gulph of Bothnia the frontier. It is to be hoped that

Sweden

Sweden now knows her real interest, which is, to be well with Ruffia, and to fuffer patiently what fhe cannot avoid. Such a fituation is humiliating; but has fhe refources in herfelf to rife above it? Certainly not, and that fhe has not is her own fault; a worfe fituation muft follow from a contrary conduct; and it is doubtful whether France and Pruffia united could, were they to turn all their force to fupport her, fave her from the talons of the Ruffian eagle.

However humiliating this ftate of dependence may be to the country, it is, undoubtedly, the only fecurity of the *crown* of Sweden. The people have received, by their connections with the French, during the minority of the prefent king particularly, fuch an augmentation of their former republican notions, that they are become, perhaps, more fanatic than many of the provinces of France. In the winter of 1795, the theatre at Norköping was fhut up; the people obliged the mufic to play *ça-ira*, of which they have an excellent Swedifh tranflation (by one of the profeffors of their univerfity) which they all fung in chorus.

It may not here be an improper digreffion, to take a flight view of the conduct of the late king of Sweden, in declaring war againft Ruffia, at a time when the emprefs

D d 4 fully

fully relied on his neutrality, and had every reaſon ſo to do, conſidering the intereſt of Sweden itſelf. That monarch, impelled by the common infatuation of ambitious princes, was eager to act a diſtinguiſhed part on the theatre of Europe, and to imitate the quixot-iſm of his illuſtrious predeceſſor, Charles XII. He ſeized the moment which appeared moſt favourable to his projects, when the armies of the empreſs were drawn down towards the ſouth, to oppoſe the Turks; but this very circumſtance made his aggreſſion ſo glaring, even to his own ſubjects, that the war was univerſally reprobated, and the Swediſh and Finland armies actually proteſted againſt it. So fully indeed had the empreſs relied on his neutrality, that the frontiers of her empire, on that ſide, were left without a force ſufficient for their defence; and it afterwards appeared that the king, could he have relied on the fidelity of his armies, might have marched without oppoſition to St. Peterſburgh, and made himſelf maſter of the imperial reſidence by *a coup de main*. Luckily for his country he only alarmed the empreſs, and the report of the cannon of his fleet only ſhook the windows of her palace. Had he effected his plan, whoever knows the empreſs, knows ſhe would never have laid down her arms till ſhe had taken ample vengeance.

The

The inconfiderate ambition of the king of Sweden appeared in the eagernefs with which he attacked the Ruffian fquadron on its way to the Mediterranean ; had he fuffered it to proceed to its deftination, the Swedifh fleet would have remained miftrefs of the Baltic.

It was in May 1788, that the Swedifh fleet failed from Carlfcrona with fealed orders, to be opened in the latitude of Gothland, to act offenfively againft Ruffia ; but the king's declaration of his motives for hoftility, though dated on the 21ft of July in the fame year, was not publifhed till Auguft. Thefe proceedings, contrary as they were in themfelves to the maxims which are generally acknowledged among civilized ftates as the law of nations, were grounded upon reafons equally nugatory and unjuft. They are conceived in the following terms : " *The declaration of war* " *made by the fublime Ottoman Porte againft* " *Ruffia was a new motive for the latter to re-* " *double its efforts in fowing confufion and trou-* " *ble in the bofom of Sweden, which, united by* " *an ancient and permanent treaty with the Ot-* " *toman Porte, concluded in* 1739, *and obliged* " *by that treaty not to abandon fo ancient an* " *ally, appeared formidable to Ruffia, &c.*"

" *His majefty, never deviating from his pa-* " *cific inclinations, is ftill defirous of peace, pro-* " *vided that the emprefs fhall offer him an ho-* " *nourable*

" *nourable one, and that the king shall be assured*
" *of procuring for the Ottoman Porte a firm*
" *and permanent peace.*"

The treaty of 1739, by which the king
pretended that he was bound to the Turks.
was not offensive, but defensive; and even
this was declared null and void by the firft
article of the treaty of Abo, concluded with
Ruffia in 1743, and the porte was, at that
time, officially informed of its abolition and
non-exiftence.

The late king of Sweden, guided by the
fame motives as the king of Pruffia, was
preparing to take an active part againft the
French republic, to fecure the friendfhip
of the re-inftated monarchy. After his death,
the regent, looking on the republican government as permanently fixed, purfued a different conduct, but having the fame view as his
brother, an alliance with France.

The conduct of Sweden during the re-
gency has been more hoftile to the allies
than is confiftent with the neutrality it profeffed; and had the allies liftened to the infinuations of the emprefs, it would have
been feverely punifhed for its partiality.
Had a war with Sweden in thefe circumftances taken place, in vain would Sweden
have relied on the co-operation of the Danifh
fleet; the emprefs might either have prevented

ed the junction, or, with a little affiftance, if not alone, have crufhed their combined force. The ifland of Bornholm lies ready for her to feize upon; and though at prefent it can boaft no harbour, that defect might be eafily remedied. From fuch a ftation the Ruf-fian fleet would be able to go to fea fix weeks earlier than the Swedifh from Carlfcrona, and confequently prevent their junction.

The Englifh politician may object, that it is the intereft of this country to prevent Sweden being fwallowed up by Ruffia: be that as it may, neither this country nor France can ferve Sweden more effentially, than by endeavouring to keep it well with Ruffia. Notwithftanding the fupport of the moft powerful allies, the ruin of Sweden muft be ultimately the refult of a conteft with its powerful neighbour.

DENMARK, we have feen, in the prefent war, which has involved the interefts of all Europe, purfuing the fame path of neutrality with Sweden, and united to it by a treaty; we have feen their combined fleets parading the Baltic and the North Sea, and profeffedly directed by the fame views, not of neutrality only, but almoft an open efpoufal of the French intereft, in defiance of the allied powers, whofe refentment they would have felt, had, as I have already mentioned, his

Britannic

Britannic Majefty not had more forbearance than the emprefs. It would have been eafy to have detached a fquadron from our fleet to have joined that of the emprefs, and put at once an end to the difpute, by annihilating the united Danifh and Swedifh navies. If they have efcaped, the danger they have run ought to make them more prudent in future.

The conduct of Denmark to the emprefs has been very ungrateful as well as imprudent.

Slefwick, which in 1762 threatened to draw upon Denmark the vengeance of the Ruffian arms, in 1776 was, at the inftance of the emprefs, guaranteed to that country by the two imperial courts, and fince, this guarantee has become ftill ftronger by the acceffion of his Britannic Majefty to it, in the triple alliance of 1795. On this fubject fhe is, therefore, perfectly eafy; but the local fituation and the relative weaknefs of that kingdom muft make it ever dependent on Great Britain and Ruffia. The alliance with Sweden can be but a temporary arrangement, however ardently the court of Copenhagen may wifh to make it permanent, through the fupport of France. Small ftates muft, in external relations, be dependent on greater; an equality of power among fovereigns is

as

as vifionary as among individuals. Has this levelling mania feized the kings of Denmark and Sweden as well as their fubjects?

SARDINIA deferves particular confideration, as its importance feems to have been falfely eftimated. To fecure the paffes of Italy againft the inroads of the French was indeed a point of the utmoft importance; but the ability of the court of Turin to fecond fuch views has long ceafed, and its interefts feem at prefent to take a contrary direction. The queftion is no longer whether Savoy fhall be preferved ; that country was difaffected long before the French revolution; it was governed with a rod of iron; the nobility and the peafantry were alike diffatisfied, and it was a general complaint, that the name of Savoyard was an infurmountable bar to promotion in every department of the ftate : fuch was its fituation when it was attacked by France; and befides this internal difaffection, it had other caufes of weaknefs, arifing from preceding political events.

During the long contefts between France and the Houfe of Auftria (the former wifhing to gain admiffion into Italy, the latter to prevent it) the alliance of Sardinia was courted, as poffeffing the command of fo ftrong a barrier. Hence arofe the importance

ance of the court of Turin, which, in changing allies as opportunity prefented itfelf, gained fomething by every treaty, and was enabled, by fubfidies, to difcipline and keep on foot a formidable force ; but when the French refigned all pretenfions to the Milanefe and the grand duchy of Tufcany, the king of Sardinia, who no longer found himfelf courted by contending parties, neglected that military force, which he had neither motive nor ability to fupport, and funk by degrees into a ftate of comparative infignificance. From this he was for a fhort time called, and enabled to act a more diftinguifhed part, by the alliance of Auftria and the fubfidies of Britain; but thefe proving infufficient, the paffes of Italy have fallen into the hands of the French. It is to be expected that Sardinia will always remain an ally, if not become a province of France, on whom it is now entirely dependent. In fact, it always was a fecret enemy to Auftria, and never favoured its caufe, but temporarily for the fake of aggrandizement, and the aggrandizement it moft coveted was at the expence of that houfe.

NAPLES is capable of poffeffing a confiderable marine, and might become a naval power of no fmall importance in the Mediterranean. The reafons which influence

Spain

Spain to take part with France have no weight with the Neapolitan court; it has no colonies to lofe, no jealoufy of our trade, or of our influence in the Mediterranean. (The former fituation of Naples, under the immediate influence of Spain, has no relation to its prefent, or to its true intereft.) To it Great Britain muft appear as a valuable ally. France has long been its fecret enemy, and has ufed every exertion to prevent it from becoming a naval power. It muft ever remain in a ftate of dependence and fubjection, if England and its allies are excluded from the Mediterranean. Every augmentation of naval force in that quarter, which can cope with the fleets of France and Spain, muft therefore be a defireable object to Naples, as on that alone her fafety and profperity depend. No country has fo much to lofe by the eftablifhment of French influence in Italy as Naples.

Austria, the ancient, and (at leaft at prefent) the moft natural ally, after Ruffia, to Great Britain, the natural protector of Germany and Italy, and the natural balance againft France, has evinced her exertions in the prefent war, her firmnefs in fupport of the common interefts fhe has with this country. The fupport which fhe derived from the finances of Great Britain was, indeed,

deed, neceſſary for her to make ſuch exertions.   Her armies were brave, well diſciplined, and numerous ; her reſources in men
inexhauſtible ; but her treaſury was inadequate, and ſhe entered upon a diſaſtrous
conteſt under circumſtances peculiarly diſ-
advantageous.   Pruſſia, without being the
friend, acted on this occaſion as the ally of
Auſtria.   If any cauſe was of ſufficient magnitude to have ſilenced their jealouſies and
conſolidated their plans, ſurely it was that in
which they were embarked, by an intereſt
hitherto unknown in the annals of hiſtory, a
general intereſt, which cruſhed all individual
intereſts of nations, and which appealed no
leſs to the paſſions of monarchs than to the
policy of all civilized ſtates.   The ſequel,
alas ! is too well known.   The French have
ſucceeded in diſſolving the alliance, by convincing the king of Pruſſia that their government was unſhakeable ; they recurred
to their old policy, *divide et impera.*

Pruſſia has entered into their project of ſe-
parating the members of the Germanic body ;
the French monarchy guaranteed their union ;
but the aim of both was the ſame, the humiliation of the Houſe of Auſtria.   This
they in part effected by the peace of Weſt-
phalia, the war preceding which, borrowing
the pretext of religion, was in effect a war

of

of policy; nor have they fince that period neglected this grand object, either in the open exertions of war or the more fubtle efforts of intrigue; hence it is, that we fhall ever find the Turks in all their contefts with the emperor, however unjuft, ftrengthened by the aid and affifted by the councils of France; and hence it is, on the other hand, that the Houfe of Auftria muft look with confidence to the fteady fupport of Great Britain. Indeed we may not only with juftice contend for the prefervation of the emperor's prefent poffeffions, but favour their extenfion, for the purpofe of ftrengthening him on the coaft of the Adriatic and 'in European Turkey, a part of which more naturally belongs to him than to Ruffia or the Greeks, were the Turks driven out of Europe.

RUSSIA, the moft powerful, the moft natural, and the moft ufeful of our allies, has fo intimate a connection of interefts with us, that the foundeft policy muft dictate to us an union of defign and a co-operation in action. Her commerce with Great Britain is of the utmoft confequence to her, as it produces a clear annual balance in her favour, from a million to a million and a half fterling. In the courfe of laft year there entered into the port of St. Peterfburgh alone 533 Britifh fhips, which carried thence Ruffian products

E e   to

to the value of £. 2,400,000 fterling; at the fame time, the greateft number of veffels employed by any other nation was eighty-fix (Danifh fhips) and the greateft value exported was £. 80,000 fterling by the Portuguefe. Yet is the Ruffian trade of great importance to England, as fhe thence draws moft of her naval ftores, and employs therein feveral hundred veffels, and many thoufand feamen. Since the emprefs has added to her dominions the reft of thofe countries where hemp is produced, we are more dependent on her than heretofore; yet not fo much, perhaps, as the Ruffian miniftry imagine, for reafons which it is eafy to point out, but which it would be foreign to the purpofe of this treatife to fpecify. When the trade of France to Ruffia is put in comparifon with this, it will be found very inconfiderable indeed. The year after their treaty of commerce, in which they had all the advantages they could wifh, the French took from Ruffia exports only to the amount of £. 50,000 fterling. They have full liberty to extend their commerce to the Ruffian ports in the Black Sea, but it has been hitherto too inconfiderable to deferve notice, or to be put in comparifon with the lofs of trade they would fuftain were the Turks driven out of Europe. Trifling however as their exports

ports

ports are, their imports are very confiderable, not only in articles which come direct from France by fea, but rich ftuffs and jewels, and other articles of luxury, which go either by land, or to the German ports in the Baltic, and thence find their way into Ruffia, a confiderable part of which are fmuggled.

Ruffia is not our rival on the feas, nor we her's on the continent; fhe ftands in need of our affiftance at fea, and we of her's by land; her intereft dictates to her the fame alliances as our intereft dictates to us; we are rivals in nothing; the profperity of the one country is the increafe of ftrength in the other; with her alliance we can protect our friends on the continent, or humiliate our enemies; with our alliance her fleets may fail in fafety to all parts of the globe, and chaftife thofe who have provoked her. Even in the trade between the two countries there is no rivalfhip; her products, partly manufactured and partly raw, brought by a long land carriage from diftant provinces to her ports (which is in itfelf a beneficial branch of commerce) find in our merchants the *only* purchafers; they tranfport them to our ports in our own fhips: neither in this is there any rivalfhip, for Ruffia has no mercantile navy; but to compenfate that circumftance the balance of trade is immenfely in her favour. In

fhort,

fhort, there is no fingle point in which we can be rivals, except it be, which fhould be more arduous in cultivating the ties of friend-fhip.

It is the intereft of this country, as muft appear from what has been faid, that the em-prefs fhould keep Sweden and Denmark in awe, as well as the Pruffian ports, to prevent them from fupplying France with naval ftores, &c. in time of war. On the other hand, our intereft requires that fhe fhould have the command in the Black Sea, in order not only to open its ports to us, but to fend us fuccours into the Mediterranean, to oppofe the formidable combination of France and Spain. Indeed it is difficult to conceive, amid the variety and difcordance of political interefts, the exiftence of two great powers, between which there are fo many mutual dependencies and fo few caufes of jea-loufy.

The emprefs of Ruffia has been accufed of inconftancy in her alliances, of inconfiftency in her politics, and of only having had in view to profit by the circumftances of the day. It muft, however, *now* be obvious, that though fhe ufed different means to ac-complifh her ends, fhe never deviated from the fyftem fhe adopted the firft year of her reign, and that, if fhe changed her friends, it it was becaufe fhe thought that fhe could no longer depend on them.

In every political connection fhe formed, fhe had conftantly in view the expulfion of the Turks from Europe, and the reftoration of the Greek empire. As long as the power fhe had allied herfelf with feemed to favour thefe projects, fhe was fteady in her attachment to it; the inftant it difcovered jealoufy of, or oppofition to them, fhe facrificed every other confideration, and became its fecret enemy. Nor has the prefent emprefs alone had in view the accomplifhing this vaft defign; Peter the Great firft conceived the idea of its being fome day practicable, and the cabinet of St. Peterfburgh have never loft fight of it during the fucceeding reigns, to this day.

The emprefs declared unequivocally her intentions, in her manifeftoes to the Greeks, during the war which took place with the Turks foon after her acceffion to the throne, in confequence of her interference in the affairs of Poland, which was only a preliminary ftep to fubjugating the Turks. It was neceffary to fecure to herfelf the refources for her armies, which Poland afforded. Subfequent accidents have indeed annihilated the government and independence of that country,

The

The ardour with which his Britannic Majefty efpoufed the caufe of the emprefs in that war, by the affiftance afforded her fleet, and in forcing France and Spain to confent to its entrance into the Mediterranean, by a pofitive declaration that a refufal would be confidered by His Majefty as an act of hoftility to him, attached her fo zealoufly to the caufe of Great Britain, and fixed in her mind a predilection, not only for its government but for individuals, that nothing could fhake it but an oppofition to her favourite meafures, which fhe confidered as her deareft interefts, and which were to crown her reign with eternal glory.

Her devotednefs to Great Britain excited in the cabinet of Verfailles the higheft jealoufy, and it laboured inceffantly, by every means, to weaken the connexion.   It would be an endlefs tafk to recite all the manœuvres of the French, till they unluckily fucceeded: they reprefented our trade with Ruffia as a monopoly, ruinous and infulting to its fubjects; they excited doubts of the fincerity of our attachment to Ruffia, and of our hearty co-operation in her favourite fchemes; they infinuated that our views were only to keep her navy in fuch a ftate of dependence as not to be able to act without our concurrence, and to proceed in its fucceffes only as far as

we

we chofe to permit it; at length they formed, at an enormous expence, a party in the emprefs's cabinet to counteract us.

The emprefs's fecond grandfon was born in January 1779. He was named Conftantine. Greek women were given him for nurfes, and he fucked in with his milk the Greek language, in which he afterwards was perfected by learned Greek teachers; in fhort, his whole education was fuch as to fit him for the throne of Conftantinople, and nobody then doubted the emprefs's defign.

In this fame year (1779) the emprefs had determined on giving his Britannic Majefty an *effective* affiftance againft his rebellious fubjects in America, fupported by the *crown of France.* Prince Potemkin, who to the laft day of his life affirmed that the fuccefs of the enterprize againft Turkey depended on the alliance with Great Britain, had the fole management of this bufinefs, and without the concurrence of Count Panin, the minifter for foreign affairs, and the partifan of the French, who, fufpecting, or having fome information of what was going on, employed a Mademoifelle Guibal, governefs to one of Potemkin's nieces, to fteal the papers from under the prince's pillow, and after feeing the contents, to replace them fo carefully that it was fometime afterwards before he difcovered how

E e 4 he

he was betrayed.   Count Panin found means, to retard the figning of the inftrument already drawn up, and produced another project, which flattered the emprefs's vanity more, the *armed neutrality*, which was firft conceived by the late king of Pruffia.   This Potemkin oppofed with all his might ; the argument he ufed was, that if the other neutral nations, who had good veffels and experienced failors, were to enjoy the fame privilege as the Ruffians had by the treaty with Great Britain, of carrying hemp, &c. to France in time of war, Ruffian fhips would never be employed; but that a contrary conduct would create a Ruffian mercantile navy, which then did not exift.   He was over-ruled.   No argument could withftand the affurance Count Panin gave, that the French entered heartily into the project of the emprefs with refpect to the Turks (whom, unable any longer to defend, they had abandoned) and that the Britifh court never would confent to it.   The conduct of the prince on this occafion was not candid : when he could not carry his point, he ranged himfelf with his adverfaries, and received from the emprefs a prefent for his fhare of the labour in bringing about the armed neutrality (as was mentioned in the ukafe.)   He did not communicate it to Sir James Harris (who had conducted the nego-

I   tiation

tiation in the moſt able manner) till it was ſigned, and a ſyſtem adopted highly inimical to the intereſts of Great Britain. The empreſs ſoon after went to Mohilov to meet the emperor Joſeph, whom Mr. de Vergennes had perſuaded, that his court had given up the cauſe of the Turks, and he led the empreſs into her error, which Prince Potemkin lamented to the day of his death.

The empreſs, and particularly Potemkin, were very anxious to obtain from His Majeſty a ceſſion of the iſland of Minorca, which was intended as a ſtation for her fleet, and a rendezvous for the Greeks. Soon after the propoſal was made it was taken from us. The empreſs might have aſked it of the king of France, had it been taken in his name, to prove the ſincerity of his friendſhip. The time it was attacked, and the circumſtance that it was ſo, and in the name of the king of Spain, ſhows that the court of France had good information from Peterſburgh.

The conduct of Mr. de Vergennes (one of the moſt indefatigable and univerſally intriguing miniſters, as well as moſt perfidious, that ever preſided in a cabinet) ſhould have opened the eyes of our coalition miniſters in 1783. After he had ſounded them, and found that they would not aſſiſt the Turks nor the Ruſſians, he not only promiſed to the

emperor

emperor the opening of the Scheld, but the exchange of the Netherlands for Bavaria; and the emprefs was fo hearty in his caufe, that fhe ordered her minifter at Frankfort to make a formal propofal of this exchange to the Duke of Deux Ponts. Had we then rightly underftood our intereft with refpect to Turkey, we fhould have joined in the league with the two imperial courts to effectuate this exchange. The offer would have been eagerly accepted; we fhould have completely duped the court of Verfailles, whofe inability to act was perfectly well known at Vienna and Peterfburgh; and Mr. de Vergennes well knew, that if Pruffia, Great Britain, and Holland, oppofed the exchange, it would not take place, notwithftanding the ferious face he might put on in the comedy he was then acting; he was not only eafy on that head, but he had the fatisfaction to widen the breach between his Britannic Majefty and the two imperial courts. The king of Pruffia faw into the true views of the French court, and was under no apprehenfion of offending it ultimately, while he was purfuing with all his might his own intereft, in preventing the very confiderable augmentation of power which would have accrued to the Houfe of Auftria.

I have fince learnt that the emprefs even then

then began to conceive fufpicions of the fincerity of the profeffions of France, and never
could be perfuaded by the emperor, that,
though their finances were in the worft ftate
poffible, they might not have lent an army to
him to prevent the Dutch oppofing the opening of the Scheld.

The emprefs, with great dexterity, on this
occafion became a guarantee to the treaty of
Weftphalia, and by it acquired a right to interfere in the internal affairs of the Germanic
empire.

From that period to the ever-memorable
Ruffian armament in England, the cabinet
of St. Peterfburgh acted in the moft unfriendly
manner to us. France had concluded a treaty
of commerce with Ruffia, from which great
advantages were expected ; but it proved that
all the encouragement given to it could not
increafe it ; on the contrary, the trade of
Great Britain, oppreffed in the moft unjuft
manner, was confiderably augmented. The
alliance between the two imperial courts and
France, and the great partiality fhown to the
latter ; the apprehenfion of the Turks being
driven out of Europe under circumftances
highly dangerous to this country, and fuch an
arrangement for a partition being made as
would have greatly increafed the power of
France, and made the bonds of amity, thus

nearer

nearer drawn together, durable, were fufficient reafons with His Majefty's minifters to
take that meafure. The dignity as well as
the intereft of the country required it at that
particular period, though that was not the
cafe before, nor has it been fince; and it muft
appear evident, that we cannot *now* reafon
on the principles we did *then*, and that we
now muft clearly fee our intereft both with
refpect to Ruffia and Turkey. After the
fleet was fitted out, and the object declared, it
became the dignity of the nation to have let
it fail, and if Mr. Fawkener was to be fent,
he fhould have gone with it.

The friends of Mr. Fox pride themfelves
much in having prevented the fleet's failing;
but let them be ever filent on the partition of
Poland, for their meafures undoubtedly occafioned it *. What might have been the
event of fuch a war it is difficult to forefee;
much conjecture may be made ; I will only
mention one circumftance, the naming of
which is alarming, however it may be treated
as romantic: the emprefs had firmly refolved
to attempt to fend an army through Bochara
and Cafhmeir, to place the Mogul on the

* Since this was written, the emprefs is dead, and I
have no fcruple now of declaring, that that unfortunate monarch accufes them of it; and if they doubt of it, there are
thofe in England who can produce proofs of it.

throne

throne of India, and drive the Britifh out of their poffeffions, and there were then in Ruffia Frenchmen, who had been fent into thofe parts by Mr. de Vergennes, and who offered to conduct the army. If Mr. Fox's friend, Mr. Adair, had the intereft of his country at heart, and not the removal of Mr. Pitt, why did he make no advantage of the ardent defire Prince Potemkin then had of feeing his court allied with Great Britain ? In fpeaking with me about Mr. Adair, he expreffed this defire in the ftrongeft terms. The emprefs then knew the treachery of France. She made the difcovery in the autumn of 1788, by the intrigues of the French at Stockholm (where fhe always had a ftrong party) and this was proved to her in a ftill ftronger manner by the difcovery that was made of the part which the Count de Choifeul-Gouffier had in the negotiating a fubfidy from the porte to Sweden; yet the emprefs was too high fpirited to confefs fhe had been duped, though fhe wifhed fecretly to change her alliance with France for one with this country. This fortunate event has at length taken place, and with no degrading circumftances to the country. His Britannic Majefty has given up the Turkifh claufe, and a war with Turkey is become a *cafus fœderis*, a condition without which fhe never would fign any

treaty

treaty with any power. That His Majefty's prefent miniftry faw the real intereft of the Britifh and the Ruffian empires, when that claufe, *fine quâ non*, of the treaty was given up, I hope muft appear evidently, as well as that their conduct has been uniformly guided by the true intereft of their country, which they followed as it varied, and neither loft fight of that nor of its honour, an object furely every true Briton confiders as dear.

To enter into a longer detail of circumftances to prove what is here advanced would be fuperfluous, as it muft appear fo very confpicuous to every one, except to thofe whom no arguments can convince, and who pronounce declamatory fentences inftead of inveftigating facts. If thofe who oppofed the vigorous and once neceffary meafures of this country will pleafe to talk of inconfiftency, I am ready to meet them on that ground, and perhaps I may be able to prove more than inconfiftency on their part.

Of later events I fhall not now fpeak: the fituation I have been in might involve me in a cenfure of breach of confidence.

How far the king of Pruffia had an underftanding in this bufinefs with the French court I have no documents to prove; but that he did fecond its views admirably well, both with refpect to Auftria and Turkey,

facts

facts prove. His conduct towards others needs no animadverfion : he firft encouraged the Poles to form their new conftitution; then he made it a crime in them to have formed it ; and laftly, he joined with the emprefs to overfet it. The emprefs accufes him of being the firft to infift on the final partition as a *fine qua non*, and as the price of his co-operation againft France ; a circumftance not then known to his Britannic Majefty's minifters. The emprefs knew too well their fentiments to rifk the communication of fuch a tranfaction. How completely the court of Berlin has duped all thofe who have been connected with it (France only excepted) not only in its engagements to his Britannic Majefty and to the emprefs, on this occafion, but in every other, is fo ftriking, that it ought by this time to have convinced the courts of London and Peterfburgh of the imperious neceffity of cementing, by every poffible tie, the prefent connection with the Houfe of Auftria, and making its intereft their own. A deviation from fuch a conduct by either of the powers muft obvioufly be the ruin of Europe.

Ruffia, however, in the eyes of the body politic of Europe, is a new power ; they ftill feem to regard her only as a huge unformed mafs,

mafs, giving a rude fhock to the countries
which her frontier touches ; they do not yet
feem to perceive her fliding into every tranfaction on the continent of Europe, and planning in the dark, and with unremitting perfeverance purfuing projects which are to
ripen at once, and to aftonifh by their effect,
not on her neighbours, not in our days only,
but on the moft remote regions of the globe,
and in future ages.   Something of this lately
flafhed on them like lightning ; they perceived that the prefent emprefs had become, they fcarcely knew how, a party in the
treaty of Weftphalia, concluded before Ruffia politically exifted, and that her guarantee
entitles her to interfere in the affairs of the
German empire.   The flafh, which afforded
a tranfitory view, dazzled the eyes of fome,
and they feem now more blind.

The means of this fovereign are vaft and
incalculable, and her will can employ them
without oppofition : her financial refources,
fo far from being exhaufted, are not touched * ; a population of more than thirty
millions, of whom not one half has been
called on to contribute to the exigencies of

---

* I do not fpeak of prefent temporary embarraffment,
but of real refources, which have not yet been recurred to,
and of which I fhall treat on another occafion.

the

the ſtate; a peaſantry looking on the monarch as a divinity, and ſtiling him *God of
the earth* (zemnoi bog); ignorant of any government but a deſpotic ſceptre, and of any
condition but vaſſalage; happily deprived of
all means of evil information, and ſecured
from rebellion by the want of communication and the diſtance of places: a ſoldier
content with rye-biſcuit and water, blindly
obedient to diſcipline, and ſuffering privation
and hardſhip with a patience unknown to
other nations; active, and peculiarly docile,
they are eaſily taught the uſe of arms; the
habit of conquering inſpires them with contempt of their enemies, and raiſes a courage
naturally inherent in robuſt conſtitutions, if
not to heroiſm, to actions worthy of heroes.
If tactics have been lately neglected, it has
been owing to the unſkilfulneſs of their officers, of late promoted almoſt entirely by
favour, and ſerving only to obtain rank and
then retire; but this may be eaſily reſtored
by a commander in chief, or a ſovereign,
poſſeſſed of much leſs military capacity than
a Frederic: a nobility unable to offer the
leaſt oppoſition to the crown, depending on
it for every honourable diſtinction of rank,
civil or military, conferred, but not inherited;
without which neither birth nor fortune
give conſideration, and which he who be-

F f   ſtows

ftows can take away, while they who fuffer muft blefs his name: not united by any common tie as a collective body, their interefts are merely thofe of individuals.

There is no law but the " *exprefs com-* " *mand*" of the monarch, who can debafe the higheft fubject to the condition of a flave, or raife the loweft to the firft dignity of the empire ; but this autocratic fceptre exercifes no defpotifm over the fubject infulting to mankind. The Ruffian monarch is not, like the ftupid Ottoman, feated on a throne involved in black clouds of ignorance, fupported by cruelty on one hand, and by fuperftition on the other, at whofe feet fits Terror, and below Terror, Death. No fovereign in Europe is poffeffed of more information, has more judgment to digeft it, or in whom the refult is more confummate wifdom. So far from the reign of the emprefs being a reign of terror, its fault is, too much lenity to her fubjects, particularly to the great. No princes have received a better education than her fon and grand-children, and the court which furrounds them is as brilliant and polifhed in manners as any in Europe.

The gloomy melancholy and folemn ftupidity of the Turks is as little obfervable on the countenance of a Ruffian, as the murderous ferocity and enthufiaftic fury which
distorts

diftorts the cadaverous phyfiognomy of the
French brotherhood; there is a fmile dif-
fufed over the face of the whole country. I
appeal to all thofe who have travelled in
Ruffia, whether they ever faw more hilarity
in any part of the world. I do not mean to
recommend for imitation fuch a ftate of
things to make men happy; thofe who have
been removed from it cannot go back again;
but I affirm, that the whole mafs of the
people appear to be more happy (and it is a
hard thing to make a man laugh when he
is not pleafed) than any I have feen in three
parts of the globe. There is no medium in
liberty with refpect to the happinefs of the
people; to be happy a nation muft be perfectly free or perfectly paffive. Perfect liberty excludes licentioufnefs: a people cannot be faid to be free where there exifts a
power to annoy with impunity either them
or their magiftrates; a little liberty, " like
" *a little learning, is a dangerous thing,*" becaufe it is not underftood. Liberty has been
no where underftood (no not in Athens) but
in this happy ifland. Here our government
is founded on reafon, and reafon will fupport,
or, if any part of it goes to decay, amend
it; it is the glory of the human underftanding; it is the pride of the moft enlightened
people on earth, whofe happinefs is its ob-

F f 2   ject,

ject, and it will stand for ever, if it have only reason to combat.

After having considered the external situation of TURKEY in various points of view, in each of which it seems little to deserve the approbation of the enlightened, or the support of the politician, we come to observe it as a member of this grand confederation of the nations of Europe, whose interests and political connections I have cursorily passed in review.

Its dominion was founded in blood; it is upheld by systematic terror and oppression, and the tyrants themselves, enervated by the licentiousness of their rapacity, and lost in the gross ignorance of habitual despotism, are as weak and ignorant at home, as they must appear abroad contemptible and insignificant. Interested views, it is true, have caused their alliance to be courted by France, but it is by no means improbable that that country, when it finds itself unable to defend its ally, may, with its usual versatility, readily join in their destruction. Great Britain can only anticipate such an event by cultivating the friendship of Russia and of the Grecian state, which must arise from the ruins of the Turkish power. Strengthened by such an alliance, we should maintain that ascendancy in the Mediterranean, of which

which the union of France and Spain threatens to deprive us.

That Turkey muſt very ſoon be over-whelmed by the empreſs, appears from a compariſon of her financial reſources, her army and her marine, with thoſe of the Ot-toman power. Conſtantinople itſelf cannot be conſidered as a tenable poſt; and when the diſaffection of the enſlaved Greeks is taken into the account, little doubt can be entertained, that the followers of Mahomet will be entirely driven from the countries in Europe which they have uſurped, whether England conſent or not.

How they came to decide on the late war appears very enigmatical. That their French counſellors were better informed than to have recommended ſuch a ſtep is certain. It has been attributed to the advice of the Engliſh ambaſſador; but this has been contradicted, both by his ſolemn denial and by the expreſs declaration of his court, that no ſuch in-ſtructions were given him. Among the Turks themſelves it was regarded, by every man of information, as raſh and impolitic; and the great captain-paſha, Gazi-Haſſan, was in the higheſt degree offended at the proceeding. The declaration of war took place while he was abſent in Egypt. His plan was, to ſubjugate the rebellious or diſ-

affected

affected provinces, which he wifely confidered as a neceffary preliminary to the engaging in any foreign conteft. He began with Egypt. The vizir Yufuf, and his party in the divan, hurried on the declaration of hof-tilities, when it was too late in the feafon for any hoftile movement to be made, except the infignificant and ill-combined attack on Kilburn, unprepared as the Turks were. In the winter, when the Bog was frozen over, the garrifon of Ochakof furprifed a Ruffian village on its banks, and murdered all its defencelefs inhabitants, confifting of above a thoufand fouls, *not one* of whom was fpared. This wanton piece of cruelty coft them dear at the capture of that place. The Ruffian army, which went in the fpring to befiege it, was led through the village in afhes, and the ftreets ftill ftained with the blood of its harmlefs inhabitants. I men-tion this circumftance, becaufe I was a wit-nefs of it, and becaufe the Ruffians have been accufed of cruelty, unjuftly *at leaft with refpect to the Turks*. Had Great Britain and Pruffia not interfered, the emprefs would not have made peace. How far that inter-ference was politic, *confidering the fituation we then ftood in with the emprefs*, has been already explained; but I think it muft be fufficiently obvious, that the exiftence of the

Turkifh

Turkifh power in Europe can *now* no longer be eonfidered as propitious, either to the particular interefts of this country, or to the general advantage of mankind.

In the condu&t of the war, a very fhort time would have led the emperor to the gates of Conftantinople, had he boldly purfued a plan of offenfive operation; but Jofeph, influenced by the irrefolution of his chara&ter, a&ted folely on the defenfive until he had loft the opportunity of crufhing his enemies, and was himfelf involved in the troubles of his Hungarian dominions.

Humanity itfelf is difgraced by the prolongation of Turkifh defpotifm, and juftice with an imperious voice demands the liberation of the oppreffed Grecians, and their re-eftablifhment in the feat of their heroic anceftors. But it is not only on the removal of exifting evils that we have to fpeculate; we may contemplate with proud exultation the fubftitution of a new fyftem of things, founded on principles more equally juft and liberal. Who can look forward without animation to the revival of learning, of arts and arms, in Greece, when the iron yoke, under which fhe now bows, fhall be broken? A Grecian ftate, the free and independent ally of Britain and Ruffia, will form a con-

F f 4   necting

necting link in the social bond of commerce; will be fitted, by the favourableness of its situation and the genius of its inhabitants, for bold and successful enterprize; and, in fine, will quickly attain a proud pre-eminence among nations. Britain is particularly interested in cherishing these hopes: her trade with Turkey is trifling and insignificant; with Greece she will stand in the relation of a favoured ally, and her commercial connections will consequently be more intimate and extensive. The free navigation of the Mediterranean, a point which this country has so long laboured to secure, will be firmly established by a confederacy of naval powers, able to resist the domineering spirit of France and Spain. How high this object has ever ranked among the views of English politicians may be inferred from their anxiety in acquiring, and pertinacity in maintaining Gibraltar, Minorca, and various other stations in that sea; but in the event to which we allude, the whole Archipelago will be friendly to us, and the support of our trade will be assured, not only by Russia, but Greece itself, which was ever a prolific nursery of seamen, and which at present supplies reluctantly the greater part of the Turkish marine forces.

Nor is it only to the Mediterranean that
we

we may look for an extenſion of our commerce : the coaſts of the Black Sea preſent a mine of wealth, hitherto untried by the Britiſh adventurer, but from which we may derive the moſt ſolid advantages, when thoſe countries are in the hands of free and independent ſtates, our friends and allies. The French had, previouſly to the preſent war, a conſiderable trade in this ſea, by their veſſels ſailing under Ruſſian or Turkiſh colours ; and this they will again enjoy on the return of peace, through the favour of their Turkiſh allies.

The concluſion then, which is moſt obvious from a view of Turkey, both in its actual ſtate, and as it preſents itſelf to the eye of ſpeculation, is, that the ſubverſion of its deſpotiſm (an event which muſt inevitably ſoon arrive, and which it requires not the gift of prophecy to foreſee) will be productive of the moſt beneficial effect, in ſubſtituting an active and commercial power, for one immerſed in ſloth and barbariſm. In theſe deductions, Britain finds herſelf particularly intereſted, from the great advantages, commercial and political, which ſuch an event holds out to her, and which, if ſhe does not embrace, her influence and weight in the Mediterranean, and, perhaps, in the ſcale of Europe, muſt ſpeedily ſink.

Turning

Turning our views again to the fide of Italy, we fhall there perceive new reafons, which dictate to Britain the neceffity of allying herfelf moft intimately with Ruffia, in accomplifhing the liberation of Greece. The influence of France muft here be almoft univerfally predominant, and in the maritime ftates fhe will find a moft prolific nurfery of feamen. She has however forefeen, that the entrance of a Ruffian fleet into the Mediterranean will prove a moft ferious obftacle to the aggrandizement of her power, and has therefore endeavoured to prevent the progrefs of the Ruffian arms. The only hope that Britain can entertain in that, as in every other quarter, muft be founded on her naval fuperiority; and this the co-operation of a Greek and Ruffian fleet promifes moft effectually to maintain. Late events have, indeed, made the danger of the French ufurpations in Italy more evident and more alarming; it appears that they aim not merely at extending their influence but their empire; their conquefts have been vaft and rapid, and refemble in every feature thofe made by their allies the Turks; fcarcely lefs ftriking is the terror which awaits on their name, than the devaftation which follows their fword; Genoa may be confidered as theirs; and even for Venice

Venice itfelf no vain apprehenfions may be entertained. What an acceffion of power is here to be acquired! By what bounds can we pretend to limit their progrefs?

If they fucceed in Italy, they will change their politics with refpect to Turkey. They are perfectly acquainted with the ftate of Greece, and the difpofitions of its inhabitants. Turkey can be of no more ufe to them; they will therefore erect Greece into a republic under their protection, and derive from it infinitely more advantages than from the porte, which is unable any longer to make a diverfion in their favour, without haftening the epocha of its own deftruction. Ruffia never can fubmit to fee fuch a ftate of things. Had the emprefs never before turned her thoughts to the liberating of Greece, as an object of glory, fhe muft now do it from motives of felf defence, and an intereft fhe had not before.

The vaft increafe of power the French will acquire, particularly in the number of failors, and the excellent ports of the Archipelago, will enable them to annihilate at their pleafure the Ruffian fleet and its eftablifhments in the ports of the Black Sea, and fhut them for ever out of the Mediterranean. All the fair views of profperity in the fouthern provinces, as well Ruffian

as

as Polifh, will vanifh and Ruffia muft depend folely on the pleafure of France for the exportation of its products.

Such a ftate of humiliation, neither the high mind of the emprefs nor the country at large will ever brook ; it would be injuftice to themfelves, cruelty to the Greeks, and ruin to all Europe. Much more even might be faid of the deftructive confequence of fuffering the French to intermeddle with the Greeks, and of not immediately feizing the opportunity of making them a free and independent nation.

POSTSCRIPT.

THESE papers, as I have faid, were written nearly two years ago, though all the political part was not meant for the prefs ; circumftances have occurred, which permit more of them being laid before the public than was at firft intended.

A great event has fince happened ; the emprefs of Ruffia is no more ! and confiderable changes have taken place in the fituation of feveral countries in Europe, but far from

weakening,

weakening, they greatly ftrengthen thefe arguments, and elucidate their deductions.

Hiftories and anecdotes have appeared of the life of that great princefs, and the revolution which placed her on the throne. It is time that the voice of truth be heard. That contemporary fycophants and vile hirelings fhould have vindicated one of the moft horrid tranfactions that ftain the pages of hiftory is not altogether to be wondered at; but indignation is raifed in the breaft of every honeft man, to fee that after the death of the emprefs there exift beings contemptible enough to traduce the memory of an unfortunate prince, a victim to the undefigning opennefs and integrity of his heart; a prince, whofe anfwer to the precautions which were recommended to him by the late king of Pruffia, was, " *I do good to all the world, and* " *with that what have I to fear ?*" a prince who was the benefactor of his country, and whofe laws (thofe very laws which were brought in accufation againft him as crimes !) have been religioufly obferved as models of wifdom and humanity, and without which the reign of the emprefs would have been lefs glorious, and her people lefs happy. That a Frenchman, that a Rulhiere, fhould abufe him, we need not be furprifed : " *Peter* " *the third was a friend to the Englifh, and he* " *dif-*

" *difcouraged the ufe of the French language at*
" *his court.* But can any man believe that
this *vindication* of the dethroning Peter the
third was the book which withftood the
temptation of Catharine's gold, ánd the me-
nace of the Baftille? Whoever has been in
Ruffia knows (or might have known) the
facts, and can contradict this ridiculous mif-
reprefentation of them—the tranfaction is
but thirty-feven years old.

Many powerful interefts were combined to
bury in oblivion this horrid event; but let
fovereigns and individuals learn, that TRUTH
will one day appear. The emperor owes a
duty to a father, to a fovereign, to his own
fecurity, and to that of other princes; the
Ruffian nation owes to its own character the
juftification of the memory of their injured
monarch, in whofe cataftrophe they were not
implicated. The ˎweight of the guilt will
fall on a few; the lapfe of time does not diminifh or change the nature of the crime.

The reign of the emprefs was a feries of
fucceffes; it was as glorious as fortunate.
She extended the frontier of her empire, and
augmented its force, by a great acquifition of
territory and population; fhe created a powerful navy, and eftablifhed a complete fovereignty in the Black Sea; fhe obtained both
by fea and land fuch a decided fuperiority
over

over the Turks, that in the very next fpring
fhe could with eafe have driven them into
Afia. The dreadful revolution which has
fhaken the governments of Europe to their
very foundations did not affect her ; in the
general madnefs her fubjects remained uncon-
taminated, and by her pofition and undimi-
nifhed ftrength fhe became the arbitrefs of
the whole continent. The document was
drawn out, the figning of which would have
decided the conteft ; would have crowned her
reign with folid and eternal glory, and have
blotted out every fpot in it ; would have
made a people, who fcarcely more than a
century ago were reckoned among the barbarous hordes of Tatars, the liberators of the
civilized world, the reftorers of order, of
juftice, of the government of laws, of the independence of nations, the protectors of property, of innocence, of religion, of morality,
and of the dignity of mankind ; the pen was
in her hand, when——myfterious Heaven !——
fhe died *.

The private character of the emprefs and
her domeftic conduct are foreign to the fub-

* That day or the next fhe was to have figned the document for furnifhing 65,000 men immediately, which
would have been only the beginning of her co-operation ;
fhe would, in all human probability, have been as fuccefsful
againft the Jacobins as fhe was againft the lefs favage
Tatars.

jeçt

ject of papers wholly political. As a fovereign, fhe will make a great figure in hiftory.
Her information proceeded from an extenfive
and minute acquaintance with the prefent
and paft ftate of nations, their actual and
relative fituations, and with the perfonal character and private interefts of fovereigns and
individuals; fhe was indefatigable in gaining
intelligence and making partizans, and fpared
neither money nor means to fucceed; fhe
was aftonifhingly rich in refources; fhe had
wonderful talents to combine and deduce, fo
as to forefee with certainty future events, or
be prepared for fuch as mere accident produces; it was thence that fhe was enabled to
profit by every fault or misfortune of other
ftates, as well as of what inevitably followed
in the common courfe of things; fhe was
never duped, but when, through complaifance or confidence, fhe had relied on the
knowledge of others; her projects were
always vaft, their object, her own glory; her
perfeverance was inexorable; oppofition or
difficulty only excited greater exertions of
talent; fhe never gave up one fingle purfuit when it was known to the world that fhe
had determined to follow it, unlefs it could
appear that fhe ceded from motives of gene-
rofity, and not from compulfion or invincible
obftacle; fuccefs never dazzled, nor danger

or

or embarrassment oppressed her ; on all occasions she had equal firmness, courage, and presence of mind ; she was always great ; even in the smallest actions she was a sovereign ; sudden impressions excited sometimes in her violent anger, as it were by surprise, though never in public ; but she commanded her passions in an instant, and put on her habitual smile. She was remarkably temperate, applied indefatigably to business, and was of a healthy constitution of body. She could temporise, and use every art of political intrigue, but she had too high notions of the dignity of a sovereign to debase herself, or prostitute publicly her word, so that whenever her honour was openly concerned in fulfilling an engagement she might be relied on. When the gratification of her personal enmity or esteem coincided with her politics it was shown, when not, silenced.

She uniformly pursued one line of politics, and she never would have changed her alliance with Great Britain, had we understood them, or our own interest, sooner. We need not say how unjustifiable her conduct has been towards Poland ; but it cannot be denied, that the whole blame does not lie on her. As to the Crim, she must have the approbation of all those who do not approve a system of rapine, and plunder, and barbarous

G g

rage

rage wreaked on poor defencelefs cottagers, whofe fons, and wives, and daughters, were conftantly expofed to be carried into flavery from all the neighbouring countries.

It is only in foreign politics that fhe appears great, and becaufe there only fhe governed alone; there her minifters were literally her fecretaries; fhe heard their advice fometimes, and fometimes took ideas from them, but fhe alone judged and decided, and no one dared propofe a meafure till they had firft difcovered her fentiments on it; to do this was the great art of keeping in favour.

As to the internal government of the empire, it was left to the great officers. The prefidents of colleges and the governors of provinces were fovereigns, and they inordinately abufed their power with impunity; hence a moft fcandalous negligence and corruption in the management of affairs in every department, and a general relaxation of government from Peterfburgh to Kamchatka. The emprefs rewarded with great munificence; but merit, unlefs it was very confpicuous to the world, had but a little fhare of it; every thing was given to favour, and what is given to favour is taken from merit: one good, however, refulted to *her*, perfonally, from the impunity which thofe in office enjoyed; fhe was fure of their attachment to

her

her government, as the more they abufed their power, the more they dreaded a fuc-ceffor. She knew their conduct, but was deaf, and almoft inacceffible to complaint.

Her code of legiflation did not contain *laws*, but *forms* of judicature ; the inftitution of general governments was a new burthen on the people of fifty millions of roubles more than the ancient fimple regulations, a fum equal to three fourths of the whole revenue of the empire ; the increafe of vexation was ftill greater.

Her finances were ill underftood, and worfe managed ; fhe got into embarraffments when fhe had incalculable refources, and the means ufed to remedy them were childifh.

Years had not impaired her talents, nor cooled the ardor of her ambition ; it feemed, on the contrary, to increafe, as other paffions gradually fubfided.

She had, in fhort, a capacity equal to the government of a vaft empire, and to give it in the world that confequence which its na-tural ftrength entitled it to. Had fhe paid the fame attention to its internal, as fhe did to its political adminiftration, her reign would have been as productive of happinefs to her people as it was of glory to herfelf.

The emprefs was at length on the eve of accomplifhing her great defign ; the Turks were left alone, without any support; all the powers in Europe were engaged in the great conteft, except the kings of Pruffia and Sweden. It was not in the power of the latter to make any diverfion. The French had paid to the court of Stockholm a confiderable fum of money to enable them to fit out their fleet, but fo low were their finances, that it was all immediately employed, except a few thoufand rix-dollars, for more preffing exigencies of the ftate. The emprefs had a fleet in the Baltic, infinitely fuperior to the combined fleets of Sweden and Denmark; fhe wifhed, as has been faid, to annihilate them; with our concurrence or confent it would have been but a fingle blow. As to the land forces of Sweden, they were then not in a condition to make the emprefs uneafy; the alarm they had occafioned in the laft war had put her on her guard. She was, however, at the fame time endeavouring, by a marriage of her grand-daughter with the young king of Sweden, to conciliate the interefts of the two countries : though fhe had no apprehenfion on that fide, yet fhe wifhed rather to avoid a quarrel, and required only a ftrict neutrality on the part of Sweden. As to Pruffia alone, in the ftate it was with refpect to the newly acquired provinces in Poland, and trembling at the refentment of the emprefs, it

certainly

certainly underftood its interefts too well to
quarrel with her. The emprefs, in a war
with the king of Pruffia, would have found
infinite refources in Poland; the king, an
enemy in every fubject he had acquired; almoft every Pole would have taken the field
againft him, fo much were they irritated at
his paft conduct. The king of Pruffia had
alfo interefts in Germany to look after, which
concerned him nearer; and certain it is, that
he paid the moft fubmiffive court to the emprefs, who on her fide was perfectly unap-
prehenfive of any oppofition from him;
all that he might have tried to effect would
have been, to obtain fome little indemnifi-
cation as the price of his complaifance in
acquiefcing in her projects.

She was now in poffeffion of every refource
fhe required of Poland for her army, in acting
againft the Turks on the European continent.
The government of the acquired provinces
was fo firmly fettled, that fhe had no apprehenfion of difturbances; her army was fo
formidable, that fhe could have marched
beyond her frontiers at leaft three hundred
thoufand effective men; and fhe had raifed
150,000 men to recruit it   Her fleet in the
Black Sea was much fuperior to the whole
Turkifh navy, and there was a flotilla of fmall
veffels built for the purpofe of landing troops in

G g 3   three

three feet water, which could have conducted, in three days, sixty thousand men within a few miles of the capital of the Turkish empire. The first blow would have been the destruction of the Ottoman fleet in its own port, and the attack of Constantinople by land at the same time. All this might have been done early last spring.

A great army had passed Derbent; an arrangement would have immediately taken place with the Persian khans, in whose quarrels, without any apparent interest, she had intermeddled; and this army would have fallen on the Turkish Asiatic provinces, the consequence of which would have been, that all the Asiatic troops, which compose the garrisons of their fortresses in Europe, would have quitted them, and fled to succour their own country, and have left the road to Constantinople defenceless.

It was a project of Prince Potemkin, in the last war, to have carried the war into Asia, and he began by taking Anapá. Had that prince not died, the war was on the point of breaking out again. I speak of this from a knowledge of the facts.

Nor would the sending an army of sixty-five thousand men to attack the French in Alsace have prevented her marching another army against the Turks. If she had any apprehensions

§

prehenfions of the king of Pruffia fiding with
the French, this meafure would have put it
in her power to have acted more offenfively
againft him. However it may have been
conftrued by fome, this meafure was a fure
indication of her intention of attacking the
Turks in the fpring; for as long as fhe was
not certain of meeting no oppofition to that
meafure, fhe conftantly declined taking an
active part by land againft the French.

In fhort, every preparation was made, and
every obftacle removed; we did not want the
publication of a manifefto to be informed of
her intentions ; and indeed the intentions of
fovereigns are better known by the ftate and
movements of their armies, or the preparations for their movements, by a knowledge
of their interefts, and the difficulties they
have to encounter in the execution of their
projects, than by manifeftoes, or by the language of their courtiers.

It is worthy of recording, that the emprefs
declared, that though His Majefty and the
Emperor of Germany made peace with the
French, fhe never would, nor acknowledge
the French republic, or any ftate that had rebelled againft its fovereign. She never would
acknowledge America to the laft, though fhe
permitted fhips coming from America, under
American colours, to enter her ports, and

trade on the fame footing as other nations having no treaty.

The prefident of the congrefs, not knowing this circumftance, appointed a conful, in 1795, to refide in St. Peterfburgh; on his arrival he requefted an audience of the vice-chancellor, to deliver his credentials; but the next day he was told, the emprefs did not know of any fuch power as the United States of America.

Since it has appeared, that His Majefty's confenting to at leaft, if not co-operating with the emprefs's projects againft Turkey, was the *fine qua non* of *an alliance with her*, and of her *taking an active part in the war againft France,* the public has fhown great anxiety to learn why fhe did not come forward immediately after figning the treaty in February 1795, in which a war with Turkey is a *cafus fœderis,* and what meafures had removed the impediment, which kept her back two years, and induced her to come forwards at laft; but thefe events are too recent to be fpoken of.

Whilft I am writing this Poftfcript, another great event has taken place.

The emperor of Germany has made peace; the emperor of Ruffia has loft a glorious opportunity to immortalize his name; it might have been faid to him:

Sire,

Sire,

You have afcended the throne of the greateft empire in the world, under fuch aufpices as never attended any monarch before you.

A glory is referved for you, Sire, fuch as never yet fhone round the throne of any fovereign on earth.

You may be the benefa&or, not of Ruffia only, but of all Europe.—Hiftory fhall fay, Alexander conquered a world, Paul faved a world.

You have begun your reign by a&s which befpeak your wifdom, your juftice, your humanity— YOU HEAR EVERY ONE *

You have felt with indignation the unneceffitated apoftacy of the court of Berlin; its alliance with regicides to difmember the German empire.

You are called on, Sire, to crufh with the irrefiftible, weight of your armies the enemies of religion, morality, and focial order.

Peace with them will be more dangerous than war. Their do&rines will have freer courfe; and their do&rines have done more than their armies. They have fubverted the order, and confounded even the names of things. Virtues

---

* Every perfon in the empire may now write to their fovereign, and if they receive no anfwer, may addrefs themfelves perfonally to him.

have

have the appellations of vices, and vices the appellations of virtues.

Can Russia, in all its extended provinces, when every foreign contact will be poison; when every breath, except from the frozen ocean, will be full of miasma, escape the contagion? None will escape but the elder brethren of Jacobinism, the Turks, whose equally monstrous, though less dangerous tyranny, has for so many centuries insulted mankind, trodden underfoot the laws of nations, and blasphemed Christianity; who, unprovoked, attacked, conquered, and slaughtered nations without number, murdered their sovereigns, and spilt every drop of royal blood, massacred their priests at the altar, extirpated nobility, plundered the opulent, and bound the wretched remains of the people in fetters of perpetual and hereditary slavery. They alone, till the reign of Jacobinism had made property a crime, the violation of property a legal resource of government, and the lives and possessions of men the right of tyranny; they alone had hitherto confounded the hereditary ranks among mankind; had depressed genius, learning, and the Christian religion, and governed their barbarous empire by slaves and assassins. Like the Jacobins, they taught Christian children to fight against their fathers and their father's God*;

* See the institution of the Janizaries, who were originally Christian children.

they

they too hold it lawful to murder prisoners in cold blood; they too possess a claim to every country in the universe, and a sacred right to subject all people to their law; they too hold all other sovereigns as usurpers, and dethroning them as the highest merit. But still the Turks have a religion, and though it permits them numberless enormities to their own sect, and all enormities to others, they acknowledge a God, and many moral duties. Not the contagion of their doctrine was to be feared, but their cruel sword, which once threatened the conquest of the universe, and the extinction of all virtue, dignity, and science in the world; yet was not this first monster so tremendous, in the insolence of his power, as an enemy, as is this second monster, in the insolence of his successes, as a brother.

To you, Sire, kings lift up their hands, and bow their anointed heads; to you, Sire, the priests of God, to you orphans of murdered nobles, to you violated virgins, despoiled possessors, enslaved nations stretch out their arms, and implore your aid; the spirits of martyred royalty call to you from above for vengeance.

The noble project of your glorious ancestor, Peter the Great, was nearly consummated when you mounted his throne; it was reserved for his nephew to accomplish the liberating of a Christian people from the most infamous bondage. It is worthy of the justice and humanity which mark

mark the beginning of a reign, on which more true glory awaits than ever was reserved for any sovereign in the records of history.

This might with truth have been said to him.

In August 1796, Prussia concluded with the French secret articles for the dismemberment of Germany. The late king of Prussia had assured the empress, " *on his word of* " *honour,*" and " *on the word of a sovereign,*" that no such articles existed. On the accession of his present imperial majesty to the throne of Russia, the king sent Count de Brühl to compliment the emperor on the occasion. This nobleman had the honour of being personally known to his imperial majesty, and, it was believed, was much esteemed by him.

The court of Berlin, soon imagining that the emperor Paul was blindly attached to its interests, ventured to give a copy of these articles. That subtle cabinet was for once mistaken. The emperor felt the indignity of the action, and, himself a man of honour, and a monarch respectful of the sacredness of a sovereign's word, he answered the communication as became the nephew of Peter the Great. Prussia submitted, and the project was abandoned. Russia was actually preparing to assist Austria effectually, when

Austria

Auftria made peace with France! I fhall make no comment on this event, which no one had reafon to expect. The emperor of Ruffia was greatly and juftly offended. If he have any predilection for Pruffia, certain it is that he is incapable of entering into meafures iniquitous in themfelves and baneful in their confequences, tending to the difmemberment of Germany; and the only obftacle which now feems to prevent his ftepping forward with that vaft weight of power he commands, is the uncertainty of the political fyftem adopted by the young king of Pruffia. While the old minifters continue in office, can it be prefumed that their fyftem is not that which the king approves? Is it to be expected that a young prince has energy of mind, and knowledge of affairs fufficient, by his arguments, to convert or to over-rule the opinions of a whole cabinet? We muft judge of the fyftem of a prince by the known fyftem of his minifters in office.

If, however, becaufe the emperor has made peace, we make peace, and fuch a peace as the bloated infolence of the enemy dictates to us, we fhall be fhut out of every port, from the Elbe to the coaft of Africa; we fhall foon be driven out of India. France, and its allies, will foon have a naval power fuperior to that of Great Britain, and, *qui mare teneat*
eum

eum neceſſe rerum potiri. Cic. Without our trade how is our navy to exiſt? how are our funds to be raiſed? If we diſband our armies, we ſhall be attacked unprepared; if we do not, what œconomy will there be in a peace?

It now remains, therefore, to be ſeen, whether the love of our country and of liberty, which fired the breaſts of our anceſtors, and led them on to thoſe glorious exertions which procured us our happy and *free conſtitution*, be tranſmitted to their deſcendants; and whether we will ſpill our blood to defend what they ſpilt their blood to purchaſe for us. It remains to be ſeen whether we are ſtill free Britons, or humiliated ſlaves, ready to receive with open arms the deathful hug of French fraternity, and ſubmit to the deſpotic five-handed ſceptre of French liberty.

February 1798.

CHAPTER XI.

Of the British Trade with Turkey.

FORMERLY the trade to Turkey was of confiderable importance to this country, but of late years it had been languifhing, and at laft dwindled into a ftate of infignificancy, when the prefent war entirely put a ftop to all communication with the ports of the Levant.

As this trade will be again opened when a peace takes place, an inveftigation of the caufes of its decline, and the means to give it its ancient extenfion, may not, in the mean time, be unimportant to the govern-ment and to the merchants of this country.

The caufes of its gradual decline are, 1ft, the rivalfhip of other European nations; 2dly, the diminution of the confumption of our manufactures in Turkey, by the impo-verifhed ftate of the country; 3dly, fome branches of trade being got into other chan-nels; and 4thly, the monopoly of the Levant company in London.

With refpect to the rivalfhip of other na-tions, that caufe will be confidered when I
fpeak

ſpeak of the Levant company. As to the impoveriſhed ſtate of Turkey, it muſt affect the trade of other European nations as well as our own ; if we are not, therefore, to expect to ſee it again in that flouriſhing ſtate it was in, when there were forty Engliſh houſes of trade at Aleppo (at preſent there is but one) we may expect to have the ſame *proportion* of it as we then had ; and if we acquire only this, our trade to the Levant will ſtill be a national object. Some branches of trade are got into other channels ; this regards principally certain imports from Turkey, and particularly of ſilk from Aleppo, whence formerly larger quantities of Perſian ſilk came, which is not now brought thither, but the Eaſt India Company ſupply our market cheaper and more abundantly. Confiderable quantities of cotton and drugs come from Holland and from Italy, which formerly came direct. This will alſo be accounted for in the next conſideration, the monopoly of the Levant company.

It is often neceſſary, and it is juſt, where merchants undertake to open to the country a new branch of trade, and where the expence and riſk is great, to grant them excluſive privileges, or monopolies, for a certain limited time, to prevent others from reaping the harveſt they had ſown, and to

ſecure

secure their laudable industry as far as possible from risk; but when that risk exists
no more, and when they have reaped their
harvest over and over again, and have had a
full compensation for their risk, their industry, and their expence, the country at large
has a right to a participation of the trade.
There may, indeed, sometimes exist circumstances of a peculiar nature, which give them
a claim to a longer indulgence in their monopoly, particularly where that monopoly is
not injurious, but, on the contrary, beneficial
to the country in general (and such is the case
of the East India company;) but in a trade
where the merchants have no *common stock*,
and can urge none of the above reasons in
defence of their monopoly; where they cannot prove that *any particular loss* would accrue to them by abolishing it; where it has
operated as a restraint on the trade, con-
fining it to narrow bounds, and giving a decided superiority to their rivals of other nations, to the almost total exclusion of the
products and manufactures of their country
from that to which their privilege exclu-
sively permits them to trade, ought in common sense such a monopoly to exist? The
Levant company is truly become the *dog in
the manger*; it does not operate so much to

H h   the

the profit of the company, as to the lofs of the country.

This monopoly is of a fingular nature: it has none of the advantages of a common ftock, in which many individuals rifk fmall fums, but which in the aggregate amount to a larger capital than any one merchant or fet of merchants poffefs, or would choofe to rifk; a common ftock to which any one may contribute, and which thereby, ftrictly fpeaking, ceafes to be a monopoly; it is a privilege granted to *certain perfons only* to trade to Turkey, each with his own capital, and for his own particular account and rifk, without any affignable reafon why they fhould be preferred to others his majefty's fubjects; it has all the difadvantages of other monopolies; it has not one of their advantages.

In fpeaking thus freely of the company, I folemnly declare that I have no private motive, no rancour againft any individual, and have no motive for writing on this fubject but the advantage of the country. The few members of the company with whom I am acquainted I perfonally refpect and highly efteem: on this fubject they muft differ with me; they are bound by oath to fupport the interefts of their body.

The trade of every other nation to Turkey

is

is free, and they have experienced the advantage of being liberated from the fetters of exclufive privileges. Let every obftacle be removed in this country to an equally free commerce, and the fuperior induftry, fkill, and riches of our manufacturers, our traders, and our navigators, will again reftore to us our loft Turkey trade.

It may be faid, that at prefent the Levant company is not a monopoly, as any one, by paying twenty pounds, may become a member of it. When the trade was already ruined, it was imagined that this regulation was equivalent to laying the trade open (a proof that government have thought it neceffary to abolifh the monopoly) but the bye-laws of the company, and the power to enforce them, were permitted to exift, and thefe fo fetter the trade to *new adventurers*, that few have found their account in purfuing it, and the trade ftill remains a monopoly in favor of the old houfes.

It will be neceffary to pafs in review thefe bye-laws, which have operated fo injurioufly to the trade in general, and to fhow how they have gradually effected the ruin of the trade, and the introduction of rivals, who have gotten poffeffion of what we have loft.

By one of the bye-laws, for inftance, it was enacted, that all merchandize brought

from

from Turkey, and imported into England, ſhould be the produce of goods exported from England to Turkey. The following are the words of the bye-law:

" That upon entering goods received in
" *England* from *Turkey* or *Egypt*, every mem-
" ber ſhall in like manner ſubſcribe the fol-
" lowing affirmation ; *videlicet :*

" *I affirm, by the oath I have taken to the*
" *Levant company, that the goods above men-*
" *tioned are for account of myſelf, or others*
" *free of the ſaid company, or of ſuch as now*
" *have their licence to trade, and are beyond*
" *the ſeas* ; *and that the ſaid goods, nor any*
" *part of them, are not, to the beſt of my*
" *knowledge, the produce of gold or ſilver,*
" *either in coin or bullion, ſent into Turkey* ;
" *but that the ſaid goods are purchaſed by*
" *merchandize, or monies ariſing or to ariſe*
" *from the ſale of merchandize ſent into Turkey*
" *or Egypt, from Europe, or from the Britiſh*
" *ſettlements in America, on account of freemen*
" *of the Levant company, or ſuch as have their*
" *licence to trade, and of which regular entries*
" *have been made with the company, or are*
" *purchaſed by freight received in Turkey or*
" *Egypt, by ſhips navigated according to law,*
" *which freight is entirely the property of*
" *members of the company, or ſuch as have*
" *their licence to trade.*"

And every merchant or factor in Turkey
or

or Egypt is required to make a fimilar af-
fidavit, on exporting goods from Turkey for
England, and to give, on oath, an exact account of every kind of tranfaction or bufi-
finefs, direct or indirect, fo that all his affairs become known.

The object of this law is evidently to encourage the exportation of cloth ; and when
we had no rivals, it produced no bad effects ; but it foon produced rivals, *and it continued in force till they had nearly got poffeffion
of the whole cloth trade.*   Such a law, indeed,
was fufficient to ruin any trade.   One houfe
may deal in exports, another in imports ;
one may combine its Italian with its Turkey
trade ; another may fend veffels for the carrying trade ; but if every individual houfe
be obliged to keep an exact regifter on oath,
and under a penalty of 20 per cent, called
" *a broke*," of all its exports and imports,
and to balance them exactly, how is fuch
a trade to profper, where the profits are reduced by the rivalfhip of foreign nations ?
This bye-law at length, when it had produced the full effect of its ill tendency, was
repealed ; but the trade was not revived ;
fo difficult is it to turn back commerce
from channels into which it has run.

It will be afked then, what are the reftraints which now lie on the trade ?

H h 3   The

The fubjection to the control of the company ; the neceffity of making entries with it of all their tranfactions on oath, and not being able to be concerned in anywife with others not free of the company, or foreigners ; the power in the company, for the leaft violation of their rules, to inflict a penalty of 20 per cent. ; the idea of reftraint, and the apprehenfion of violating a folemn oath, have made many determine to trade with Turkey through foreign and circuitous channels, without becoming free of the company ; witnefs the very large quantities of cottons and drugs, &c. which come from Holland and Italy, as the cuftom-houfe books prove. This was the cafe till our trade to Holland and the Mediterranean was ftopped by the war, and in that fame fituation we fhall be when a peace takes place.

The drugs, &c. which are imported from Italy, were carried thither from Turkey ; they had already given a profit to the Italian merchant in Turkey, to the importer, and to the purchafer in Italy, who cleans, afforts, repacks, and often adulterates them ; to the commiffioner, who purchafes them for his correfpondent in England ; to which add charges, and intereft of money for fo long a difburfement, which the different people through whofe hands the merchandize has

gone

gone have all calculated, as well as their profits, double freights, and loading and unloading, &c. &c.

Cottons are imported from Holland, becaufe the company cannot import themfelves enough for the confumption ; and the reafon why they do not is, becaufe the old members, who are under no apprehenfions of the bye-laws, *find other articles enough to employ their whole capital, and beyond that the trade cannot increafe.* This is the reafon, as will be feen hereafter more fully, why the trade in exports as well as imports is confined within fuch narrow bounds.

The Britifh merchants in Italy and other foreign countries, not being members of the company (and to become free of the company they muft come to England) cannot trade with Britifh houfes in Turkey, and thefe, if they will trade to Italy, muft trade with foreigners : thus all combinations of the trades are prevented. Englifh veffels in the Mediterranean might often make a voyage to Turkey, inftead of lying in an Italian port, and return time enough to take in their cargoes for England.

The great preference given to Britifh veffels in the Mediterranean would affure them an employment whenever they want freights. This carrying or caravan trade is fo exten-

five,

five, that befides the French, the little ſtate of Ragufa has no leſs than 400 veſſels in it.

Were the *maſters of ſhips*, *their owners*, and the Engliſh *merchants in Italy* and Turkey, under no reſtraint in regard to the Levant company, people would riſk more readily the ſending their veſſels to the Mediterranean to get employment in this carrying buſineſs, and their ſpeculation in trade being free, they would find means to employ their veſſels in the intervals of their being without freights ; the maſters, owners, and correſpondents might combine their *own ſpeculations* in merchandize with their carrying buſineſs, and thus keep them conſtantly employed. It is the want of theſe reſources to our ſhips, that prevents Engliſh owners from ſending their ſhips into the Mediterranean to ſeek freights, and prevent the few which do go thither from profiting ſo much by it as thoſe of other nations, whoſe houſes of trade are nearer.

Had the Turkey trade in England never been a monopoly, the French would never have got poſſeſſion of almoſt all the cloth trade, and the laying it open will be the only means of our coming in again for any conſiderable ſhare of it. There is a greater demand in Turkey for the light Languedoc cloths, than for any other ſort. The Turks clothe their ſervants twice a
year,

year, and the French cloth, made into loofe garments (which laft much longer than the tight European drefs) is ftrong enough for their purpofe, and its cheapnefs makes its preferable ; poorer people, who form the great body of confumers, buy it alfo for œconomical reafons. Englifh broad cloth, called mahoot (of a light quality, made purpofely for the Turkey market) is only worn by thofe in eafier circumftances. Confiderable quantities of cloth have alfo of late years come to Turkey *from Germany.*

It is the opinion of many people well acquainted with thefe matters, that the Englifh manufactories might make the fame fort of cloth as the Languedoc, and as cheap as the French ; but as long as the Levant company exifts, who is to undertake it? Were the trade laid entirely open, it is probable that all kinds of Englifh manufacturers would fend people (called riders) to Turkey to feek for commiffions, as they do to all parts of Europe. This practice, *though not very agreeable to Englifh merchants* (which however may not be the cafe in Turkey, as they may find the mediation of merchants neceffary) would greatly increafe the vent of Englifh commodities, and thefe induftrious people might poffibly be the means of our regaining the cloth trade.

5

The

The few merchants who are in the true secret of the Levant trade, can employ in it their WHOLE CAPITAL *advantageously, and therefore do not seek for new branches, or how to recover old ones which are lost.*—This is the great secret.

The French do not get their wool cheaper than we do; the price of labour may be less; but will not superior skill and industry, with larger capitals, compensate this single circumstance against us? Experience in other articles shews it, as in the manufactures of Manchester, Sheffield, and Birmingham.

It is very worthy of attention, that the French cannot make so cheap as we can the same kinds of cloth, which our people bring to the Turkey market; it is not that they cannot make them *so fine*, for they make in France much finer cloth than that kind of broad cloth made in England purposely for the Turkey market. There is also a coarse strong cloth brought to Turkey from England, called *londras*; these the French cannot *make so cheap* neither; nor are their *shalloons so cheap*. In short, there is no sort of woollen stuff made in the two countries, of the same quality, which the English do not sell cheaper than the French. The fact seems to be, that the French invented a kind of cloth more proper for the general consumption confumption of Turkey than that which the Englifh had brought thither, and the Englifh never attempted to follow their example, but continued carrying to the market a fort of cloth, which at laft got almoft out of ufe. *Whenever the English shall have made and brought to Turkey the same kind of cloth as the French, and cannot afford it so cheap, then with certainty we may conclude that the French have an advantage over us*; but till then it ought to be doubted, and certainly it merits the trial; but a fair trial never can be made till the Levant trade is entirely free.

But even fuppofing that we cannot regain the cloth trade, there are very many other objects worth attending to, and *which may be of greater national advantage.*

The Manchefter ftuffs would find a great vent in all parts of Turkey. The manufactories of Aleppo and Damafcus are almoft ruined, and if the Manchefter people were to imitate the Turkifh patterns of their ftuffs, they could certainly afford them cheaper. Imitations of the Surat and Bengal goods of filk and cotton, which are enormoufly dear, would find alfo a ready fale in Turkey, and cotton velvets, velverets, &c. Birmingham and Sheffield wares would be articles of importance. The Turks, both in Europe

Europe and Afia, have a great partiality for all thefe kinds of Englifh manufactures, and in general the epithet Englifh is fynonimous with excellent.

Thefe articles at prefent are not attended to ; but the mafters of fhips, who bring out their *little ventures* to Turkey in a contraband manner, in thefe kind of things, make great profits ; they can, however, bring only fmall quantities, left the Levant company fhould take umbrage at it. A few of thefe goods alfo find their way to Turkey from Italy, but greatly enhanced in their price from the many hands they go through, and therefore this channel does not afford a great vent for them. Linen may likewife be an article of exportation for Turkey. The Turks wear linen of a hard twifted thread, very open and unbleached, which comes moftly from Egypt, and is exceedingly dear, but is the moft pleafant kind to wear in hot weather. No European nation has yet undertaken to imitate it, but it is probable it might be made in Ireland infinitely cheaper than in Egypt : if this was the cafe, it would be of great importance. The German linens begin to be fold in confiderable quantities in Turkey, but they never will fupply the place of the Egyptian, on account of their quality. Vaft quantities of the above mentioned articles come

come from Venice and Germany, where they are dearer, and of worfe quality, than thofe manufactured in England.

Were I to enter into an enumeration of all the Englifh manufactures that would find a vent in Turkey, and particularly in the interior parts of Afia, and point out the different ports to which they might be fent, the detail would be too long for a general reprefentation ; but collectively it muft be very obvious to every perfon acquainted but generally with the trade of Turkey, that our exportations to that country muft become of great importance in a few years, were the monopoly removed, and the agents of the manufacturers fent to travel through the country, and get certain information of the ftate of its trade and manufactories.

Salt fifh, could the Newfoundland fhips, &c. go directly to Turkey as they go to Italy, would be a very important branch.

The Eaft India company could fupply the Turkey market with muflins much cheaper than they are brought by the way of Baffora, of Gidda, and Suez, which trade is entirely in the hands of their fervants : the trial has been fuccefsfully made ; but the company have other articles enough in which to inveft their whole capitals.   Other nations now bring large quantities of muflins to Turkey.

Turkey. The British muslins also fell to considerable profit.

Let all this be mere suppofition, is not the object of importance enough to give it a fair trial? and does not common fenfe fay, that a trade freed from obſtacles muſt flouriſh more than when clogged with the moſt unfupportable ſhackles? May it not be aſked, what juſt right have the members of the Levant company to lay reſtraints on this trade by their bye-laws? I have heard this ſubject diſcuſſed in Turkey, where people certainly underſtand the trade of the country better than in England, and I never heard one plauſible reaſon alledged in favour of the company. Sophiſtical arguments may be produced in London, which may appear plauſible to thoſe who are not informed of the real ſtate of matters in Turkey.

To ſhow what little efforts have been made by the company to extend the trade, and how little they deviate from the footſteps of their forefathers, I will cite two ſtriking inſtances:

Mr. John Humphrys, of Conſtantinople, was the firſt, who, a few years ago, imagined that Engliſh ſhalloons might be ſold in Conſtantinople, and they ſoon became a very important article for exportation to Turkey. The French have not been able to make them ſo cheap.

Mr.

Mr. Peter Took, of Conſtantinople, only about twenty years ago, diſcovered that he might buy raw ſilk in Bruſa (the hills behind which are viſible from their houſes in Conſtantinople) from the firſt hands, and thus make his returns direct to England. Before that period, from the firſt exiſtence of the company, the merchants of Conſtantinople had always ſent their money to Smyrna to be inveſted in ſilk, which the Turks and Jews of Smyrna bought at Bruſa.

There is a great demand in Turkey for Staffordſhire earthen-ware, which would become a very important article of commerce.

Perhaps the greateſt importation of Britiſh articles in Turkey would be by foreigners, or natives of the Turkiſh provinces, as is the caſe in many branches of our commerce, where ſuch reſtraints on foreigners do not exiſt; for inſtance, every one knows that not one-tenth part of our exports to Ruſſia are on account of the Ruſſia company in London, or the Britiſh factory in Ruſſia. Theſe articles are ſent to Ruſſia for account of foreigners ſettled in Ruſſia, or Ruſſians, and ſome part for account of our manufacturers. With reſpect to Germany this is ſtill more the caſe.

The Levant company exact a duty on all merchandize exported to and imported from Turkey,

Turkey, befides a confulage in the ports of Turkey on all the exports and imports in Britifh veffels. This confulage is a very heavy burthen on our trade, and particularly when it is confidered that fome other nations *pay none.* The following are the words of the company's bye-law :

" *At a general court, &c. the following* " *orders were eftablifhed as proper and expe-* " *dient for the* SUPPORT OF THE COMPANY'S " AFFAIRS, *and for the government of the* " *trade ; and they were confirmed at a general* " *court, held 3d of March* 1775*.*

" *It was refolved and ordered, That all* " *goods exported from Turkey or Egypt for* " *Great Britain fhall pay three confulages and* " *one-half, or feven in the hundred, according* " *to the rates of the company's tarif, in fuch* " *fpecies of the grand feignior's coin as his of-* " *ficers receive for cuftoms ; which confulage* " *fhall be paid, one-half in thirty days, and the* " *other half in fixty days after the departure of* " *the fhip, &c. ; and the company's treafurers* " *are not to take any notes or obligations for the* " *payments of confulages, but they are to infift* " *upon being paid in money when it is due.*

" *That all goods imported, &c. into Great* " *Britain, fhall pay one impofition according to* " *the company's rates, &c. except cotton and* " *emery ftones, &c.*

" *That*

" *That all goods imported into Turkey or*
" *Egypt, from Leghorn, or any other Port or*
" *Ports of Chriftendom,* BY BRITISH SUB-
" JECTS OR BRITISH SHIPS, FOR ACCOUNT
" OF FOREIGNERS, *fhall pay a confulage of*
" TWO *in the hundred, &c."*

" *That all goods exported from Conftantino-*
" *ple, Smyrna, and Aleppo, to Leghorn, or any*
" *other foreign port or ports of Chriftendom, by*
" *Britifh fubjects,* ON FOREIGN SHIPS, *on ac-*
" *count of Britifh fubjects, fhall pay a confulage*
" *of* ONE *in the hundred, &c.*

" *That all goods imported into Turkey or*
" *Egypt, by ftrangers, upon Britifh fhips, from*
" *any foreign port, &c. fhall pay two in the hun-*
" *dred, &c. and in like manner exported,* TWO
" *in the hundred, &c."* and feveral other regulations for the paying of confulage, of leffer
importance, which I omit for brevity.

" *April 29th,* 1785. *It is refolved and or-*
" *dered, &c.*

" *That all goods, excepting raw filk, mohair*
" *yarn, and drugs, exported from Turkey and*
" *Egypt, in the time of the plague, to Malta,*
" *Ancona, Venice, Meffina, Leghorn, Genoa, or*
" *Marfeilles, for the purpofe of performing qua-*
" *rantine, and which are to be re-fhipped on the*
" *fame fhip for Great Britain or Ireland, fhall*
" *pay a confulage of two in the hundred only."*

Befides

Befides this revenue, the company have for many years received an affiftance from government of five thoufand pounds a year. All thefe fums are expended for paying a part of the falary of the ambaffadors at Conftantinople, the confuls at the feveral ports in Turkey, the chancellors and drogomans (or interpreters) and for defraying of the expences attending vifits from the ambaffador to the porte, and of the confuls to pafhas, befides extraordinary prefents made at the firft audience of a new ambaffador and of a conful; for paying *avanias* (or money extorted by falfe accufations) and public entries of confuls, which were formerly very coftly; and finally, for the expences of the company and its officers at home.

Were our trade put on the fame footing as the Ruffian, a very little (perhaps five hundred pounds) more than the five thoufand pounds government now pays, would fuffice for all the expences which then would be neceffary. The Ruffian trade to Turkey is free to every one; there is no tax on it, either under the appellation of confulfhip or otherwife; no fee is taken at any ambaffador's, conful's, or chancellor's office, for documents neceffary for the difpatch of trade; no prefents are made by confuls to pafhas or other officers; no avania is fubmitted to.

A conful

A conful at Smyrna only is neceffary. Vice-confuls in the other ports would anfwer every purpofe for the protection of trade; and there would be found merchants enow, who would be glad of the office without pay, for the honour of it, which in Turkey is confiderable. There is at this day no neceffity for confuls living in fuch great ftate as they did a few years ago. The foreign minifters at Conftantinople have very confiderably retrenched their expences.

The power of an ambaffador and of a conful in Turkey is very great; it extends even to life and death. By one of the articles of the *capitulations* (or treaty with the porte) it is ftipulated, that in all criminal cafes wherein fubjects of the porte are not concerned, ambaffadors or confuls fhall punifh the criminal according to the laws of their country. In the Dutch capitulations this is expreffed ftill ftronger. As crimes committed in a ftate are crimes immediately againft that ftate, the cognizance of them belongs to it alone. The fultan delegates his power to the ambaffadors and confuls; and if in punifhing the criminal they exceed the rule prefcribed by the laws of their own country, they are only anfwerable for their conduct to the fultan; but the fultan takes no cognizance of it, therefore they are without control, and their

I i 2   power

power is defpotic. It is indeed true, that they generally fend fuch offenders home to their country ; there have, however, with other nations, been examples where an European has killed a fubject of the porte, and juftice being demanded, the ambaffador or conful has put the criminal to death. Should it happen that an Englifhman killed a Turk, it would certainly be better that the ambaffador or conful caufed him to be hanged, than to deliver him up to the Turks, for juftice being demanded, there is no other alternative; if he efcaped, the confequence might be a general maffacre ; we have lately had an example at Smyrna exactly of this nature, which coft the lives of many hundreds, and caufed the European quarter to be reduced to afhes. There is no poffibility of fending the criminal home if the populace demand juftice.

The company have given alfo another power to the ambaffadors and confuls over merchants, which free traders may not approve of. Their bye-law is, " *If any factor* " *or factors fhall have any dealings with any* " *perfon* battulated *by the lord ambaffador, or* " *the conful of any of the* Scales *(ports,* Scala " Italian) *in Turkey, with the advice of the re-* " *fpective factories, fuch factor or factors fhall* " *pay a fine for every offence to the amount of*

I

" *three*

" *three confulages upon the value of the tranf-*
" *action by or with fuch* battulated *perfon,*
" *without appeal, &c.*"   *Battulation* with
them fignifies interdiction of all commerce
with the perfon *battulated.*   The intention
was to prevent the factors or merchants having dealings with litigious perfons of the country ; but this power has been abufed.

The ambaffador formerly had a confiderable revenue from protections granted to fubjects of the porte ; but this protection having
been totally difregarded by the prefent fultan,
both that income and that fource of conftant
litigation with the porte are done away.   It
were to be wifhed that this privilege was
wholly abolifhed.   The French feveral times
propofed giving it up, and at a time when it
was refpected, and lucrative to their ambaffadors.

The French alfo, on the reprefentation of
their ambaffador, M. de St. Priefte, laid the
Levant trade open; the confequence was, that
immenfe quantities of French goods were
carried to Turkey by fubjects of the porte ;
but the company at Marfeilles found means
to get their exclufive privilege renewed ;
they had fuffered, but the country had
gained.   At prefent every one has liberty
to trade, and fince our fleet has left the Mediterranean, their commerce is revived, and,
except the trade to Great Britain be equally

I i 3   free

free when a peace takes place, we fhall have little chance of being able to rival them ; but we muft not wait till that period to lay our trade open ; it muft be done immediately.

As all communication with the Levant by fea is cut off, there remains no refource to our merchants, but to carry on their trade through Ruffia ; and though this be a circuitous way, it is by far not fo expenfive as might be imagined. The freights to the Baltic are very low, as half the fhips go out empty. The carriage from Riga to Cherfon, or Niccolai on the Bog, is moftly by water, and the land carriage in Ruffia is not one fourth of the price it is in Germany. The expence on cloth would be trifling, and on cheap and bulky goods even would not be equal to the enormous price of infurance paid for armed fhips, which *run the voyage* at prefent, and which is not equal to the rifk ; it is indeed fo great, that government fhould, perhaps, interfere. At Cherfon there are good veffels to be found, which in three days may carry the goods to Conftantinople at a reafonable freight.

But in order to open fuch a communication, liberty muft be obtained of the emperor of Ruffia to fend merchandize in *tranfito* (without paying duty) acrofs Ruffia ; and there is no doubt but that fovereign, who has ftudied

Adam

Adam Smith's book on the Wealth of Nations, and who is perfectly acquainted with
the principles of commerce and navigation,
would fee the very great advantage which
would accrue to Ruffia by fuch a trade, both
on account of the fums which would remain
in the country for expences of carriage, the
employment of a number of people, and alfo
the encouragement it would be to the Ruffian
navigation in the Black Sea; but he never
would *grant* fuch a privilege to a part of the
Britifh nation exclufively, and fhut out from
it the Ruffia merchants, who carry on a
branch of commerce fo advantageous to his
empire, nor exclude his own fubjects from
it. Before this can be done, the Turkey
company muft be abolifhed.

At prefent a few goods, I am informed,
have been fent to Hamburgh, thence to
Vienna, and down the Danube, where they
are fhipped for Conftantinople. The freight
to Hamburgh is dearer than it is to Riga; the
charges acrofs Germany ten times as much as
acrofs Ruffia. At the mouth of the Danube
there are only bad Turkifh or Greek veffels to
be freighted, on which no regular infurance
can be made. At Cherfon there are fome
hundreds of veffels, among which many equal
thofe to be found in the ports of other

feas,

feas; and a reafonable infurance may be made by fafe underwriters ; but the route through Germany does not neceffitate an abolition of the Levant company.

Refpecting the Inefficacy of the **Quarantine Re-** *gulations in* **Great Britain.**

IT may be faid, if every kind of veffel have leave to go to the Levant, we fhall run a greater rifk of having the plague imported, than while the company exifts. "In the latter cafe there are fewer veffels, and thofe veffels belonging to the company, who having an intereft that they perform the voyages pre-fcribed to them, it can always be known where they have been, and under what cir-cumftances, and fuch veffels being addreffed to factors in Turkey, members of the com-pany, and under its direction and the control of the confuls, they cannot in an irregular manner leave Turkey without their defti-nation being known, and with atteftations from the confuls, fhowing the ftate of the health of the port of the Levant they failed from."

In

In anfwer to this it may be obferved, that in the ports of the Mediterranean, not only veffels of the country, but of all other nations, arrive without any previous notice to perform quarantine, and the length of their quarantine is regulated by the bills of health which they bring, and the knowledge which the officers of the health offices have of the ftate of the plague in every part of Turkey.

Can it be fuppofed that veffels can arrive in the ports of Great Britain, without its being known whence they came? The regulations of the quarantine and the cuftom-houfe, as they now exift, are fufficient to put this beyond doubt; befides, free veffels muft bring from the Levant the fame papers, fhowing the ftate of the country with refpect to health, as are now required of the company's fhips; the rifk will not therefore be augmented by laying the trade open.

But it may be neceffary to examine a little more narrowly how far our quarantine regulations fecure us at prefent from the plague. After all that has been faid by Dr. Ruffel, it may appear indeed fuperfluous to touch this fubject again, but fince his excellent treatife has produced no amelioration of thefe regulations, his arguments cannot be

too

too much enforced *. I affirm, not only from my own knowledge of the nature of lazarettos, but from the opinion of officers of the health offices at Malta, Leghorn, and Marfeilles, whom I confulted on the fubject, THAT OUR QUARANTINE REGULATIONS ARE WHOLLY INEFFECTUAL, AND THAT WE ARE CONSTANTLY EXPOSED TO THE DANGER OF HAVING THE PLAGUE IMPORTED FROM TURKEY, BY EVERY VESSEL WHICH COMES DIRECTLY FROM THAT COUNTRY.

1ft. It is beyond all doubt eftablifhed, that the miafm, effluvia, or whatever it may be called, which produces the plague, may remain in an active ftate, fo as to occafion infection, for a much longer time than is required for a veffel to load in Turkey, make her voyage, and perform quarantine in Great Britain.

2. It is equally certain that thefe fomites, or the impregnation of fubftances with peftilential miafmata, cannot be deftroyed but by

* Dr. Miltzer, a phyfician of Mofcow, has written in German a large book on the plague, which contains a great number of cafes which came under his obfervation ; but as they all tend to fupport a fyftem he has adopted, it is to be feared that the power of prepoffeffion in favour of his fyftem has often mifled his judgment.

airing '

airing a certain time, by fumigating, by wafhing, by moiftening with fuch liquors as are
anti-peftilential, or by expofing to a fevere
cold. Some of thefe deftroy the miafm in
a fhort time, fome require a longer.

3. It appears from Dr. Ruffel's remarks
(and he has been delicate on this fubject too)
that notwithftanding all the fidelity and di-
ligence of confuls, infected goods may be
fhipped for Britain, and the fhip which carries them have a *fair bill of health.*

Now as merchandize performing quarantine in Britain and in Holland (where the
regulations are ftill worfe) are never opened
and properly aired, it follows that fuch quarantines are not fufficient to deftroy the fomites; nor are thefe quarantines fafe with
regard to other circumftances; for communication with thofe who fupply the paffengers
and fhip's crew with provifions, &c. is not
fufficiently guarded, and the paffengers and
the crew, though they were not infected in
Turkey, are liable every day, by touching the
cargo or their effects, to catch the plague, and
to communicate it to others; nor is fmug-
gling impoffible as the lazarettos now are
eftablifhed.

It does not appear that the laws of this
country will permit fuch a police to be observed

ſerved in lazarettos as is indiſpenſably neceſſary to ſecure the country from the
plague.

The officers of health have, in the Mediterranean, a power of putting to death immediately all thoſe who violate the laws of the
quarantine in ſuch a manner as that contagion may be communicated, and their
power is independent of the civil magiſtrate
or any other authority. For the moſt trifling
thing ſmuggled, or endeavoured to be ſmuggled, out of the lazaretto, the offenders are
ſhot dead the inſtant they are detected. A
perſon eſcaping from the lazaretto, were it
one hour before the expiration of the quarantine, is equally puniſhed with immediate
death, &c. &c. &c. *

There are neither proper places, nor buildings, nor regulations, for performing quarantine in ſafety in Great Britain, nor is the
nature of quarantine underſtood in our lazarettos.

It may be aſked, how have we eſcaped the
plague ſince the year 1666, when the laſt
plague in London entirely ceaſed. I anſwer,
chiefly by not admitting ſhips with foul bills

* The humane Leopold, when Grand Duke of Tuſ-
cany, though he would not ſuffer a murderer to be put to
death, did not alter the quarantine laws.

of

of health from the Levant, and obliging them to perform quarantine in the Mediterranean since that regulation took place, and by God's mercy only that veſſels with clean bills of health have not brought it.

What are we to do to be more ſecure in future, will then be aſked. The anſwer is very ſhort and obvious; to oblige all veſſels coming from the Levant, whether with *fair* or with *foul bills of health*, to perform quarantine in Malta, in Leghorn, or in Marſeilles, &c. and then with the proper atteſtations of the health officers, ſigned alſo by His Majeſty's conſuls in other ports, to admit them into Great Britain without performing a ſecond and uſeleſs quarantine.

Trade would gain by this regulation, and we ſhould be under no apprehenſion of the plague. The charges are ſmall in the Mediterranean, and not more for us than for our rivals in trade.

Malta is by far the beſt port to perform quarantine in; the regulations are even more to be relied on than at Leghorn, as they are in ſome reſpects more ſcrupulous; it lies more in the road of veſſels coming home from any part of Turkey. It is true that maſters of veſſels, for many private reaſons, which do not benefit their owners or the freighters,

prefer

prefer Leghorn ; but it is confiderably out of the track of their voyage.

With refpect to Holland, moft certainly, Turkey goods, and cottons in particular, ought not to be admitted thence till they have been well aired; nor need we ever have imported fuch vaft quantities, or any quantity at all from Holland or any other place, had the Turkey trade been free in Britain.

APPENDIX.

MISCELLANEOUS PAPERS.

THESE fragments are extracts and tranflations from original documents; they will ferve to elucidate and confirm fome paffages in the preceding pages.

Of EGYPT.

THE French have it in their power either to feize Egypt, or to make fuch an alliance with the begs as will open to them a communication with India.

The begs would eagerly embrace any offer which would fecure to them a perfect independence of the Ottoman porte; or they would even become tributary to any other fovereign or ftate, who would maintain them in their feparate governments, and protect the one againft the other, and the whole country againft the Turks.

Had not the domeftic affairs of France engaged all the attention of that cabinet, the effects of M. de Truguet's miffion to Cairo would, long ago, have been vifible.

Were the Turks driven out of Europe, their force would be more concentrated; they would be ftronger, and more able than they are now, to reduce to obedience thofe provinces, which at prefent are either in a ftate of open rebellion or virtual independence, and from which the porte draws neither troops nor money; they would then be able to reduce Egypt, and to defend it againft the French. In
fuch

such a state of affairs, the French would easily obtain from the Turks a communication through Egypt to India, which then would be attended with less risk, though not with much less expence than it now is. It is not, however, probable that the porte would, so readily as the begs, permit troops to be sent across Egypt *.

Volney says, that memorials have been laid before the French cabinet, on the expediency of obtaining possession of Egypt. These memorials are now no secret.

The principal force of Egypt consists in 8,000 horse; the janizaries are not to be estimated as soldiers. There are not four cannons to defend the Pharos of Alexandria, which, according to the regulations, should be garrisoned by 500 janizaries, but there are never half the number. A single frigate might beat down these fortifications. The greatest difficulty a foreign army would have to encounter in keeping possession of Alexandria, is the want of water; this city has none but what is brought in canals to their cisterns when the Nile overflows; it would, therefore, be necessary to make a conquest of the country, at least as far as the river.

The revenues of the begs consist in a tax on land and the customs, which produce about two millions sterling, of which the porte receives very little. Uncertain revenues are extortions under various pretexts, and these are not inconsiderable.

Suez is a most miserable and defenceless place; it has no

---

* Abolishing the Levant company in England, and supplying, by means of the East India company, all parts of the Turkish empire with India goods (as some of the foreign India companies do in part) would put an end to the clandestine trade of the company's servants, and to the commercial speculations of the French, except so far as regard their own consumption; because the English East India company is able to send from|London, and sell in Turkey, these goods at a cheaper rate than they can be brought by the Red Sea or the Persian Gulph, which always must be attended with much expence and considerable risk.

When Great Britain is at war with France, this communication may easily be stopped, and the necessary steps may be taken during a peace. The extraordinary expence would not be great.

water

water nearer than ten miles, and that is very brackifh, and drawn from a well. No fhips can approach Suez nearer than three miles.

Egypt produces a confiderable quantity of fugar of a very good grain. Were that country under a better government, it might fupply Europe with a great quantity. The fugar cane grows alfo very well in Candia and in Sicily, where, if the inhabitants were more induftrious, or were there enter-prifing people of capital among them, this would become a product of great confequence. The fame may be faid of a great part of the coaft of Barbary.

There is a coffee tree growing in the open air at Malta, in the garden of the French minifter, and the fruit ripens perfectly. The French have tried the experiment in Can-dia, and it fucceeded; probably it would grow in Sicily. It is thought that it would become more hardy, and ripen ear-lier, were it engrafted on other trees or fhrubs, and that it might be naturalized to climates lefs warm than thofe in which it is now produced in the greateft perfection. We know that re-production has made many plants refift a colder climate better than when the parent plant was firft imported. There can be no doubt of the coffee tree's growing in Egypt. Egypt alfo produces excellent flax and hemp.

Indigo has been cultivated with fuccefs on the eaftern coaft of the Adriatic, near Zante, till the planter, it is not known by whom or for what reafon, was affaffinated. Were the French poffeffed of Egypt, they might abandon their Weft India iflands.

The French court, a very few years ago, paid much at-tention to thefe fpeculations.

1/t. Refpecting PERSIA.

THE internal diforders of Perfia are favourable to Great Britain, and to affift any party, fo that it fhould gain a pre-ponderance, which might end in a fubjugation of the whole

country,

country, is acting contrary to the English interest. The weakness of Persia is the security of India.

The Agwans (or Afgans) and Abdali, being of the sect of Omar, are enemies to the other Persians, who are followers of Ali ; they are now distinct nations, and have their own independent sovereigns. They are not concerned in the civil wars in Persia. They are powerful enough to impede the marching of a Russian army through Bochara to India, or the Persians from crossing the Indus. They themselves may, however, be dangerous, acting in concert with any Indian power. England should avoid quarrelling with them ; but prevent, as much as possible, their having any connection with India, or receiving artillery from any quarter.

While Great Britain is firmly allied with Russia, she need not fear either the Persians, Afgans, or Abdali. A diversion made by Russia would prevent, at all times, their sending an army to India, or meddling with the disputes in that country.

A war with these Asiatic nations should be a *casus fœderis* in the treaty with Russia. At present it is an exception.

2d. *Respecting* PERSIA.

THERE are three Persian ambassadors in Russia : one from the khan of Ghilan, one from the khan of Derbent, and one from Jafeer, khan of Ispahan.

These two last came to Kremenchuk, in the summer of 1787, after the departure of the empress, and had a pompous public audience of Prince Potemkin. The minister of the khan of Derbent was exceedingly well received by the prince ; but the other, not conforming entirely to an etiquette, which he thought was to be observed only in an audience of the empress herself, was received, and afterwards treated with great coolness. The minister from the khan of Ghilan did not obtain permission from the prince to come to him, or to go to Peterſburgh, till a little time before his death, when he ſent for him to Yaſſy; but on the road, hearing of the prince's death, he ſtopt, and obtained leave of the empreſs to go to Peterſburgh.

The object of the miſſion of all theſe miniſters was, to ſolicit the aſſiſtance of the empreſs for the party of their maſters, *on her own conditions.* Probably the prince kept them in ſuſpenſe till he ſaw which party would prevail. That of Derbent will be always of importance on account of the paſs it commands, and which is the only one on that ſide of the Caſpian by land.

Almoſt every governor of a province in Perſia has ſet up for himſelf, and refuſes to take part in the quarrel, which has greatly leſſened the power of the two great competitors, Mahomed Khan (ſon of Haſſan Khan) of Mazanderan, and Jafeer Khan, in the ſouth, and who reſides at Iſpahan. Mahamud Khan is of the race of the ancient family of the Shahs, but was made an eunuch by the late Karim Khan, regent of Perſia.

Since the death of Achmet Shah, of the Afgans, the country is much weakened by the partition he made of it among his three ſons. Prince Naſſau and Mr. de St. Genie propoſed to gain over the Afgans to the intereſt of Ruſſia, in 1791, during the diſpute with Great Britain, and they propoſed to the empreſs to ſend an army through Bochara to the north of India.

They want artillery very much in Perſia, and the Ruſſians refuſe ſelling them any at Aſtrakan.

Tibet Shah, of the Abdali, near Bochara, aſked a train of artillery of the Engliſh Eaſt India company, about the time that Count Ferrieres was ſent into Perſia by Mr. de Vergennes. He intended to employ it againſt the Bocharians, who, doubtleſs, would have been aſſiſted by Ruſſia. He offered to the Engliſh a body of 25,000 cavalry to act againſt the Mahrattas. This cavalry is excellent, and 15,000 beat near 200,000 Mahrattas in a pitched battle ſome years ago.

The French offered, by Mr. de Ferrieres, a large train

of

of artillery to Jafir, khan of Ifpahan, to fecure his friendfhip. A fmall French fleet did actually come up the
Perfian gulf, in June 1781, with a confiderable number of
cannon on board, but Ferrieres, for want of addrefs, did
not fucceed in his miffion, which was as hoftile to Ruffia
as Britain.

Bochara, at prefent, is divided into almoft as many fovereignties as there are villages, and there is no union among
them. It is a country without ftrength, except fome enemy
were to attack them in fuch a manner as to oblige them to
unite.

The friendfhip of this Tibet Shah may be of confequence
to the Englifh to cultivate, as the moft effectual check on
the Bocharians, or on thofe who would pafs through their
country to invade India.

The Perfians, diftracted as their ftate is, ftill remember
that they have conquered India. Timur entered India
in 1398, Nadir Shah in 1738, Abdallah feveral times from
1748 to 1765.

3d. *Refpecting* PERSIA.

IN 1780, Prince Potemkin framed a project of opening
a trade through Perfia to Bender-Bufhier, and India. Count
Mark Wainovich failed in July 1781, with a fquadron of
four frigates and two armed floops from Aftrakan. He
ftopped and examined the iflands of Shiloy and Oguzzin,
but found them barren fpots; he proceeded to Afterabad;
the commodioufnefs of the harbour and the fruitfulnefs of the
country, induced him to enter into a negociation with the
khan of Afterabad, who deceived him. The Ruffians, however, erected, to defend the harbour, a fmall fort about
fifty miles from the city of Afterabad. The caravans from
Bochara, Tibet, and India, pafs through Mefhd. The
fleet wintered there, and returning, furveyed the bay of
Bulkan, and the inlet of Karabogas.

The death of the regent (Vakiel) Karim Khan, having
thrown Perfia into fuch a diforderly ftate, that the prince

　　　　　　　　　　　　　　　　　　　　　　abandoned

abandoned his project, but there still exists a Russian fortress at Zinzeli, with a small but sufficient garrison to defend it. A consul resides there, who is the commandant.

Of a Project, which the Empress of Russia had formed to attack the English in India.

WHEN the British fleet was about to sail for the Baltic, to force the empress to make peace, Prince Nassau, who was then in favour with her imperial majesty, presented a project of sending an army through Bochara to Cashmir, and thence to Bengal, to drive the English out of India. This project was conceived and drawn up by a Monsieur de St. Genie (the person whose agents set fire to the Dutch arsenal, &c. and had formed a similar project for destroying the British dock-yards and ships, &c.)

By a manifesto to be published, the empress declared that she sent the army to re-establish the mogul on the throne of India.

Little difficulty was foreseen in passing through Bochara; it was even hoped, seeing the object was to re-establish on the throne of India a prince of their religion, that they would be friendly to the enterprize: however, were they not, little apprehension was entertained of a people so disunited among themselves, and who tremble at the name of Russia.

St. Genie pretended, that there were passes through the mountains, and that he had people who had been in the country, sent by Mr. de Vergennes. He presented with his project a map, and a *marche-route* for the army.

The empress highly approved the plan: Prince Potemkin turned it into ridicule. Had a war taken place, it is difficult to say what the empress might not have undertaken, if not effectuated, at that period.

They counted on being joined in the north of India by the discontented from all parts.

Respecting

Respecting some PROJECTS *of the* RUSSIANS *on* CHINA *and* JAPAN.

1*st* PAPER.

CAPTAIN BILLINGS, who was formerly with captain Cook round the world is returned to St. Peterſburg, from the north-eaſt part of Ruſſia, and the continent of America, whither the empreſs ſent him nine years ago.

One of his inſtructions was, to find a port for eſtabliſhing an admiralty; *i. e.* a port for building, putting into dock, and ſtationing ſhips of war and other veſſels.

A captain of the navy was alſo ſent to join him in 1787, and to examine the coaſt as far as the mouth of the river Amur, and to fix on a port. Oud, not far from the mouth of the Amur, was fixed on. Alſo, 200 werſts to the ſouth of Oud, they found a very fine port beyond the Chineſe frontier. At length, it was determined to fix the admiralty on the American coaſt, either at Prince William's Sound, or Comptroller's Bay. They alſo found many other very fine harbours on the American coaſt. The empreſs wrote, in 1787, to theſe captains, and to the commander of the Ruſſian fortreſſes, that ſhe had ſent ſix ſhips from the Baltic to Kamchatka, to co-operate with a powerful army that was to go down the Amur, and take poſſeſſion of its banks to its mouth, and all the country to the left.

A great ſaving would accrue to the Ruſſians by ſending by water proviſions for their ſettlements, which now go by land to Kamchatka, &c. at a great expence, and two thirds of them are often ſpoiled. Beſides, they propoſe to open this way a trade with Japan, China, and India, and to have in thoſe ſeas a naval force ſufficient to make themſelves reſpected.

Two ſmall ſquadrons were fitted out at Cronſtadt, for Kamchatka, but were prevented from ſailing by the Swediſh war. One of them was commanded by captain Trevanion, an Engliſhman, and was to go round Cape Horn; the other

by

by captain Malofskoi, who was to go round the Cape of Good Hope.

The emprefs acted in conjunction with the court of Spain, it feems, for Malofskoi was to go to the Philippines, and to purchafe large veffels from the Spaniards.

The Ruffians claim the coaft of America to a confiderable diftance fouth; they have not themfelves determined how far; this probably will be fixed by the utility the claimed country may promife to be of.

2d PAPER.

IN Auguft 1792, Profeffor Laxman conducted to St. Peterfburg, a Japanefe mafter of a veffel, that had fome years ago been fhipwrecked on the Ruffian coaft; they were in all fixteen failors and the mafter; five of the failors only are now alive. It was not thought proper to fend them back till they had learned enough of the Ruffian language to communicate what knowledge of their own country they were poffeffed of. The mafter is a very intelligent man, but it is only by ftealth that he can be fpoken with, as the government is very watchful over him. He has brought with him a chart of the coaft of Japan, which widely differs from thofe made in Europe.

3d PAPER.

THE emprefs has appointed the fon of Profeffor Laxman to conduct the Japanefe, in a Ruffian fhip, back to their own country, and to refide there as her chargé d'affaires, if he is received. He has confiderable prefents with him, and is accompanied by feveral engineers.

4th PAPER.

THE chargé d'affaires is returned from Japan, and has obtained leave for the Ruffians to fend a veffel every year, to trade with the natives under the fame reftrictions as the Dutch.

K k 4   The

The iſlands on which the Ruſſians have poſſeſſions extend within 300 miles of Japan. They think *ſome day or other* they may be maſters of the iſlands of Japan alſo (for Japan is not one, but two large iſlands) as they conceive the force they could bring could not be withſtood by ſuch a people.

With reſpect to China, an attack was much nearer; preparations were actually making for taking poſſeſſion of the Amur at Narſhinſk, where the Ruſſian gold and ſilver mines are; the chief difficulty was want of timber. The death of Prince Potemkin put a ſtop to this expedition:—when it will be reſumed is not known; it is ſuppoſed that 10,000 Ruſſians could march through China *.

A Project *of the late* Prince Potemkin's, *of purchaſing from a private proprietor the Iſlands of* Lampedosa *and* Linosa, *in the Mediterranean, and obtaining the Suzerainity of the Court of* Naples.

WHETHER any overture was made to the court of Naples reſpecting this object I do not know. The project was drawn up, ſome time after Minorca was taken by the French, and was much approved of by Prince Potemkin, as well as by the empreſs. The following particulars were extracted from the original paper in his poſſeſſion. It probably was laid aſide when the king of Naples conſented to receive the Ruſſian fleet into his ports in Sicily.

It was propoſed to eſtabliſh an order of knighthood, ſimilar to that of Malta, for Ruſſians and Greeks, but proofs of ancient nobility were not to be required. The particular inſtitution of the order I never ſaw; but the empreſs was to be the grand maſter, and the governor of the iſland for the time being her deputy.

* A particular account of all theſe matters, and a deſcription of the countries here alluded to, from original documents, will ſhortly be publiſhed by Mr. Arrowſmith, with valuable maps, charts, &c.

Description

DESCRIPTION *of the Island of* LAMPEDOSA.

THIS iſland is in Africa, in 35 degrees and 30 min. latitude; it is about twelve miles long and five to eight broad; it is flat, exceedingly fertile, and has plenty of water; the ſea on the ſouth ſide is not very deep, and a veſſel may anchor at a conſiderable diſtance from land; to the north it is deep all round, and the ſhore very bold. There is a rock a league from the W. S. W. point, but it is eaſily known, and may be marked: a ſhip may ſail ſafely between it and the land. Three leagues off there is a high great round rock in the ſea, which is a good mark. To the ſouth there is an exceedingly fine bay, where veſſels may anchor in fifteen to eighteen fathoms water, ſhut in from all winds except the ſouth and ſouth-weſt; the bottom is a ſoft ſand. There is a great abundance of fiſh in this bay.

The ſhore may be eaſily defended all round by forts and entrenchments. At the bottom of the bay is a creek, which is capable of being made a very fine harbour, and at a ſmall expence, nature having already done the greateſt part of the work. The entrance is from the S. S. W. There is fifteen fathoms water at its mouth, ten in the middle, which gradually decreaſes to ſix, and at the extremity there is only one fathom. To the left, halfway up the creek, there is a point which projects half acroſs it, behind which ſmall veſſels may anchor with ſafety, when the wind blows ſtrong directly into the harbour, at which time there is a great ſwell in other parts of it. To the left, from the entrance to the part where there is ten fathoms water, there is a ſhallow bay, land-locked, in which there is only three to five feet water, with a ſoft ſandy bottom: this bay may be ſhut up with a temporary wall, and the bay ſunk to any depth, at a ſmall expence, and continued a great way into the iſland, ſo as to form a large port for ſhips of any draught of water, the land being but a little above the ſurface of the water, and of a proper kind to admit of digging. Docks may alſo be formed

by

by fimply excavating the earth. The furface of this bay is never ruffled by the moft violent gales of wind.

The entrance of the creek or port is ninety fathoms broad, and half a mile in length; the right hand fhore is a rock, and near it is a hill of ftone with a church on it; this being fortified, would defend the harbour and command the land.

Veffels may anchor in the bay all the fummer; and in winter, when too violent a ftorm comes on from the fouth or fouth weft, they may go to the north, round the ifland, and keep in as clofe under fhore as they pleafe; when the port is fit to receive them, they may fafely run in; they may alfo bear away for Linofa, about twenty miles diftant, and which lies exactly in the direction thefe winds blow. The coaft of Linofa is fo bold, that fhips may faften on fhore; large veffels are, however, not more expofed at Lampidofa than in the road of Leghorn.

There are only ten or fifteen inhabitants on the ifland: they are Maltefe; one of them is a prieft, and they have a paffport of protection from France. The Barbary cruizers go often into this port as well as the Maltefe veffels, and fhips which come from Turkey with the plague on board, till the ficknefs has ceafed, when they return to Turkey, and thus fave their fhip and cargo from being burnt, which would be the cafe were they to go into any harbour where there is a quarantine.

The fituation of Lampidofa is the moft advantageous poffible; it is 100 miles from Sufa in Barbary, from Giorgenti in Sicily, and from the great port of Malta; 600 from Toulon, from Algiers, and the entrance into the Archipelago; from Gibraltar, Alexandria, and Conftantinople, 950; from Tripoli, Tunis, and the fouth point of Sicily, 160 miles.

ADVANTAGES *to* RUSSIA, *in poffeffing this Ifland.*

IT is the beft fituation of any in the Mediterranean; in that refpect it has all the advantages of Malta for the ftation

of

of a fleet in time of peace or war; Leghorn is quite out of the way; every thing is exceedingly dear there, and the motions of the fleet are almoſt immediately known in Italy and France. It is farther from France than from the Archipelago, and is in the paſſage of all veſſels that go to or come from the Levant.

In time of war, if the iſland ſhould be in danger of an invaſion, and being attacked by a ſuperior fleet, the veſſels ſtationed there may retire to Malta or Sicily, &c. however, a fleet drawn up near the ſhore may be protected by the land batteries.

It is the beſt ſtation for protecting trade. Veſſels coming either from the ſtraits of Gibraltar or from the Levant may be met by frigates, this iſland being in the middleway.

Magazines of naval ſtores may be formed here from the Black Sea, inſtead of purchaſing them at enormous prices in Italy, in war time.

Proviſions will be produced in the iſland, but till that is the caſe, they may be had from Sicily or the coaſt of Barbary, even in time of war, as Malta is ſupplied thence, and more than two thirds of the coſt at Leghorn ſaved.

The Barbary powers will be kept in great awe by its vicinity, and prevented from ever daring to commit hoſtilities againſt Ruſſia: their ports may be kept blocked up. If Malta would cruize *ſeriouſly* againſt theſe ſtates in conjunction with the Ruſſians, the Algerine cruizers could never paſs beyond theſe iſlands, and Tunis and Tripoli may be continually blocked up.

It is alſo the beſt ſituation for an emporium for Ruſſian products brought from the Black Sea, for ſupplying the Mediterranean, and for collecting articles of return.

A lazaretto muſt be built, and thereby the expences of quarantine will be ſaved to Ruſſia.

Maxims of Government to be obſerved.

A colony and a province of the empire are to be governed by oppoſite maxims.

1. The

1. The colony muſt manufacture nothing that can be manufactured in Ruſſia, not even the raw products of the colony.

2. The colony muſt produce only raw articles, which Ruſſia does not produce, or ſuch as Ruſſia is in need of, or its veſſels.

3. The colony muſt take from Ruſſia every thing it wants, if Ruſſia can furniſh them.

4. The colony muſt trade with no other country. Ruſſia muſt receive its products, and either conſume them or ſend them to other nations, and muſt reap the advantage of exportation and navigation.

5. The inhabitants muſt be drawn as much as poſſible from other countries, not to diminiſh the population of the mother country.

6. A colony muſt be diſtant enough from the mother country to become a nurſery for ſeamen, but not ſo far off as that the voyage may injure their health ; its climate muſt be healthy, that its advantages may not be counterbalanced by the loſs of · thoſe of the mother country who viſit it. It muſt be in a different climate than the mother country, or theſe maxims will be oppreſſive.

Laws for the Colony.

IN eſtabliſhing the government, regard muſt be had to the genius, cuſtoms, and morals of the neighbouring Chriſtian nations.

1. No duty whatever ſhall be paid, neither on importation nor exportation of any kind of merchandize. Duty is to be paid in the Ruſſian ports as now, or with ſuch diminutions as ſhall be judged neceſſary.

2. It is prohibited to make uſe of, or to have any utenſil or inſtrument of iron, braſs, &c. or any cloth, linen, or ſail cloth, not made and imported from Ruſſia, with the exception of ſilks and other merchandize not produced or manufactured in Ruſſia, which may be had from the neighbouring countries, of which a liſt ſhall be made.

3. No

3. No foreign veſſel (except in time of war and by ſtreſs of weather) ſhall be permitted to enter the port, except it be empty of all kind of merchandize, and then it ſhall have no communication with the coloniſts, till after it has been viſited. Veſſels loaded, in need of aſſiſtance, ſhall receive it, but they ſhall be conſidered as in quarantine as long as they ſtay. Paſſengers, after the quarantine has been performed, according to the place they came from, may land with their baggage, but not with merchandize.

4. Foreigners may purchaſe merchandize in the iſland, except the products of the iſlands, and export them in their own veſſels, which arrived empty.

5. Foreigners or Ruſſians may import into Lampidoſa merchandize from Ruſſia or elſewhere, only in Ruſſian veſſels.

6. Only Ruſſian veſſels may export products to Ruſſia. The cargo unloaded in Ruſſia muſt correſpond to the note of the cargo given by the government of the iſland, and they muſt not carry it elſewhere, nor ſell any to pay charges in ports they may by diſtreſs put into, but they may mortgage the produce of the ſale in Ruſſia.

7. The products of the iſland muſt be regiſtered before the harveſt, or the bringing them into warehouſes from the fields.

8. Any perſon, of whatever nation or religion, may become an inhabitant of the iſland, and leave it when he thinks proper; but his reſidence in it ſhall not give him a right to have the Ruſſian flag for a veſſel, large or ſmall.

9. Every individual, who ſhall be poſſeſſed of a houſe, or land cultivated, to the value of five hundred roubles, ſhall be entitled to have the Ruſſian flag for one veſſel of forty tons; if he poſſeſs houſe or land to the value of 1,000 roubles, one of eighty tons; and for larger poſſeſſions, one or more veſſels in the ſame proportion. Who lends his name to others ſhall forfeit the value, and the borrower ſhall forfeit the veſſel. Property, which has given a right to have the flag, ſhall not be ſold before the paſſports of the veſſels have been delivered up to the government, and the veſſels return

to

to the port of the ifland. No proprietor of a veffel is obliged to go himfelf to fea with his veffel.

10. He who fhall fend his family to Ruffia, or another family in its ftead, confifting of a male under thirty-five years of age and a woman under twenty-five, or a man of any age and a woman under thirty years of age and one child, or of thirty-five with two children, or the man and woman of any age with three children, who fhall become naturalized fubjects of the emprefs, and fhall buy in Ruffia immoveable property for 500 roubles, under the fame re-ftrictions as property in the ifland with refpect to the fale, fuch fender fhall have the Ruffian flag for a veffel of any fize under 200 tons, and for a larger veffel in proportion, or for feveral. Neither the perfons fent to Ruffia fhall be anfwera-ble for the conduct of the fender, nor the fender for the con-duct of the fent.

In the year 1779, a project of a peace with the Barbary States, was prefented to the emprefs by Prince Potemkin, who was at that time very ardent in promoting the trade of the Black Sea to the Mediterranean in Ruffian veffels. There were no humiliating conditions in this arrangement, as there are in moft of the treaties of other nations. The emprefs gave for anfwer, that fhe would never make any arrange-ment whatever with thofe powers; that if they took her mercantile veffels fhe would know how to force the porte to oblige them to obferve the ftipulations of the treaty of peace; and that rather than fend a negotiator to them, fhe would fend a fleet of frigates.

The number of failors in the different ports of Italy is much greater than is generally imagined; there are above 10,000 in the two Sicilies. Malta generally furnifhes to Spain 6,000 excellent feamen.

From the coaft of the Adriatic, about Ragufa, Prevafa, &c. the French have for many years imported a great quantity of the moft excellent oak timber, there is, indeed, no finer timber any where to be found for the purpofe of fhip building, than that which grows in thofe parts in great abundance.

A PLAN

A Plan *for attacking the* Turkish Fleet *in the Port of* Constantinople.

IT will ferve no good end to publifh the details of the intended operations of the Ruffian fleet in the laft war. The following particulars will fufficiently fhow the probability there was of their being crowned with fuccefs.

The channel of Conftantinople is of different breadths, from about one to three miles, and runs between high hills, at the foot of which are batteries, from the entrance at the Black Sea to Serrieri (a village near Buyukderé.) The north and north eaft winds blow down the channel nine or ten months in the year. The foutherly winds, which blow up the channel when they reign, feldom laft more than two or three days at a time; the north and north eaft winds, on the contrary, are generally conftant for two or three months, fo that a fleet coming from the Black Sea at the proper feafon is almoft certain of a fair wind to enter the channel and the port of Conftantinople.

The current is very ftrong from the Black Sea, except when the wind has blown two or three days from the fouth, when there is a current from the fea of Marmora. The ftream divides at the point of the feraglio; a part of the water runs into the fea of Marmora, and a part is forced into the port, making, on the Conftantinople fide, a tolerably ftrong current, which runs towards the bottom of the port, and coming out again on the Galata fide, and by an under current, occafions an eddy or ftill water in the middle; hence it is, that fhips cannot fail at once from the port, but muft be towed or warped in the ftill water clofe to the fhore of Tophana, till they are fo far up the ftream (that is, to the northward) that they can make fail without danger of being carried againft the feraglio point (as has fometimes happened) and where there is a perfect torrent.

From this defcription it is evident, that a fleet coming from the Black Sea down the channel of Conftantinople, with the wind and current in its favour, could with eafe

fail

fail ftraight into the port; that the Turkifh fleet in the port cannot go out to meet it in the middle of the channel, but by towing flowly up the fhore, while the enemy's fleet coming down will have, within a few fathoms of it, the wind and current in its favour, and will be able to caft anchor, and form in whatever manner the commander may judge moft advantageous.

If the Turkifh fleet is not in the port, but lies in the channel in the ftream, where it ufually is ftationed before it fails in the fpring for the Archipelago, three or four miles above the port, the Ruffian fleet may anchor at what diftance it pleafes from it, either to attack or not, while the Turkifh fhips cannot poffibly advance againft the current, not even by warping. In fuch a fituation they are expofed to fire-fhips, and if any part flip their anchors to avoid being burnt, they cannot again get into the line; the reft muft follow them if they will preferve their line.

As to the batteries on the two fhores, they may be paffed fo rapidly, and at fuch a diftance, that nothing is to be feared from them; but as the water is deep enough to admit line-of-battle fhips to lie quite clofe to them, and the fhore is perfectly clean, they may be foon filenced, and particularly as only one or two guns in the flanks can bear on a fhip before it comes oppofite to them. The ftones of which they are built are hard and exceedingly brittle; they are alfo fo low and fo expofed, that a fhip with grape-fhot may foon drive out the gunners.

In the firft winter of the laft war, a Ruffian fixty-four gun fhip was difmafted in a violent ftorm in the Black Sea, and the officers being ignorant of the Turkifh ports on the coaft of Anatolia, faw no other means of faving their lives than by running into the channel of Conftantinople. The fhip entered it with a fair wind, but having only jury-mafts, fhe failed very flowly, yet the Turkifh batteries, though they kept up a conftant fire on her, did her not the leaft injury; when fhe had run by all the batteries, fhe caft anchor in the bay of Buyukderé, and furrendered herfelf. The captain was afterwards blamed for not failing by Conftantinople,

nople, and attempting to run between the forts of the Dardanelles, and get into the Archipelago.

This example puts the matter beyond doubt, as to the poffibility of a fleet's failing by thefe batteries, reputed fo tremendous.

STATE of the RUSSIAN ARMY, January 1795, according to the Regifters of the College of War, from the Reports of the different Corps.

Regiments.	Number of Men in pay.
19 of artillery . - - -	38,110
11 grenadiers, of 4,075 men each - - ⎱	
3 grenadiers, of 1,000 to 3,000 men each - ⎰	51,048
51 mufketeers, compofed of 10 companies of mufketeers and 2 companies of grenadiers, each regiment being compofed of 2,424 men - - - - -	
7 mufketeers without grenadiers - -	139,592
1 mufketeers, of 4 battalions, 4,143 men -	
New arquebufiers, fo called - -	5,879
12 battalions of mufqueteers, of 1,019 men - ⎱	
3 battalions of mufqueteers, of 1,475 men - ⎰	16,653
48 battalions, infantry in garrifon on the frontiers - - - - ⎱	
10 in the country - - - - ⎰	82,393
9 corps of chaffeurs (jäger) of 4 battalions of 998 men, each 3,992 - - -	35,928
3 battalions of chaffeurs - - -	2,994
5 cuiraffiers (of 6 fquadrons) of 1,106 and 1,125 men - - -	5,490
10 dragoons (of 10 fquadrons) of 1,882 men ⎱	
2 with huffars and grenadiers mounted - ⎰	23,573
8 carabiniers (of 6 fquadrons) of 1,106 men ⎱	
8 carabiniers (of 5 fquadrons) of 938 men - ⎰	16,352

L l

2 huffars

Regiments.	Number of Men in pay.
2 huffars of 1,119 men	
3 fquadron huffars	2,722
1 fquadron huffars de corps	
4 regiments chaffeurs à cheval, of 1,838 men	7,352
5 light horfe (of 6 fquadrons) of 1,047 men	5,235
6 cavalry of the Ukraine, of 1,047 men	6,282
16 regular Cofack cavalry	30,883
Troops to guard the country (marechauffée)	22,216

In the new provinces acquired from Poland at the firft partition, viz.

6 brigades of 1,819 men	
5 brigades light horfe, of 1,098 men	23,360
4 of infantry, of 1,447, &c. in all	
Invalids in garrifon	3,864
Soldiers fons at fchool for fervice	16,816
Troops to affift the commiffaries, &c.	1,258

Total regular troops - - Men	541,731
Irregular Coffaks cavalry - - 21,625	
Irregular troops of the Don Coffaks cavalry, all in actual fervice - 24,976	46,601
A great number of other irregular troops, all cavalry, as Calmuks, Bafkirs, &c. &c. not enrolled, but ready when called out; they receive no pay; at leaft	100,000

Men -	688,332

Of the regular troops there are about 300,000 men, which may be fpared for foreign fervice.

The cavalry is never complete, and particularly thofe in Poland.

The irregulars are generally over-complete in time of war.

In 1796, there were 150,000 recruits raifed for the infantry.

A very

A very great part of the empire has not yet contributed in furnifhing troops for the army, fo that the number of regular troops may be greatly increafed, whenever a ftill more formidable military eftablifhment may be neceffary.

LIST of the RUSSIAN FLEET, fitted out at Cronftadt, to cruize in the Baltic, in 1795.

100 gun fhips.	74 gun fhips.
Evfevie.	Pobedoflav.
Vladimir.	Prince Guftaf (Swedifh)
Saint Nicholai.	Boris.
Saratov.	Sophia Magdalena(Swedifh)
Rafteflav.	Vfeflav.
Ire Erarkov.	Jaroflav.

74 gun fhips.	66 gun fhips.
Makfim Izpovednik.	Omgeten (Swedifh)
Sifoi Velikoi.	Proxor.
Conftantine.	Pobedonocets (hofpital fhip)
Saint Peter.	

FRIGATES.

Archangel Gabriel.	Pomofhnoi.
Simeon.	Raphael.
Patrick.	Venus.

2 cutters, Volkov and Sokole.

A LIST of the AUXILIARY FLEET, which the Emprefs of Ruffia fent to England, in 1795.

74 guns.	66 guns.
Pamit Eftafei.	Jona.
Kleb.	Philip.
Peter.	Pimen.
Helena.	Parmen.
	Nikonor.
66 guns.	Revifan (Swedifh fhip) of
No. 82 (fo called)	oak.
Graf Orloff.	

FRIGATES,

FRIGATES.

The Archangel Michael	The Narva.
The Reval.	The Archipelago.
The Riga.	The Cronstadt.

CUTTERS.

Mercury.	Letúchie.

STATE of the RUSSIAN FLEET at Sebaſtopolis, in the Spring of 1796, all the old veſſels being condemned.

		Number of guns.
1 ſhip of 90 guns - - - -		90
1 — 80 - - -		80
3 — 74 - - -		222
6 — 64 - - -		384
11 ſhips of the line - - -		776
8 large frigates - - -		362
19		1,138 guns.

Beſides thoſe on the ſtocks, which are now finiſhed.
The flotilla at Odiſſa, or Khogia-bay.
Twenty-five very large and ſixty ſmaller veſſels to tranſport troops.
They are ſixty-four to ſeventy feet long, draw ſix feet water when loaded, and carry one very large gun. They have a latine main ſail and gib, and twenty-four oars; beſides theſe, there are a great number of other tranſports, bomb veſſels, &c.

F I N I S.

THE *Middle East* COLLECTION

Arno Press

Abbott, Nabia. **Aishah: The Beloved of Mohammed.** 1942

Addison, Charles G. **Damascus and Palmyra.** 1838. 2 Vols. in 1

[Adivar], Halidé Edib. **Turkey Faces West.** 1930

Baddeley, John F. **The Rugged Flanks of Caucasus.** 1940. 2 Vols. in 1

Barker, Edward B. B., ed. **Syria and Egypt Under the Last Five Sultans of Turkey.** 1876. 2 Vols. in 1

Bell, Gertrude Lowthian. **Syria: The Desert & The Sown.** 1919

Bowring, John. **Report on the Commercial Statistics of Syria.** 1840

Brydges, Harford Jones. **The Dynasty of the Kajars.** 1833

Churchill, [Charles H.] **The Druzes and the Maronites Under the Turkish Rule from 1840 to 1860.** 1862

Denon, Vivant. **Travels in Upper and Lower Egypt.** 1803. 3 Vols. in 1

Donaldson, Bess Allen. **The Wild Rue: A Study of Muhammadan Magic and Folklore in Iran.** 1938

Eton, W[illiam]. **A Survey of the Turkish Empire.** 1798

Forbes-Leith, F. A. C. **Checkmate:** Fighting Tradition in Central Persia. 1927

Fraser, James Baillie. **Narrative of the Residence of the Persian Princes in London, in 1835 and 1836.** 1838. 2 Vols. in 1

Fraser, James Baillie. **A Winter's Journey (Tâtar) from Constantinople to Tehran.** 1838. 2 Vols. in 1

Gobineau, Joseph Arthur. **Romances of the East.** 1878

Islamic Taxation: Two Studies. 1973

Kinneir, John Macdonald. **A Geographical Memoir of the Persian Empire.** 1813

Krusinski, J[udasz Tadeusz]. **History of the Late Revolution in Persia.** 1740. 2 Vols. in 1

Lane-Poole, Stanley. **Cairo:** Sketches of Its History, Monuments, and Social Life. 1898

Le Strange, G[uy], ed. **Don Juan of Persia: A Shi'ah Catholic, 1560-1604.** 1926

Leeder, S. H. **Modern Sons of the Pharaohs:** A Study of the Manners and Customs of the Copts of Egypt. 1918

Midhat Bey, Ali Haydar. **The Life of Midhat Pasha.** 1903

Miller, Barnette. **The Palace School of Muhammad the Conqueror.** 1941

Millspaugh, A[rthur] C[hester]. **The American Task in Persia.** 1925

Naima. **Annals of the Turkish Empire from 1591 to 1659 of the Christian Era.** 1832

Pasha, Djemal. **Memories of a Turkish Statesman, 1913-1919.** 1922

Pears, Edwin. **Life of Abdul Hamid.** 1917

Philby, H[arry] St. J[ohn Bridger]. **Arabia of the Wahhabis.** 1928

St. John, Bayle. **Village Life in Egypt.** 1852. 2 Vols. in 1

Sheil, Lady [Mary]. **Glimpses of Life and Manners in Persia.** 1856

Skrine, Francis Henry and Edward Denison Ross. **The Heart of Asia:** A History of Russian Turkestan and the Central Asian Khanates from the Earliest Times. 1899

Sykes, Mark. **The Caliphs' Last Heritage:** A Short History of the Turkish Empire. 1915

Sykes, P[ercy] M., ed. **The Glory of the Shia World.** 1910

De Tott, Baron. **Memoirs of Baron de Tott.** 1785. 2 Vols. in 1

Ubicini, M. A. **Letters on Turkey.** 1856. 2 Vols. in 1

Vambery, Arminius. **Arminius Vambery:** His Life and Adventures. 1914

Vambery, Arminius. **History of Bokhara.** 1873

Waring, Edward Scott. **A Tour of Sheeraz by the Route of Kazroon and Feerozabad.** 1807

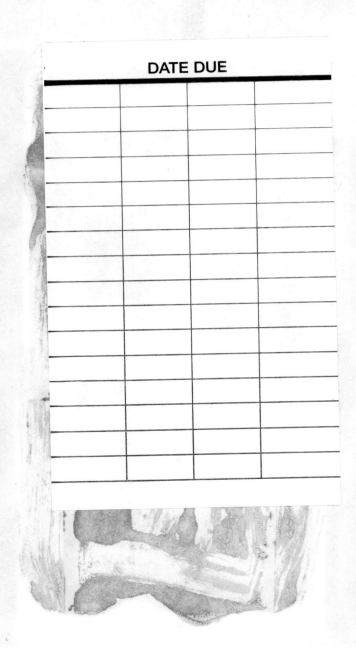

DATE DUE